THE POLITICS OF
CLIMATE CHANGE

THE POLITICS OF
CLIMATE CHANGE

A SURVEY

FIRST EDITION

Editor: Maxwell T. Boykoff

Routledge
Taylor & Francis Group

LONDON AND NEW YORK

First Edition 2010
Routledge
Albert House, 1–4 Singer Street, London EC2A 4BQ, United Kingdom
(Routledge is an imprint of the Taylor & Francis Group, an **informa** business)

ISBN 978-1-85743-496-5

Development Editor: Cathy Hartley

Typeset in Times New Roman 10.5/12

Typeset by Taylor & Francis Books
Printed and bound in Great Britain by CPI Antony Rowe, Chippenham, Wiltshire

Foreword

TIM O'RIORDAN

Just over a decade ago I edited a book entitled *The Politics of Climate Change –
A European Perspective* (with Jill Jager, Routledge, 1996). This looked at the
journey taken by climate change science and politics in the European Union
over the previous decade. At that time there was no Kyoto Protocol, the
Intergovernmental Panel on Climate Change (IPCC) was mostly mysterious,
and climate change had not hit the news waves. In essence, climate change as
a political issue had not arrived.

It has been a remarkable period of rising attention and awareness since
then. The notion of climate change has entered the consciousness of almost
all citizens of the developed world, the IPCC is now deeply politicized yet the
most powerful and effective voice of interdisciplinary science, and politicians
cannot avoid the issue. The fact that climate change is part of day-to-day
conversation, and that it appears almost ubiquitously in newspapers and television bulletins, as well as in the 'blogosphere', tells us that at least as a
concept of profound social interest and of ordinary life, climate change has
definitely arrived.

This evidence provides a necessary but incomplete beginning. What Maxwell Boykoff and his colleagues tell us in this important volume, *The Politics
of Climate Change: A Survey*, is that all of this frenzy is by no means sufficient to generate the necessary action to wean us off our heretofore wholly
indispensable carbon fix. What is so scary is that we probably have just a
short time to clean out this habit of carbon dependency before the devastating
consequences of global warming become unavoidable. There has never been a
period of social and economic change where such a step in cultural transformation has had to be made in such a short period of time, involving so many.

In a whole series of ways climate change is testing our citizenship, our
humanity and our globalism. I am not sure the body politic – the planetary
human race – is ready and able to meet this call. Nor am I confident that our
politicians can rise to meet the huge challenges we all face. This is a particularly
stressful period in global markets in the aftermath of a truly profound recession, where jobs are on the line and where the resources for technological
response are being sucked away by the need to overcome the huge indebtedness
that our financial leaders have bequeathed to us. What is even more troubling
is that the world is being populated annually by 70 million more stomachs to
feed and 70 million more demands on already stretched planetary life support
services.

This volume provides the basis of the challenge to come. Looming on the horizon are the 'tipping points' of unknown changes to planetary life-enabling processes. These include the functioning of a healthy ocean and its critical store of biota, the loss of ice in mountains and around the poles, the melting of the once permanently frozen methane-rich tundra, and the drying of the tropical forests, with their huge storage of carbon and their indispensable role in cooling the equatorial regions and of transferring moisture to the temperate lands. We are unsure of the resilience of these functions, as well as the possible repercussions for the already battered global economy in the face of climate change. We also must not underestimate the plight of vulnerable peoples, who have already endured profound poverty and fundamental disruptions to the functioning of their lives.

Climate change is nowadays of direct interest to those dealing with the top order priorities of international relations. It will buffet the economy. It will create civil/military violence. It has huge implications for the future of food security and water availability. It chafes away at the most troublesome dilemmas of the day. It will test our governance beyond endurance.

Yet there are signs of hope. The USA is newly led by a President who expresses concern about the science and the wider geopolitical implications of climate change. Meanwhile, the Chinese are learning that climate change will hurt them more than any other country of similar magnitude. They already realize that the low carbon economy is a social and political necessity if widespread dislocation and violence are to be avoided.

There are serious discussions taking place in the Office of Climate Change in Bonn over the workability of the proposed programme for financing the safeguard of all tropical forests under a plan named Reducing Emissions from Deforestation and Degradation (REDD). There are the beginnings of thoughtful debates on what kind of new social values, and what mix of globalism and localism, will move us to a carbon-neutral world, beyond the comfort blanket of 'technical fix' and fanciful geo-engineering. The conference of the parties to the UN Framework Convention on Climate Change in Copenhagen in December 2009, to which the noble contents of this book are geared, will make progress at least in focusing the political minds on the need for a full-bodied Protocol for global action.

Three themes that will persist in troubling us as these processes continue are:

1. What to do about financing adaptation to the effects of climate change, especially for the less-developed nations and their peoples who do not contribute to the drivers, but who are uniquely targeted by the consequences. One cannot help reflecting that this critically important matter will remain unresolved for too long. No one can prove what stresses to people and to natural processes are climate change driven. No one can find a means for financing adaptation that is equitable and sustainable. No one can feel confident about targeting funds so that they really have the effect on the most vulnerable as intended. Finally, no one has the skills to

define property rights in forests that are not corruptible, and to ensure that the livelihoods of forest dwellers are in synchrony with the needs to store carbon and divert forest removal from short-term but income-generating agriculture. We simply do not have the tools to do this. I see the need to fill these voids with credible evidence and reliable recommendations as one crucial test case for climate change interdisciplinary science in the coming years.

2. How to finance the transition to a low-carbon and sustainable economy in the aftermath of a deep and troubling recession where the political instinct is to recreate 'business as usual', and to return the unemployed and lost consumers to the familiar economic frame. Already we see signs of deep contradiction: stimulating the car producers yet facing a crisis in guaranteeing safe and reliable sources of petroleum. Trying to store carbon from newly constructed and long-lasting coal-burning power plants when there is as yet no proven technology: creating a whole new generation of electric vehicles when there is no 'super' grid of renewable electricity available, or even on the horizon; promoting biofuels in an age of food insecurity and water scarcity. There is no appetite for a credible carbon tax, or for a workable method of delivering personal carbon credits and trading schemes in the foreseeable future, when such initiatives may become vital in the coming decade. Here again is a void that 'smart' science needs to fill.

3. How to instill a social morality in the practice of carbon neutrality as strong as the established ethics of revering life and caring for one's neighbour, so that the prospect of living 'carbon neutrally' is regarded as a civic virtue. There is no precedent for such a shift in outlook. Here is where there will have to be a whole new approach to the manner of introducing schools to truly sustainable living, and to promoting community-level approaches to human well-being in the context of maintaining and enhancing ecological resilience. Nothing short of virtue in both government and citizenship, coupled with a common governing unity and backed by the diversity and vibrancy of local action, will do the trick.

This powerful volume sets out the challenges to come. It is thoughtfully edited and presented by the best in the business. It should be read with care and its suggestions acted upon with enthusiasm and unwavering commitment.

Acknowledgements

This book is a volume in an ongoing series of edited books by Routledge. The editor wishes to express gratitude to Europa Development Editor Cathy Hartley for her outstanding help, assistance and support through the various stages of the project. Thanks also to those who helped to compile the maps (the Cartographic Unit, School of Geography, University of Southampton), tables and figures that appear in this volume, and to the compilers of the A – Z glossary section of *The Environment Encyclopedia and Directory 2009* (Routledge, 2009) for their assistance.

Many thanks also go to Kamal Kapadia, Saffron O'Neil, Anabela Carvalho, Sam Randalls, Emma Tompkins, Roopali Phadke, John Cole, Adam Bumpus, Nathan Hultman, Brian Gareau and Steve Clark, as well as to the chapter authors themselves, who were very collegial as they provided immensely valuable peer reviews of chapters for the volume.

The editor also extends thanks to Margaret Fitzsimmons, David E. Goodman, E. Melanie Dupuis, Simon Batterbury, Scott Prudham, Mark Sheehan, Michael Loik, Roberto Sanchez-Rodriguez, Roger Pielke, Jr., Polly Ericksen, Maria Mansfield and Monica Boykoff for advice, support and insights along the way of producing this book. Each of these people has subtly yet importantly shaped the considerations and formulations you see in the book you now hold.

The editor wishes to thank the James Martin 21st Century School, the Environmental Change Institute and the School of Geography and the Environment for institutional support during part of the process of assembling this volume.

Of course, this book is an inherently collaborative volume, so sincere and profound thanks from the editor go to chapter contributors Emily Boyd, Ian Curtis, Michael K. Goodman, Maria Carmen Lemos, Michael D. Mastrandrea, Susanne C. Moser, Peter Newell, Chukwumerije Okereke, Bradley C. Parks, Matthew Paterson, J. Timmons Roberts, Stephen H. Schneider, Heike Schroeder and Hans von Storch.

In addition, thanks go to Chukwumerije Okereke for his co-authoship (and mentoring) on the A–Z dictionary.

Finally, the Editor thanks Elijah A.M. Boykoff and Calvin I.M. Boykoff for providing ongoing happiness.

Contents

MAPS

STATISTICS

The Editor and Contributors

Maxwell T. Boykoff is an Assistant Professor in the Center for Science and Technology Policy, and Fellow in the Cooperative Institute for Research in Environmental Sciences (CIRES) at the University of Colorado–Boulder. In Boulder he also teaches in the Environmental Studies programme. For the three years previously, he was a James Martin Research Fellow in the Environmental Change Institute and a Departmental Lecturer in the School of Geography and the Environment at the University of Oxford. He researches issues involving transformations of carbon-based economies and societies, as well as cultural politics and the environment. Cutting across these themes, his research has concentrated on interactions between state and non-state actors at the interface of environmental science, policy and practice. His research includes analyses of media coverage of climate change, how certain discourses influence environmental policy considerations, the role of celebrity endeavours in climate change issues, and links to ethics, environmental justice movements, climate adaptation and public understanding. Among his ongoing writing, he is working on a book called *Who Speaks for Climate? Making Sense of Mass Media Reporting on Climate Change* for Cambridge University Press (due out in 2010).

Emily Boyd is a Lecturer at University of Leeds and co-leader of the adaptive governance theme at the Stockholm Resilience Centre. She has a PhD in Development Studies from the University of East Anglia, Norwich. She has research interests in the climate change development interface, focusing on governance and politics of natural resource management in the context of global environmental change, questions of property rights, accountability and power dynamics between different agents and governance structures and how these interplay with ecological systems, and in complexity and feedbacks and their relation to resilience. She is currently researching resilient climate adaptation in Mumbai, India, and the development consequences of carbon offset projects in India and China. She has researched in Latin America (Bolivia and Brazil) and in Indonesia, Zimbabwe and Namibia. She has published in *Global Environmental Change*, *Journal of International Development*, *Ecology and Society*, *Development*, *Environment and Planning A*, *Philosophical Transactions of the Royal Society*, and *Environmental Science and Policy*. She is co-editing a forthcoming book (with Professor Carl Folke) on adaptive governance and transformations in socio-ecological systems (SES) (Cambridge University Press) and has co-edited an introduction to climate change (with Dr Emma Tompkins), which focuses on living with, and adapting to, climate change. She is an associate sub-editor of *Ecology and Society*.

Ian Curtis is Head of Development and Communications at the Environmental Change Institute (ECI), University of Oxford. He is founder of the Oxfordshire ClimateXchange, an experiment in community engagement, particularly focused on generating a positive attitude in society's response to climate change. ClimateXchange's Ecorenovation project was awarded the innovation poster prize at the 2009 Conference of the European Council for an Energy Efficient Economy. Ian Curtis is playing a leading role in boosting the role of non-state actors in climate governance in Oxfordshire, which has one of the highest concentrations of climate community groups in the world. He has also been closely involved in a variety of public engagement projects at ECI. These include Tipping Point, which brings together climate scientists with artists and other cultural professionals; the Nielsen global climate and consumer surveys; and the visit of the *Earth from the Air* Exhibition to Oxford. Ian Curtis has a BA (Hons) in Agriculture and Forest Sciences and an MSc in Forestry and its relation to Land Management, both from the University of Oxford. Ian was closely involved in the initial development of the then Environmental Change Unit in 1988. Prior to this he worked for Oxfam, for a public sector management consultancy, and as a professional cricketer. He is a trustee of the Oxfordshire Nature Conservation Forum and Northmoor Trust.

Michael K. Goodman is a Senior Lecturer in the Geography Department, King's College London. He is interested in the shifting cultural politics of environment and development, consumption cultures and the alternative geographies of food. Recent work includes a paper with Max Boykoff on celebrity politics in the journal *Geoforum*, and the edited volume *Contentious Geographies: Environmental Knowledge, Meaning and Scale* (Ashgate, 2008) with Max Boykoff and Kyle Evered. He is currently preparing *Consuming Space: Placing Consumption in Perspective* (Ashgate) with David Goodman and Michael Redclift, and a monograph on alternative food spaces with David Goodman and Melanie DuPuis. He currently sits on the editorial board of *Geography Compass* and edits the *Critical Food Studies* book series for Ashgate.

Maria Carmen Lemos is an Associate Professor of Natural Resources and Environment at the University of Michigan, Ann Arbor and Senior Policy Scholar at the Udall Center for the Study of Public Policy at the University of Arizona. She currently serves as the Vice-Chair. of the Scientific Advisory Committee for the InterAmerican Institute for the Study of Climate Change (IAI) and as a member of the America Climate Choice Science Panel and of the Human Dimensions of Environmental Change

Committee, National Research Council/US National Academy of Sciences. She has MSc and PhD degrees in Political Science from the Massachusetts Institute of Technology (MIT). During 2006–7 she was a James Martin 21st Century School Fellow at the Environmental Change Institute at the University of Oxford. Her research focuses on public policy-making in Latin America and the USA, especially related to the human dimensions of global change, the co-production of science and policy, and the role of techno-scientific knowledge in environmental governance and in building adaptive capacity, especially of water systems, to climate variability and change. Recent publications include papers in *Climatic Change, Ecology and Society, Global Environmental Change* and the *Annual Review of Natural Resources and Environment*. She is a contributing author to the Intergovernmental Panel on Climate Change (IPCC) and the US Climate Change Science Program Synthesis Reports. Maria Carmen Lemos is originally from Brazil, where she still carries out most of her research.

Michael D. Mastrandrea is a Consulting Assistant Professor at the Stanford University Woods Institute for the Environment. His research focuses on the physical, biological and societal impacts of climate change, policy strategies for reducing climate risks, and their accurate and effective translation for the general public, policy-makers and the business community. His research includes projects on integrated modelling of the climate and society as a tool for international and domestic policy analysis; climate change impacts and vulnerability assessment in California and world-wide based on observed climate data and climate model projections; treatment of uncertainty in climate change projections and climate policy decision-making. His work has been published in several journals, including *Science Magazine* and *Proceedings of the National Academy of Sciences*, and he is a co-author of chapters on key vulnerabilities and climate risks, and long-term mitigation strategies for the 2007 IPCC Fourth Assessment Report. He also serves on the editorial board for the journal *Climatic Change*.

Susanne C. Moser is Director and Principal Researcher of Susanne Moser Research & Consulting in Santa Cruz, CA and a Research Associate at the Institute of Marine Sciences at the University of California—Santa Cruz. Her current work focuses on local and state adaptation planning in the USA, developing guidance for participatory adaptation planning in conservation areas, and improving the communication of climate change to facilitate societal response. Her research interests include effective decision support, science-policy interactions, uncertainties in decision-making and management, and community/regional resilience in the face of rapid change. Previously, Dr Moser was a Research Scientist at the National Center for Atmospheric Research in Boulder, Colorado; a staff scientist for climate change with the Union of Concerned Scientists; a post-doctoral researcher at the Heinz Center in Washington, DC and at the Kennedy School of Government at Harvard University; and she received her PhD in geography in 1997 from Clark University. Susanne Moser is co-editor with Lisa Dilling (University of Colorado—Boulder) on a groundbreaking anthology on climate change communication, *Creating a Climate for Change: Communicating Climate Change and Facilitating Social Change* (Cambridge, 2007). She contributed to the Fourth Assessment Report of the IPCC, and is a fellow of the Aldo Leopold Leadership and Donella Meadows Leadership Programs.

Peter Newell is Professor of International Development at the University of East Anglia and an Economic and Social Research Council (ESRC) Climate Change Leadership Fellow. Prior to this he held posts including James Martin Fellow at the University of Oxford Centre for the Environment, Principal Fellow in the Centre for the Study of Globalisation and Regionalisation at the University of Warwick, Fellow at the Institute of Development Studies, University of Sussex, associate researcher at FLACSO Argentina, and researcher and lobbyist for Climate Network Europe in Brussels. He has worked on climate change issues for more than 16 years and conducted research and policy work for the governments of the UK, Sweden and Finland as well as international organizations such as the United Nations Development Programme (UNDP) and the Global Environmental Facility (GEF). He is author of *Climate for Change: Non State Actors and the Global Politics of the Greenhouse* (Cambridge University Press, 2000), co-author of *The Effectiveness of EU Environmental Policy* (Macmillan, 2000), and co-editor of *Development and the Challenge of Globalization* (ITDG, 2002), *The Business of Global Environmental Governance* (MIT Press, 2005) and *Rights, Resources and the Politics of Accountability* (Zed Books, 2006). He has two co-authored books forthcoming on *Climate Capitalism* (with Matthew Paterson) and *Governing Climate Change* (with Harriet Bulkeley).

Chukwumerije Okereke is a Research Fellow at the Smith School of Enterprise and Environment at the University of Oxford. He also an affiliate fellow of the Said Business School and the Centre for International Studies, both at the University of Oxford. His research interests lie broadly in the links between global environmental governance systems and international development. His current research focuses on the relationship between business climate strategies, government policies and international climate governance. He also explores the roles of equity norms and economic ideas in global environmental governance, drawing from political philosophy and international relations theories. Before joining the Smith School, Chukwumerije Okereke was a Senior Research Associate at the Tyndall Centre for Climate Change Research in the School of Environmental Sciences at the University of East Anglia. His recent books include *Global Justice and Neoliberal Environmental Governance* (Routledge 2008) and as editor of *The Politics of the Environment* (Routledge 2007).

Tim O'Riordan is Emeritus Professor of Environmental Sciences at the University of East Anglia. He is a Deputy Lieutenant of the County of Norfolk, Sheriff of Norwich (2009–10) and a Fellow of the British Academy. He holds an MA in Geography from the University of Edinburgh, an MS in Water Resources Engineering from Cornell University, and a PhD in Geography from the University of Cambridge. He has edited a number of key books on the institutional aspects of global environmental change, policy and practice, led two international research projects on the transition to sustainability in the European Union (1995–2002) and edited two editions of the text book, *Environmental Science for Environmental Management*. Professor O'Riordan is a member of the UK Sustainable Development Commission and of Sustainability East, the East of England Sustainable Development Round Table. His research deals with the themes associated with better governance for sustainability. He is also active in the evolution of sustainability science partnerships. His direct work relates to designing future coastlines in East Anglia so that they are ready for sea level rise, and the creation of sound economies and societies for a sustainable future. He is a core member of the Prince of Wales' seminar on Business and the Environment. He has many contacts with the business world. He is an assessor for the Prince of Wales Accounting for Sustainability project. He sits on the Corporate Responsibility Body for Asda plc and also on the Growth and Climate Change Panel for Anglian Water Group. Professor O'Riordan is also Executive Editor of *Environment Magazine*.

Bradley C. Parks is a PhD Student in the Department of International Relations at the London School of Economics and Political Science (LSE). He holds an MSc in Development Management from the LSE and a BA in International Relations from the College of William and Mary. He has written and contributed to several books and articles on global environmental politics, international political economy, and development theory and practice. Most recently, he co-authored *A Climate of Injustice: Global Inequality, North-South Politics, and Climate Policy* (MIT Press, 2007) with J. Timmons Roberts and *Greening Aid: Understanding Environmental Assistance to Developing Countries* (Oxford University Press, 2008) with Michael Tierney, J. Timmons Roberts and Robert Hicks. In 2005–9 he was an Associate Director of Development Policy in the Department of Policy and International Relations at the Millennium Challenge Corporation (MCC). He helped design and monitor the implementation of policy reform action plans in partner countries; document the MCC's impact on policy and institutional reform in compact, threshold and candidate countries; and administer the MCC's annual country selection process. As an Acting Director for MCC Threshold Programmes, he was also responsible for overseeing the implementation of a US $35m. anti-corruption programme in Indonesia and a $21m. customs and tax reform programme in the Philippines. Additionally, Bradley Parks was a founding member of the

MCC's Climate Change Working Group, which has sought to integrate more effectively climate considerations into project selection, design and implementation. Prior to joining the MCC, he was a Visiting Scholar in the Government Department at the College of William and Mary and an independent consultant to the European Commission, the UK Department for International Development, and ActionAid International.

Matthew Paterson is Professor of Political Science at the University of Ottawa. His research focuses on the political economy of global environmental change. In addition to a book developing a general theoretical approach out of these interests, he has developed them in relation to global climate change and the politics of the automobile. His publications include *Global Warming and Global Politics* (Routledge 1996), *Understanding Global Environmental Politics: Domination, Accumulation, Resistance* (Palgrave 2000) and *Automobile Politics: Ecology and Cultural Political Economy* (Cambridge University Press 2007). He has recently completed a book with Peter Newell (University of East Anglia) entitled *Climate Capitalism*. He is working on a series of articles on the political economy of climate change governance, especially its 'market-led' character, and has recently started a research project entitled 'Governance and legitimacy in carbon markets' with Matthew Hoffmann, Steven Bernstein and Michele Betsill.

J. Timmons Roberts is the Director of the Center for Environmental Studies at Brown University, where he is also Professor of Sociology. His research focuses on the role of foreign aid in climate negotiations and solutions, and a major area of recent work has been as part of the Project-Level Aid (PLAID) research project at the College of William and Mary, where he taught in 2001–9. He is the author of six books and more than 50 articles, including *A Climate of Injustice: Global Inequality, North–South Politics and Climate Policy* (MIT, 2007), co-authored with Bradley Parks.

Stephen H. Schneider is the Melvin and Joan Lane Professor for Interdisciplinary Environmental Studies, Professor of Biological Sciences and a Senior Fellow in the Woods Institute for the Environment at Stanford University. He served as a National Center for Atmospheric Research (NCAR) scientist in 1973–96, where he co-founded the Climate Project. He focuses on climate change science, integrated assessment of ecological and economic impacts of human-induced climate change, and identifying viable climate policies and technological solutions. He has consulted for federal agencies and White House staff in six administrations. Involved with the IPCC since 1988, he was Co-ordinating Lead Author, WG II, Chapter 19, 'Assessing Key Vulnerabilities and the Risk from Climate Change' and a core writer for the Fourth Assessment Synthesis Report. He, along with four generations of IPCC authors, received a collective Nobel Peace Prize for their joint efforts in 2007. Elected to the US

National Academy of Sciences in 2002, Dr Schneider received the American Association for the Advancement of Science/Westinghouse Award for Public Understanding of Science and Technology and a MacArthur Fellowship for integrating and interpreting the results of global climate research. Founder/editor of *Climatic Change*, he has authored or co-authored more than 500 books, scientific papers, proceedings and legislative testimonies, edited books and chapters, reviews and editorials, and has been featured in numerous televisions and film productions. Dr Schneider counsels policy-makers, corporate executives and non-profit stakeholders about using risk management strategies in climate-policy decision-making, given the uncertainties in future projections of global climate change and related impacts. He is actively engaged in improving public understanding of science and the environment through extensive media communication and public outreach.

Heike Schroeder is a Research Fellow with the Tyndall Centre for Climate Change Research and the James Martin 21st Century School at the Environmental Change Institute, University of Oxford. Her research focuses on analysing options for international action on climate change; the roles of non-nation-state actors and emerging countries in a post-2012 international policy framework; and international forest governance and the evolving REDD mechanism. She is also a member of the Scientific Steering Committee of the Earth System Governance Project under the International Human Dimensions Programme on Global Environmental Change (IHDP). In 2003–7 she was a researcher at the University of California—Santa Barbara and the Executive Officer of a 10-year international research project on the Institutional Dimensions of Global Environmental Change (IDGEC), a core project of the IHDP. Her latest publications include O.R. Young, L.A. King and H. Schroeder (editors) *Institutions and Environmental Change* (MIT Press 2008) on the findings of the IDGEC project.

Hans von Storch is a Director of the Institute of Coastal Research, GKSS Research Centre (Geesthacht, Germany) and Professor at the Meteorological Institute of the University of Hamburg; he is also a member of the steering committee of the centre of excellence CLISAP (Integrated Climate System Analysis and Prediction) at the University of Hamburg, and a member of the advisory board of the German Climate Computing Centre (DKRZ). He was a lead author of the Third Assessment Report of the IPCC. In 2008 Hans received an honorary doctorate from the University of Gothenberg. His scientific focus is on regional climate dynamics and change, coastal change, coastal defence, climate modelling, and scientific and public construction of climate change. He is author and/or editor of 13 books, more than 145 peer-reviewed articles, and a frequent author of articles in public daily and weekly newspapers.

Abbreviations

a.m.	ante meridiem (before noon)
BAU	Business as Usual
CA	California
CBD	Convention on Biological Diversity
CD ROM	Compact Disc read-only memory
CDM	Clean Development Mechanism
CEO	Chief Executive Officer
CFC	Chlorofluorocarbon/s
CITES	Convention on International Trade in Endangered Species of Wild Fauna and Flora
CO	Colorado
CPR	Committee of Permanent Representatives
CSD	Commission on Sustainable Development
CT	Connecticut
CTE	Committee on Trade and Environment
DC	District of Columbia
DNA	Deoxyribonucleic acid
DSB	Dispute Settlement Body
EC	European Commission
ECOSOC	United Nations Economic and Social Council
EDA	Environmental Direct Action
EJ	Environmental Justice
EMAS	Eco-management and Audit Scheme
EMG	Environmental Management Group
EMIT	Group on Environmental Measures and International Trade
EMS	Environmental Management Systems
est.	estimate/estimated
EU	European Union
FAO	Food and Agriculture Organization
FBI	Federal Bureau of Investigation
FCCC	Framework Convention on Climate Change
FEMA	Federal Environmental Management Agency
FoE	Friends of the Earth
FoEI	Friends of the Earth International
GATT	General Agreement on Tariffs and Trade
GDP	Gross Domestic Product

GEF	Global Environmental Facility
GEG	Global Environmental Governance
GEMS	Global Environmental Monitoring System
GEO	Global Environmental Outlook
GHG(s)	greenhouse gas(es)
GM	genetically modified
GMEF	Global Ministerial Environmental Forum
ha	hectare
IAEA	International Atomic Energy Agency
IBRD	International Bank for Reconstruction and Development (World Bank)
IL	Illinois
IMF	International Monetary Fund
IMO	International Maritime Organization
INFOTERRA	Global Environmental Information Exchange Network
IPCC	Intergovernmental Panel on Climate Change
IPE	International Political Economy
ISO	International Standards Organization
IUCN	International Union for Conservation of Nature (formerly World Conservation Union)
JI	Joint Implementation
JPI	Johannesburg Plan of Implementation
kg	kilogram
KS	Kansas
MA	Massachusetts
MBIs	Market-Based Instruments
MD	Maryland
MDGs	Millennium Development Goals
MEAs	Multilateral Environmental Agreements
MLG	Multi-Level Governance
MNC	Multinational Companies
NATO	North Atlantic Treaty Organization
NEPIs	New Environmental Policy Instruments
NGO	Non-governmental Organization
NJ	New Jersey
ODA	Official Development Aids
OECD	Organisation for Economic Co-operation and Development
PA	Pennsylvania
PRSP	Poverty Reduction Strategy Papers
SUV	Sports Utility Vehicle
SWMTEP	System-Wide Medium-Term Environmental Programme
TEU	Treaty on European Union
TRIPS	Trade-related aspects of intellectual property rights
TX	Texas
UN	United Nations

UNCED	United Nations Conference on Environment and Development
UNCHE	United Nations Conference on the Human Environment
UNCLOS	United Nations Conference on the Law of the Sea
UNDP	United Nations Development Programme
UNEP	United Nations Environment Programme
UNESCO	United Nations Educational, Scientific and Cultural Organization
UNFCCC	United Nations Framework Convention on Climate Change
UNFPA	United Nations Population Fund
UNGA	United Nations General Assembly
UNIDO	United Nations Industrial Development
US(A)	United States (of America)
VAs	Voluntary Agreements
vs.	versus
WCED	World Commission on Environment and Development
WHO	World Health Organization
WI	Wisconsin
WMO	World Meteorological Organization
WRI	World Resources Institute
WSSD	World Summit on Sustainable Development
WTO	World Trade Organization
WWF	World Wide Fund for Nature

Essays

Introduction

MAXWELL T. BOYKOFF

Climate change is a defining theme for the 21st century. Changes in the climate permeate our lives in multifarious ways, affecting critical functions in economic, political and social systems upon which we base our lives and our well-being. Alluding to this dynamism and prominence, climate scientist and geographer Mike Hulme has commented, 'climate change has more potency now as a mobilising idea than it does as a physical phenomenon' (2009, 328).

In response, the interdisciplinary nature of engagement here in *The Politics of Climate Change: A Survey* reflects the contemporary conditions where climate politics penetrate all aspects of our lives. 'Politics' here are considered as the management and contestations of policies, through social relations infused with power, authority and varying perspectives. 'Politics' involve proposals, ideas, intentions, decisions and behaviours, with a focus on processes that prop up, challenge, lurk behind, support and resist explicit actions. By directing inquiries in this way, the authors in this volume unpack and examine varied influences that expand as well as constrict the spectrum of considerations for ongoing climate politics, deliberations and governance.

Moving headlong into the 21st century, this period of time has been dubbed the 'Anthropocene Era' due to the unprecedented scale of human influence on the environment (Crutzen 2002).[1] Since the beginnings of the Industrial Revolution in the 1700s by way of iron smelting in the coal-rich Shropshire region in the United Kingdom (UK), heavy reliance on carbon-based sources for energy and materials in industry and society have contributed to substantial changes in the climate. In this contemporary milieu, anthropogenic sources of CO_2 are primarily attributed to transportation, industry, household use/infrastructure, and land use and land-cover changes. Emissions from these activities thus contribute to increases in concentrations of atmospheric CO_2 and associated climate changes (IPCC 2007).

An expansive genealogy of the 'discovery' of climate change or global warming in Western science begins with inquiries by German astronomer Frederick William Herschel in the 1700s. Herschel examined how sunspots may have an effect on cooling and warming periods of planet earth (Weart 2003). Histories of modern scientific inquiries more specific to anthropogenic climate change often look to work initiated by French physicist Jean-Baptiste Joseph Fourier, who examined the earth's energy budget and worked to explain heat-absorptive processes in the atmosphere (Fleming 1998). Furthering this work, in the late 1800s British scientist John Tyndall experimented with various atmospheric gases in order to understand their unique heat-trapping capacities, while Swedish physicist Svante Arrhenius looked specifically at the heat absorption of CO_2 and the connections to (warming) atmospheric temperature (Bolin 2007). From these foundational observations and experiments, physical scientific examinations of changes in the climate continued through the mid-20th century by way of notable researchers such as Guy Stewart Callendar, Milutin Milanković, Gilbert Plass, Willard Frank Libby, Hans Seuss, Roger Revelle and Charles David Keeling.

This edited volume is a collaborative effort that seeks to address associated pressing and formidable questions in the area of climate politics. The collection draws on a vast array of authors' experience, expertise and perspectives; contributors have backgrounds in climate science, environmental studies, geography, biology, sociology, political science and psychology. In this book, authors offer keen insights, observations and analyses as they work through salient questions along themes such as politics at the science-policy interface, the politics of markets and economics, the politics of climate ethics and justice, the politics of adaptation and development, and the politics of public engagement.[2] Chapter authors interrogate the many webs of negotiations, from formal and codified policy actions to informal ways of understanding, considering and engaging with climate change.

In the Foreword to the book, Tim O'Riordan points out how over the last three decades we have seen concerns regarding human contributions to climate change move from obscure scientific inquiries to the fore of science, politics, policy and practice at multiple levels. These developments have been accompanied by growing recognition that physical science identification of 'climate change' in the 18th century has opened up over time to interdisciplinary challenges linking to social sciences and the humanities, in turn interacting with contemporary politics, governance and policymaking. It is here, in the interstices of human institutions and the environment – referred to by Simon Dalby as 'Anthropocene Geopolitics' (2007) – where critical decisions about a collective future rapidly unfold. Such decisions pose significant challenges for the resilience of institutions and society. In his recent book (with a similar name to this one), Anthony Giddens commented, 'responding to climate change will prompt and require innovation in government itself and in the relations between the state, markets and civil society' (2009, 94). Chapters in this volume demonstrate that while much more is needed, a great deal is already under way. In the aggregate, these endeavours are highly contentious as they cut to the heart of industry and society in the 21st century. From local adaptation strategies to international treaty development, the power-infused 'politics of climate change' are as pervasive and contested as ever.

The first three chapters in the volume provide a solid foundation for understanding these politics of climate change. Chapter 1, by Stephen H. Schneider and Michael D. Mastrandrea, begins by working through the tenets of climate science, such as climate cycles and processes, historical climate patterns, the scientific basis for attribution of current climate change to human activities, and climate change models. They discuss how these aspects of the science are treated in politics and policymaking, as well as how climate science has become increasingly politicized in recent decades. In a section entitled 'mediarology', the chapter then focuses on the role of mass media as an important link between science, policy actors and the public. Drawing from a combination of prominent illustrations and personal experiences, the authors then offer suggestions as to how scientists and the media can improve representations of various dimensions of climate science.

Chapter 2, by Heike Schroeder, situates these interactions in a 30-year history of climate politics and policy since the 1979 World Climate Conference in Geneva, Switzerland. She identifies four phases through which climate politics have moved up to the present negotiations unfolding through the United Nations Conference of Parties talks. These might be referred to in shorthand as the emergence of climate change in the political realm (through the formation of the Intergovernmental Panel on Climate Change—IPCC), regime creation (through the development of the United Nations Framework Convention on Climate Change—UNFCCC), regime strengthening (centred on the Kyoto Protocol), and regime maturation (by way of the development of a post-2012 architecture). Schroeder wades through the acronym soup that has developed in climate politics over time to clarify the key issues, processes and institutions involved in these arenas of international climate politics. She insightfully clarifies what have become increasingly murky waters, where international climate regimes and supporting institutions have grown in sophistication and complexity.

Chukwumerije Okereke picks up these discussions in Chapter 3, in the context of present political activities, and further delineates prominent issues in these high-profile and highly-politicized climate negotiations. Also, while Schroeder emphasizes on history through the institutions in Chapter 2, Okereke turns a critical gaze to the actors – particularly nation-states and coalition groups. He focuses on elements of leadership and trust as he lays out the details of how certain compromises have been vital to the functioning of ongoing climate negotiations in the theatre of treaty negotiations. Most prominently, Okereke discusses these politics through the constructions of affinity groups in 'developed' and 'developing' countries, of countries in the 'Global North' and 'Global South'.

In Chapter 4, Hans von Storch examines how various features of the climate science-policy interface shape consequent dimensions of policy advice and public understanding. He describes two competing frames of knowledge he calls 'cultural constructs' and 'scientific constructs' in order to help analyse how misunderstandings and discrepancies have developed between the science and policy communities over time. Drawing on experiences primarily in the German context, von Storch analyses how to improve connectivity at the climate science-policy interface, particularly as we move into negotiations for a post-2012 international climate policy regime. He draws usefully on science-policy insights from Roger Pielke, Jr and Peter Weingart, as well as the tenets of postnormal science (also discussed in Chapter 1) as they relate to environmental decision-making.

In Chapter 5, Peter Newell and Matthew Paterson expand considerations to those of political economy and finance as well as relations between the states and markets. They survey an increasingly hegemonic arena of climate politics governed by markets through the carbon economy. The authors characterize the carbon economy as an inter-related web of climate governance systems tied into processes of commodification of the atmosphere, and fetishization of markets. This is manifested through emissions trading and carbon offsets (both voluntary and through the Clean Development Mechanism—CDM), as well as carbon disclosure schemes. They trace the history of the carbon economy to key developments in neoliberalism, concurrent to the institutional history outlined by Schroeder (Chapter 2). Their critical analysis is then cast upon what the future implications of this emergent form of climate governance might be, and whether and under what conditions the carbon economy might enable a transition to climate capitalism, in which capitalist imperatives of accumulation are achieved through low-carbon economic growth. They argue that it remains unclear whether the carbon economy will follow a path towards unregulated and privatized 'cowboy climate capitalism' or a more regulated, state-managed 'climate Keynesianism'. None the less, they outline how these routes will have critical consequences for constraining or expanding possibilities for significant greenhouse gas (GHG) emissions reductions and decarbonization in the post-2012 regime.

In Chapter 6, Maria Carmen Lemos and Emily Boyd shift our attention from climate mitigation to the multi-dimensional politics of adaptation. Mitigation and adaptation initiatives are often overlapping and inter-related in climate politics and governance. However, in general, mitigation activities tend to be those that protect the climate and environment from humans, while adaptation activities are those that protect humans from the environment. As Lemos and Boyd work through many pertinent elements of adaptation politics, they focus on the crucial questions of justice, resource distribution and development. The authors argue that for adaptation strategies to engage successfully with goals of vulnerability reduction and resilience capacity building, policy negotiators and leadership must commit financial resources that match the scale of need, agree upon a realistic conception of 'additionality', achieve a substantive accountability framework, and better co-ordinate these activities with the ongoing work in development communities. In this burgeoning web of governance, Lemos and Boyd effectively work through what might be seen as daunting complexities, and clearly delineate the vital issues at stake in these processes.

Further along these discussions of vulnerability, risk and resilience, in Chapter 7 Bradley C. Parks and J. Timmons Roberts interrogate questions of global North–South relations, and associated issues of responsibility, equity and justice. They focus their comments on the ambitious objective of a just and equitable post-2012 climate agreement. Their essay takes us through many reasons why it is important to account for equality and justice when formulating these policy agreements. In so doing, they point to many challenges that divergent viewpoints, perspectives and interests may pose on fostering an atmosphere of trust, which is fundamental to success. They posit that unconventional, heterodox and hybrid forms of climate politics and interventions are needed in order to overcome histories of troubled North–South environmental relations. They argue that mitigation discussions to date have overlooked longer-term issues of inequality in global North–South relations. Therefore, they turn to adaptation in particular as a way to promote civic and co-operative norms, and to inspire poor country participation in a climate treaty. To finish, the authors offer hopeful words for building a global, just, trusting and long-term co-operative climate accord.

The final two chapters emphasize interactions in the spaces of everyday. Chapter 8, by Maxwell T. Boykoff, Michael K. Goodman and Ian Curtis, explores the workings of how formal climate science, policy and politics meet the everyday lived experience. The chapter looks to how these interactions are contested, negotiated and ever-changing in both the discursive realm (e.g. what political discussions on climate action are dominant and legible) and material spaces (e.g. how these activities relate to issues of consumption). The chapter addresses how climate phenomena are framed in various contexts and thus who effectively is authorized to 'speak for the climate'. They trace how the range of 'actors' speaking out about climate change mitigation and adaptation has expanded – particularly into popular culture – as climate change has earned increasing attention in public and policy arenas. Like Chapter 1, this chapter also points out the importance of mass media. Boykoff, Goodman and Curtis specifically explore how mass media stitch together developments in art, music, sport and through a range of celebrity voices. The authors then ask questions about what these developments may have achieved so far in terms of keeping or taking GHGs out of the atmosphere, and related themes of consumption in increasingly 'naturalized' neoliberal contexts.

Chapter 9, by Susanne C. Moser, addresses climate politics as they relate to public understanding and engagement. Moser posits that no matter what treaty or accord is ultimately implemented, public support and engagement are critical to its ultimate success (or failure). In the chapter, Moser situates potential citizen action in a complex landscape of political economics, ideologies, structural forces, habitual behaviour, and the agency of nature across scales and places. She appraises the state of these interactions at present, and surveys awareness, understanding, concern, personal action and policy support across a number of social contexts. In so doing, the chapter assesses various ways that inspire or disillusion people to take part in mitigation or adaptation activities. Moser draws on research on climate communications through imagery, emotions and our 'rational' self in order to work through what communication strategies tend to empower people and inspire participation, as well as what information may overwhelm them and lead to disengagement. The chapter ultimately argues that leadership seeking successful climate governance must commit to consider carefully these factors on public engagement, and initiatives must commit resources in ways resembling wartime mobilizations to combat the sources and impacts of anthropogenic climate change effectively.

Taking these contributions together, this project has been carried out during a pivotal time in climate politics, at multiple scales and in countless communities. As one example we can look to both multilateral and bilateral negotiations at the international level. This book goes to press while the world is on the cusp of a possible new multilateral commitment to international architectures that address GHG emissions through mitigation and adaptation actions (a potential agreement at the December 2009 UN Climate Conference in Copenhagen, Denmark). Much is at stake in terms of the structure and function of the carbon economy and society (e.g. Boykoff et al. 2009), as leaders seek a climate treaty to follow on from the 1997 Kyoto Protocol, which expires in 2012. Meanwhile, rhetoric from the recently elected US President Barack Obama and his staff has indicated a shift in US climate policy stance. Many participants in climate politics view this change as signalling a significant break from the preceding President, George W. Bush, who was an oft-considered climate villain as he withdrew US participation in the Kyoto Protocol.

In terms of concurrent bilateral negotiations at the international level, in the first months after coming into office, President Obama sent US Secretary of State Hilary Clinton to the People's Republic of China to open a dialogue on climate mitigation. These US–China talks seek to overcome what has become an entrenched impasse on commitments for climate actions to mitigate anthropogenic GHG emissions (Goldberg 2009). This dialogue — and possible progress from the two greatest contributors to climate change on planet earth — may be a profound step forward for climate politics in symbolizing movements beyond North–South differences discussed in Chapters 6 and 7. Will these bilateral talks take on the significance of the historic 'Nixon goes to China' trip in 1972 if the USA and China broker a partnership? Will these developments inspire as well as foster more co-ordinated multilateral climate policy action in Copenhagen? Time will tell. None the less, whether the potential strength of President Obama's commitments derived from promising early rhetoric and actions will be significant remain an open question, as the Copenhagen negotiations unfold.

This does not mean to suggest that the signing, ratification and entry into force of a successor treaty would represent the 'solution' to anthropogenic climate change. Rather, it calls attention to a dominant mode of climate action unfolding at the international level at this time. Former British Prime Minister Winston Churchill once said, 'It has been said that democracy is the worst form of government except all the others that have been tried'. This might usefully be applied to ongoing international climate politics and policy in their present form and function. In 2007, in a paper entitled 'Time to Ditch

Kyoto', Prins and Rayner put forward a critique of the Kyoto Protocol when they wrote (2007, 973):

'The Kyoto Protocol is a symbolically important expression of governments' concern about climate change. But as an instrument for achieving emissions reductions, it has failed. It has produced no demonstrable reductions in emissions or even in anticipated emissions growth. And it pays no more than token attention to the needs of societies to adapt to existing climate change ... the Kyoto Protocol was always the wrong tool for the nature of the job.'

Among others, climate scientist John Schellnhuber responded to this Prins and Rayner critique by commenting that these are well-known deficiencies in the Kyoto process; however (2007, 346):

'Kyoto is simply a miserable precursor of the global regime intended to deliver genuine climate stabilization — and was never expected to be more. 'Ditching' it now would render all the agonies involved completely meaningless after the event, denying the entire process of policy evolution the slightest chance to succeed.'

These exchanges point to some of the highly-contentious politics and debates that often undergird explicit policy statements.

This example represents an indisputably compelling and contingent space of climate politics. Many related questions of critical importance are taken up to varying degrees throughout this volume: what are the most effective architectures for addressing climate mitigation and adaptation challenges? How can related concerns such as poverty, consumption, population and biodiversity protection be incorporated effectively into climate politics and governance? Can sustainable development objectives be harmonized with transitions to renewable energy pathways? In what ways do certain groups benefit from currently constructed global governance structures with heavy reliance on economic markets and the authority of the nation-state? What voices are not at the policy negotiating table and whose interests may not be represented in dominant conceptions of climate politics? How might stakeholders with a range of interests, vulnerabilities and resilience capacities differentially address, accept and adopt climate policy measures? In what ways might varied social movements align interests to promote climate mitigation and adaptation goals?

As indicated by these many questions, the comments above and the chapters in this volume, climate change is no longer merely an environmental issue. In the years to come, the contours of climate politics will undoubtedly continue to be fiercely contested. Meanwhile (strong) political leadership and (progressive) institutional actions will rapidly reconfigure these spaces. Once more, the collective intention here with *The Politics of Climate Change: A Survey* is that the contributions herein offer foundational information, insights and analyses that will prove useful to all readers, from academic researchers, business actors and government representatives, to policy negotiators, activists, students and interested members of the public. These essays that you hold in your hands seek to help make sense of these contemporary contexts, and catalyse our collective thinking about how the future of climate science, policy, politics and governance intersect with our lives, livelihoods, happiness and well-being.

The chapters are supplemented by an extensive A–Z glossary section of terms, organizations and issues of note, cross-referenced for ease of use; a selection of maps offering graphic representation of issues affecting climate change; and statistics for reference.

NOTES

1 Through improving detection and attribution work (e.g. Allen et al. 2000, Tett et al. 1999), a consensus has emerged in the climate science community that human activity has largely driven climate changes in the past two centuries, and changes are not merely the result of natural fluctuations (see Chapter 1 for more).
2 To cover all the dimensions of the politics of climate change would require an encyclopaedic accounting, so some issues are not addressed in as much detail as we might have desired.

REFERENCES

Allen, M.R., Stott, P.A., Mitchell, J.F.B., Schnur, R. and Delworth, T.L. (2000) 'Quantifying the uncertainty in forecasts of anthropogenic climate change', *Nature* 401, 617–20.

Bolin, B. (2007) *A History of the Science and Politics of Climate Change: The Role of the Intergovernmental Panel on Climate Change.* Cambridge: Cambridge University Press.

Boykoff, M., Bumpus, A., Liverman, D. and Randalls, S. (2009) 'Theorising the carbon economy: introduction to the special issue', *Environment and Planning A* 41 (10), 2299–2304.

Crutzen, P.J. (2002) 'The Anthropocene', *Journal de Physique IV France* 10, 1–5.

Dalby, S. (2007) 'Anthropocene geopolitics: globalisation, empire, environment and critique', *Geography Compass* 1, 1–16.

Fleming, J.R. (1998) *Historical perspectives on climate change.* Oxford: Oxford University Press.

Giddens, A. (2009) *The politics of climate change.* Cambridge: Polity Press.

Goldberg, S. (2009) 'Clinton tries to build China climate pact', *The Guardian*, 14 February, 12.

Hulme, M. (2009) *Why we disagree about climate change: understanding controversy, inaction and opportunity.* Cambridge: Cambridge University Press.

IPCC (2007) *Climate Change 2007: The Physical Science Basis.* Geneva, Switzerland.

Prins, G. and Rayner, S. (2007) 'Time to ditch Kyoto', *Nature* 449, 973–75.

Schellnhuber, J. (2007) 'Kyoto: no time to rearrange the deck chairs on the *Titanic*', *Nature* 450, 346.

Tett, S.F.B., Stott, P.A., Allen, M.R., Ingram, W.J. and Mitchell, J.F.B (1999) 'Causes of twentieth-century temperature change near the Earth's surface', *Nature* 399, 569–72.

Weart, S.R. (2003) *The Discovery of Global Warming.* Cambridge, MA: Harvard University Press.

The Politics of Climate Science

STEPHEN H. SCHNEIDER AND MICHAEL D. MASTRANDREA

There is growing world-wide momentum to address the problem of climate change. Scientists now have high confidence that rapid, human-induced climate change and many measurable impacts are already at hand, and that further, more severe impacts can be expected in the future as changes continue, with the potential for catastrophic changes if the drivers of human-induced climate change are not curbed. Thus, we face immediate societal choices about how to reduce both the drivers of climate change, primarily greenhouse gas emissions from fossil fuel burning, and the harmful consequences that cannot be avoided for vulnerable populations and regions. This chapter examines how the interactions between science, policy, politics and the media have shaped the course of the public policy debate over climate change, with a specific focus on the USA (where many of the most contentious and influential debates over climate change have played out). Given the essential need for the USA to 'walk the walk' of domestic climate policy before most other nations in the world will commit to serious long-term reductions, what happens in the USA is a bellwether for what will likely occur internationally in the formal negotiating process. We discuss the different standards by which scientific and political debates are governed, how these debates are portrayed by the media (which often serve as a conduit by which the public and politicians learn about scientific information), and how political considerations have often overwhelmed scientific considerations. We also comment on ways to improve the interaction between science and politics in the context of climate change. To clearly distinguish between consensus and contention, and to understand what consensus actually means in a complex systems science like climate change, are tasks incumbent on us all.

First, though, it is important to understand the current state of scientific knowledge of climate change.

THE BASIC CLIMATE SCIENCE

Since the second half of the 19th century, the global average surface air temperature has risen unequivocally. Through 2005, this increase is estimated by the Intergovernmental Panel on Climate Change (IPCC) to be 0.76°C above the average for the second half of the 19th century, with a 90% confidence interval of 0.57–0.95°C, accounting for measurement and sampling errors (Solomon et al. 2007). Although the decade from 1998 to 2008 has not seen a rapid rising trend in global surface temperature (whereas the decade before that had a dramatic trend), nevertheless, 12 of the previous (to 2009) 13 years rank among the 12 warmest years on record. There is now overwhelming scientific evidence that the primary driver of this observed global-scale warming, particularly the rapid warming over the last 40 years, is emissions of infrared-trapping gases such as carbon dioxide and methane, from human activities—primarily, the burning of fossil fuels, but also agricultural practices, deforestation and cement production. Warming temperatures have been linked to a number of other changes around the world, such as melting of mountain glaciers, the Greenland ice sheet and polar ice, rising and increasingly acidic seas, increasing frequency and/or severity of droughts, intensified heat waves, fires, hurricanes, and changes in the lifecycles and ranges of plants and animals as spring advances toward winter.

The potential of carbon dioxide in the atmosphere to trap solar radiation was proposed as early as 1827 by the mathematician and physicist Joseph Fourier. This mechanism is called the greenhouse effect, a term coined by Svante Arrhenius in 1896, who first argued that changes from human activities in the level of carbon dioxide in the atmosphere could have a significant effect on surface temperature (see, e.g., Weart 2003). The greenhouse effect is now scientifically well-established, and is rooted in basic radiative transfer physics and thermodynamics. The gases that comprise the earth's atmosphere are moderately transparent to short-wave, visible light. About half of the radiant energy from the Sun penetrates the atmosphere and is absorbed by the surface, while the other half is absorbed by the atmosphere or reflected back to space by clouds, atmospheric gases, aerosols and the earth's surface. This absorbed energy warms the surface and atmosphere, which re-emit energy as infrared radiation. To stay in energy balance, the earth must radiate away the same amount of energy it absorbs, but the atmosphere is much less transparent to infrared radiation. Carbon dioxide and other greenhouse gases and clouds absorb 80–90% of the infrared radiation emitted at the surface and re-emit energy in all directions, both up to space and back down towards the surface. This trapping of infrared energy adds heat to the lower layers of the atmosphere, warming the surface layer further, which emits infrared radiation at a still greater rate, and so on, until the emitted infrared radiation to space is in balance with the absorbed short-wave radiant energy from sunlight and the other forms of energy coming and going from the surface (for example, rising plumes of convective energy, or evaporated water vapour that carries a great deal of latent chemical energy from the surface to the clouds, where it is released in the condensation process).

The natural greenhouse effect makes our planet much more habitable, about 33°C warmer, than it otherwise would be. However, human activities, predominantly the burning of fossil fuels, are increasing the concentrations of greenhouse gases in the atmosphere directly and indirectly, thus intensifying the greenhouse effect. The indirect effect is primarily the extra evaporation of water from a warmed surface, a feedback that adds more of the greenhouse gas water vapour to the atmosphere, warming the surface further. These amplifying influences are called positive feedbacks in radiative forcings since the net effect of the addition of greenhouse gases when averaged over the globe is to trap extra heat, which in turn increases temperatures in order to eventually restore energy balance. Human-induced emissions of greenhouse gases include carbon dioxide, methane, nitrous oxide, a host of industrial gases, such as chlorofluorocarbons, that do not appear naturally in the atmosphere and, indirectly, ozone in the lower atmosphere, formed as a health-damaging component of smog from fossil fuel burning (such ozone formation is also increasing with atmospheric warming). Fuel combustion and, to a lesser extent, agricultural and industrial processes, also produce emissions of aerosol particles, many of which, such as sulfate aerosols, directly reflect incoming solar energy upward toward space, a negative radiative forcing. Some dark aerosols, such as soot, absorb solar energy, a positive forcing if they darken the planet enough to cause more sunlight to be absorbed. Aerosol particles also affect the colour, size and number of cloud droplets, in aggregate, a negative forcing, though some black carbon particles can darken cloud drops and even lead to their evaporation if the darker droplets absorb enough extra solar energy. The effects of aerosols on the optical properties of clouds are known as 'indirect aerosol radiative forcing'. Another indirect effect is soot falling on snow and ice, darkening it and thus accelerating melting.

Many land-use activities, such as deforestation, contribute to greenhouse gas emissions, a positive forcing, and can change the earth's albedo, or reflectivity by, for example, replacing 'dark' forest by 'light' agricultural land, in aggregate, a negative forcing. However, deforested surfaces may warm locally since the removal of evapo-transpiring vegetation can reduce evaporative cooling of the surface even more than the loss of absorbed solar energy from increased surface albedo. Current estimates of the effect of all of these non-carbon dioxide radiative forcing factors indicate that the combined influence of all human activities to date is roughly equivalent to the positive radiative forcing of increased carbon dioxide concentrations alone, with the positive forcing of the non-CO_2 greenhouse gases and dark aerosols roughly offset by the negative forcing of direct and indirect aerosol effects and land use changes. While scientists have very high confidence that the net human forcing is positive (heating), uncertainty remains regarding its magnitude and the magnitude of various components, particularly the negative forcing from direct and indirect aerosol effects (Forster et al. 2007).

Climate has varied greatly in the more distant past and natural processes, such as changes in the energy output of the Sun or volcanic eruptions, also affect the earth's energy balance. Aerosols injected into the stratosphere from large volcanic eruptions, where they can remain for several years, can lead to a temporary lower-atmospheric cooling of generally up to a few 10ths of a degree Celsius during that period. Medium-term variations in solar output on decadal time scales from variability in the Sun itself are implicated in temperature changes of up to a few tenths of a degree Celsius, whereas changes in the earth's orbital elements such as tilt or eccentricity (known as Milankovitch cycles), have substantially affected the earth's climate on the timeframe of many thousands of years. The sunspot cycle also has a small effect on solar output (~0.1%). Natural processes alone, though, do not cause a sufficiently sustained radiative forcing to explain more than a small fraction of the observed warming of the past 40 years. On the other hand, anthropogenic forces can explain a much higher fraction of what has been observed over the past half century (Hegerl et al. 2007).

Examining past climate allows scientists to compare the current changes with past naturally-induced changes. Scientists use 'proxies' that vary depending on temperature and other climatic variables as a window into climates of the past. Proxies such as tree rings and pollen percentages in lake beds indicate that current temperatures are the warmest of the millennium, and that the rate and magnitude of warming over the past 150 years are likely greater than any previous changes during this period (Hegerl et al. 2007). Ice cores bored in Greenland and Antarctica provide estimates of both temperature and atmospheric greenhouse gases going back hundreds of thousands of years, spanning several cycles of shorter periods of warmth (5,000–20,000-year interglacials) separated by longer (up to 100,000 years), colder ice ages (Jansen et al. 2007). Not only do they indicate a strong correlation between temperature and atmospheric greenhouse-gas concentrations, particularly carbon dioxide and methane, they also indicate that current levels of carbon dioxide and other greenhouse gases in the atmosphere are far above any seen in at least the past 650,000 years at least. Ice cores also provide information about volcanic eruptions and variations in solar energy, furthering understanding of these natural forcing mechanisms described above.

Scientists have found overwhelming evidence of the human 'fingerprint' on observed warming trends. For example, the earth's stratosphere has cooled while the surface has warmed—a fingerprint of changes owing to increased atmospheric greenhouse gases and stratospheric ozone-depleting substances rather than, for example, a fingerprint of an increase in the energy output of the Sun, which should warm all levels of the atmosphere (Hegerl et al. 2007). This growing body of evidence has led the IPCC to conclude that it is *very likely* (at least a 90% chance) that human activities are responsible for most of the warming observed over the 20th century, particularly that of the last 40 years.

There are two general sources of uncertainty in projecting future climate change: the future trajectory of human-induced greenhouse-gas emissions and how the natural climate system will respond to those emissions. Policy decisions can strongly influence the first source of uncertainty (future emissions), but will have little influence on the second source (climate response to emissions) as that is a (still not precisely known) property of the complex climate system.

Uncertainty regarding these two sources makes projecting future climate change a complex, imprecise task, meaning that there are a range of plausible projections for future climate conditions. Scientists employ computer models of the global climate system, describing mathematically the physical, biological and chemical processes that determine climate to project the response of the climate to scenarios for future greenhouse-gas emissions. The ideal model would include all processes known to have climatological significance and would involve spatial and temporal detail sufficient to model phenomena occurring over small geographic regions and over short time periods. Today's best models strive to approach this ideal, but they still entail many approximations because of computational limits and incomplete understanding of climatically important small-scale phenomena, such as clouds (Randall et al. 2007). Global climate models are currently limited by a combination of data availability and computational power to a geographic grid-box resolution of roughly 50–100 km horizontally and 1 km vertically. Because all physical, chemical and biological properties are averaged over a single grid cell, it is impossible to represent these 'sub-grid-scale' phenomena *explicitly* within a model. However, they can be treated *implicitly* by a parametric representation or 'parameterization'. A parameterization connects sub-grid-scale processes to explicitly-modelled grid-box averages via semi-empirical rules designed to capture the major interactions between these scales. Developing and testing parameterizations to assess the degree to which they can reliably incorporate sub-grid-scale processes is one of the most arduous and important tasks of climate modellers.

The best models reproduce approximately, though not completely accurately, the detailed geographic patterns of temperature, precipitation and other climatic variables seen on a regional scale, and can project changes in those patterns given scenarios for future greenhouse-gas emissions. The IPCC Fourth Assessment Report (AR4) includes climate model projections based upon six 'storylines', possible future worlds with different assumptions about future population growth, levels of economic development and potential technological advancement, as well as the rate at which such advancements are actually deployed around the globe (Meehl et al. 2007). For a scenario in which heavy reliance on fossil fuels drives emissions so that they continue to increase significantly during the century, the IPCC AR4 projects further global average surface warming of 2.4–6.4°C by the year 2100. For a scenario in which emissions grow more slowly, peak around the year 2050 and then fall (with concentrations in 2100 still reaching around a doubling of pre-industrial CO_2), the IPCC projects further warming of 1.1–2.9°C by the year 2100. The difference between these ranges is an indication of the influence of different trajectories for future greenhouse-gas emissions on projected climate change. The ranges themselves represent uncertainties associated with feedbacks within the climate system—how much temperatures will increase for a given level of greenhouse-gas emissions (the so-called climate sensitivity), and how the carbon cycle and the uptake of carbon dioxide by the ocean and by terrestrial ecosystems will be altered by changing temperature and atmospheric greenhouse-gas concentrations.

These different ranges and rates of warming imply very different risks of climate change, affecting both projected changes in other climatic variables (for example, precipitation patterns) and the projected intensity and likelihood of occurrence of a variety of climate impacts (Parry et al. 2007). While warming at the low end would be relatively less damaging, it would likely still be significant for some communities, sectors and natural ecosystems, as some systems have already shown concerning responses to the ~0.76°C warming over the past century. Warming at the high end of the IPCC range could have widespread catastrophic consequences and very few positive benefits, save perhaps shipping routes across the ice-free Arctic Ocean, or oil exploration in that sensitive region. A temperature change of 5–7°C on a globally averaged basis is about the difference between an ice age and an interglacial period occurring in merely a century, not millennia like ice-age interglacial transitions. The rapidity of such a change would risk many dangerous impacts (see, e.g., Schneider et al. 2007).

THE INTERFACE OF SCIENCE AND POLICY

The acknowledgement of global concern has not been achieved without a lot of bumps and bruises along the way. The greenhouse effect and its intensification by human-induced emissions of greenhouse gases are well understood and solidly grounded in basic science. Nevertheless, climate change is not just a scientific topic but also a matter of public and political debate. Responding to climate change will fundamentally affect natural systems, energy production, transportation, industry, government policies, development strategies, population-growth planning, distributional equity, and individual freedoms and responsibilities around the world (see Chapter 5 by Newell and Paterson, and Chapter 7 by Parks and Roberts for more). Decisions on the scale and timing of climate policy will imply an array of costs and/or benefits for stakeholder communities with conflicting priorities. Moreover, vulnerable populations threatened by unequally distributed climate impacts can benefit from climate policies that reduce the magnitude of their exposure to harmful climate trends, but their vulnerability also depends on trends in adaptive capacity, improvements which, within limits, can reduce their susceptibility to climate impacts (see Chapter 6 by Lemos and Boyd for more).

Policymakers, lobbyists, financial interests, environmental advocates and climate contrarians have struggled mightily to turn the weight of public opinion—and the funds controlled by it—in their preferred directions. Most mainstream scientists have countered with the methods at their disposal: research to increase understanding and predictive capacity, responsible reporting of research data, best practice theory, international co-operation and calls for policy consideration. The battle is by no means won—extensive and sustained global action is required to reach the goal of coping with climate impacts already in the pipeline, let alone preventing even more damaging climate change in the coming decades.

Why haven't we made more progress in reducing greenhouse gas emissions, given that the current threats have been articulated in nearly the same terms for at least three decades? Why are alternative sources of energy still only a small percentage of production relative to polluting fossil fuels and why do politically charged calls for new drilling in sensitive environments continue to be made? What has been going on for 40 years since this problem first was put under the noses of government officials all over the world? The answers are both simple and complicated. The simple can be summed up as ignorance, greed, denial, tribalism and short-term thinking—and the growing number of people for whom to feed, house and fashion productive lives. The complicated will require sustained in-depth analysis of many examples (see Schneider 2009 for a personal history of this 35-year climate debate).

Assessing climate science, impacts and policy issues rarely involves certainties, but rather requires assessment of risks—defined as a function of the likelihood of the occurrence of a specific event and its consequences. The climate problem is filled with 'deep uncertainties', uncertainties in both likelihoods and consequences that are not resolved today and are very unlikely to be resolved to a high degree of confidence before we have to make decisions regarding how to deal with their long-term and, in some cases, potentially irreversible, implications. These decisions often involve very strong and conflicting stakeholder interests and high stakes. Sociologists Funtowicz and Ravetz (e.g., Funtowicz and Ravetz 1993) have called such problems examples of 'post-normal science'. In Kuhn's 'normal science' (Kuhn 1962), the practice is to strive to reduce uncertainty through standard science: data collection, modelling, simulation, model-data comparisons and so forth. The objective is to overcome the uncertainty—to make known the unknown. New information, particularly reliable and comprehensive empirical data, may eventually narrow the range of uncertainty. In this way, further scientific research into the interacting processes that make up the climate system can reduce uncertainty in the response of the system to increasing concentrations of greenhouse gases. Post-normal science, on the other hand, acknowledges that while normal science continues its progression, some groups want or need to know the answers well before normal science has resolved the deep inherent uncertainties surrounding the problem at hand. In that case, there will not be a clear consensus on all important conclusions. Even the most optimistic 'business-as-usual' emissions pathway is projected to result in some dramatic, and potentially dangerous, climate impacts. Therefore, there is a clear need to consider policy decisions before this uncertainty is resolved, rather than using it as a justification for delaying action and preserving the status quo (see Chapter 4 by von Storch for more). Assessing risk is primarily a scientific issue for scientists to resolve, but deciding which risks to tolerate and which to try to avoid—so called 'risk-management'—is primarily a value-laden, normative activity for the political process to resolve.

Sometimes a post-normal scientific debate happens unconsciously inside the scientific tent. Such events are not rare, and occurred in the IPCC AR4 over sea-level rise projections in two different working groups. Because Greenland ice was melting much faster than models predicted, the Working

Group 1 scientists projected about 1–2 feet of rise this century from thermal expansion of the oceans and ice sheet mass balance (Solomon et al. 2007), and chose not to project sea-level rise contributions from dynamical ice sheet melting (which was believed to be an important component of the observed melting), and just added a caveat. On the other hand, Working Group 2, required by governments to take a risk-management approach, assigned a medium confidence—one-third to two-thirds chance—that 4–6 m of sea-level rise could occur over centuries to millennia (Schneider et al. 2007). In debates with Working Group 1 colleagues, we from Chapter 19 of Working Group 2 argued that paleoclimatic history and the fact that melting is going much faster than predicted requires us to estimate, but not with high confidence, the potentially concerning metres of potential rise in centuries—a time frame for which ports and cities would not like to have to face dislocation. 'But there is no scientific consensus on this conclusion', we were told by Working Group 1 scientists, and indeed there wasn't consensus on the conclusion itself. However, the consensus that is important in this case is not consensus on one specific outcome, but rather over the *confidence* we have in the scientific basis for the range of possible outcomes, even less likely ones if they imply significant impacts like metres of sea-level rise with a 50/50 chance. Society, not scientists, should decide how to react to more uncertain, but highly significant, potential risks. Therefore, we believe scientific information about the range of possible outcomes needs to be communicated to decision-makers, since what to do about the prospect of low-probability/high-consequence outcomes is a normative risk-management judgement that only society should make.

The multiply peer-reviewed, government-approved IPCC Assessment Reports present the best approximation of a world-wide consensus on climate change science every five to six years (most recently in 2007). One important feature of IPCC reports is the quantified assessment of the likelihood of each major conclusion, and the explicit assignment of the authors' confidence in the underlying science to back up each conclusion. This practice clearly separates out aspects that are well established, from those that are better described by competing explanations, and from those best labelled as speculative.

The plethora of uncertainties inherent in climate change projections clearly makes risk assessment difficult (see, e.g., Morgan and Henrion 1990). In this context, some fear that actions to control potential risks could unnecessarily consume resources that could be used for better purposes, especially if impacts turned out to be on the benign side of the range. This can be restated in terms of Type I and Type II errors. If governments were to apply the precautionary principle and act now to mitigate risks of climate change, they'd be said to be committing a Type I error if their worries about climate change proved unfounded and anthropogenic greenhouse-gas emissions didn't greatly modify the climate and thus lead to dangerous change. A Type II error would occur if serious climate change did occur, after insufficient hedging actions had been taken because uncertainty surrounding the climate change projections was used as a reason to delay policy until the science was 'more certain'. Deciding whether to be Type I versus Type II error averse is not only a scientific activity (i.e., assessing risk), but also a personal value preference (choosing which risk to face).

Decision-makers must weigh the importance of climate risks against other pressing social issues competing for limited resources. Therefore, they must have information about potential climate impacts associated with different levels of climate change (consequences), and the range of future climate change that could be induced by different levels of future emissions (the likelihood of those consequences occurring).

'MEDIAROLOGY'

The IPCC reports provide an important conduit for scientific research to be accurately communicated to policy-makers and the general public, who rarely directly see 'raw science' from the lab, the field, or computer models. Universities, non-governmental organizations (NGOs), private businesses, government agencies, and other groups and organizations play a dynamic and often influential role in the interactions between science and policy. However, in general, science reaching the general public is filtered through the media (see Chapter 8 by Boykoff, Goodman and Curtis for more). This filtering process plays the critical role of communicating scientific information in clear and relevant terms. However, it can also (and often has in the past) play a distortionary role. In reporting political, legal, or other advocacy-dominated stories, it is both natural and appropriate for fair and honest journalists to report 'both sides' of an issue. In science, there are rarely just two polar-opposite sides, but rather a spectrum of potential outcomes, which are often accompanied by a history of scientific assessment of the relative credibility of each possibility. When journalists attempt to force scientific debates into this bi-polar mould, competing claims sampled from the extreme ends of the spectrum of opinions often get disproportionate time as either/or options. What needs to be conveyed to the public is the relative credibility of each claim. The political balance model often results in well-established conclusions given equal weight in a story with speculative ones, resulting in public confusion regarding both scientific knowledge and appropriate societal responses. This is an important aspect of what we call 'mediarology', a discipline everyone interested in climate change and public policy needs to understand.

Such a framing has also been dominant in political debates in the USA. For example, in a 17 April 2007 hearing of the US House of Representatives Science and Technology Committee (110th Congress House Hearings 2007), Congressman Dana Rohrabacher from Orange County, California tried to challenge the testimony of four IPCC Lead Authors, co-author of this chapter Stephen Schneider among them, by noting that temperatures since 1998 had not risen, thus suggesting human-induced global warming is not occurring. Schneider explained that climate is about trends over many decades. A record from 1992 to 2000 would have suggested a catastrophic rate of warming much more rapid than the longer-term trend. All such short-term runs have little to do with climate trends and predominantly reflect natural variability—long-term averages are needed to separate a real trend from climatic noise.

A snippet of fact disembodied from fair context, such as the example above, is typical of 'courtroom epistemology'—in short, 'it is not one's job to make an opponent's case'. Expert witnesses spouting opposing views—in Congress, courtrooms, or on editorial pages—often obscure an issue more than they enlighten juries, congressional representatives, or the general public. They often refuse to acknowledge that an issue is multifaceted and present only their own argument, ignoring—or denigrating—opposing views.

In the popular media, Congressman Rohrabacher's testimony would appear as a short phrase soundbite such as, 'it hasn't warmed since 1998 though greenhouse gases have increased, so global warming is refuted', followed by Schneider saying, 'it is too short a time to see any significant trend and what happened since 1998 proves nothing'. It is likely that such a tit-for-tat soundbite 'debate', where a mainstream, well-established consensus of climate experts is 'balanced' against the opposing views of a few contrarians, would likely cause an audience of non-experts to come away confused and not ready for endorsement of strong measures to address climate change—each position may seem equally credible. A typical reaction is to say, 'well, if the experts don't know, how can I know, so let's just wait a while until they figure it out'. That is precisely the strategy of the climate contrarians, to ensure public confusion that saps the political energy needed to fashion meaningful policies that help the planet and future generations, but hurt the special interests that are vested in the status quo.

This situation is not helped by the fact that scientists are often untrained in communication to non-scientists. Scientists do not make their reputations by repeating what is well-established, but rather by arguing at the cutting edge where much speculation remains. Thus any journalist looking for controversy has to go no further than a scientific conference to find all they can scratch down on their note pads. What is often missing at such conferences are survey talks that summarize what is shared knowledge and well-established conclusions in the broad scientific community, where a preponderance of evidence drives a consensus—or at minimum a partial consensus.

Polemics such as those described above have been a staple in most Congressional hearings on climate change for quite some time (see, e.g., Mooney 2005). In 1981, at Congressman Albert Gore, Jr of Tennessee's first contentious climate change hearing (97th Congress House Hearings 1981), there was a nasty debate with the newly-elected Reagan Administration, which cut the climate impacts research at the US Department of Energy (DOE) because the administration perceived it had a mandate to reduce 'wasteful' spending, which included societal research related to the environment. The following are a few excerpts from this hearing:

> After several witnesses defended the DOE programme (Dr Roger Revelle, Dr Lester Lave, Dr Joseph Smagorinsky and Dr Schneider), Congressman

Gore questioned the Administration official who was sceptical about the impacts research programme. Congressman Gore said: 'let me ask you, do you share the sense of urgency that I feel about getting a firmer grip on whether or not this problem is in fact occurring?'

'No', Dr N. Douglas Pewitt, the new DOE official, said.

When Congressman Gore asked why, Dr Pewitt said: 'I think that in running a scientific research program, we have a responsibility to the Congress and the American people to act in a fashion that is not alarmist. We have been down this road in similar areas before; for example, in aerosols and in the SST's [supersonic transport] disturbing of the atmosphere. It clearly is the prerogative of the Congress and policymakers to set a higher priority than the scientific programs can produce research results. There is a natural approach to scientific research that probably would not justify much of the more alarming carbon dioxide statements. I absolutely refuse as an official in a responsible position to engage in the type of alarmism for the American public that I have seen in these areas time and time again, and I do not think that I can responsibly encourage that sort of alarmism'. (The ozone 'alarmism' Dr Pewitt mentioned turned out to be much worse than scientists had forecast at the time, when the ozone hole was discovered in the mid-1980s.)

Congressman Gore took a few steps over to a chart documenting carbon dioxide levels that had been gathered over the past 23 years, remarking that the chart reflected a consistent pattern, 'quite unlike the skimpy evidence upon which the SST and aerosol debate was based'. The record shown was collected at Mauna Loa in Hawaii by Scripps Institution of Oceanography chemist, Dr David Keeling and initiated by the efforts of Gore's college mentor, Dr Revelle, who was there testifying that day. Congressman Gore asked Dr Pewitt, 'Doesn't that lead you to look at it in a different light?'

Dr Pewitt countered, 'I am not an atmospheric scientist ... I am a high energy physicist, a particle physicist. I understand false correlations; until one understands fundamental mechanisms of how things happen, they can be trapped into false correlations. Twenty-three years is not exactly a significant timeframe in the weather'.

'We have it going back to 1958 with reliability but the same pattern goes all the way back to 1880, and you can see fluctuations for the Great Depression, for two world wars', Congressman Gore said. The chart clearly showed the dramatic drop in emissions during the Depression and the rapid increase following the period of industrialization after World War II.

Dr Pewitt: 'You have several different effects going on here at the same time. It is a very difficult system to understand; this is a very complex physical system ... We have some bright people advising us on this program ... You can't have bureaucrats dictating science, but at the same time you can't have scientists using alarmism in order to justify bigger research budgets. That is irresponsible, too ... Nobody predicts anything to happen in less than 50 years. It is important not to waste the next decade, but it is also important not to stop everything in the world, on the basis of misinformation'.

Congressman Gore parried, agreeing that 'while we ought to avoid alarmism, we also ought to avoid a head-in-the-sand attitude at the same time'.

In the advocacy arena, everybody knows the game—spin for the client—and is alert to the practice. In science, though, where many don't know that game, the playing field for public discussions is not level. Scientists tend to think that advocacy based on a 'win for the client' mentality that deliberately selects 'facts' out of context is highly unethical. Those practising full disclosure while ignorant of the methodology of courtroom epistemology are often imputed to be spinning the facts by those who only know the advocacy rules—spin or lose—but are unaware of the damage to one's reputation that detectable spin would cause a scientist. When a scientist merely acknowledges the credibility of some contentious information or endorses actions that affect stakeholders differentially, opposing advocates often presume the expert (scientist) is spinning the information for some client's benefit. Even when the scientist points out that there is a wide range of possibilities and refers to extensive peer-reviewed assessments, the opposition accuses the expert of currying favour. After all, isn't that what everybody else is doing?

It's not that reporters, politicians, lawyers and others, or their methods, are wrong or that 'impartial' scientists are morally superior; the question is whether the techniques of advocacy-as-usual are suited to a subject like climate change. Indeed, just as it would be a breach of scientific ethics to deliberately spin the facts, it would be a breach of ethics for a professional advocate, lobbyist, or lawyer *not* to advance his or her client's interests, even if it means self-consciously picking and choosing from the full range of data available.

The fundamental question related to climate change and mediarology, then, is: how can we encourage advocates to convey a balanced perspective when the 'judge' and 'jury' are Congress or public opinion, the 'lawyers' are the media, and the polarized advocates get only 10-second soundbites each on the evening news or five minutes in front of a congressional hearing to summarize a topic that requires hours just to outline the range of possible outcomes, much less convey the relative credibility of each claim and rebuttal? How do we deal with this bubbling cauldron of special interests, paradigmatic misunderstandings, and time-honoured and entrenched professional practices?

TRANSCENDING MEDIAROLOGY

There are no simple answers, but there are some guidelines that can help. First, it is indeed a scientist's responsibility to honestly report the range of plausible cases (what can happen) and their associated (usually at least partially) subjective probability distributions (what the odds are) and confidence levels, so that the risks of climate change can be assessed. At the same time, a scientist could have a personal opinion on what society ought to do with a particular risk assessment. Can a scientist who expresses such value preferences about a controversial topic also provide an unbiased assessment of the factual components? This may be a feasible tightrope to walk, but even if one is scrupulously careful to separate factual from value-laden arguments, will the outside world of advocates and advocate institutions buy it as 'objective'?

The more scientists discuss their initial assessments with colleagues of various backgrounds, the higher the likelihood we can illuminate unconscious biases. We may not ever reach the archetype of 'pure objectivity'—but 'pure objectivity' is, of course, a myth in science. The path to objectivity does not involve scientists holding back their opinions in order to maintain a pretense of some higher calling as 'objective scientist'. Rather, only active effort to make our biases conscious and explicit via outside review is likely to effectively keep our science-advocacy more objective and allow us to better manage the 'advocacy-truth' conundrum by doing both.

Scientists can take a more proactive responsibility for the public debate. If scientists fail to address the public arena, claiming it is 'dumbed down' and beneath our lofty 'objectivity', we will only add to the miscommunication (see Chapter 9 by Moser for more). It is also important to use accessible language and metaphors. Scientific jargon is effective for communicating with other scientists, but is often misunderstood in the public arena and increases the probability that a scientist will be 'boxed in', misquoted, or ignored altogether. Scientists can write review papers from time to time and present talks that stress well-established principles at the outset of meetings before the debate turns to the more speculative, innovative science, deliberately outlining the *consensus* before revealing the *contention*. This should not be a threat to the careers of daring young scientists who, in addition to contributing to new knowledge, also report on the state of the science writ large.

It would be worthwhile for scientists, reporters and policy-makers to better understand each other's paradigms. Public dissemination of scientific knowledge would be improved if science graduate students were required to take a course in public communication, including the process of political advocacy and science policy formulation. Similarly, journalism schools need to explore with their students the consequences of misapplying 'balanced' reporting techniques from political arenas to complex issues in which not all opinions deserve—nor should receive—equal billing in a story. An approach that elaborates on the relative credibility of a range of views on complex issues—not just the extreme opposites—is what is needed to properly inform the public. Finally, literate citizens can take responsibility for educating themselves about all 'sides' of the climate change debate and their relative probabilities, so that they can see past biased media opinions or bi-polar 'duelling scientists'.

That is why the IPCC adopted in its Third Assessment Report a consistent guidance on uncertainty language (Moss and Schneider 2000), in which terms such as 'likely' or 'high confidence' were linked to a quantitative scale of expert subjective probabilities to ensure consistency in terminology across the assessors. With scientists assessing risks in consensus probabilistic language, it makes it simpler for decision-makers who require such information to do their job: fashioning risk-management actions that make explicit their values over priorities for public policy attention better informed by a consistent assessment of risks.

These are complex and confusing times and it is important to be able to clearly express values when it is time to make policy. It is the job of *all* citizens, including scientists, policy-makers and journalists to understand the distinction between consensus and contention and where each exists, and to maintain a willingness to change current beliefs in light of challenging new evidence.

REFERENCES

97th Congress House Hearings (1981) *Carbon Dioxide and Climate: The Greenhouse Effect*, Hearing before the Subcommittee on Natural Resources, Agriculture Research and Environment, and the Subcommittee on Investigations and Oversight of the Committee on Science and Technology, Washington, DC: US Government Printing Office.

——(2007) *The State of Climate Change Science 2007*, Hearing before the Committee on Science and Technology, Serial No. 110–20, available at: frwebgate.access.gpo. gov/cgi-bin/getdoc.cgi?dbname = 110_house_hearings&docid = f:32966.wais

Forster, P., V. Ramaswamy, P. Artaxo, T. Berntsen, R. Betts, D.W. Fahey, J. Haywood, J. Lean, D.C. Lowe, G. Myhre, J. Nganga, R. Prinn, G. Raga, M. Schulz and R. van Dorland (2007) 'Changes in Atmospheric Constituents and in Radiative Forcing', in S. Solomon, D. Qin, M. Manning, Z. Chen, M. Marquis, K.B. Averyt, M. Tignor and H.L. Miller (eds), *Climate Change 2007: The Physical Science Basis*, Contribution of Working Group I to the Fourth Assessment Report of the Intergovernmental Panel on Climate Change, Cambridge and New York: Cambridge University Press, 129–234.

Funtowicz, S.O. and J.R. Ravetz (1993) 'Three Types of Risk Assessment and the Emergence of Post-Normal Science', in S. Krimsky and D. Golden (eds), *Social Theories of Risk*, Westport, CT: Greenwood, 251–73.

Hegerl, G.C., F. W. Zwiers, P. Braconnot, N.P. Gillett, Y. Luo, J.A. Marengo Orsini, N. Nicholls, J.E. Penner and P.A. Stott (2007) 'Understanding and Attributing Climate Change', in S. Solomon, D. Qin, M. Manning, Z. Chen, M. Marquis, K.B. Averyt, M. Tignor and H.L. Miller (eds), *Climate Change 2007: The Physical Science Basis*, Contribution of Working Group I to the Fourth Assessment Report of the Intergovernmental Panel on Climate Change, Cambridge and New York: Cambridge University Press, 663–746.

Jansen, E., J. Overpeck, K.R. Briffa, J.-C. Duplessy, F. Joos, V. Masson-Delmotte, D. Olago, B. Otto-Bliesner, W.R. Peltier, S. Rahmstorf, R. Ramesh, D. Raynaud, D. Rind, O. Solomina, R. Villalba and D. Zhang (2007) 'Palaeoclimate', in S. Solomon, D. Qin, M. Manning, Z. Chen, M. Marquis, K.B. Averyt, M. Tignor and H. L. Miller (eds), *Climate Change 2007: The Physical Science Basis*, Contribution of Working Group I to the Fourth Assessment Report of the Intergovernmental Panel on Climate Change, Cambridge and New York: Cambridge University Press, 433–98.

Kuhn, T. (1962) *The Structure of Scientific Revolutions*, Chicago, IL: University of Chicago Press.

Meehl, G.A., T.F. Stocker, W.D. Collins, P. Friedlingstein, A.T. Gaye, J.M. Gregory, A. Kitoh, R. Knutti, J.M. Murphy, A. Noda, S.C.B. Raper, I.G. Watterson, A.J. Weaver and Z.-C. Zhao (2007) 'Global Climate Projections', in S. Solomon, D. Qin, M. Manning, Z. Chen, M. Marquis, K.B. Averyt, M. Tignor and H.L. Miller (eds), *Climate Change 2007: The Physical Science Basis*, Contribution of Working Group I to the Fourth Assessment Report of the Intergovernmental Panel on Climate Change, Cambridge and New York: Cambridge University Press, 747–846.

Mooney, C. (2005) *The Republican War on Science*, New York: Basic Books.

Morgan, M.G. and M. Henrion (1990) *Uncertainty: A Guide to Dealing with Uncertainty in Quantitative Risk and Policy Analysis*, New York: Cambridge University Press.

Moss, R.H. and S.H. Schneider (2000) 'Uncertainties in the IPCC TAR: Recommendations to Lead Authors for More Consistent Assessment and Reporting', in R. Pachauri, T. Taniguchi and K. Tanaka (eds), *Guidance Papers on the Cross Cutting Issues of the Third Assessment Report of the IPCC*, Geneva, Switzerland: World Meteorological Organization, 33–51.

Parry, M.L., O. Canziani, J.P. Palutikof, C. Hanson and P. van der Linden (eds) (2007) *Climate Change 2007: Impacts, Adaptation and Vulnerability*, Contribution of Working Group II to the Fourth Assessment Report of the Intergovernmental Panel on Climate Change. New York: Cambridge University Press.

Randall, D.A., R.A. Wood, S. Bony, R. Colman, T. Fichefet, J. Fyfe, V. Kattsov, A. Pitman, J. Shukla, J. Srinivasan, R.J. Stouffer, A. Sumi and K.E. Taylor (2007) 'Climate Models and Their Evaluation', in S. Solomon, D. Qin, M. Manning, Z. Chen, M. Marquis, K.B. Averyt, M. Tignor and H.L. Miller (eds), *Climate Change 2007: The Physical Science Basis*, Contribution of Working Group I to the Fourth Assessment Report of the Intergovernmental Panel on Climate Change, Cambridge and New York: Cambridge University Press, 589–662.

Schneider, S.H. (2009) *Science as a Contact Sport: Inside the Battle to Save Earth's Climate*, New York: National Geographic Press.

Schneider, S.H. et al. (2007) 'Assessing key vulnerabilities and the risk from climate change', in M. Parry et al. (eds), *Climate Change 2007: Impacts, Adaptation, and Vulnerability*, Contribution of Working Group II to the Intergovernmental Panel on Climate Change Fourth Assessment Report, Cambridge and New York: Cambridge University Press, 779–810.

Solomon, S., D. Qin, M. Manning, Z. Chen, M. Marquis, K. B. Averyt, M. Tignor and H. L. Miller (eds) (2007) *Climate Change 2007: The Physical Science Basis*, Contribution of Working Group I to the Fourth Assessment Report of the Intergovernmental Panel on Climate Change. Cambridge and New York: Cambridge University Press.

Weart, S.R. (2003) *The Discovery of Global Warming*, Cambridge, MA: Harvard University Press.

The History of International Climate Change Politics: Three Decades of Progress, Process and Procrastination

HEIKE SCHROEDER

INTRODUCTION

International climate change politics turned 30 in 2009. At its hour of birth at the first World Climate Conference in 1979, an already large constituency of 400 scientists from 50 countries appealed to 'the nations of the world ... to foresee and to prevent potential man-made changes in climate' (Gupta 2001, 12). Some 30 years later, anthropogenic greenhouse gas (GHG) emissions continue to rise unabatedly; no country has yet managed to reverse its upward emissions trend, except through fortunes of history. The collapse of the former Soviet bloc and the outcome of the United Kingdom's 'dash for gas' policy under Thatcher just before the United Nations Frameworks Convention on Climate Change (UNFCCC) emissions baseline year of 1990 are the exceptions, and the current economic crisis may come to have a similar effect. The climate regime is at a crucial juncture now; will it continue at a slow pace, following the 'law of the least ambitious program' (Underdal 1980, 36), or will it take scientific emissions scenarios to heart and recreate itself in a way to achieve deep cuts in emissions in the order of 50%–85% by 2050 (IPCC 2007, 20)? This chapter takes stock of this 30-year history, identifying four distinct phases. The first phase covers the process of politicization of the issue and the creation of the Intergovernmental Panel on Climate Change (IPCC). The second phase spans the regime formation process and the adoption of the UNFCCC. Third, the negotiation and implementation of the Kyoto Protocol are examined. Lastly, the fourth phase covers the negotiations toward a post-2012 deal. The chapter provides the chronology and a critical assessment of key features shaping the four phases in terms of the effectiveness and broader consequences of the climate regime.

PHASE ONE: INSTITUTIONALIZING THE SCIENCE—THE IPCC

From the 1950s, the USA invested heavily in meteorological research to aid the development of computer technology, aviation and weaponry (Harper 2003). In 1957, the Mauna Loa Observatory, an atmospheric baseline station, was set up in Hawaii and has been continuously monitoring and collecting data. There, Charles David Keeling and his team developed the Keeling Curve, which shows the rise in concentration of atmospheric CO_2 since 1958. It observed for the first time the rapidly increasing levels of CO_2 and visualized the effects of human activity on the earth's atmosphere.

As scientific data began to suggest a gradual warming of the earth's atmosphere, a number of international scientific conferences were held from the 1970s onward. Scientists gradually built up evidence that human-induced emissions had already begun to affect the climate. In 1979 the World Meteorological Organization (WMO) organized the first World Climate Conference in Geneva, where some 400 scientists from 50 countries appealed to policy-makers to consider precautionary action concerning possible anthropogenic interference with the global climate (Paterson 1996, 27–28; van Beukering and Vellinga 1996, 198; Brenton 1994, 165). It was the first conference to recognize climate change as a serious problem.[1] This new political 'threshold' (Lunde 1991, 14) was further marked by a conference in Villach in 1985, when scientists declared that a rise in global mean temperatures 'greater than any in man's history' could occur in the first half of the 21st century as a result of the increasing concentrations of GHGs in the atmosphere. The participating scientists recommended that 'scientists and policy makers should begin active collaboration to explore the effectiveness of alternative policies and adjustments' (Skodvin 2000).

The first conference where climate change was dealt with as a major political issue took place in 1988 in Toronto, with participation of over 300 scientists and policy-makers from 48 countries. It recommended that governments and industry should reduce emissions by 20% of 1988 levels by 2005 as an initial global goal (Paterson 1996, 33–34). At the 1990 Second World Climate Conference in Geneva, with scientific and ministerial participation from 137 countries, ministers agreed to a global strategy based on the precautionary principle (van Beukering and Vellinga 1996, 201).

The first major institutional milestone was the establishment of the IPCC in 1988 (Skodvin 2000). The IPCC was set up by the United Nations Environment Programme (UNEP) and the World Meteorological Organization (WMO) with the objective of assessing 'the scientific, technical and socio-economic information relevant for the understanding of the risk of human-induced climate change' in a 'policy relevant', rather than a 'policy prescriptive' manner.[2] The IPCC does not have a mandate to carry out its own research. Rather, it assesses peer-reviewed and published scientific and technical literature to produce policy-relevant, state-of-the-art scientific reports. Its main publications are the assessment reports and their summaries for policy-makers (SPMs) and synthesis reports, which are published every five-to-six years. The main bodies of the organization are the three Working Groups on science, impacts and responses, respectively, and the IPCC Plenary, which includes government representatives and experts from intergovernmental organizations (IGOs) and non-governmental organizations (NGOs).[3]

The latter is where the SPMs are negotiated, line by line, oftentimes word by word. IPCC lead authors and government representatives, including policy-makers and scientists, take part in this process, enabling, at best, the emergence of political acceptance of the knowledge produced by the scientists, at worst a watering down of the science to politically acceptable levels. However, substantive changes to the text cannot be made without consent from the lead authors, as they can veto changes they regard to be unsubstantiated. The only means of influencing the results then is through utilizing the rules of procedure as a tool for delaying the process.[4] Unlike the IPCC's voluminous assessment reports (some 750–900 pages per Working Group), the short SPMs (some 10–20 pages) are widely circulated, referenced and reported on by the media.

Although there has been a relatively high level of acceptance of the scientific knowledge base provided by the IPCC and its political neutrality among national delegates,[5] scientific debates and controversies have prevailed. One such debate has been over the validity of human-induced warming as opposed to naturally occurring climate change or the ability to attribute changes to human activity. In this regard, the First Assessment Report (Houghton et al. 1990) concluded that the increasing atmospheric GHG concentrations were largely due to human activities and that an international climate change agreement should be negotiated. This led to the adoption of a UN General Assembly resolution in late 1990 and the creation of an Intergovernmental Negotiating Committee (INC) in 1991, which was charged with negotiating the UN Framework Convention on Climate Change.

The Second Assessment Report (Houghton et al. 1996) then formulated it in this way: 'The balance of evidence suggests a discernible human influence on global climate' and 'the observed warming trend is unlikely to be entirely natural in origin'. It helped to put debate over the validity of anthropogenic climate change more or less to a close (Depledge 2002; Brack and Grubb 1996), and it may have influenced the change of position by the USA, which, in 1996, began to endorse the idea of a legally-binding protocol (Schröder 2001). The Third Assessment Report (Houghton et al. 2001) determined that there 'is new and stronger evidence that most of the [global] warming observed over the last 50 years is attributable to human activities', and the Fourth Assessment Report (IPCC 2007) concluded that while 'difficulties remain in reliably simulating and attributing observed temperature changes at smaller scales[,] warming of the climate system is unequivocal'. According to some calculations, to stabilize global anthropogenic GHG emissions at 445–490ppm (parts per million) (without an overshoot in emissions)—resulting in an estimated global temperature rise of 2.0–2.4°C above the pre-industrial average—emissions would need to peak before 2015 and be reduced by 50%–85% of 2000 levels by 2050.

Being a boundary organization (Guston 1999, 2) at the interface of the scientific and the political realm, there is always a tension in the assessments between 'a dedication to notions of truth and credibility in the scientific world and claims of interest, power and legitimacy in the political world'

(Siebenhüner 2003, 113). The IPCC publications also remain biased by under-representation from the Global South in the working groups. Also, the body of literature reviewed remains mainly an English-language one. Despite these shortcomings, the IPCC has made some important improvements during its first two decades in progressing on what it was established to do, to provide authoritative and policy-relevant assessments of the science, impacts and possible responses to climate change.

PHASE TWO: CREATION OF A CLIMATE REGIME—THE UNFCCC

The UNFCCC was completed after 16 months of negotiations; there was a deadline of adopting an agreement in time for signature at the UN Conference on Environment and Development (UNCED) in Rio de Janeiro, and it entered into force in March 1994. Some 15 years after its adoption, 192 states plus the European Community have ratified and acceded to or approved the treaty, amounting to almost universal membership.[6] However, this came at the price of a weaker, non-binding agreement. The Convention established the institutional and procedural architecture—the rules of the game—with an objective, a set of principles and reporting obligations for all parties.

The UNFCCC's long-term objective is the 'stabilisation of greenhouse gas concentrations in the atmosphere at a level that would prevent dangerous anthropogenic interference with the climate system'. It should be 'achieved within a time-frame sufficient to allow ecosystems to adapt naturally to climate change, to ensure that food production is not threatened and to enable economic development to proceed in a sustainable manner' (Article 2). What would constitute 'dangerous' and what time-frame would be sufficient was not specified at the time. This gave the interpretation of the objective some flexibility but has also made it a highly political issue given that determining the level of 'dangerous' can hardly be done on scientific grounds alone. It is bound to an assessment of risk given that 'answers to some scientific questions become less accurate over decadal timescales' (Oppenheimer 2005; see also Mastrandrea and Schneider 2004; Keller et al. 2005).

To achieve its objective, the Convention emphasizes five principles in Article 3 to guide the actions and measures undertaken by parties: 1) common but differentiated responsibility, implying that industrialized countries should take the lead in mitigating climate change as they bear the historical responsibility; 2) the specific needs of developing countries should be given full consideration, especially those countries that are particularly vulnerable to the adverse effects of climate change; 3) the precautionary principle, suggesting that lack of full scientific certainty should not be a reason for postponing measures to mitigate climate change; 4) sustainable development and that policies and measures to protect the climate should be commensurate with national circumstances and promote economic development; and 5) that parties should co-operate in promoting an open international economic system that would lead to sustainable economic growth, especially in developing countries.

These principles were not translated into any legally binding targets for industrialized countries, mainly due to US resistance (Oberthür and Ott 1999, 34). As a compromise, in Article 4 a non-binding 'aim' for industrialized countries to return 'individually or jointly to their 1990 levels' was agreed. In addition, industrialized countries were subjected to obligations to adopt national policies and report on their progress periodically. The Conference of the Parties (COP) was required to review the adequacy of these commitments at its first session, and undertake a 'second review' by no later than 31 December 1998.[7] In addition, all parties to the Convention were obligated to publish national inventories of emissions and national programmes to address their emissions, as well as promoting and co-operating in the development and diffusion of technologies and practices, exchange of information and education, training and public awareness related to climate change.

The Convention's institutional structure includes a secretariat, located in Bonn, Germany, the COP and two subsidiary bodies to the COP, the Subsidiary Body for Implementation (SBI) and the Subsidiary Body for Scientific and Technical Advice (SBSTA), as shown in Figure 1 below.

The Convention also established practices and processes to support a constant development and implementation of the regime (Oberthür and Ott 1999, 37). Three are particularly noteworthy. First, delegation power and size are hugely disparate across parties. This leads to richer countries sending larger delegations with specialists who can cover all issue items on the agenda and poorer countries sending small delegations with generalists who need to pick and choose on which issue areas to focus their attention. Second, the dichotomy of Annex I versus non-Annex I countries is increasingly unhelpful and arbitrary, taking for granted the large diversity of countries within these two groups (Okereke and Schroeder 2009). This does not equitably reflect the principle of common but differentiated responsibilities and respective capabilities as the differences among countries are much more fluid than the static list of Annex I versus non-Annex I countries would suggest. This has made the regime considerably less flexible as a result. Third, the existence of negotiating blocs has somewhat helped overcome the two points mentioned above. By negotiating as part of larger blocs, countries are able to increase their power in the negotiations, which is especially useful for countries with smaller delegations. Countries are able to associate with like-minded countries, who share negotiating positions.

PHASE THREE: STRENGTHENING THE CLIMATE REGIME—THE KYOTO PROTOCOL

After the Convention entered into force in 1994, the first COP took place a year later in Berlin. COP-1 reviewed the adequacy of commitments under the Convention and decided that they were not adequate in view of the Convention's objective. It adopted the Berlin Mandate, in which an Ad Hoc Group on the Berlin Mandate (AGBM) was charged with negotiating a protocol to

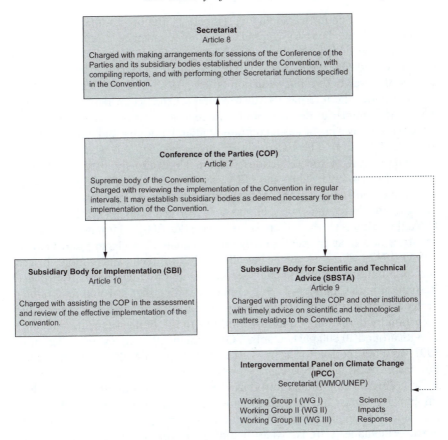

Figure 1 Institutional Structure of the IPCC

the UNFCCC by COP-3 in 1997. This was achieved only after heated debates between two camps, the European Union (EU) and the 'Green Group' of developing countries versus JUSSCANNZ[8] and the Organization of Petroleum Exporting Countries (OPEC), which were put in separate rooms during the last stretch of the conference. The conference Chair, German Environment Minister Angela Merkel, conducted 'shuttle diplomacy' between the two blocks until finally the US delegation agreed to a compromise, which also included a statement that any new commitments for non-Annex I Parties would be ruled out in the next round (Jäger and O'Riordan 1996, 21–25; Oberthür and Ott 1999, 46–47).

Although the USA came to agree to legally-binding emissions reduction targets by COP-2 in 1996, the period up to COP-3 was marked by conflict between the negotiating blocks and general doubt that an agreement could be reached. The USA demanded that all Annex I Parties should commit to stabilizing emissions at 1990 levels by the period between 2008 and 2012, and that developing countries should participate in the commitments. However, the G77 and the People's Republic of China remained resolute that they should not be pulled into the commitments in the first commitment period (Oberthür and Ott 1999). The EU proposed that all Annex I Parties should commit themselves to a flat reduction target of 15% from 1990 levels by 2010, but that under the internal EU distribution scheme, countries' commitments would be commensurate with ability to reduce emissions; this was harshly criticized by other parties as a contradiction and a double standard (Oberthür and Ott 1999, 143). The EU preferred strong policies and measures (PAMs) to achieve most of the reductions domestically and submitted its proposal early in March 1997, while the USA sought maximum flexibility and cost-effectiveness in implementing its commitments. Japan's position as host was that of a mediator, placing itself between the positions of the EU and the USA, but closer to the US position (Schröder 2001). However, these two countries had their proposals ready only in September (Japan) and October (USA) 1997, which is somewhat illustrative of their much more hetero-geneous domestic setting. The US Senate unanimously passed the Byrd-Hagel Resolution in the summer of 1997, explicitly stating that it would only ratify a protocol that had maximum flexibility built in and required meaningful par-ticipation by developing countries, contrary to the Berlin Mandate.

With around 10,000 participants, COP-3, taking place in Kyoto in December 1997, adopted the Kyoto Protocol. It includes a total GHG emissions reduc-tion target of 'at least 5 percent below 1990 levels in the commitment period 2008 to 2012'. The protocol introduces the concept of commitment periods to smooth out annual fluctuations in emissions arising from uncontrollable fac-tors such as economic cycles. Annex A of the protocol lists six gases: carbon dioxide, methane, nitrous oxide, hydrofluorocarbons, perfluorocarbons and sulphur hexafluoride. The baseline for the first three main gases is 1990, while a 1995 baseline for calculating the emissions of the other three gases is allowed. The gases are taken together as a basket and compared according to their global warming potential (GWP), i.e., the radiative, or warming, impact of a molecule relative to carbon dioxide within a 100-year time horizon.

Annex B of the protocol lists the 'assigned amount' for each Annex I Party, relative to 1990 levels, such as 8% for EU countries, 7% for the USA, and 6% for Japan and Canada, and increases of emissions for Norway, Iceland and Australia. These figures came about entirely politically; pressure was high on the EU, USA and Japan to negotiate and bargain out meaningful targets, while all other countries got away with lenient targets as 'voluntary pledges' based on their 'willingness to pay' (Oberthür and Ott 1999, 120), due to their relatively small populations and, therefore, small overall emissions. Also, sur-prisingly, Russia and the Ukraine got away with a stabilization target despite its drastic drop in emissions after the collapse of the Soviet Union in 1990, generating a cushion of 'hot air' from which countries with stricter targets could benefit through emissions trading. This brought down the overall reductions to 'at least 5 percent', which was included in the treaty text.

Moreover, the protocol included provisions for a compliance regime as well as three flexibility mechanisms to reach emission reductions cost-effectively. However, the details concerning the operability of these provisions remained unresolved. The 'nitty-gritty' work was adjourned to future meetings and finally completed with the 2001 Marrakech Accords, adopted at COP-7.

Regarding compliance, the Kyoto Protocol requires that procedures and mechanisms entailing legally-binding consequences—such as a compliance mechanism—have to be adopted by amendment. COP-7 created a Compliance Committee of 20 members and divided into two branches: facilitative and enforcing. This enables the Committee to both promote compliance with commitments and to take action when Parties are not in compliance. Parties in breach of their commitments have to make up shortfalls at 1.3 tons to 1, have their right to sell credits suspended and are issued a compliance action plan by the Committee (Wang and Wiser 2002). Given that there is not yet a second commitment period with a new set of assigned amounts for parties, the compliance scheme is rather vague.

The flexibility mechanisms include Joint Implementation (JI), the Clean Development Mechanism (CDM) and emissions trading. JI is the oldest of the mechanisms, having been in the 1992 Convention as AIJ, and because of this longer history it has received the least attention of the three (Oberthür and Ott 1999, 158). JI allows emission reductions or sink[9] enhancement to be undertaken where they are cheapest within the group of Annex I countries, including economies in transition, through the implementation of projects.

The CDM was dubbed 'the Kyoto surprise': it evolved from a Brazilian proposal for a Clean Development Fund, which was controversial because it sought to penalize countries for not complying with their emissions reductions through a levy that would fund mitigation and adaptation projects in developing countries. It was when this scheme was flipped that the idea for the CDM was born: Annex I countries could fulfil their Kyoto commitments by investing in projects in developing countries. With that the scheme offered 'geographical flexibility', which was much to the liking of the USA (Oberthür and Ott 1999, 166). The CDM rules establish that the host country has to verify that a project meets the objective of contributing toward its sustainable development, that projects must lead to emissions reductions that are additional to any reductions that would have occurred in the absence of these projects, and that resources for the CDM cannot be diverted from existing Official Development Aid (ODA) funds.

Lastly, emissions trading allows parties to buy or sell emission rights,[10] to make it easier for a party facing higher costs to reach its assigned amount under the Protocol. It provides an incentive for countries or companies that find it relatively easy to cut emissions to go further than required under the Protocol. They would then profit financially by selling their surplus to countries or companies that face relatively high reduction costs.

Participation in the mechanisms is open only to countries that have ratified the Kyoto Protocol and that are in compliance with their general provisions, such as having in place a national registry. They are fungible, meaning that they are equivalent and interchangeable, and Parties are allowed to trade between them as long as they are in compliance with the Protocol's provisions. This allows the units to be traded on a single market, resulting in more liquidity and lower transaction costs. The units are all equal to one metric tonne of carbon dioxide equivalent, calculated using GWPs. The four units are as follows:

1) Assigned amount units (AAUs) allocated under the Kyoto Protocol on the basis of national targets.
2) Certified emission reduction units (CERs) generated by CDM projects.
3) Emission reduction units (ERUs) generated by JI projects.
4) Removal units (RMUs) generated by JI sink projects.

Parties to the Protocol can authorize legal entities, such as companies, to trade. However, the Party itself remains responsible for meeting its Kyoto commitment. If a Party fails to meet its eligibility requirements, its legal entities are excluded from trading under the accounts of that country.

The years leading to the Marrakech Accords were marked by serious procrastination, which became especially poignant during COP-6 in 2000 in The Hague. The conference, where the outstanding details of the Kyoto Protocol were to be finalized, ended in complete deadlock and was suspended. This was due to many things, among them lost momentum, weak leadership, hardened positions and reduced willingness for compromise among parties (Hirono and Schroeder 2004). The Kyoto Protocol finally entered into force in early 2005. It survived not only the political deadlock of COP-6, but also the withdrawal from the process of the USA in early 2001 under the George W. Bush Administration. Perhaps spurred to action because of the intransigence of the USA, the Europeans took it upon themselves to bring the other wavering countries back on board—or rather entice them through one deal or another. Japan, Russia, Canada, New Zealand and eventually also Australia under new Prime Minister Rudd in 2007 ratified the Kyoto Protocol, while the USA has remained on the sidelines.

PHASE FOUR: TOWARDS DEEP CUTS?—THE EMERGING POST-2012 REGIME

In 2005 at the first COP/MOP in Montréal, parties initiated a discussion of possible processes for post-2012 talks in accordance with the Kyoto Protocol (Article 9) and launched two tracks for deliberating on the future of the climate regime. This was done to include the USA in the discussions on future commitments. Therefore, in addition to the Ad Hoc Working Group on Further Commitments for Annex I Parties under the Kyoto Protocol (AWG), a series of four workshops ('Dialogues') was started under the UNFCCC to lead to COP-13 in Bali in 2007.

Prior to COP-13, the release of the IPCC's fourth Assessment Report (AR-4) and the IPCC and Al Gore winning the Nobel Peace Prize that year, as well as Al Gore winning an Oscar for his film 'An Inconvenient Truth', gave the issue of climate change a probably unprecedented sense of urgency and opportunity for progress. In addition, the Stern Review, published in 2006, made a compelling case that doing nothing on climate change would be significantly more expensive than taking action (Stern 2006). The review has been both appraised and criticized, the latter, for example, for the discount rate it used in its calculations and the treatment of adaptation of future generations to a changed global climate (Weitzman 2007).

At COP-13, parties adopted the Bali Roadmap, also referred to as the Bali Action Plan, which is a two-year process toward finalizing a new treaty. The Bali Roadmap under the Convention sets out the steps 'to reach an agreement on long-term cooperative action up to and beyond 2012', to be adopted in Copenhagen, Denmark in December 2009, 'recognizing that deep cuts in global emissions will be required to achieve the ultimate objective of the Convention' (UNFCCC 2007). It created a new Ad Hoc Working Group on Long-term Cooperative Action (AWG-LCA) under the Convention for this purpose. Meanwhile, the other track, now referred to as AWG-KP, continued its meetings.

The aim is to adopt a post-2012 agreement at COP-15 in Copenhagen at the end of 2009. It is likely that, as in the case of the Kyoto Protocol, the agreement will take a few years beyond 2009 to be fleshed out. The main elements of this new agreement are likely to include: a revised CDM; an adaptation fund and additional financial flows for adaptation; a mechanism on avoided deforestation; technology transfer; and targets and timetables or agreement on some type of emissions trajectory.

The CDM has been hailed a success as a cost-effective new market mechanism involving developing countries, but it has also received criticism for not delivering on the sustainable development objective for which it was established. Shortfalls include that projects are unevenly distributed, both geographically and by sector, that the approval process is slow and cumbersome, benefiting large over small-scale projects and projects in more- over less-developed countries, that there is concern over leakage, i.e. emissions saved in one place happen somewhere else instead, and that there is concern whether reductions for which CERs are issued are always additional (e.g. HFC-23 from refrigerant manufacturing) (Wara 2007; Boyd et al. 2007; Clémençon 2008). Also, the bureaucratic process of project registration and CER issuance has been criticized as extremely slow (ENB 2008). It is expected that the CDM will continue to play a leading role in the post-2012 regime, but its effectiveness into the future will be largely dependent on overcoming the shortcomings addressed above.

Adaptation has come onto the international agenda relatively late, and a shift has taken place from thinking of adaptation as opposed to mitigation toward the realization that both have equally important roles to play only in the last decade (Verheyen 2002) (see Chapter 6 by Lemos and Boyd for more).

COP-11 in 2005 adopted a Least Developed Countries Fund and a Special Climate Change Fund, both under the Convention and managed by the Global Environmental Facility (GEF). In addition, COP-13 adopted an Adaptation Fund under the Kyoto Protocol to finance adaptation projects in developing countries through a share of proceeds of 2% of CERs from CDM project activities, as well as additional, voluntary sources. COP-13 in 2007 agreed on an Adaptation Fund Board as the operating entity for the Fund. COP-14 adopted rules of procedure of the Adaptation Fund Board so it can become operational. Despite these first steps, financing adaptation is all but secured as the needs by far outstrip the current availability of funding. According to UN estimates, US $50–$80 billion a year is needed, while the current fund collects only around $200–$300 million annually from a 2% levy on the CDM. A proposal to increase the 2% levy to 5% was thwarted in Poznań, Poland, as was a proposal to extend the share of proceeds to joint implementation and emissions trading (under the second review of the Protocol under Article 9) (Okereke and Schroeder 2009).

Under the Kyoto Protocol, crediting for emission reductions resulting from land-use change was limited to afforestation and reforestation, leaving out avoided deforestation, mainly for reasons of uncertainty regarding the measurability, reportability and verifiability of reductions. The fact that around one-fifth of global emissions are due to deforestation activities—mainly in the Global South—has brought this issue to the top of the political agenda. A new approach has been developed since COP-11, now referred to as REDD (reducing emissions from avoided deforestation and forest degradation). The idea behind this emerging mechanism is that countries that are able and willing to avoid deforestation should be financially compensated for doing so. There is now a general consensus among Parties that avoided deforestation should be addressed separately from afforestation and reforestation under the CDM in order not to overwhelm the CDM carbon offsetting market, and that this mechanism should include both deforestation and forest degradation. Also, only developing countries should participate in REDD and participation should be on a voluntary basis only (GCP 2008). Proposals include market and fund-driven approaches, as well as project and country level accreditation, and countries remain divided over which approach to adopt (GCP 2008; Bellassen et al. 2008; Ebeling and Yasue 2008).

There is some debate over whether a cap-and-trade system on its own would be sufficient to mitigate climate change (Keohane and Raustiala 2008), but while emissions trading may work well among large businesses and industries, it may not be an effective instrument for addressing emissions from smaller businesses and industries, and it may be difficult to apply to the transportation and housing sectors (Clémençon 2008). The EU-ETS in its first phase of operations (January 2005 until December 2007), with its national allocation plans and mostly grandfathered (i.e. given away freely) allocations, has been criticized for being inefficient and giving rather little incentive to reduce emissions to participating companies (Igielska 2008). These issues have been addressed for subsequent phases.

The decision on targets and timetables, or at least an agreement on some type of emissions trajectory, is likely to be another highly political game compared with that during the Kyoto negotiations. What is different now is that there is a stronger consensus around the scale of decarbonization needed to stabilize the global climate. While the long-term or mid-century target is likely to be around 50%–85% reductions from 1990 levels, the mid-term, or 2020, target is more contentious. It is important because it can deliver on the pledge made in the 1995 Berlin Mandate that industrialized countries would make the first step toward meaningful reductions. However, whether the majority of industrialized countries can shift their economies onto more sustainable production and consumption paths quickly enough to reach a target of this magnitude is uncertain.

To solve the problem of climate change the following three points also need to be considered in designing a new agreement: first, the informal arena of actors other than national governments has been remarkably active on climate change relative to nation-states over the past decade or so. For example, cities are pledging reductions that far outstrip those of their national governments (Schroeder and Bulkeley 2009). Despite the lack of a top-down mandate, non-nation-state actors have demonstrated entrepreneurship and reduced emissions in cost-effective and co-beneficial ways (Lovell, Bulkeley and Liverman 2009; Okereke 2007). To understand this difference in approach might help overcome this divide. Second, the current approach looks only at aggregate country emissions, not the differences within countries or the different drivers for emissions. China is often pointed to for its rapid increase in emissions, but the fact that they are to a large extent export-driven is overlooked. Also, embodied carbon is omitted from current calculations (Wang and Watson 2008). Third, to find a way toward including developing countries, the diverse approaches already adopted by key developing countries could be indicators of ways forward, such as Mexico's trans-sectoral cap-and-trade scheme, China's renewable energy goals and Brazil's efforts to address deforestation.

CONCLUSION

Many commentators have blamed the Kyoto Protocol for being ineffective and flawed (Prins and Rayner 2007; Victor 2001), but the major hurdle is not the institutional design per se that was created, above all, by its biggest critic, the US Government under President Bush. To reach deep cuts in emissions in the order of 80% or more by mid-century, the politics of climate change need to change. This will only happen if there is a substantive change in climate change politics in the USA. Much hope now rests on the new politics of the Barack Obama Administration.

The large oil-dependent nations as producers and consumers alike, including the USA, many OPEC countries and Japan, have contributed much to procrastinating on climate change; the EU and many developing countries have contributed to keeping the Kyoto process alive. There is now a window of opportunity for all countries to make progress in terms of a concerted effort to design a post-2012 regime that is effective, equitable and inclusive of all stakeholders at all levels of governance.

NOTES

1 Certain individuals were ahead of the game, writing books on the need for a political response, such as Stephen Schneider (1976), *The Genesis Strategy* and Crispin Tickell (1977), *Climatic Change and World Affairs* (Paterson 1996, 30).

2 See the IPCC's homepage at www.ipcc.ch/about/about.htm.

3 The organization of the Working Groups has changed several times. For a detailed account of the history of the IPCC, see Agrawala 1998.

4 For example, countries such as Saudi Arabia and Kuwait have argued that 'these scientific findings may well be true, but they have not come about in the correct manner. We can therefore not be certain that they are true, and they should therefore be deleted'. They have thus been able to accuse the IPCC of violations of their own rules and procedures in the development of the knowledge base and on those grounds demand that conclusions and findings are deleted (Skodvin 2000, 173).

5 According to a survey carried out by the United Nations University's Institute of Advanced Studies (UNU/IAS) at COP-3 (1997) and COP-4 (1998), 80% of the delegates interviewed at COP-3 and 84% at COP-4 agreed that the IPCC provides scientifically credible information, while 3% at COP-3 and 2% at COP-4 disagreed. Moreover, 60% of the respondents at COP-3 and 57% at COP-4 agreed that the IPCC provides politically neutral information, while 18% at COP-3 and 10% at COP-4 disagreed (Barrett et al. 2001).

6 See *www.unfccc.int* (accessed December 2008).

7 This second review has not yet taken place.

8 Negotiating alliance consisting of Japan, the US, Switzerland, Canada, Australia, Norway and New Zealand.

9 Carbon sinks are carbon dioxide-absorbing ecosystems such as forests and soils. The Kyoto Protocol allows for the inclusion of absorption by sinks resulting from post-1990 changes in forestry-related activities, including afforestation and reforestation, but they were not defined at the time. The protocol omitted other sink sources such as agricultural soils and avoided deforestation. Annex I Parties for whom land-use change and forestry (LUCF) constituted a net source of GHG emissions in 1990 were allowed to include LUCF emissions when calculating their 1990 base-year emissions, treating them almost like an additional source (Yamin 1998).

10 The term emissions trading is somewhat imprecise; it is not the emissions, but rather the right to emit that is traded.

REFERENCES

Agrawala, S. (1998) 'Structural and Process History of the Intergovernmental Panel on Climate Change', *Climatic Change* Vol. 39, No. 4, 621–42.

Barrett, B.F.D., W.B. Chambers and H. Schröder (2001) 'Delegate perspectives of science and politics at COP3 and COP4 of the UNFCCC process', UNU/IAS working paper series, Tokyo: Institute of Advanced Studies, United Nations University.

Bellassen, V., R. Crassous, L. Dietzsch and S. Schwartzman (2008) 'Reducing Emissions from Deforestation and Degradation: What Contribution from Carbon

Markets?', *Climate Report*, Issue 14, Mission Climat of Caisse des Dépôts, www. caissedesdepots.fr/missionclimat.

Benedick, R. E. (1998) *Ozone diplomacy: New directions in safeguarding the planet*, Cambridge, MA: Harvard University Press.

Beukering, P. van and P. Vellinga (1996) 'Climate change: From science to global policies', in P. B. Sloep and A. Blowers (eds), *Environmental Policy in an International Context: Environmental Problems as Conflicts of Interest*, London: Arnold Publishers.

Bodansky, D. (1993) 'The United Nations Framework Convention on Climate Change: A commentary', *Yale Journal of International Law* Vol. 18, No. 2, Summer.

Boyd, E. et al. (2007) 'The Clean Development Mechanism: An assessment of current practice and future approaches for policy', Tyndall Working Paper No. 114.

Brack, D. and M. Grubb (1996) 'Climate change: A summary of the Second Assessment Report of the IPCC', Royal Institute of International Affairs (RIIA) briefing paper 32, July.

Brenton, T. (1994) *The Greening of Machiavelli, The Evolution of International Environmental Politics*, London: RIIA.

Clémençon, R. (2008) 'The Bali Roadmap: A First Step on the Difficult Journey to a Post-Kyoto Protocol Agreement', *The Journal of Environment & Development* Vol. 17, No. 1.

Depledge, J. (2002) 'Climate change in focus: The IPCC Third Assessment Report', Royal Institute of International Affairs (RIIA) briefing paper, new series 29, www. riia.org/Research/eep/climateinfocus.pdf, February.

Ebeling, J. and M. Yasue (2008) 'Generating carbon finance through avoided deforestation and its potential to create climatic, conservation and human development benefits', *Philosophical Transactions of the Royal Society B*, 363.

ENB (2008) 'COP-14 Final', www.iisd.ca/download/pdf/enb12395e.pdf.

GCP (2008) *The Little REDD Book*, London: GCP.

Goldberg, D. and K. Silverthorne (2002) 'The Marrakech Accords', section of Environment, Energy and Resources, American Bar Association website, www.abanet. org/environ/committees/climatechange/newsletter/jan02/goldberg.html, January.

Grubb, M., C. Vrolijk and D. Brack (1999) *The Kyoto Protocol: A guide and assessment*, London: RIIA/Earthscan.

Gupta, J. (2001) *Our Simmering Planet: What to Do about Global Warming?*, London: Zed Books.

Guston, D.H. (1999) 'Stabilizing the boundary between US politics and science: the role of the office of technology transfer as boundary organization', *Social Studies of Science* Vol. 29, 1–25.

Harper, C. (2003) 'Research from the Boundary Layer: Civilian Leadership, Military Funding and the Development of Numerical Weather Prediction (1946–55)', *Social Studies of Science* Vol. 33, No. 5.

Hirono, R. and H. Schroeder (2004) 'The Road to and from the Kyoto Protocol: The Perspectives of Germany and Japan', *International Review for Environmental Strategies* Vol. 5, No. 1.

Houghton, J.T., G.J. Jenkins and J.J. Ephraums (eds) (1990) *Climate Change: The Scientific Assessment – Contribution of Working Group I to the First Assessment Report of the Intergovernmental Panel on Climate Change*, Cambridge: Cambridge University Press.

Houghton, J.T., L.G. Meira Filho, B.A. Callander, N. Harris, A. Kattenberg and K. Maskell (eds) (1996) *Climate Change 1995: The Science of Climate Change –*

Contribution of Working Group I to the Second Assessment Report of the Inter-governmental Panel on Climate Change, Cambridge: Cambridge University Press.

Houghton, J.T., Y. Ding, D.J. Griggs, M. Noguer, P.J. van der Linden, X. Dai, K. Maskell and C.A. Johnson (eds) (2001) *Climate Change 2001: The Scientific Basis – Contribution of Working Group I to the Third Assessment Report of the Inter-governmental Panel on Climate Change*, Cambridge: Cambridge University Press.

Igielska, B. (2008) 'Climate Change Mitigation: Overview of the Environmental Policy Instruments', *International Journal of Green Economics* Vol. 2, No. 2.

IPCC (2007) *Climate Change 2007 Synthesis Report: Summary for Policymakers*, Cambridge: Cambridge University Press, www.ipcc.ch/pdf/assessment-report/ar4/syr/ar4_syr_spm.pdf.

Jäger, J. and T. O'Riordan (1996) 'The History of Climate Change Science and Poli-tics', in J. Jäger and T. O'Riordan (eds), *Politics of Climate Change: A European Perspective*, London: Routledge.

Kameyama, Y. (2003) 'Climate change as Japanese foreign policy: From reactive to proactive', in P. Harris (ed.), *Global warming and East Asia: The politics and foreign policy of climate change*, London: RoutledgeCurzon.

Keller, K., M. Hall, S.-R. Kim, D.F. Bradford and M. Oppenheimer (2005) 'Avoiding Dangerous Anthropogenic Interference with the Climate System', *Climatic Change* Vol. 73, 227–38.

Keohane, B. and K. Raustiala (2008) 'Toward a Post-Kyoto Climate Change Archi-tecture: A Political Analysis', Discussion Paper 08–01, Harvard Project on Interna-tional Climate Agreements.

Lovell, H., H. Bulkeley and D. Liverman (2009) 'Carbon Offsetting: Sustaining Con-sumption?', *Environment & Planning A*, 41(10), 2357–2379.

Lunde, L. (1991) 'Science or Politics in the Global Greenhouse? The Development Towards Scientific Consensus on Climate Change, Energy, Environment and Development', Publication No. 8, Oslo: Fridtjof Nansen Institute.

Mastrandrea, M. D. and S. Schneider (2004) 'Probabilistic integrated assessment of "dangerous" climate change', *Science* Vol. 304, 571–75.

Michaelowa, A. (2001) 'Rio, Kyoto, Marrakesh—Groundrules for the global climate policy regime', HWWA discussion paper 152, Hamburg: Hamburgisches Welt-Wirtschaft-Archiv (HWWA), Hamburg Institute of International Economics.

Oberthür, S. and H. Ott (1999) *The Kyoto Protocol: International climate policy for the 21st century*, Berlin: Springer-Verlag.

Okereke, C. (2007) 'An Exploration of Motivations, Drivers and Barriers to Carbon Management: The UK FTSE 100', *European Management Journal* Vol. 25.

Okereke, C. and H. Schroeder (2009) 'How can the objectives of justice, development and climate change mitigation be reconciled in the treatment of developing coun-tries in a post-Kyoto settlement?', *Climate & Development* Vol. 1, No. 1.

Oppenheimer, M. (2005) 'Defining Dangerous Anthropogenic Interference: The Role of Science, the Limits of Science', *Risk Analysis*, Vol. 25, No. 6.

Paterson, M. (1996) *Global Warming and Global Politics*, London: Routledge.

Prins, G. and S. Rayner (2007) 'Time to Ditch Kyoto', *Nature* Vol. 449, 973–75.

Schröder, H. (2001) *Negotiating the Kyoto Protocol: An analysis of negotiation dynamics in international negotiations*, Münster: Lit Verlag.

Schroeder, H. and H. Bulkeley (2009) 'Global cities and the governance of climate change: What is the role of law in cities?', *Fordham Urban Law Journal* Vol. 36, No. 2.

Siebenhüner, B. (2002) 'The changing role of nation states in international environmental assessments—the case of the IPCC', *Global Environmental Change* Vol. 13, No. 2.

Skodvin, T. (2000) 'The Intergovernmental Panel on Climate Change', in S. Andresen et al. (eds), *Science and politics in international environmental regimes. Between integrity and involvement*, New York: Manchester University Press.

Stern, N. (2006) *Stern Review: The economics of climate change*, London: UK Treasury.

Underdal, A. (1980) *The Politics of International Fisheries Management: The Case of the Northeast Atlantic*, Oslo: Universitetsforlaget.

UNFCCC (2007) 'Decision-/CP.13. Bali Action plan. Advanced unedited version', unfccc.int/files/meetings/cop_13/application/pdf/cp_bali_action.pdf.

Verheyen, R. (2002) 'Adaptation to the Impacts of Anthropogenic Climate Change – The International Legal Framework', *Review of European Community and International Environmental Law* Vol. 11, No. 2.

Victor, D. (2001) *The Collapse of the Kyoto Protocol and the Struggle to Slow Global Warming*, Princeton, NJ: Princeton University Press.

Wang, T. and J. Watson (2008) 'Carbon Emissions Scenarios for China to 2100', Tyndall Working Paper 121.

Wara, M. (2007) 'Is the global carbon market working?', *Nature* Vol. 445, 595–96.

Wang, X. and G. Wiser (2002) 'The Implementation and Compliance Regimes under the Climate Change Convention and its Kyoto Protocol', *Review of European Community and International Environmental Law* Vol. 11, No. 2.

Weitzman, M. (2007) 'The Stern Review of the Economics of Climate Change', book review, *Journal of Economic Literature*, www.economics.harvard.edu/faculty/weitzman/files/JELSternReport.pdf.

Yamin, F. (1998) 'The Kyoto Protocol: Origin, assessment and future challenges', *Review of European Community and International Environmental Law* Vol. 7, No. 2.

The Politics of Interstate Climate Negotiations

CHUKWUMERIJE OKEREKE

INTRODUCTION

A great deal of the politics of interstate climate negotiations can be described, following Mathew Paterson, in terms of 'two great conflicts' (Paterson 1996, 73). One is the conflict between the USA and the rest of the world over the nature of commitment and type of governance instruments that should be used in limiting greenhouse gas emissions (Biermann 2005; Paterson 1996). The other and more pervasive is the North–South conflict that is implicated in virtually every aspect of the development of an international climate regime (Anand 2004; Biermann 2005; Okereke 2008a; Paterson 1996). The objective of this chapter is to provide a shorthand account of the climate politics of nation-states from the optic of these 'two great conflicts'. The narrative here focuses on the development of the international climate regime—the United Nations Framework Convention on Climate Change (UNFCCC) and its Kyoto Protocol—but also touches on issues that are defining interstate climate politics in the run up to a post-Kyoto agreement. Unlike the account of Schroeder (Chapter 2), the specific emphasis here is on the key issues in the negotiations and the positions/influences of nation-states and their negotiating blocs. The account indicates that the development of the global climate regime is characterized by a series of trade-offs and compromises amongst three key actors—the USA, the European Union (EU) and the developing countries under the aegis of G77/the People's Republic of China. These trade-offs and compromises might be considered necessary in a bid to ensure that a functional global climate agreement subsists. However, ultimately, it is doubtful that the process would lead to the development of a regime robust enough to propel deep emission reductions by states and other autonomous actors. The chapter proceeds as follows. First, I provide a brief account of states' involvement in the politics of climate change at the international level starting from the 1980s when global warming first became an international political issue. Second, I sketch the key questions that have confronted states in their effort to design an effective and equitable global climate regime and indicate the influences of specific nation-states and their coalition groups. Finally, I look at the negotiating dynamics of both the developed and developing countries going forward to future negotiations before making some concluding remarks.

Before proceeding any further, it is important, I believe, to make two quick clarifications. One is that while a great deal of the global climate politics revolves around—and can be understood by focusing on—the activities of nation-states, a comprehensive understanding of global climate politics would require an account of the activities of a range of non-nation-state actors seeking to govern at multiple scales and geographies. I do not attempt to engage with this dimension in this chapter. The other is that the following analysis, for the sake of space, only touches on the key issues in the global climate change negotiations. No attempt is made to be either comprehensive or exhaustive (for fuller analysis, see among others Depledge 2005; Oberthür et al. 1999; Mintzer and Leonard 1994; Paterson 1996).

STATES' INVOLVEMENT IN CLIMATE POLITICS

The involvement of nation-states in climate politics started from the late 1980s, with a number of national governments joining in the environmental and scientific community-led initiative to foster political consensus on global warming through a series of international conferences (see Chapter 2). However, actual interstate politics of climate change can be said to have truly begun in the last four months of 1988 with two related key events. The first was the establishment of the Intergovernmental Panel on Climate Change (IPCC) by the Executive Council of the World Meteorological Organization (WMO) and United Nations Environmental Programme (UNEP). The second was the introduction of a motion on global climate change on the floor of the United Nations General Assembly (UNGA) by the government of Malta.

Prior to the establishment of the IPCC, there had been several assessments and conferences organized by the scientific and environmental communities, which call attention to human influence on the climate system and on the need for urgent action by governments to stabilize the atmospheric concentrations of greenhouse gases (Oberthür 1999; Paterson 1996).[1] However, while a number of these pre-IPCC events, as stated, had government officials in attendance, they were viewed with some suspicion in selected governmental circles, with many officials believing that 'the conclusions drawn at these meetings promoted environmental activism more than they reflected sound science' (Bodansky 1994, 51). The USA was a prominent example of such states that had deep suspicion of the prevailing process, with many state officials, especially those in the economic department, arguing for the need for sound science,[2] greater co-ordination and a guarded approach (Borione and Ripert 1994; Oberthür et al. 1999). The establishment of the IPCC—a move strongly supported by the USA—was born not simply out of a quest for internationally co-ordinated and reliable independent advice on climate change. Instead, the creation of the intergovernmental scientific body had a lot to do with the desire of nation-states to bring a process that had been largely in the hands of the scientific community under 'the control of state decision-makers' (Paterson 1996, 124). The action was, in the words of a former US climate negotiator, a move at least in part 'intended to re-assert governmental control and supervision over what was becoming an increasingly prominent political issue' (Bodansky 1994, 51). It is, in a sense, one of the great ironies of international climate politics that the IPCC has today become arguably the most important voice among those calling for radical reductions in global greenhouse gas emissions.

The second key event marking the involvement of states in climate politics was the proposal by the government of Malta at the UNGA meeting of September 1988 seeking a UN resolution proclaiming the global climate as the common heritage of mankind (Dasgupta 1994, 130). This move by the Maltese government was hugely significant not only because it brought climate change squarely to the UNGA, but also because the motion sought to link the climate to the previously politically charged and contentious issue of seabed mineral resources which occupied the international community between 1973 to 1994 (Bodansky 1994, 53; see Okereke 2008a; Ramakrishna 1990).[3] Following heated debate, the UNGA eventually declared the climate a 'common concern' rather than the common heritage of mankind as proposed by Malta. However, the motion served to prompt a much stronger UN engagement with the issue, as expressed in a resolution which *inter alia* called on the IPCC to recommend 'options for possible strengthening of relevant existing international legal instruments having bearing on climate and elements for inclusion in a possible future international convention on climate' (UNGA Resolution 43/58, 1988).

Following the adoption of the first IPCC report in 1990 and in line with other UN declarations on the issue, the UN on 21 December 1990 adopted a resolution establishing an intergovernmental negotiating committee (INC) under the auspices of the UNGA with the mandate to negotiate a convention containing appropriate commitments. Such negotiations would be co-ordinated with the preparations for the UN Conference on Environment and Development (UNCED) in Rio de Janeiro in 1992 (Depledge 2005). Critically, by establishing the INC as the single intergovernmental negotiating medium, the UN effectively took the political process out of the direct purview of the more technical UNEP and WMO and under the control of state decision-makers. This purpose was further consolidated by the establishment, through the same Resolution 45/212, of an *ad hoc* independent secretariat for the INC and a mere invitation to UNEP and WMO to make contributions to the negotiating process. The INC negotiations eventually started in February 1991 and concluded just in time to present a draft convention, which was eventually adopted for ratification during the UNCED in Rio. Over the years, climate change has grown in significance and the regime has witnessed many important landmarks. There are now over 195 nation-states that are Parties to the convention. The Kyoto Protocol, which contains quantified emissions reduction targets, was signed in 1997 and came into force in 2005 and each of the last three Conference of the Parties (COP) meetings has attracted over 10,000 participants.

KEY ISSUES IN THE NEGOTIATIONS, INITIAL POSITIONS AND INFLUENCE OF STATES

Interstate negotiation for the global governance of the climate is probably the most complex environmental diplomacy ever undertaken by the global political community.[4] The complexity of climate negotiations results from the very many intricate issues it involves. These include: 1) abiding scientific uncertainties about the magnitude of future climate change and its potential consequences; 2) the ubiquity and deep embeddedness of carbon in a broad array of vital human activities including transport, agriculture and energy use; 3) extreme asymmetry in relative contributions and burden of consequences; 4) the time-bound and significant economic costs involved in dealing with the issue; and 5) the divergent views over institutions and actions best required to deal with the challenge (cf. Rayner and Okereke 2007, 116–18; Stern 2006; Toth and Mwandosya 2001). Focusing on key issues in the negotiations, this section offers a simplified account of the diplomatic battle that shaped (and to a large extent is still shaping) the development of the global climate regime. I organize these key issues around seven broad questions. Some of these questions have been addressed decidedly, while others continue to generate controversy today. However, the character of the global climate change regime that exists today has been more or less defined by these subject matters.

1. Who should organize and conduct the negotiations: the UN or a technical body?

The first issue of contention amongst states regarding the development of an international climate regime was about who should have the authority to organize and conduct the negotiations (Hyder 1994; Bodansky 2001). Clear indications emerged that the international community would negotiate an agreement having a bearing on climate in 1989 but up until the last months of 1990, the question of how the negotiation should be conducted and who should have the authority to organize the process remained unclear. The front running option strongly favoured by the USA and many other Western countries was for the negotiation to be conducted by a special committee under the auspices of UNEP and WMO (Borione and Ripert 1994, 81; Bodansky 2001). The aim of developed countries in choosing this option was to have a neat technical agreement that specifically addressed the subject matter of stabilizing global atmospheric greenhouse gas concentration. The pattern proposed here was that of the Basel Convention on Hazardous Waste and the Vienna Convention on Ozone Layer Protection, the negotiation of which were both conducted under a specialized UN agency (Oberthür et al. 1999). The developing countries, though, had a different view. Led by a vocal Brazil, India and Mexico, they rejected the idea of a UNEP/WMO-led technical agreement, and instead expressed preference for a UN-organized and supervised conference. In adopting this position developing countries argued firstly that climate change was not just a technical environmental issue but a political issue as well (Depledge 2005; Okereke 2008a). Indeed, they considered that the wide-ranging economic implications of climate change made the negotiation of a global climate agreement an auspicious opportunity to address background issues of injustice in the international economic system (Anand 2004; Paterson 1996; Okereke 2008a). This sentiment was, for example, well captured by a leader of the Indian delegation when he expressed the view that 'the sharing of costs and benefits implied in the convention could significantly alter the economic destinies of individual countries' (Dasgupta 1994, 131). Developing countries preferred to negotiate under the UN umbrella given that only the UN was considered to have the commitment and the authority to preside over the deeply political and sensitive issues involved.

Moreover, in opting for a UN-organized process, the developing countries wanted to ensure that the negotiations were conducted in a transparent manner and under a forum that afforded them the opportunity for maximum participation (Okereke 2008a). For the developing countries, the 'one country one vote' system of the UN and the universality of representation the system offers were both seen as crucial conditions in securing a climate change agreement that would be sensitive to their peculiar needs and circumstances. Tariq Osman Hyder, the head of the Pakistan delegation to the INC puts it well: 'the UN system permits all sides to express their opinions from a position of sovereign equality and [...] countries acknowledged to have dominant economic, political and military power are forced to take into account the contrasting views of many other countries, however weak those countries may be' (Hyder 1994, 203).

After much political wrangling and horse-trading, the developing countries got their way with the UN Resolution of December 1990 mandating that the climate negotiation should proceed under one negotiating process—the INC—and under the direct authority of the UN. The feeling remains very strong among many today that the negotiation of the global climate regime under the UN has helped to create a sense of universality and an atmosphere of solidarity needed for real interstate co-operation to take place (Borione and Ripert 1994; Hyder 1994; Dasgupta 1994). What is less clear, though, is the extent to which this process would actually facilitate a regime under which rapid emission reduction and international justice could be achieved.

2. What kind of regime should be developed: a target-based protocol or a framework convention?

The second issue of serious debate in the early days of the development of the regime related to the nature of the agreement that might be developed to deal with the threat of changing global climate. Here the battle was mainly between the USA and members of the European Community (EC) mostly led by Germany, the Netherlands and Denmark (Biermann 2005; Depledge

2005). The USA was clear from the outset that it wanted a fairly general agreement without targets and binding commitments (Borione and Ripert 1994). The US negotiating team based its position on the grounds that there were so many scientific uncertainties about climate change, that a target-based protocol with quantified reduction commitments was unwarranted (Bodansky 1994). The team expressed preference for a gradual and cautious approach calling for the need for a better understanding of the economic and social consequences of change and response options before discussing commitments and targets (Borione and Ripert 1994, 82). The EC members on their own part pressed for urgent and ambitious action and called for strict quantified targets to be included in the convention (Paterson 1996, 54). Indeed, some European countries like Germany and the Netherlands had before the start of the negotiation made unilateral pledges to reduce emissions and were pushing hard for the convention to reflect similar commitments at least for the rest of the developed countries (Oberthür et al. 1999). There was division among the developing countries on this issue. One the one hand, a group of small island states mindful of their vulnerability to potential sea-level rise called for ambitious targets and commitments. On the other hand, many oil producing countries, led by Saudi Arabia, fearing the consequences of a possible global energy/carbon tax wanted a weak regime or no regime at all.

Ultimately, it was the US position that prevailed. Rather than risk having a regime without US involvement, the EC members eventually agreed to negotiate a general framework convention with neither commitments nor emission reduction targets apart from a vague reference to a desire to cut emissions to 1990 levels. Subsequently, Parties to the UNFCCC have gone ahead—mostly propelled by the EC—to agree a Kyoto Protocol with commitments, quantified targets and a timetable, despite US reluctance and even outright opposition. The US position on the issue of quantified emission targets in the run up to a post-Kyoto agreement remains unclear even under the presidency of Barack Obama. The George W. Bush Administration was adamant that strict quantified emission reduction targets remain a bad policy in that they do not discount reductions produced by economic decline or policies that simply shift greenhouse gas emitting activities from one location to another. Instead, the Administration favoured what it called 'near term policies and measures that harness the power of the market to reduce emissions' (US Department of State 2006, 1). In practice, this means placing emphasis on investments, voluntary initiatives, and the development and deployment of clean energy technologies rather than absolute targets. The new president has spoken of the need for 'a global response to climate change that includes binding and enforceable commitments to reducing emissions' (Obama 2007, 13); however, it has since become clear that the USA is not keen to back the Kyoto Protocol as a basis for post-2012 international action on climate change. Instead, the USA is calling for an 'implementation agreement' under the Framework Convention that allows governments to voluntarily formulate, implement and regularly update nationally appropriate mitigation actions subject to countries' domestic laws. None of this, of course, addresses the question of how sufficient the commitments might be or how to ensure that states meet the pledges under such a regime.

3. What will the convention's objective be: environment and/or development?

Closely related to the debate about who should have the authority to organize and conduct the negotiations was the question about what the convention's objective should be. As stated, developed countries had a mind to negotiate a fairly narrow treaty specifically focused on finding ways to limit global greenhouse gas emissions. In contrast, though, developing countries wanted a convention that clarifies the link between climate and international development, including issues of poverty reduction, debt cancellation and North–South technology transfer (Dasgupta 1994; Hyder 1994).

The differences in opinion here merely reflect an ongoing argument between developed and developing countries which started during the preparation for the United Nations Conference on the Human Environment in 1972 on how to contextualize international co-operation for the protection of the environment (von Weizsäcker 1994, 4–5; Ramakrishna 1990). Broadly, the developed countries tend to divide neatly between development and the environment. Furthermore, there is also a tendency to split environmental problems between 'global' and 'local' impacts (Hyder 1994, 205; von Weizsäcker 1994, 4–5). Instances of 'global' environmental problems would include climate change and ozone layer depletion. These arise mostly from industrialization and have the potential of causing harmful effects world-wide. On this frame, local environmental problems would include land degradation, water pollution and other such problems that are closely related to poverty and underdevelopment. Developed countries not only tend to separate between the two types of environmental problems mentioned, but also to invite concerted global action in addressing the challenges posed by the 'global' problems. The expectation, on the other hand, is that (developing) countries that are usually more weighed down by poverty-related problems should be left to deal with the 'local' issues as best they can.

However, developing countries consider such separation between global and local environmental problems, as well as the divide between environment and development, very artificial and unhelpful. They contend that issues of poverty and environmental problems are closely related and that environmental protection in developing countries must be viewed as an integral part of the development process and in the context of international economic relations (Ramakrishna 1990; Okereke 2008b). To this effect, developing countries reject the prioritization of environment over development and argue that both should be dealt with as a package.

With respect to climate change, developing countries made a link between climate change and a host of other economic issues such as access to energy, transportation, technology development, and deforestation and land use.

Following this, they sought an agreement that addresses not just ways of reducing greenhouse gas emissions, but also means of improving the welfare of people in the poor countries of the world.

Owing to these differences and following also the debate on whether or not to have targets in the convention, the negotiation of the convention's objective ended up being one of the most difficult in the development of the regime (Cooper 1998; Hyder 1994:204; Mintzer and Leonard 1994, 17). In the end, the result was a muddled compromise (Panjabi 1993, 5,407). An unusually lengthy objective was crafted which includes the aim to stabilize global atmospheric greenhouse gas concentration and promote economic growth, but the convention makes no mention of the need for deeper structural changes to achieve a more equitable world economic order (Okereke 2008a).

The question of what the appropriate ambition and objective of the convention should be remains a very contentious one to date. Some argue that a narrower focus or even smaller number of countries is needed in order to get an effective deal. They point out that only about 25 countries account for 80% of global greenhouse gas emissions. However, others are pressing for a much broader convention with clear links to other issues like trade, biodiversity and international property rights regimes (e.g. Biermann and Bauer 2005).

4. Who should take responsibility for the cause and effort of dealing with climate change: the West or the world?

The issue of who should bear the responsibility for the cause and effort of dealing with the challenges posed by climate change has been at the heart of interstate politics of climate change since the time that global warming became a political issue (Hayes 1993; Paterson and Grubb 1992; Ramakrishina 1990). The initial position of developing countries was that Western industrialized countries should assume full and complete responsibility for the dangers posed by climate change and the effort needed to solve the problem. The argument was quite simply that since climate change has been caused by the long-term historic emissions of developed countries in their pursuit of industrialization and economic growth, it makes sense for those who are responsible for the problem to pick up the bill (Shue 1993; Hayes 1993). Developing countries were adamant that their more immediate problems were those of poverty alleviation and socio-economic development. They insisted that they have no moral obligation or resources to devote to the fight against climate change. Indeed, developing countries viewed any suggestion that they should undertake any emission reduction responsibilities as a calculated attempt by the developed countries to place further burden on poor countries and limit their economic development (Agarwal and Narain 1991). This sentiment was so strong that some actually expressed the fear that climate change might well be another clever contrivance by the North designed to perpetuate existing inequalities and retain patterns of colonial domination, which were instrumental to the present prosperity of the North (Guha and Martinez-Alier 1997).

However, the industrialized countries were unconvinced by this argument. While they were willing to accept responsibility for a higher share of the historic and current global greenhouse gas emissions, they pointed that the balance could possibly soon tilt as a result of rapid industrialization and population growth in developing countries. Industrialized countries further sought to undermine the argument directly linking previous industrialization activities with culpability for climate change, arguing that it is not particularly just to hold a generation responsible for the 'sin' of their fathers. Accordingly, the industrialized countries strongly argued for an approach that incorporates efforts from all countries of the world. At the very least, they proposed that developing countries should prepare reports on their national sources and sinks of greenhouse gas emissions in preparation for future quantified reduction targets. The USA was especially insistent (and largely remains so) that it was not going to back any political process that did not oblige big developing countries like China, India and Brazil to cut their own emissions. Against the argument that climate change was contrived to limit Southern development, the North replied that poverty in developing countries is, more than anything else, due to mismanagement and lack of fiscal discipline on the part of the poor countries. The North argued that it is unfair for developing countries to attempt to exploit the new demands for closer co-operation towards effective global environmental governance, to extract money, technical aid and the transfer of other resources in terms outside the existing rules and market conditions. Developing countries on this account are thus seen as 'kleptocrats' (Singer 1992), bent on using their number and majority votes to foster, cajole or co-opt the rich countries into subsidizing their voluntarily incurred expenses.

Following months of deep political wrangling, the Parties eventually agreed to the concept of common but differentiated responsibility (CDR) as the basis for North–South co-operation on climate change. While this innovative concept enabled the Parties to find an agreement they could all sign in Rio de Janeiro, though, working out what it means in practice has continued to prove an extremely difficult balancing act.

5. How should the burden and benefits of co-operation be shared: aid or justice?

Having accepted that countries have different degrees of responsibility for causing climate change and varying levels of capabilities for response, the challenge before states has centred on how best to reflect this in the commitments and obligations under the regime. The key question in this regard relates to what (if any) duty the North owes the South and how such responsibilities might be best met (Hayes 1993; Paterson 2001). Basically, the underlying source of tension is that the North and the South vary fundamentally in the way they each seek to interpret the CDR principle—with one group seeing it in terms of aid or assistance and the other seeing it in terms of equity or justice (Harris 1999; Stone 2004; Okereke 2008b) (see Chapter 7 by Parks and Roberts for more).

For the developed countries, the CDR is simply a way of recognizing that their stronger financial and technological capabilities offer them opportunities to play a greater role in an issue of common global concern. This understanding, in other words, accords with the interpretation of the CDR in terms of capability rather than obligation (Harris 1999; Okereke 2008b, 32; Stone 2004, 276). Developed countries maintained (and this remains their position in the post-Kyoto negotiation) that any assistance given to the developing countries must be seen in terms of aid rather than arising out of any obligation of global justice. The North feels, as Hyder puts it, that emphasizing culpability and historical responsibility 'would amount to finger pointing and such unnecessary accusations would make it difficult for them to sell any resulting convention or declarations to their citizens and to their treasuries' (Hyder 1994, 207).

Developing countries, on the other hand, view the CDR from the optic of culpability and clearly see in the concept an endorsement of global equity as the touchstone of the climate regime. Following this, they insist not only that developed countries must take the lead in cutting emissions, but also that substantial North–South resource transfers are required to help the poor countries take part in fighting climate change. Developing countries further emphasize that such transfer must be in *addition* to the previously existing official development assistance (ODA). The following extracts from the speech of the Malaysian Prime Minster, Dr Mahathir Mohamad, during the 1992 Earth Summit in Rio illustrates the debate:

> Obviously the North wants to have a direct say in the management of forests in the Poor South at next to nothing cost to themselves. The pittance they offer is much less than the loss of earning by poor countries and yet it is made out as a generous concession […] The Poor are not asking for charity [but] for the need for us to co-operate on an equitable basis. Now the rich claim a right to regulate the development of the poor countries. And yet any suggestion that the rich compensate the poor adequately is regarded as outrageous.

> (Mohamad 1992)

The UNFCCC documents recognize historical responsibility of emissions, and make the participation of the developing countries conditional of the provision of additional financial resources. The convention text also has provisions for capacity building and technology transfer. Furthermore, during the development of the Kyoto Protocol, the developing countries were exempted from quantified emissions reduction targets (even though this proved a major reason for the USA refusing to ratify the treaty). All of these points would suggest that the developing countries have so far been largely successful in their demand that international co-operative arrangements for the climate should reflect the need for global equity and justice. However, despite this success, the convention, as Bodansky (2001, 212) cleverly notes 'does not actually require any particular country to contribute any particular amount'.

In preparing for the future climate regime, deciding how exactly to share emission reduction targets (if there is a target at all) is proving very contentious. The developing countries continue to argue that their prevailing poor economic condition makes it untenable for them to take on targets. Moreover, they point out that the developed countries have not done enough to fulfil the obligations they took on in the existing treaty. Developed countries, on the other hand, point to the rising emissions in some developing countries (especially China and India) and argue that it would be worthless from a global atmospheric stabilization point of view to exempt the developing countries from taking on emission reduction obligations. In the Nairobi and Bali meetings, parties agreed to pursue action on the basis of a 'globally shared vision', but just as in the case of the CDR, it is not at all clear exactly what this should mean in practice. Looking forward to post-Kyoto negotiations, the indications are that the EU is no longer prepared to accept an agreement that places it under a separate obligation to those borne by the USA and Canada. At the same time, it is also certain that the developed countries led by the USA will be stepping up pressure to see that a post-2012 climate regime recognizes the diversity of countries and economic circumstances within the G77 and, in particular, that some rapidly industrializing countries such as China, India and Brazil take on emission reduction targets. This is likely to prove one of the most contentious issues in the Copenhagen round of negotiations in December 2009.

6. What policy instruments should be used: money or market?

Even before the UN endorsed the idea that an international framework convention on climate change should be negotiated, a number of suggestions were already making the rounds as potential options for dealing with the issue (Bodansky 1994, 50–52; Paterson 1996). One of these suggestions—perhaps the most radical one—came from The Hague conference on climate change and environmental protection organized jointly by the governments of the Netherlands, Italy and Norway in 1989. Considering that the governance of climate change would pose unprecedented challenges to the existing international governance system, The Hague conference called for the establishment of a world authority or governing body to protect the atmosphere. This suggestion did not gain traction, as many considered the idea of a world government rather too drastic (Bodansky 1994; Borione and Ripert 1994). While the idea of world government faded, another equally innovative idea—that a Multilateral Atmosphere Fund should be established to fund global action on climate change and especially oversee the North–South resource transfer—attracted the support of many in the developing countries. The idea was that in order to finance programmes for dealing with the impacts of climate change (adaptation) and the shift to a clean energy low-carbon development path (mitigation) in developing countries, hundreds of billions of new and additional US dollars would need to be provided annually. A multilateral fund was seen as the best way to gather and disburse such monies. It was proposed that such a funding mechanism could be financed through some form of tax or levy on fossil fuel consumption in industrialized countries. Other proposals that figured in pre-negotiation summits include a climate change stamp, a climate fund based on a percentage of a country's gross national product (GNP), and a 'planet protection fund' under UN control, proposed by the late Indian Prime Minister, Rajiv Gandhi. In general, the developing countries tied the idea of a global climate fund to their argument on historical responsibility of climate change and suggested that contributions to the fund could be based on the countries' historical and current contribution to global warming and their respective capabilities. Earlier in 1987, the international community had established a small multilateral fund to help developing countries in the replacement of CFC substances with less dangerous compounds. The South was, in effect, asking for a much bigger fund than the one established by the Montréal Protocol to cater for the huge transfers needed to deal with climate change (Depledge 2005).

However, as the negotiation gained momentum, the idea of a multilateral fund came under serious attack by the developed countries. Instead of direct transfers of money from the North to the South, the developed countries proposed a range of convoluted market and economic mechanisms involving especially emission trading schemes and 'joint implementation' (Paterson 1996). The USA was at the forefront of those pushing the argument that traditional command and control strategies or direct transfers represent bad approaches to dealing with climate change (Yamin et al. 2001). They emphasized the need for flexible approaches that do not commit states to specific ways of either reducing emissions or assisting developing countries. The rationale was that such flexible market mechanisms were more efficient as they allow action to be taken without compromising economic growth.

After much argument, the Parties agreed on a number of policy instruments including bubbles, joint implementation, emissions trading and the CDM (collectively called the flexible mechanisms), all of which were designed to enable states to enter into different kinds of special economic ventures with the aim of meeting the Convention's objectives. These market-based mechanisms continue to form the thrust of the policies for actions against climate change by the international community to date (Bodansky 2001, 209; Cooper 1998, 67; Yamin et al. 2001). However, the door is not completely closed, as some developing countries in the post Kyoto negotiations have renewed their call for the establishment of some kind of climate fund for mitigation and adaptation in poor countries (see Okereke and Schroeder 2009). In fact most of the questions confronting government negotiators currently relate to the kind of financial instruments that should be used to fund adaptation and mitigation, including emissions from avoided deforestation (REDD) in developing countries. For example, the developed countries prefer some form of market approach to REDD, while Brazil leads a number of other developing countries that insist on a fund-based approach (Ebeling and Yause 2008).

7. How should efforts between prevention and cure be divided: mitigation or adaptation?

Although the concept of adaptation has been part of the discussion of a global climate agreement from the outset, it was mitigation that attracted the greater focus in both the UNFCCC and the Kyoto Protocol (Burton et al. 2002; Dessai and Schipper 2002). Three related reasons account for this. First, it was difficult for the developing countries to draw attention to adaptation at a time when the EU and the USA were hotly debating whether or not there should be some quantified base targets and emission reduction commitments. Second, developing countries were largely confident that the argument on historical reasonability would secure them the financial and technological transfers they required to deal with climate change. Third, and critically, science was not sufficiently robust to back up the case for a concerted effort on adaptation. However, starting from the 7th COP meeting in Marrakech, Morocco in 2001, developing countries have been pressing for adaptation to be accorded equal attention with mitigation in the development of the institutions and policies for climate governance. Of course, it is generally recognized that the two issues are linked in theory, but developing countries consider that the frame on which the two aspects are currently discussed does not allow for the establishment of policies that effectively address the need for urgent action on adaptation.

Since Marrakech 2001, adaptation has continued to gain a prominent position in international climate politics, to the extent that the Nairobi Conference of the Parties meeting (COP/MOP 2) in 2006 was unofficially dubbed the adaptation conference. Earlier in the 11th COP meeting in Montréal, Canada in 2005, developing countries have won a major concession with the establishment of a Work Programme on Adaptation and Adaptation Fund, both designed to support a wide range of activities on adaptation in developing countries (Burton et al. 2002; Najam et al. 2003). The Adaptation Fund is generally seen as a unique achievement because the idea is to generate revenue through a 2% levy on the emission permits ('Certified Emission Reductions', or 'CERs') generated by emission reduction projects under the Kyoto Protocol's Clean Development Mechanism (CDM). Because many of the CDM projects are carried out by private enterprise and given that the 2% share of the CERs generated by the projects is to be collected directly and monetized by an intergovernmental agency (the CDM Executive Board), the Adaptation Fund comes very close to an international private sector tax. This makes the Adaptation Fund in a sense very close to the kind of multilateral fund for which developing countries were clamouring during the early days of the regime.

During the Nairobi meeting several discussions were characterized by drawn-out bickering, as developing countries argued over the relative placement of paragraphs that emphasize mitigation and ones that highlight adaptation. The debate was so heated that by the end of the meeting a number of developing country delegates were proposing the establishment of a separate protocol for adaptation (Okereke et al. 2007). Even now, debate continues over what sort of institution should be created for the management of the Adaptation Fund and, perhaps more importantly, over the framework conditions which any institution (existing or new) that would like to operate the Adaptation Fund would have to satisfy. One major issue complicating the debate is that developed countries are keen to ensure that a clear distinction is made between the small climate-vulnerable developing countries and big rapidly industrializing developing countries in the disbursement of the Adaptation Fund. This is fuelled by a growing suspicion that, as opposed to some smaller countries that have a genuine urgency to enhancing adaptive capacity, some of the more technologically advanced developing countries could be attempting to use adaptation as a route to the compensation debate (see Chapter 6 by Lemos and Boyd for more).

This divide between mitigation and adaptation in a sense reflects the debate over what the appropriate objective of the climate regime should be, and how best to achieve an optimum level of integration between efforts to curb emissions and other concerns such as energy, land use and sustainable development, which are so closely related and yet addressed in completely different ways in international regimes (Beg et al. 2002). It appears that as the climate regime develops, the need to strengthen the links between climate efforts and other regimes dealing with related issues, in the pursuit of 'win-win' or 'no regrets' options becomes more apparent. At the same time, the need to determine what should be included and what should be left out in order to have a regime that works in practice remains a pressing one. Future negotiators will continue to face the challenge of working out how best to deal with these inter-linkages without making the climate regime too complicated or unwieldy to operationalize, or even completely ineffective.

LOOKING AHEAD: THE NEGOTIATION OF A POST-KYOTO CLIMATE AGREEMENT

The Developing Countries

It is now over 20 years since the North–South political wrangling over climate change began, but there is hardly any change yet in the negotiating dynamics between the developed and the developing countries (Biermann 2005; Dessai and Schipper 2002; Grubb and Yamin 2001; Mintzer and Leonard 1994; Najam et al. 2003). Recent negotiations have more or less proceeded practically on the basis of the blocs and coalitions that existed from the start. The developing countries continue to band together as a negotiating bloc under the aegis of G77 and China, despite huge and widening variations in the socio-economic differences of the individual countries. Of course, a number of issues like carbon capture and storage (CCS) and avoided deforestation add some strain to the internal discussions of the group with, for example, the small island states supporting CCS and the oil producing countries pressing for caution and more scientific research (Okereke et al. 2007). However, in the end, the developing countries always manage to present a common negotiation front while skirting over internal differences. There is a sense amongst developing countries that what ties them is far greater than whatever internal differences might exist. They are aware, for example, that presenting a common front is critical in any bid to extract resource transfer-related concessions from the group of developed countries normally determined to hold back as much as they possibly can.

However, it is likely that future climate negotiations could very well produce a deeper split between the developing countries in the G77/China bloc. Some of the issues that may generate fissures might involve the rules on the CDM, including how to ensure the equitable distribution of CDM projects, the issue of carbon capture and storage, and the issue of graded 'soft' commitments by some of the key developing countries (Okereke and Schroeder 2009). For example, there is already some indication that some of the poorest countries are beginning to feel that most of the important rules of the UNFCCC and Kyoto that are designed in principle for the benefit of the developing countries, in practice tend to favour only the more advanced within this group (Najam et al. 2007). The guidelines relating to the ·CDM and the Financial Mechanism are usually cited as prime examples. Although there are moves to amend some of these rules or to make special provisions for the least developed countries, it is not difficult to imagine that in the future some of these developing countries will increasingly feel marginalized within the big G77/China bloc if they are unable to secure appropriate amendments and/or special provisions that suit their purposes.

Developed Countries

Many developed country Parties face a huge dilemma in international climate politics. The problem they face has two dimensions. First, most are willing to recognize the moral issues involved in climate change, the need for an equitable climate regime and the argument for helping the most vulnerable countries to establish robust adaptation measures. However, there remains a great reluctance to fully support these measures, especially given the innate desire to remain dominant in the international political system. Second, many of the developed countries feel the need to show themselves as progressive and willing to move quickly on climate change on a national level. The ones in this camp are also eager to project themselves as international leaders pushing for a bold international effort on climate change. However, many of these same countries are struggling with their national mitigation commitments and are seeing rising emissions within their own borders. Furthermore, they are also reluctant to support radical changes in the ways some of the vital international climate institutions are currently structured. For example, many government officials from the Nordic countries recognize the need for equitable geographical distribution of CDM projects and the need to give special attention to the plight of the African and the least-developed countries. However, most of these governments are opposed to a climate fund and to suggestions for a radical change in the structure of the GEF, which is the main funding mechanism of the convention.

This apparent double standard attracts a lot of commentary from developing country Parties, who feel that the singular most important barrier to progress in international climate co-operation is the hypocrisy and lack of action on current commitments by Annex I countries. It is on this basis that many in the developing countries see the regular references to the growing emissions in China and India by the North Annex I Parties as mere diversionary tactics. The former Pakistani permanent representative to the UN and chairman of the G77 group in New York, Munir Akram, captured this sentiment well, saying: 'Unless the North comes to grips with its responsibility it will be difficult to come to an international consensus by which all of us can contribute to halting the degradation of the environment, and certainly stopping the development of developing countries is not the answer'.

Another interesting aspect of the negotiating dynamics among developed countries relates to the internal relationship within the EU countries and the relationship between the EU and the USA. Until recently, the EU has managed to present a common climate-proactive front despite, as in the case of the G77, huge variations in domestic circumstances. However, with the expansion of the EU and more recently the incidence of the global financial crisis, the EU is feeling great pressure from its new eastern and central European members (e.g. Poland) to water down the EU's climate change ambitions. Furthermore, there are indications that even some of the key climate-proactive countries like Germany may be considering beating a retreat from the more ambitious emission reduction plans. This wrinkle was highly visible at the last COP in Poznań (COP/MOP 4), with the EU presenting a somewhat diluted message from the ones it had offered at preceding conferences. It has to be said that so far (and despite internal wrangling) the EU still tries as much as possible to: 1) present a common front; 2) push hard for ambitious targets; 3) carry the USA along into the climate mitigation process; and 4) serve as a broker between the USA and the South (Biermann 2005). However, the sentiment within the EU is that the commission would no longer be prepared to sacrifice the economic growth of member countries just to get a global deal, unless the USA were prepared to accept a comparable set of actions. In a sense, whether the EU will be willing to ditch Kyoto because of the USA, or whether it can broker an agreement under which the USA can take Kyoto-comparable targets is one of the biggest questions of the forthcoming Copenhagen negotiation.

CONCLUSION

This chapter has attempted to provide a summary account of the involvement of nation-states in the international politics of climate change. An attempt has also been made to provide a simplified account of the politics of interstate negotiations of the climate regime from the point of view of the intractable and pervasive conflict between the North and the South. The narrative indicates that the development of the climate change regime is characterized by a series of compromises and trade-offs between three sets of actors—the EU, the USA and the group of developing countries under the aegis of G77/China. On the one hand, the diplomatic trade-offs among these three actors appear necessary in order to secure international co-operation for action on climate change. On the other hand, though, the consequence of these trade-offs appears to be a bloated and convoluted regime that hardly satisfies the aspirations of any of the Parties.

Developing countries have been successful in bringing the negotiation of the global climate change under the authority of the UN, linking climate change with development, and highlighting the issue of equity and historic responsibility for greenhouse gas emissions. They have also been successful in raising the profile of adaptation, securing the establishment of an Adaptation Fund, effecting changes in the structure of the GEF, and rebuffing any suggestion that they will consider taking either hard or soft emission reduction targets. However, they have so far failed to achieve substantial North–South transfers or any deep changes in the structure of the international economic system.

The developed countries have been successful in establishing flexible market-based instruments as the dominant policy approach to combating climate change and have also successfully managed to retain control over the financial mechanism of the convention, especially the GEF. However they have not yet succeeded in their bid to get some developing countries to take on emission reduction targets.

Overall, there has been a growing sense of distrust among both parties, with developed countries complaining that developing countries are being unco-operative in refusing to take on emission reduction targets and the developing countries accusing developed countries of eroding the foundation of trust by consistently failing to keep their obligations within the convention. The EU has in the past worked hard to project itself as an honest broker, but recently increasingly caught within the politics of its own internal consensus and weakened by the lingering economic crisis, it is not clear to what extent the EU can really offer the bold leadership needed to break the diplomatic impasse. There is some hope that the incoming President Obama in the USA might provide impetus for renewed diplomatic re-engagement and bold climate steps, although seasoned commentators have highlighted how domestic and constitutional problems in the USA might stand in the way of any speedy ratification of a post-2012 accord—no matter how hard the new president pushes. As the diplomatic log-jam over the climate negotiations continue, scientists continue to warn that urgent action is required to avoid dangerous climate change.

NOTES

1 Perhaps the most prominent of these pre-IPCC events was the Toronto Conference, which recommended a 20% reduction of carbon dioxide emissions by 2005.
2 Sound science—at least in global environmental governance circles—is a tremendously loaded term. Many governments, especially the US Administration under President George W. Bush, have manipulated the term for various ends (see Boykoff 2007)
3 The third UN Conference for the Law of the Sea was signed in 1982, but the politics of seabed mining continued well into 1994 when the USA eventually succeeded in amending some of the most contentious provisos to make them consistent with its political ideology and economic interest.
4 The only other serious contender would be the third UN Conference on the Law of the Sea, which lasted nearly 14 years from 1962 to 1982.

REFERENCES

Agarwal, A. and S. Narain (1991) *Global Warming in an Unequal World*, New Delhi: Centre for Science and Environment.

Anand, R. (2004) *International Environmental Justice: A North South Dimension*, Aldershot: Ashgate Publishing.

Beg, N., J.C. Morlot and O. Davidson (2002) 'Linkages between climate change and sustainable development', *Climate Policy* 2 (2–3), 129–44.

Biermann, F. (2005) 'Between the USA and the South: Strategic choices for European climate policy', *Climate Policy* 5, 273–90.

Biermann, F. and S. Bauer (2005) *A World Environment Organization: Solution or Threat for Effective International Environmental Governance?*, Aldershot: Ashgate Publishing.

Bodansky, D. (1994) 'Prologue to Climate Change Convention', in I. Mintzer and J. A. Leonard (eds), *Negotiating Climate Change: The Inside Story of the Rio Convention*, Cambridge: Cambridge University Press.

——(2001) 'International Law and the Design of a Climate Change Regime', in U. Luterbacher and D. F. Sprinz (eds), *International Relations and Global Climate Change*, Cambridge, MA: MIT Press.

Borione, D. and J. Ripert (1994) 'Exercising Common but Differentiated Responsibility', in I. Mintzer and J. A. Leonard (eds), *Negotiating Climate Change: The Inside Story of the Rio Convention*, Cambridge: Cambridge University Press.

Boykoff, M. (2007) 'From convergence to contention: United States mass media representations of anthropogenic climate science', *Transactions of the Institute of British Geographers*, 32 (4), 477–89.

Burton, I, S. Huq, B. Lim, O. Pilifosova and E.L. Schipper (2002) 'From impacts assessment to adaptation priorities: the shaping of adaptation policy', *Climate Policy* 2 (2–3), 145–59.

Cooper, R. N. (1998) 'Towards a Real Global Warming Treaty', *Foreign Affairs* 77 (2), 66–79.

Dasgupta, C. (1994) 'The Climate Change Negotiations', in I. Mintzer and J. A. Leonard (eds), *Negotiating Climate Change: The Inside Story of the Rio Convention*, Cambridge: Cambridge University Press.

Depledge, J. (2005) *The Organization of Global Negotiations: Constructing the Climate Change Regime*, London: Earthscan.

Dessai, S. and E.L. Schipper (2002) 'The Marrakech Accords to the Kyoto Protocol: analysis and the future prospects', *Global Environmental Change* 13, 149–53.

Dowdeswell, E. and R. J. Kinley (1994) 'Constructive Damage to the Status Quo', in I. Mintzer and J. A. Leonard (eds), *Negotiating Climate Change: The Inside Story of the Rio Convention*, Cambridge: Cambridge University Press.

Ebeling, J. and M. Yause (2008) 'Generating carbon finance through avoided deforestation and its potential to create climatic, conservation and human development benefits', *Philosophical Transactions of the Royal Society B* 363, 1,917–24.

Grubb, M. and F. Yamin (2001) 'Climatic Collapse at The Hague: What Happened, Why, and Where do we go from Here?', *International Affairs* 77 (2), 261–76.

Guha, R. and J. Martinez-Alier (1997) *Varieties of Environmentalism*, London: Earthscan.

Gupta, J. (1997) *The Climate Change Convention and Developing Countries*, Kluwer Academic Press.

Harris, Paul G. (1999) 'Common but Differentiated Responsibility: The Kyoto Protocol and United States Policy', *NYU Environmental Law Review* 17 (1), 27–48.

Hayes, P. (1993) 'North–South Transfer', in P. Hayes and K. Smith (eds), *The Global Greenhouse Regime: Who Pays?*, London: Earthscan.

Hyder, T. O. (1994) 'Looking Back to See Forward', in I. Mintzer and J. A. Leonard (eds), *Negotiating Climate Change: The Inside Story of the Rio Convention*, Cambridge: Cambridge University Press.

Mintzer and J. A. Leonard (eds) (1994) *Negotiating Climate Change: The Inside Story of the Rio Convention*, Cambridge: Cambridge University Press.

Mohamad, M. (1992) 'Statement to the U.N. Conference on Environment and Development', *Environmental Policy and Law* 22, 4, 232.

Najam, A., S. Huq and Y. Sokona (2003) 'Climate negotiations beyond Kyoto: developing countries concerns and interests', *Climate Policy* 3, 221–31.

Obama, B. (2007) 'Renewing American Leadership', *Foreign Affairs* Vol. 86, Issue 4, 2–16.

Oberthür, S., H. Ott, R.G. Tarasofsky and E.U. von Weizsäcker (1999) 'The Kyoto Protocol: International Climate Policy for the 21st Century', Springer.

Okereke, C. (2007) 'The Ethical Dimensions of Global Change', in C. Okereke (ed.), *The Politics of the Environment*, London: Routledge, 136–57.

——(2008a) *Global Justice and Neoliberal Environmental Governance: Ethics, sustainable development and international co-operation*. London: Routledge.

——(2008b) 'Equity Norms in Global Environmental Governance', *Global Environmental Politics* 8 (3), 25–50.

Okereke C., P. Mann, H. Osbahr, B. Müller and J. Ebeling (2007) 'An Assessment of the Nairobi conference and what it means for future climate regime', *Tyndall Centre for Climate Change Research Working Paper 106*, www.tyndall.ac.uk/publications/working_papers/twp106.pdf

Okereke, C. and H. Schroeder (2009) 'How can the objectives of justice, development and climate change mitigation be reconciled in the treatment of developing countries in a post-Kyoto settlement?', *Climate and Development* 1, 10–15.

Panjabi, R.K.L. (1993) 'Can International Law Improve the Climate? An analysis of the United Nations Climate Change Treaty Signed at the Rio Summit in 1992', *North Carolina Journal of International Law*, 18, 491–549.

Paterson, M. (1996) *Global Warming and Global Politics*, London: Routledge.

——(2001) 'Principles of Justice in the Context of Global Climate Change', in U. Luterbacher and D. Sprinz (eds), *International Relations and Global Climate Change*, Cambridge, MA: MIT Press.

Paterson, M. and M. Grubb (1992) 'The International Politics of Climate Change', *International Affairs* 68 (2), 293–313.

Ramakrishna, K. (1990) 'North South Issues, Common Heritage of Mankind and Global Climate Change', *Millennium Journal of International Studies* 19 (3), 429–45.

Rayner, T. and C. Okereke (2007) 'The Politics of Climate Change', in C. Okereke (ed.), *The Politics of the Environment*, London: Routledge, 116–35.

Rowlands, I. H. (1997) 'International Fairness and Justice in Addressing Global Climate Change', *Environmental Politics* 6 (3), 1–19.

Shue, H. (1993) 'Subsistence Emissions and Luxury Emissions', *Law and Policy* 15 (1), 39–59.

Singer, S. F. (1992) 'Earth Summit Will Shackle the Planet, Not Save it', *The Wall Street Journal*, 19 February 1992.

Stern, N. (2006) *The Economics of Climate Change*. Cambridge: Cambridge University Press.

Stone, Christopher D. (2004) 'Common and Differentiated Responsibilities in International Law', *The American Journal of International Law* 98 (2), 276–301.

Toth, F. and M. Mwandosya (2001) 'Decision-Making Frameworks', in B. Metz et al. (eds), *Climate Change 2001: Mitigation*, contribution of Working Group III to the Third Assessment, Report of the Intergovernmental Panel on Climate Change, Cambridge: Cambridge University Press.

US Department of State (2006) *USA Energy Needs, Clean Development and Climate Change*, Washington, DC: US Department of State Publications.

von Weizsäcker, E. U. (1994) *Earth Politics*, London: Zed Books.

Yamin, F., J. Burniaux and A. Nentjes (2001) 'Kyoto Mechanisms: Key Issues for Policy Makers for COP-6', *International Environmental Agreements* 1, 44, 187–218.

Protagonists in the Market of Climate Change Knowledge[1]

HANS VON STORCH

KNOWLEDGE ABOUT CLIMATE CHANGE

Science has established that processes of human origin are influencing the climate—that human beings are changing the global climate. Climate is the statistics of the weather. In almost all localities, at present and in the foreseeable future, the frequency distributions of the temperature continue to shift to higher values; sea level is rising; amounts of rainfall are changing. Some extremes, such as heavy rainfall events, will change. The driving force behind these alterations is above all the emission of greenhouse gases, in particular carbon dioxide and methane, into the atmosphere, where they interfere with the radiative balance of the earth system.

This is the *scientific* construct of human-made climate change. It is widely supported within the relevant scientific communities, and has been comprehensively formulated particularly owing to the collective and consensual efforts of the UN Intergovernmental Panel on Climate Change (IPCC).[2]

Of course, there is no complete consensus in the scientific community, so that speaking of the 'scientific construct' is a simplification, which is applied in this essay for describing the contrast with the cultural constuct, which is equally not just one construct but features many different variants. What is stated in the previous paragraph is the core of the consensus and may, therefore, represent the core of 'the' scientific construct.

What else do people know about climate and climate change? Here is what may be called the social or cultural construct, which guides perceptions and understanding (cf. Stehr and von Storch 1995). Climate really is changing because of human activity—due to deforestation, for example, as well (von Storch and Stehr 2000). The weather is less reliable than it was before, the seasons more irregular, the storms more violent. Weather extremes are taking on catastrophic and previously unknown forms.

The cause? Human greed and stupidity. The mechanism? The justice, or the revenge, of a nature that is striking back. For large chunks of the population, at least in Central and Northern Europe, the mechanism is obvious.[3] In olden times, the adverse climatic developments were the just response of a God angered by human sins (e.g. Kershaw 1973; Stehr and von Storch 1995); this approach is also sometimes invoked today, in particular in the USA or possibly in the United Kingdom. An example is provided by the former Chair of the IPCC, Sir John Houghton, who expressed his conviction that God would speak to the public through disasters (Welch 1995). Or, as it is put on the back cover of an alarmistic book 'Our Drowning World' (Milne 1989): ' ... we shall be engulfed by the consequences of our greed and stupidity. Nearly two thirds of our world could disappear under polar ice cap water [...] For this will be the inevitable outcome of industrialization, urbanization, overpopulation and the accompanying pollution'. An enlightened variant is suggested by Lovelock in the framework of his Gaia hypothesis, when he speaks about 'The revenge of Gaia – why Earth is fighting back ... ' (Lovelock 2006).

Finally, there is also the idea of 'climatic determinism' (see Stehr and von Storch 1999; Hulme 2008), which can be traced back to classical Greek literature and was widely accepted in Western thinking in the 18th century up to the middle of the 20th century. Some elements of this school of thought continue to have an effect upon our Western culture. One of these elements is the understanding that human beings have to live in balance with that climate that is suitable for them. If this climate changes, civilization is at risk; whole cultures perish on such an occasion—for instance, Native American cultures in North America, the Viking settlements in Greenland. No wonder, then, that in German usage, the term is *Klimakatastrophe*, 'climate catastrophe' and not 'climate change'.

This is the *cultural* construct of climate change, particularly in the German-speaking countries, but similarly, and widely, in other areas of the West as well. It has to be stressed, again, that referring to just one well-defined construct is a simplification; obviously, the cultural construct takes many different forms; displays various nuances—but what is described above represents something like a standard core of such statements. Different perceptions prevail in, for instance, Germany and the USA (von Storch and Krauss 2005).

Obviously, the scientific construct is hardly consistent with such cultural constructs.

There is another rather different construct of climate change, namely that of so-called sceptics (e.g. Demeritt 2001, 2006), according to whom climate has changed naturally since ancient times so that the present change is not cause for alarm; that human influence would be much too weak, and that claims about anthropogenic climate change would mostly reflect vested political interests. While claims of the fossil-fuel industry being the main driver are often made (e.g. Demeritt 2001), case studies (Lahsen 2008) indicate that the root of such claims is more in traditional scientific circles, chiefly physicists, chemists and geologists, who find the widespread usage of models and indirect evidence hard to accept (e.g. Kellow 2007). In the following chapter, we will not deal with this school of thinking, even though it would certainly be worth examining why so often older scientists find it difficult to accept the many arguments supporting the understanding that man is currently changing, and will continue in the foreseeable future to change, the climate to a significant extent.

The two constructs, scientific and cultural, are competitors in the interpretation of a complex environment; two protagonists on the market of knowledge. Their inconsistency makes them incompatible, but sometimes the two forms are, nevertheless, mended, the efficacy of the modernized construct so formed increases; its scientific basis, however, becomes narrower. Public acceptance rises; its robustness in the face of scientifically verifiable facts sinks; but its utility for pursuing certain value-driven politcal agendas is improved; at the same time, science is corrupted. Of course, scientific practice—and thus its construction of explanations and theories—are influenced by the cultural construct in any case; after all, we simply cannot live free of our culture. Our culture conditions us in our point of view, steers us in our formulation of questions, in our willingness to regard answers as sufficient to build an argument. Needless to emphasize, there is no pure scientific construction in reality but at least a kind of approximation of such.

THE ARENA OF PUBLIC ATTENTION

In the 1970s the idea of *Bringschuld of science* was created in Germany[4]—when related to science this term *Bringschuld* denotes the ethical obligation of scientists to pay their debt to society by informing it about existing, arising and possible future dangers. In the past, science had all too often turned a blind eye to such dangers, and instead made itself a willing servant of such scientific and technological developments as eugenics and nuclear power. Rewarded with financial incentives, recognition and the satisfaction of a sometimes perverse curiosity, science looked on without lifting a finger and without taking responsibility. It was time to put an end to such inaction, the argument said. Scientists were to see their activities in a social context, to inform the public on their own initiative, without waiting to be asked—so that the public could then decide, democratically, what made sense and what did not.

What do we scientists—who may well be experts in our field, but who are otherwise laypeople like anyone else—know about the dangers at hand? It often happens that the perceived dangers lie outside the realm of our expertise; that is, we 'experts' operate with culturally constructed knowledge—not, however, as the onlooking public believes, with scientifically constructed knowledge. Thus it is not the best knowledge that is put into action, but rather knowledge claims. Pretensions to interpretation, and to power, disguised as science.

It is not that there are few dangers, real or perceived; rather, there are many such dangers. They vie with one another in competition for public attention. The public, incuding scientists, is only able to 'process' a limited number of topics at length; just how many is unclear, but it seems implausible to me that there would be at the same time more than 10 or maybe 20. Some of these topics are 'givens', such as the national soccer league, for instance. How are the topics that come to the fore chosen? One would hope that the deciding factor might be the urgency of the topic, the social or economic relevance, but that is most certainly not the case. Perhaps it is their entertainment value, even their fear-mongering value, the challenge they pose, or even, in terms of the interpretive order, their assurance that all is well with the cultural construct.

Of course, one can attempt to 'push' one's own field of expertise into the arena of public attention. The attributes needed to accomplish this must then be added—by means of exaggeration, perhaps; by implicit associations; by exploiting the cultural construct, that is to say, what the public in any case recognizes as being 'correct'. Forest dieback, or 'Waldsterben',[5] was certainly one such topic.

Whether fulfilling the terms of *Bringschuld* is beneficial or harmful for the individual certainly depends upon the social context. When everyone was enthusiastic about scientific and technological progress—when the German weekly 'Micky Maus' comics,[6] in the series 'Our Friend, the Atom', described a golden future of ubiquitous nuclear energy to their young readers—then no one paid any heed to the possible drawbacks of these advances. Today, though, with a sceptical attitude towards scientific and technological progress, particularly when it seems to be documented in our immediate environment in the form of masts, noises or smells, a scientifically presented assessment of the dangers is appreciated by society, particularly when such an assessment confirms prior knowledge and thus is recognized *a priori* as correct in any case. This appreciation can take a multitude of forms: a career, public attention and recognition, better working conditions, personal satisfaction in the belief that one has made the world a better place.

Satisfying the demands of *Bringschuld* is no longer an altruistic act nowadays, but rather a productive element in a marketing strategy. *Bringschuld* of science has led to a massive influx of proclaimed dangers into the arena of public attention. Environmental science, and not just environmental science, has become 'postnormal'.

POSTNORMAL SCIENCE BETWEEN THE REQUIREMENTS OF POLICY AND THE MEDIA

The quality of being postnormal was introduced into the analysis of science by the philosophers Silvio Funtovitz and Jerry Ravetz (1985). In a situation where science cannot make concrete statements with high certainty, and in which the evidence of science is of considerable practical significance for formulating policies and decisions, this science is impelled less and less by the pure 'curiosity' that idealistic views glorify as the innermost driving force of science, and increasingly by the usefulness of the possible evidence for just such formulations of decisions and policy. It is no longer being scientific that is of central importance, nor the methodical quality, nor Popper's dictum of falsification, nor Fleck's idea of repairing outmoded systems of explanation (Fleck 1980); instead, it is utility that carries the day. The saying 'nothing is as practical as a good theory', attributed to Kurt Lewin, refers to the ability to facilitate decisions and guide actions. Not correctness, nor objective falsifiability, occupies the foreground, but rather social acceptance.

In its postnormal phase, science thus lives on its claims, on its staging in the media, on its congruity with cultural constructions. These knowledge claims are raised not only by established scientists, but also by other, self-appointed experts, who frequently enough are bound to special interests, be they Exxon or Greenpeace.

Currently, climate research is postnormal (Bray and von Storch 1999). The inherent uncertainties are enormous, since projections of the future are required, or rather: of futures—such futures that can only be represented using models, where conditions will prevail that no one has yet observed. We simply do not know exactly how the cloud cover will alter if temperatures and water vapour content change, or which will win the upper hand in terms of the balance of the Antarctic ice mass—increased precipitation in the heights, or melt-off at the edges. Our knowledge is inadequate not because the scientists are incapable, but rather due to the meagre facts available, the incomplete data, which moreover span too short a time period. Certainly there are arguments that point to one answer or the other, and considerations of plausibility allow us to exclude certain developments as unlikely or even impossible. There remains, though, a residual uncertainty that will possibly never be resolved, or will be reduced only in the course of years, or even decades. In this situation, the representatives of social interests seek out those knowledge claims that best support their own position. One need only recall the Stern report (see the critique by Pielke 2007a, or Yohe and Tol 2008), or the regular press releases of US Senator Inhofe. Not only are those knowledge claims that seem suitable picked out and placed into a matching overall picture, but new and idiosyncratic knowledge claims are also constructed, so that in the end a bizarre accumulation of claims is produced—claims that sometimes seem arbitrary, such as that the number of patients with kidney stones will increase (Brikowski et al. 2008), for instance, as a result of human-made global warming. The scientifically untenable film 'The Day after Tomorrow' is praised by high-profile scientists as an aid to awareness-raising; political and scientific achievements are intermingled by awarding the Nobel Peace Prize simultaneously to Al Gore and the IPCC; politicians disguised as professors pronounce to the public necessary reactions to climate change. Along with these alarmist tendencies, there is also the sceptical counterpart, represented in such grossly misleading products as 'State of Fear', by the otherwise admirable Michael Crichton, or the film 'The Great Swindle'. All of this is typical of a postnormal science.

In the daily course of events, there are many opportunities for both the individual and powerful scientific organizations to draw public attention to themselves. There remains, though, not only among natural scientists, a gnawing sense that this practice simply cannot be that which we describe as more or less 'good science', where it is the argument, the critical enquiry, the well-constructed test, the unconventional idea that lies outside the prevailing paradigm, that effect progress, rather than science's usefulness for putting through a policy perceived or described as correct. What appears in *Science* and *Nature* is often prematurely published research; it stimulates the educated readership's imagination—and sometimes its fears—and after a few years it often proves to be in need of revision anyway. However, this revision is ultimately the mechanism that extricates science from the whirling eddy of postnormality. When the caravan of public attention turns to other topics, then normal science takes hold again and compromises with the required usefulness, the *Zeitgeist* and political correctness can be revised. On a smaller scale, we can already see this revision of details (but not the overall assessment) in the field of climate research: for instance, in the case of the so-called 'hockey stick', the premature closure of debate on the question of historical temperature fluctuations;[7] or of the perception, pushed by some re-insurance companies, that the risk of storms has increased; or the perspective that anthropogenic climate change would be associated with the break-down of the gulf stream or the disintegration of the West-Antarctic Ice Shield within decades.

A ROLE FOR THE SOCIAL AND CULTURAL SCIENCES

For us, as scientists involved in this matter, the question is: how do we deal, here and now, with this postnormal situation, for we accept both demands—good science and good advice for the public—as justified. The solution can actually only be this: that we do what we do best, at least in principle: namely, analyse the situation scientifically. However, we natural scientists can do this only to a limited extent. We already suspect that the process of science is a social process; that we are not always quite objective, at least when we frame questions and accept explanations; that we are conditioned by our different cultures; that the advance of individuals into important positions often has less to do with science, and rather more to do with social and political acceptance.

In order to give our analysis depth and substance, we need the skills of the social and cultural sciences. My personal experience, which is admittedly limited, informs me that up to now these sciences have largely kept their distance. What I have heard are occasional and general hints that everything would be socially constructed and relative—which I consider mostly signs of an unfortunate refusal to go into concrete detail, which would be unavoidable for any real synergy. It is disappointing when colleagues from these fields obviously fail to notice that the scientific and cultural constructs are falling away from each other; instead, they content themselves with cultural constructions as circulated by the popular media and vested interests.

However, even if the overwhelming majority of social and cultural scientists, whom I came across in recent years, continue to close their minds to a transdisciplinary[8] approach to the topic of human-made climate change, there are, none the less, outstanding successful examples of the required research collaboration with the social sciences. I refer to the exemplary work of the German media scholar Peter Weingart, and to the US political scientist Roger Pielke, Jr. There are others of similar or even greater calibre, but having found their work relevant for my practical task of communicating climate science with stakeholders, I will describe some of their work in the following paragraphs in some detail.

The Honest Broker of Knowledge

In his book 'The Honest Broker', Roger Pielke, Jr (2007b) has constructed a provisional typology of scientists. Further, he has described how politics degrade science to a theatre of war by proxy, in order to solve problems that the political system itself cannot solve—no more than science can.

Pielke differentiates five types of scientists, who enter into communication with the public in various ways. The 'pure scientist' is essentially driven by curiosity and has hardly any interest in seeing his new scientific insights placed into a social or political context. The 'scientific arbiter' enables an accurate understanding of indisputable scientific facts. Both types are well suited to those situations when a 'normal' science can answer questions with great certainty, and these answers, if they come to be socially implemented, are as a rule uncontroversial.

As I have just explained, though, at present climate research is not normal, but rather postnormal. As a result, we often see the 'issue advocate', who applies his scientific competence not to the impartial[9] extension of knowledge, but rather to promoting a value-oriented, and thus also political, agenda. This means that the results of scientific insight are narrowed down to a few, or even to only one 'solution', consistent with his values. The last few decades in particular have produced many scientists of this type, who work and speak for economic or (socio-)political interests. The fourth type of scientist, and the one that Pielke clearly sees as a model to emulate, gives his book its name: 'The Honest Broker'. This type distinguishes himself in that, unlike the 'issue advocate', he broadens the scope of the deductions he draws from his findings, rather than constricting it. Thus he enables the political process to choose the 'solution' that society desires (and not that which is favoured and promoted by the issue advocate). The fifth type is the 'stealth issue advocate', who performs the functions of an 'issue advocate', but who cultivates the image of a 'scientific arbiter' or 'honest broker'. Due to his fraudulent self-representation, in essence, he benefits neither science nor society.

Pielke recommends that science choose the path of the 'honest broker', who explains the complexity of the problems and contributes to weighing up the implications of possible decisions. In doing so, he puts society in a position to choose solutions for its controversies, even on the basis of uncertain knowledge regarding the connections and possibilities, but rationally, and in a manner consistent with its values—for instance, in order to deal with the prospect of climate change, which society itself has caused.

The other question is that of the proxy battlefield. Again and again, we see situations in which politicians run aground, coming to decisions that are perceived negatively by significantly large or influential groups. In this case, it happens that a factual constraint is built up, so that policy-makers, in accordance with the scientific analysis, purportedly can come to only one decision. Politics then portrays itself as subordinate to science. This is the case particularly in the field of climate policy, where the 'two-degree goal' for avoiding catastrophic climate change, as formulated by scientists, is depicted as an *ultima ratio* to which policy-makers simply must yield. In accordance with Lewin's rule that nothing is as practical as a good theory, because it guides the action to be taken, this depiction is indeed extremely useful politically, precisely because it does indeed guide the action to be taken. Further discussions are not required; the goals of climate policy will be met by means of energy policy, the concept informs. The problem is, though, that the confrontation has been transferred from the visible political stage to the less visible scientific discussion. In that realm, just as little consensus has been reached among scientists as among the politicians, and the resulting argumentative conflict among the scientists degenerates into a political confrontation, fought according to the rules of politics, and ultimately 'won' by one party or another.

This process is useful to policy-makers—after all, they come to their decisions more easily—but science is done an injury by being thus politicized. This is not a sustainable use of the resource we call science, the service of which to society by rendering an interpretation of complex facts is ultimately barely distinguished, in the public perception, from the political information disseminated by interest groups.

From this, Pielke derives two normative demands: namely, that the responsible scientist should act as an 'honest broker', and that policy-makers should concentrate on posing only scientifically solvable problems for science, and not on evading their own responsibility—to find a 'solution' consistent with society's values in normatively difficult situations.

Risks of Communication

In their book, Peter Weingart and his colleagues (2000, 2002) have reconstructed how the topic of climate moved from science to the realm of politics and the media in Germany.

Initially, within scientific circles there was a phase of 'anthropogenization and politicization', according to which human beings were to blame for climate change in the first place, and they could also guide and manage this change by means of responsible behaviour. Those responsible, those affected and the options for action were clearly named. Thus, as it was put in the 1986 declaration by the Energy Study Group of the German Physical Society: 'in order to avert the threatened climate catastrophe, we must now begin drastically to reduce the emission of trace gases'.

This description quickly found its way into the political discussion, because it was also suited to a broader environmental policy discourse. Thus, the concept of catastrophe, once brought into the world, was taken up into the political language. At the same time, the 'climate catastrophe' and the struggle to avert it came to be understood and described as an object of policy-based regulation.

The topic was picked up by the mass media, resulting in a further dramatization and intensification. Here, Weingart describes the elements of the 'manufacture of climate change as an event', 'the staging of the relevance of climate change for day-to-day life', and finally the transformation of the scientific hypothesis into the 'certainty of the coming catastrophe'.

Weingart substantiates all of these steps by means of examples. Then he poses the question of the risks involved for the three actors: science, politics and media.

For science, the principal risk is the 'loss of credibility due to the particular dynamic of the catastrophe metaphor'. This concept enabled climate research to enter onto the stage of politics and the media, but due to its parallel cultural construct this communication also smuggled along with it a number of connotations. Science is now confronted with these connotations, in statements such as: you made this claim and that claim; how does that match up with this current development, or that one? Klaus Hasselmann analysed this phenomenon in his response, 'The Moods of the Media', (Hasselmann 1997) and lamented that the evidence science was presenting would first undergo a metamorphosis, and science would then have to let itself be measured by these now altered messages. This certainly is not fair, but it is political and social reality. Or, as a journalist once said to me: 'whoever hitches a ride upwards with the media, will meet them again when going down'. In both cases, the elevators function according to the same rules.

The risk for policy-makers is in the possibility that the goals set in this manner cannot be achieved. Weingart speaks of a 'loss of legitimacy due to taking on too much'. That Kyoto was unable to prevent the perceived 'climate catastrophe' was foreseeable from the outset; that focusing one-sidedly on energy policy was indeed useful in staging the event for the public, but did not do justice to the facts of the matter.

The media primarily fear the 'loss of public attention', due to concepts and conceptual fields becoming worn out. In 2005 it was declared that there remained only 13 years more in which the climate could be rescued (McCarthy 2005), and in the following years very little happened other than rhetoric and symbolic acts on both the scientific and the political side; then the media, for their part, attempted to gain the public's attention by other means, for example, by propagating a sceptical counter-discourse (Spiegel 2007). This is exactly what we have observed in the last few years. This counter-discourse, staged by the media, follows the logic of Hasselmann's 'Moods of the Media', but also corresponds to the attempt within scientific circles to limit the acceptance of the misleading cultural construct in favour of the more realistic scientific construct. Weingart and his collaborators describe this as follows: 'The object and trigger of this [climatic] scepticism are, not least, the correcting and relativising of scientific climate scenarios by established climate research itself. In the sciences this is a normal process; in the media, it becomes an incentive to mistrust'.

Science, or more precisely the scientific institutions, react to this risk by implementing professional 'press relations', which are oriented to 'representational principles of the mass media'. Policy-makers protect themselves by creating a 'hierarchy of knowledge, or of advice', with advisers to the Chancellor, Climate Service Centres and the like. The mass media seek the attention of the public by selectively presenting scientific findings that either agree or conflict with the cultural construct, or else by staging controversies, by which means yet another cultural construct is served; namely, the construct of the allegedly arbitrary nature of scientific evidence.

CHALLENGE TO SCIENTIFIC INSTITUTIONS

Most scientific institutions around the world dealing with climate research, I presume, are confronted with requests by the public, decision-makers and the media for information about the 'climate problem', and options available for 'action'. The heads of these institutions travel throughout the country, talking to the media, the public and, sometimes, to politicians.

This is also the case in my own institution, the Institute for Coastal Research of the Helmholtz Association of German Research Centres (GKSS), which sees itself faced with a demand for advice, above all in the realm of coastal protection, but also about marine traffic, tourism and other sectors. Just as important is the demand for interpretation on the part of the public, particularly in the form of the media, regarding climate change and the classification of conspicuous events, above all storms and storm surges. In other institutions, the situation is similar. We have developed a strategy to deal with these needs, foremost at the regional and sectorial level. At first, this process was conducted *ad hoc*. Since then, we have attempted to structure the task more broadly and approach it more systematically. We believe that our approach may also be useful for other institutions in other cultures.

The elements of this approach are (von Storch and Meinke 2008):

1) A systematic consideration of the significance of adapting to climate change and the possibilities of mitigating climate change; for instance, in the form of the 10-point 'Zeppelin Manifesto', by Stehr and von Storch (2009). Apart of the obvious options, such as enlarging the rainwater system, or increasing the height of dykes along rivers and coast, conceptually different and intriguing options emerge upon closer scrutiny, such as redesigning urban planning (Gill et al. 2007) to deal with the effects of heatwaves or geo-engineering estuaries (von Storch et al. 2008) to reduce the hazard of storm surges.

2) A survey of the scientifically legitimate knowledge claims regarding present and future climate change in relevant regions. 'Scientifically legitimate' in this context refers to publications by recognized scientific institutions, corresponding to current good scientific practice. This is not a matter of representing the 'best knowledge', which is often a problematic claim in any case, but rather of identifying a consensus, including the consensual determination of those areas where there is, as yet, simply no consensus: a consensus of disagreement (BACC 2008; Reckermann et al. 2008).

3) The availability of descriptions of regional climate changes in the recent past, detailed in terms of time and place. For Northern Europe,

such a data set is CoastDat (www.coastdat.de), which covers the period from 1948 to today. In addition to other commonsense applications (Weisse et al. 2009), such a data set allows us to assess to what extent current changes can be seen as consistent with the changes indicated to us by climate models, in the form of scenarios (e.g. Bhend and von Storch 2009). This helps to overcome a frequent and highly counterproductive element in public communications: the fondness for frequent—and negligent—assertions that this or that event is a harbinger of what is in store for us. As a rule, there is hardly a basis for such claims. Data sets of climate variability and weather extremes of the past decades allow deconstruction of such claims. (An example of the case of hurricanes making landfall in the USA is provided by Pielke et al. 2008; for Northern European storms see Weisse et al. 2005.)

4) This catalogue of the knowledge on offer is rounded out by a knowledge broker, a regional climate office. Within the framework of the Helmholtz Association, we have set up four such regional climate offices in Germany (www.klimabuero.de); the office at GKSS takes care of the northern German area, especially aspects of the coast, that is storms, storm surges and swells. Researchers in Karlsruhe look after the south, those in Leipzig the central region, and the Alfred Wegener Institute for Polar and Marine Research looks after the Arctic regions. All of these activities are carried out in association with related activities of the German Weather Service and the Climate Service Centre, as of 1 January 2009.

The fundamental idea of the regional climate offices is based on the observation that communication about the climate is not a question of 'knowledge speaks to power', or the coaching of an uneducated public, as many naive physicists and meteorologists still like to believe. This challenge cannot be met with a pedagogically inspired website, or a climate game. Rather, the primary necessity on the part of science is to understand what exactly the questions from the public and the policy-makers entail, how these questions are connected to other complexes, whether the answers given by climate research have any bearing at all on these questions, and to what extent our ideas are in competition with cultural constructs.

The North German Climate Office at the GKSS, which is managed in tandem with the Hamburg Centre of Excellence for climate research (CLISAP), is thus designed with bilateral communication in mind.

CONCLUDING REMARKS

This article is a personal account of a climate scientist, who is often engaged with the need to communicate with stakeholders and with the media, mainly in Germany. During this communication I was confronted with a number of problems, which obviously are not specific to my own practice, but which I found to be similar to those of other natural scientists.

The key element of my summary is the insight that we have two competing knowledge claims, or, to formulate more precisely, two classes of knowledge claims. For cultural scientists this is no surprise, but for many natural scientists, this statement is almost an affront.

Scientific knowledge, in social practice, is only one form of knowledge; it must compete with other forms and it will not automatically 'win this competition', or perhaps better described 'be accepted as superior knowledge'. What would be the 'best' outcome of such an encounter? ('best' in the sense of instituting the most rational available understanding of phenomena and their dynamics). It does not imply the availability of immediate practical advice for designing policies, but the presentation of a solid basis of the natural science issues of such policies. A separation of science and values, to the extent possible. If this goes along with nudging of cultural constructions towards the scientific construction, a gradual rationalization, that would also be a favourable cultural result—for me.

The outlook of this discussion is related to my unfortunate limitation of drawing mostly on Central and Northern European experience. Plausibly, in other cultures, say in Asia or Africa, different attitudes and constructions will prevail and compete with scientific views. This may be so in the USA and People's Republic of China (this was nicely reflected by the very different reviews I received for this manuscript, prior to its publication in *Environmental Science and Policy*, *Leviathan* and now in this book; see also von Storch and Krauss 2005). We need urgently cultural scientists and scientific platforms, which bring the natural and cultural approaches together.

If scientific actors do not recognize this dynamic, they often attempt to 'optimize' the dissemination of their 'message' by means of propagandistic tricks, such as emphasizing or selectively communicating information to suit their purpose. As a result, first, the public will be disenfranchised; and second, science as a socially accepted institution will be damaged. I consider it our task to pursue science on a sustainable basis.

The insight of two competing types of knowledge has a number of practical implications for science. One is that science itself is under permanent influence of non-scientific knowledge claims, such as ideological or pre-scientific claims. They influence the scientist in his way of asking and in his request for evidence before accepting answers. Claims that are consistent with cultural constructed knowledge are more easily accepted as accurate than results that contradict such claims. Another issue is the transfer of scientific understanding into the policy process. Here, the scientific understanding should help to prepare policy design—which must not be misunderstood as enforcing certain designs—by clarifying the natural science part of the issues.

NOTES

1 Paul Malone has done an inital translation of the German manuscript. Comments provided by Max Boykoff and Mike Hulme are acknowldeged. Discussions with

Jerry Ravetz, Silvio Funtovicz, Roger Pielke and Peter Weingart were most helpful. This is a slightly modified version of the talk 'Klimaforschung und Politikberatung – zwischen Bringeschuld und Postnormalität', presented 21 November 2008 in Potsdam. Two different versions of the manuscript have been published: in English (von Storch 2009a) and in German (von Storch 2009b). The publication of the revised manuscript in this collection has been kindly permitted by the Publisher of *Enviromental Science and Policy*, Elsevier.

2 To avoid misunderstanding: I am a natural scientist, I have contributed to the IPCC process as lead author and consider the 'scientific construct' realistic. I do not ascribe to the cultural construct as a useful and realistic concept for understanding climate, climate change and climate impact, which I try to describe in the following paragraphs. The cultural construct is, though, a powerful concept, which deserves scientific analysis and attention.

3 On 14 August 2002, the reputable Swedish daily newspaper 'Dagens Nyheter' wrote: 'Naturen slår tilbaka våldsamt' [Nature strikes back violently], when reporting about disastrous flooding in the Czech Republic.

4 According to Frese (1994) the then-Chancellor of the Federal Republic of Germany, Helmut Schmidt, brought the issue up during his speech to the annual meeting of the Max Planck Society (MPG) in Hamburg, 1975. Later Helmut Schmidt came back to this issue several times, e.g. twice in 2004: Schmidt (2004a, 2004b).

5 'Forest dieback', which was around in the 1970s and 1980s, is an icon of human destruction of the environment. It was most popular in Germany, and the German term 'Waldsterben' was introduced into the French and English languages.

6 This weekly journal addressed children and juveniles with Walt Disney's comics since 1951 in Germany. Facing opposition to the comic characters, which were considered inferior to 'real' literature, the editor added a supposedly informative article-style mid-part on social and technological issues.

7 This conflict about the methodical validity of the methodology behind the hockey stick – which, according to our analysis, suffered from significant underestimation of low-frequency variability (e.g. von Storch 2009a, 2009b) – represents an interesting case for the cultural scientists. The conflict was driven to large extent by the utility and significance of the hockey stick for political arguing, and much less by the need of sorting out methodical issues.

8 In the sense of a collaboration between natural sciences on the one side, and social and cultural scientists on the other side, or more generally a co-operation beyond the modern division of disciplines.

9 This wording does not imply that strict impartiality would be possible. Certainly, all scientists unavoidably exhibit, or suffer from, some partiality, but most try to constrain this subjectivity to the limited extent possible. Indeed, the building of two opposing separate constructions, scientific and cultural, in this essay represents an oversimplification, which helps to work out the argument more easily.

REFERENCES

BACC (2008) *Assessment of Climate Change in the Baltic Sea Basin*, Heidelberg: Springer Verlag Berlin.

Bhend, J. and H. von Storch (2009) 'Consistency of observed temperature trends in the Baltic Sea catchment area with anthropogenic climate change scenarios', *Boreal Env. Res.* 14, 81–88.

Bray, D. and H. von Storch (1999) 'Climate Science. An empirical example of postnormal science', *Bull. Amer. Met. Soc.* 80, 439–56.

Brikowski, T.H., Y. Lotan and M. S. Pearle (2008) 'Climate-related increase in the prevalence of urolithiasis in the United States', *Proceedings of the National Academy of Science* 105, 9, 841–46.

Demeritt, D. (2001) 'The Construction of Global Warming and the Politics of Science', *Annals of the Association of American Geographers* 91, 2, 307–37.

——(2006) 'Science studies, climate change and the prospects for constructivist critique', *Economy and Society* 35, 3, 453–79.

Fleck, L. (1980) *Entstehung und Entwicklung einer wissenschaftlichen Tatsache: Einführung in die Lehre vom Denkstil und Denkkollektiv*, Frankfurt-am-Main: Suhrkamp Verlag.

Frese, W. (2004) 'Die Treibhausfenster schließen sich ... und die Ozonschicht versprödet weiter. Ozon-und Klimaforscher haben vergeblich "Bringschuld" geleistet', *MPG Presseinformation*, 14 February 2004.

Funtowicz, S.O. and J.R. Ravetz (1985) 'Three types of risk assessment: a methodological analysis', in C. Whipple and V.T. Covello (eds), *Risk Analysis in the Private Sector*, New York: Plenum, 217–31.

Gill, S.E., J.F. Handley, A.R. Ennos and S. Paulett (2007) 'Adapting cities for climate change: The role of the green infrastructure', *Built Environment* 33, 115–33.

Hasselmann, K. (1997) 'Die Launen der Medien', *ZEIT* Nr. 31, 25 July 1997; www.rz.shuttle.de/rn/sae/warming/klima972.htm.

Hulme, M. (2008) 'The conquering of climate: discourses of fear and their dissolution', *The Geographical Journal* 174, 1, 5–16.

Kellow, A. (2007) *Science and Public Policy*, Edgar Elgar Publishing.

Kershaw I. (1973) 'The great famine and agrarian crisis in England, 1315–22', *Past Present* 59, 3–50.

Lahsen, M. (2008) 'Experience of modernity in the greenhouse: A cultural analysis of a physicist "trio" supporting backlash against global warming', *Global Env. Change* 18, 204–19.

Lovelock, J. (2006) *The revenge of Gaia – Why Earth is Fighting back – and How We Can Still Save Humanity*, London: Penguin Group.

McCarthy, M. (2005) 'Countdown to global catastrophe', *The Independent* online, 24 January 2005.

Milne, A. (1989) *Our Drowning World*, London: Prism Press.

Pielke, Roger A., Jr (2007a) 'Mistreatment of the economic impacts of extreme events in the Stern Review Report on the economics of climate change', *Global Environmental Change* 17, 302–10.

——(2007b) *The Honest Broker*, Cambridge: Cambridge University Press.

Pielke, R.A., Jr, J. Gratz, C.W. Landsea, D. Collins, M. Saunders and R. Musulin (2008) 'Normalized Hurricane Damages in the United States: 1900–2005', *Natural Hazards Review* 9, 29–42.

Reckermann, M., H.-J. Isemer and H. von Storch (2008) 'Climate Change Assessment for the Baltic Sea Basin', *EOS Trans. Amer. Geophys. U.* 161–62.

Schmidt, H. (2004a) 'Uns selbst mit den Augen der Nachbarn sehen', *ZEIT* 1 April 2004, 15.

——(2004b) 'Mischt Euch ein, Professoren!', *Hamburger Abendblatt* 18/19, December 2004, 3.

Spiegel (2007) 'Abschied vom Weltuntergang', 19, 2007.

Stehr, N. and H. von Storch (1995) 'The social construct of climate and climate change', *Clim. Res.* 5, 99–105.

——(1999) 'An anatomy of climate determinism', in H. Kaupen-Haas (ed.), *Wissenschaftlicher Rassismus – Analysen einer Kontinuität in den Human-und Naturwissenschaften*, Frankfurt-am-Main and New York: Campus-Verlag, 137–85.

——(2009) *Climate and Society*, World Scientifc Publisher (forthcoming). See also in German, www.spiegel.de/wissenschaft/natur/0,1518,576032–11,00.html.

Tol, R.S.J. (2007) 'Europe's long-term climate target: A critical evaluation', *Energy Policy* 35, 424–32.

von Storch, H. (2009a) 'Climate Research and Policy Advice: Scientific and Cultural Constructions of Knowledge', *Env. Science Pol.*

——(2009b) 'Klimaforschung und Politikberatung – zwischen Bringeschuld und Postnormalität', *Leviathan, Berliner Zeitschrift für Sozialwissenschaften* 37, 305–17.

von Storch, H., G. Gönnert and M. Meine (2008) 'Storm surges – an option for Hamburg, Germany, to mitigate expected future aggravation of risk', *Env. Sci. Pol.* 11, 735–42.

von Storch, H. and W. Krauss (2005) 'Culture Contributes to Perceptions of Climate Change. A comparison between the United States and Germany reveals insights about why journalists in each country report about this issue in different ways', *Niemann Reports* (winter 2005), 99–102.

von Storch, H. and I. Meinke (2008) 'Regional climate offices and regional assessment reports needed', *Nature Geosciences* 1 (2), 78.

von Storch, H. and N. Stehr (2000) 'Climate change in perspective. Our concerns about global warming have an age-old resonance', *Nature* 405, 615.

Weingart, P., A. Engels and P. Pansegrau (2000) 'Risks of communication: Discourses on climate change in science, politics and the mass media', *Public Understanding of Science* 9, 261–83.

——(2002) *Von der Hypothese zur Katastrophe*, Leske + Budrich Verlag.

Weisse, R., H. von Storch and F. Feser (2005) 'Northeast Atlantic and North Sea storminess as simulated by a regional climate model 1958–2001 and comparison with observations', *J. Climate* 18, 465–79.

Weisse, R., H. von Storch, U. Callies, A. Chrastansky, F. Feser, I. Grabemann, H. Guenther, A. Pluess, T. Stoye, J. Tellkamp, J. Winterfeldt and K. Woth (2009) 'Regional meteo-marine reanalyses and climate change projections: Results for Northern Europe and potentials for coastal and offshore applications', *Bull. Ameri. Met. Soc.*

Welch, F. (1995) 'Me and My God', *Sunday Telegraph*, 10 September 1995.

Yohe, Gary W. and Richard S.J. Tol (2008) 'The Stern review and the economies of climate change: An editorial essay', *Climatic Change* 89, 231–40.

The Politics of the Carbon Economy

PETER NEWELL AND MATTHEW PATERSON

INTRODUCTION

Climate politics are increasingly conducted by, through and for markets. Business and financial actors have become central in the construction and management of an elaborate and increasingly intermeshed system of climate governance. Central to these are a series of markets, constructed to facilitate investment in carbon abatement and to create incentives for states and firms to limit their carbon emissions. Emissions trading systems, the Kyoto flexibility mechanisms, voluntary carbon offset projects and projects by investors to get other companies to disclose their carbon emissions are the key elements in this governance system. All amount to the creation of what is sometimes called the carbon economy; they all subject climate change to a market logic. They do this by allocating property rights to carbon emissions, by getting firms to incorporate their carbon emissions into their routine calculations of profit and risk, and by subjecting firms to a logic of transparent information by which investors and consumers can make decisions through the market that are compatible with the goal of reducing greenhouse gas emissions.

This way of responding to climate change is increasingly hegemonic, gaining a taken-for-granted character. Two things are worth noting, though, which we address in this chapter. First, that as with all forms of hegemony, it is highly contested: many people object fundamentally to the idea of 'commodifying the atmosphere', and those involved in carbon markets thus have to work hard to legitimize their practices. This contestation and response is fundamental to the politics of the carbon economy, as we show later on. Second, the hegemony of these ways of dealing with climate change (or any other environmental problem) is only a recent phenomenon. Had climate change become seen as an acute problem in 1950 rather than from the late 1980s onwards, anyone proposing emissions trading as the principal means to deal with it would have been subject to ridicule. Even in the late 1980s, as the international community was responding to ozone depletion, market-based policies only played a minor role in the response. The rise of the carbon economy, as one manifestation of a broader trend towards the 'marketization' of environmental governance (Newell 2005), evolves alongside and is a product of the entrenchment of neo-liberal politics throughout the 1990s (Harvey 2005).

What we claim in this chapter is that we may be in the early stages of witnessing the emergence of what we call climate capitalism. We refer to this as a form of capitalism that is based on a fundamental and transformative shift away from the use of fossil fuels to underpin economic development in which decarbonization is defined as an opportunity to reconcile capitalist accumulation with the requirements of climate change mitigation. It is still capitalism—organized through markets, private property, wage labour and so on, and with economic growth as imperative to its survival. It is, of course, possible that such a world is impossible to achieve (Kovel 2002). But if it is possible, and effective climate policy genuinely entails the reorganization of global capitalism towards decarbonization, the scale of the challenge—not only in narrow economic and technological terms, but more importantly in political terms—should not be underestimated.

Our claim is not only a normative one; that we need such a transformation of capitalism to occur. This much is fairly obvious. We also claim that a wide range of contemporary climate governance activities, from the Kyoto system to the voluntary offset markets, are starting to imagine and aim for such an economic transformation, and that such a transformation is thus, at least potentially, in its early stages of emergence. Given the time frame within which sweeping action to forestall the worst effects of climate change have to take place, it is clear that, like it or not, neoliberal capitalism(s) will provide the context and historical moment in which action has to take place. This implies engagement with prominent actors in neoliberalism from business and finance, whose strategies need to be aligned with the goal of climate protection.

What matters, then, is to understand how it is that such a potential decarbonization of the global economy is being shaped. What we seek to explain in this chapter is why it is that the construction of carbon markets has become the preferred mode of governing climate change, and the extent to which they *may* drive a process of decarbonization. If it would have been unimaginable even 50 years ago to deal with a large policy problem in this way, what has changed to make it seem normal now? Telling this story of a historical change also enables us to identify which political forces underpin climate governance, how those forces are contested, and what the consequences might be for future responses to climate change.

A BRIEF HISTORY OF NEOLIBERALISM

Our answer to the first question is that the character of responses to climate change has been conditioned principally by the way in which the global economy is organized. This is, of course, general to most environmental problems; but climate change is also unique in how its origins are embedded in almost all practices that underpin contemporary economic development: most obviously through energy use but also, for example, transport and agriculture. This means powerful economic actors have had much more direct influence on the sort of regime than they have in other environmental issue areas which do not touch on the core operation of the global economy so strongly (Newell and Paterson 1998).

The organization of the global economy is widely understood to have undergone a massive shift from the mid-1970s onwards, from what was called a Fordist-Keynesian model to a neoliberal one. This transformation was effected in the aftermath of the various economic crises of the 1970s, including the oil crisis and the end of the Bretton Woods system of pegging currencies to the dollar and the high levels of indebtedness faced even by leading industrialized countries. These events of the 1970s had four key consequences.

One is the shift rightward in economic ideology. There was a political struggle to identify the main causes of the various economic problems of the period, but the version that won was best exemplified by Thatcherism (from British Prime Minister Margaret Thatcher) and Reaganomics (from US President Ronald Reagan), usually known academically as 'neoliberalism'. This was promoted by a group of economists at the University of Chicago (the 'Chicago boys') who went on to hold influential positions in governments and international institutions (Harvey 2005). The broad argument was that the crisis occurred because the state had become too involved in the detail of economic management and the 'natural' effects of markets had thus been distorted. The solutions proposed were thus an emphasis on free markets, on 'rolling back the state', privatization of publicly owned industries, and the retrenchment of the welfare state in what has been known as the 'Washington consensus'. This sort of economic management, though started in the USA and the United Kingdom, has progressively become the norm across the world, in part because of the dominance of those countries in the global financial markets (and on the growing power of finance, see below), and in part because of their use of the International Monetary Fund (IMF) and World Bank to promote neoliberal reform agendas in developing countries and after 1989 in the so called 'economies in transition'. This ideological preference for markets provided the frame of reference for the sorts of climate change policies being proposed from the late 1980s onwards.

The second consequence is the shifts in power between different elements of business produced by this liberalization of markets. In the Bretton Woods period (after the Second World War, through to 1971 when US President Richard Nixon unilaterally ended the fixed exchange rate system), finance was tamed through direct controls on the movement of money around the world, and the major firms in the global economy were those associated with manufacturing, in particular petroleum and car firms. The regulatory systems at both international and national levels were designed to enable them to flourish—for example the fixed exchange rate system that removed a key source of uncertainty for investors. Neoliberalism aimed to set finance free and stimulated an extraordinary expansion of global financial markets. Thatcher and Reagan, followed by other governments, deregulated financial markets, removing controls on the movement of money, as well as on who can operate in financial markets, and blurring boundaries between different types of financial institutions. This has had well-known consequences in terms of global volatility (the various currency crises induced by speculation, for example in Brazil, Russia and East Asia) and crises of corporate governance (classically Enron). However, the other key element that becomes important to understand climate politics is the shift in the power among different sectors of business. As Kees van der Pijl establishes, whereas in the 1970s the key firms in the global economy (as measured not only by size, but their place in the networks of interlocking directorships of the large transnational companies) were oil and car firms, by 2000 or so the key firms were in finance and information technology (IT) (van der Pijl 1998). This shift in the balance of power manifested itself in climate politics in the way in which firms in the financial sector positioned themselves to benefit from the creation of carbon markets as carbon traders (such as Eco-securities and Climate Care), and latterly as investors (such as JPMorgan and Barclays).

The third consequence of neoliberalism is that the world became a significantly more unequal place between and within nations. This was part of deeper and multi-faceted historical processes described in more detail in Chapter 7, borne of European colonialism and entrenched North–South conflicts, but levels of global inequality became dramatically more acute after 1980. One of the immediate consequences of neoliberal management was a dramatic rise in interest rates. Part of the neoliberal diagnosis of the problem of the 1970s was that governments had not paid enough attention to the problem of inflation, or had attempted to manage it by highly intrusive measures such as direct controls on wages and prices. The neoliberal solution was to 'control the money supply' (hence the name monetarism) on the basis of the idea that if you reduced the amount of money in the economy you would reduce the rate that prices could increase. In a deregulated system, however, where banks and other institutions are much freer to lend money (in effect to create it), the main, if not the only, way to do that is to use interest rates. If you raise the interest rate, you make borrowing more expensive, so people won't do so much, and thus won't be able to spend so much. A further move to limit unnecessary 'interference' in the setting of interest rates was to hand over control of them to a central bank. One of the first policy announcements of the incoming 'New Labour' government in the United Kingdom in 1997 was to seek to reassure the markets of the credibility of their handling of the economy by handing over control of interest rates to the Bank of England.

However, the immediate effect of increased interest rates was what became known as the debt crisis. In a period of two years, 'real' interest rates (actual interest rate minus inflation) in the USA and United Kingdom went from 1.4% to 8.6%. In the meantime, developing countries had borrowed significant amounts of money in the 1970s, in part spurred on by the rise in raw material prices like those of oil and the availability of 'petro-dollars', and by investment in their economies by Western firms looking for profitable investments during the stagnation of that decade. The repayments on these debts soared simply because of the rise in interest rates, and many economies were plunged into crisis. Mexico made the crisis a global one when it threatened to default on its debt in 1982, prompting emergency action to reschedule its debt and shore up the world's banking system. Many other developing countries during this period ended up paying the majority of their export earnings just to service the interest on their debt. To add insult to injury, many had to go to the World Bank and the IMF to get emergency loans to stabilize their economies, and those institutions used this new-found power to force neo-liberal 'structural adjustment' and austerity measures on them, frequently making their crisis worse, and almost always turning the economic crisis into a social one. For example, forcing the removal of subsidies on basic foodstuffs provoked 'food riots' against the IMF in a number of places (Walton and Seddon 1994), while in Argentina, once the 'star pupil' of the IMF for following its policy proscriptions to the letter, the IMF found itself the target of widespread protests when it was in part blamed for the economic crisis that hit the country in 2001–2.

The debt crisis and its management by the Bretton Woods institutions produced a dramatic reorganization of power between North and South. It also contributed to increasing complexity in the patterns of growth and inequality among countries in the South. Those countries that escaped the IMF's clutches (as well as one or two that did not) were able to set in train a strong process of growth (Stiglitz 2003). This started with the East Asian tigers, but in the climate change context what is most significant is the rapid growth of the People's Republic of China, from around 1980, and India, from around 1990. These two, the most populous countries in the world, have experienced 9.4% and 5.4% average growth rates, respectively, since those dates. The power shift produced by this growth has both had the obvious knock-on effects on carbon emissions (keeping the overall trajectory of global emissions going up, while also changing the global distribution of emissions between different regions), but also changed the diplomatic landscape on climate change as elsewhere, in ways we come back to later.

The fourth consequence stimulated by the events of the 1970s is in the way that organizations operate. If globalization has changed the nature of international inequalities, it is also frequently described through changing forms of organizations (for different ways of understanding this, see Harvey 1989, Castells 1996). Business, governments, non-governmental organizations (NGOs) and others have all undergone shifts in the ways they work, both on their own and with others, both as cause and consequence of globalization. These changes can be characterized as shifts from clear bureaucratic hierarchies, organized through rules and clear procedures, towards much more fluid forms, such as networks and partnerships. Boundaries between different parts of firms, between different firms, between firms, governments and NGOs, are broken down as actors seek new ways of solving problems. For firms, this is often both a response to the (perceived) competitive pressures produced by globalization, but also serves as a means to globalize their operations, as they build partnerships with other firms globally in the search for novel sources of economic advantage. The story of these organizational changes is often told through the language of the 'new economy', but it is important to recognize that the changes are not to be associated narrowly with the emergence of information and telecommunications, as among the most dynamic areas of the economy. It is also necessary to understand the claims about a 'network economy' as having an ideological component— business has presented itself as organized through networks for branding reasons.

At the same time, for governments, traditional regulatory and bureaucratic solutions are increasingly seen as ill adapted to the accelerated pace of economic life or to the resolution of problems of ever-greater complexity, of which environmental problems are almost paradigmatic. The discourse of 'governance' is in large part due to an attempt to reorganize government in ways that go beyond trying to pursue the goals of government through simple bureaucratic fiat. They are forced to reorganize themselves internally as well as build partnerships with firms and other social actors to achieve their goals. We find evidence of this in the plethora of public–private partnerships and other similar arrangements, not only at the national level, but also at the international level in the form of the Renewable Energy and Energy Efficiency Partnership or the Asia-Pacific Partnership on Clean Development and Climate. In the case of finance, the move to embrace voluntary codes of conduct is evident with the Equator Principles, which stipulate how and why financial institutions should consider environmental and social issues in their project finance operations (Wright and Rwabizambuga 2006). This emphasis on partnership can also be understood as an ideology—classically, in former British Prime Minister Tony Blair's 'Third Way', partnerships are presented as a way of overcoming 'old' social conflicts and political divisions, but also at a strategic level as a way of managing opposition.

These changes in governmental practice may well be regarded as an extension of neoliberal politics, notably the revived power of business, especially finance. Certainly the language of partnerships often serves to obscure the lack of will on the part of governments to regulate powerful firms. Indeed, self-regulation is often a convenient way for governments to lighten their regulatory load and outsource responsibilities to the private sector. 'Voluntary agreements' are a weak substitute for clearly set rules, though they often try to pre-empt them, as we have seen in the case of climate change with car companies in Europe arguing that regulation should be invoked as a last resort after their own voluntary programmes to increase fuel efficiency have failed.

Whatever their merits or otherwise, partnership approaches have been influential in the way that actors have responded to climate change—as we will see below. This is not only because they fit with dominant neoliberal logic, but because climate change itself exemplifies the sorts of new complex problems that require novel organizational forms focused more on 'problem-solving', 'puzzling through', or 'learning by doing', than the rule-setting that is the focus of more traditional organizations. Enrolling different actors, public and private, with diverse capacities, across scales creates in its wake, nevertheless, other problems of accountability, transparency and legitimacy (Bäckstrand 2008; Newell 2008a; Pattberg 2007).

NEOLIBERALISM AND CLIMATE CHANGE: CONSTRUCTING CARBON MARKETS

As with many other environmental problems (see for example Mansfield 2008; Heynen et al. 2007; Castree 2008), the character of neoliberal capitalism has fundamentally shaped how we have responded to climate change. Four key elements—its ideological fixation with markets, the dominance of finance in neoliberal capitalism, the widening global economic inequalities, and the focus on networks as means of organizing—have all combined to shape the character of responses to climate change.

When people started to talk about climate in political and policy terms in the late 1980s, there was a great proliferation of proposals as to how to respond. Much of this was at the technical level—the prospects for different energy technologies, for renewable energy, whether there was a role for nuclear, and so on. How might societies best promote these various options? Here we see that, from early on, the debate reflects this broad shift in the global economy towards the power of finance and neoliberal ideology. In environmental policy debates more generally, there were changes during the 1980s towards the idea of using economic analysis and markets to achieve environmental goals. People talked of the 'New Politics of Pollution' (Weale 1992) and 'ecological modernisation' (Mol 2003), which argued that economic growth and environmental protection could be made compatible. This was important in seeking to discredit earlier claims made by the Club of Rome and echoed by environmentalists from the 1970s onwards that there existed environmental limits to economic growth. Markets, in other words, could be made to work for the environment. Cost-benefit analysis, it was argued, could allow us to weigh up the pros and cons of particular paths to pollution control, and allocate values to them accordingly. In this way, governments could calculate the optimal rate of pollution. United Kingdom economist David Pearce was a key figure here, promoting the idea that rather than develop policies that specified what technologies business and individuals must use, or to simply ban particular substances or processes (through so-called 'command and control' policies), it would be better to use markets to achieve environmental goals ('market mechanisms'). His book 'Blueprint for a Green Economy', published in 1989, widely known as the 'Pearce Report', advocated basing policy on the criterion of 'sustainability', valuing environmental effects and making use of market incentives (Pearce et al. 1989). The two key pillars of this approach are environmental taxation measures (where the government imposes taxes on particular pollutants like carbon dioxide) and emissions trading schemes (where permits are distributed to actors to meet an overall emissions limit, and then actors are allowed to trade the permits among themselves). With both, the main rationale is that it leaves the decisions about how to achieve particular environmental goals up to individuals and firms; governments set either general incentives (in the cases of taxes) or overall limits to pollution levels (in the case of emissions trading) and leave markets to work out who will reduce emissions. In climate change, emerging in the late 1980s as a political issue, we find these neoliberal ideas leave a powerful impact. Their legacy can be seen by focusing on emissions trading and asking 'why did emissions trading become the preferred policy approach?'

Proposals for emissions trading (ET) were made as a means to respond to climate change as early as 1989, in a paper by Michael Grubb (1989) and subsequently picked up by others (Lunde 1991). His original ET proposal and its trajectory encapsulates many of the big economic changes going on at that time. In Grubb's hands, and those of many who took it up, like Michael Hoel, Scott Barrett or Frank Joshua at the United Nations Conference on Trade and Development (UNCTAD), it was designed both to be efficient and equitable. The former was fast becoming the most important value in neo-liberal ideology, while the latter is the legacy of a dominant framing of global environmental politics since the Stockholm Conference in 1972 and emble-mized in the Brundtland Commission's report of 1987. ET systems, in Grubb's or UNCTAD's hands, would enable North–South transfers of wealth and technology, and thus respond to the challenge of growth in countries like China and India. Their assumption was that a principle of per capita emis-sions would be the only legitimate principle for allocating emissions, and thus countries in the North would be short on permits, while those in the South would have excess, and thus earn income by selling permits to the North.

Once it became a formal part of the negotiations, however, it became clear that the emphasis on equity was to be marginalized. In part this was a result of the diplomatic impasse it provoked—Northern countries baulked at the financial transfers implied, while Southern countries resisted steadfastly the implicit limit on their emissions. The legacy of widening inequalities produced this impasse in climate diplomacy (see Chapter 7). However, it also reflects two other elements in our dynamics of neoliberal politics. On the one hand it reflects the ideological priority of efficiency and the way that markets are assumed to produce such efficiency. This also explains the way that ET came to be favoured over carbon taxes. Such taxes have also been proposed and debated (and implemented in countries such as Sweden and the Netherlands, and the United Kingdom's climate change levy is a quasi-carbon tax), but have failed to get off the ground elsewhere, even in the European Union (EU), for example, where a long carbon tax debate was stalled by industry opposi-tion (Newell and Paterson 1998). In the UN Framework Convention on Cli-mate Change (UNFCCC) process, occasional proposals for harmonized introduction of such taxes never got anywhere. Everyday political processes of interest groups defending their interests is important here—big firms success-fully resisted on the grounds of the increased costs, and new taxes are not popular anywhere. In a more open global economy the prospect of relocation also meant that 'carbon leakage' might occur, where a tax would simply have the effect of driving the most polluting companies or parts of the production process overseas, resulting in no overall reduction in emissions. This was an argument successfully used by industry groups to prevent taxes from being used in the first place. In the economic debates though, purists also argued that ET systems are more efficient than taxes, in part because they permit the setting of an absolute limit on emissions (and thus act on a determination of the optimal rate of pollution), and in part because they entail the actual creation of a market, rather than the attempt by governments to affect behaviour within existing markets. So by contrast with the stagnation of proposals for carbon taxes, the establishment of emissions trading systems is expanding rapidly. At the latest count, there are now 34 sites at which such systems have been seriously considered, and a substantial number of these have been, are, or are in the process of becoming operational (Betsill and Hoffmann 2008).

ET became the preferred solution because of its ideological fit with neo-liberal logic, but it was also successful because of its fit with the interests of newly dominant financial actors. The USA first formally proposed ET in the UNFCCC process in December 1996, though it met with widespread resistance at the time. The USA's rationale was initially to create flexibility for countries in implementing their commitments. The political resistance to emissions reductions in the USA was considerably stronger than in Europe, and the Administration of President Bill Clinton, while favourable itself to action, was heavily constrained by a Congress that was hostile. Economists in the USA also insisted that the costs of reductions to the US economy were very high, and Clinton was, in any case, a strong proponent of market-based mechanisms. These combined to make the USA propose ET as a means to pursue reductions in a manner that minimized the costs associated with them.

In the Kyoto negotiations, countries ended up agreeing to ET mostly because of the USA's determined support for the idea, and the desperate desire of others to keep the USA on board. The interesting period, though, was the next three years, to around 2000. In this period, there was a dramatic transformation in ET's fortunes. The Kyoto process plodded on slowly because of the many unresolved questions about its various innovative elements, but the EU changed its mind about ET shortly after Kyoto, during 1998–99. In the period before Kyoto, most EU countries had been of the view that countries ought to reduce their own emissions domestically and that flexibility mechanisms were a distraction from this goal. The EU shifted its position after Kyoto, becoming a proponent of ET in the Kyoto process, but also starting to plan its own system. It did so in part because of personnel changes in key positions in the Commission, in part because of a continued desire to accommodate the USA (through to the President George W. Bush Administration's withdrawal, at least), and in part because of an increasing realization of the potential of ETS to help with achieving the EU's internal greenhouse gas reduction goals. Individual European countries like the United Kingdom and Denmark started also to plan their own ET systems.

Most importantly, a whole range of private market actors started to emerge. New firms were created, such as Ecosecurities (1997), CO2e.com (2000) and Point Carbon (2000). They became key actors in the voluntary carbon markets. Existing banks, such as Barclays or Dresdner Kleinwort, developed their own carbon trading offices. Annual carbon finance and carbon market conferences were started, and a Carbon Expo has been held every year in Cologne since 2004. In 2005 alone emission reduction purchase agreements for more than 100 projects were signed or reached advanced negotiations at Carbon Expo according to the organizer's website (www.carbonexpo.com). New associations of actors, like the International Emissions Trading Association (IETA) or the Emissions Marketing Association, and more recently the Carbon Markets and Investors Association, were created or expanded considerably in reaction to the growing momentum of ET systems. IETA is now one of the most active organizations at UNFCCC negotiations, organizing substantial numbers of side events. They haven't only reacted to the pressure from politicians, however; they have become crucial to why politicians didn't abandon ET in the face of various pressures—notably the ongoing difficult negotiations in the Kyoto process and the withdrawal of the USA from the process in 2001.

ET thus became almost unstoppable once the newly dominant financial actors realized its potential as a new market, with its derivatives, options, swaps, insurance and so on, and thus as a profitable enterprise. While the key period of take-off of this dynamic was 1996–2000, after that date the process continued to mushroom. The point to underscore here is that ET 'gained traction' because of this alignment between the need that policy-makers had for flexibility in meeting commitments and the realization by financial firms that the emissions market could be the source of significant growth and profits.

Some financial actors also became interested in climate change for another reason. Insurance companies started to worry in the early 1990s about large-scale payouts to extreme weather events (principally hurricanes and flooding), which had already increased by that point, and were projected in many models to become even more frequent and intense. Jeremy Leggett at Greenpeace International was particularly active in courting insurers to persuade them to get active in climate politics. They started to act through the 1990s, in conjunction in particular with the UN Environment Programme (UNEP), and then their activity exploded in the 2000s, particularly through the Carbon Disclosure Project (CDP). Insurers were joined by banks and pension funds during this period. The CDP is a project whereby investors attempt to shape the activities of other firms by getting them to disclose their carbon intensity and their strategies to limit emissions. The CDP now has US \$57 trillion of assets behind it. It claims:

> The CDP provides a secretariat for the world's largest institutional investor collaboration on the business implications of climate change. CDP represents an efficient process whereby many institutional investors collectively sign a single global request for disclosure of information on

Greenhouse Gas Emissions. More than 1,000 large corporations report on their emissions through this web site. On 1st February 2007 this request was sent to over 2400 companies.

(CDP 2007)

Financial firms, thus, have complicated interests in relation to climate change. They are exposed to all sorts of risks from climate change itself—direct insurance risks to homes and businesses, but also indirect risks to banks of loans going bad because of weather-related risks. However, they have also become the power brokers in contemporary capitalism, capable of moving money around, putting pressure on manufacturing firms, governments and other social actors. Their power has become a crucial element in the politics of climate change.

Similarly, public financial institutions like the World Bank became interested in climate change as a new means to extend their influence and secure a role for themselves in the new carbon economy. The World Bank has been important in North–South dimensions of climate politics for some time through the Global Environment Facility, but increasingly seeks to position itself as one of the main players in carbon markets through its portfolio of Climate Investment Funds (Newell et al. 2009; World Bank 2008a; World Bank 2008b). Just as its role in development has attracted considerable controversy and critique in the past, so too there is some evidence that its role in funding climate projects in the South similarly transforms climate policy into social crises—as, for example, in those Clean Development Mechanism (CDM) or Prototype Carbon Fund projects, which displace indigenous or marginalized communities (Bachram 2004), working on a logic of what Bumpus and Liverman (2008) call 'accumulation by decarbonization'.

The final thing to note about the way that neoliberalism has shaped climate politics has to do with the organizational forms many of these projects take. Neoliberal capitalism is often described as being organized through networks and partnerships. Climate governance reflects this tendency well. From the approach of Greenpeace's Jeremy Leggett to insurers, through to the fully-fledged CDP, collaborative partnerships have been formed across a range of actors to identify means of pursuing common goals. The CDM, for example, has often been described as a huge 'public–private partnership', while the World Bank's Prototype Carbon Fund (PCF) is described by Streck (2004) as an 'implementation network', bringing together interested parties from North and South under the rules set out by the CDM. In some ways it functioned as a learning network, providing participants with an opportunity to learn about the CDM and Joint Implementation. It was also intended to have demonstration effects that project-based investments under the Kyoto Protocol could earn revenue for developing countries and increase the profitability of cleaner energy options. Other governance experiments have brought together cities, firms and NGOs to produce climate action plans that go above and beyond the formal forms of institutional response (Betsill and Bulkeley 2004). The general point is that climate governance operates less in terms of traditional hierarchical authority relations, but through more horizontal relations between diverse actors, seeking both to learn with others and to influence them to their advantage.

At a national level, many organizations have emerged that operate in this fashion. Sometimes arm's-length organizations (like the Carbon Trust in the United Kingdom), which are used by governments to implement policy, also act as sites of collaboration among firms and between them and NGOs, as bodies which aim to foster learning about best practices and enable the exchange of ideas. Many transnational groups have emerged that defy conventional categorization. The Climate Group, for example, is a body which is technically a non-profit organization based in London, but which cannot be understood as a traditional NGO organized around research and lobbying. Rather, it has members that are transnational firms and subnational government units, which apply to join in order to be regarded as 'leaders' in their CO_2 reductions strategies, to use the Climate Group both to promote their public image but also to gain access to a network of other such organizations. The group acts then to promote CO_2 reductions among other firms and subnational actors. The group's close ties to Tony Blair have also provided a high-profile national platform for projecting their ideas into global policy debates on climate change.

These sorts of networks are highly fluid, expanding and changing focus rapidly, aiming to mobilize people in ways that neither traditional regulation nor exhortation from governments can. It is certainly the case that some of these can be understood as the result of efforts by private firms to avoid such regulation—to show their 'good behaviour' to prevent a stricter form of action imposed by governments. Climate change has become a leading CSR issue for firms, but given that climate change presents such fundamental challenges to the organization of capitalist economies, flexible networks, focused on 'learning by doing' are surely a necessary component of strategies for reducing CO_2.

POLITICAL DYNAMICS OF THE CARBON ECONOMY

What, then, of our second question, about the politics and consequences of this neoliberal way of organizing responses to climate change?

Like the neoliberalism more generally out of which it has grown, the carbon economy is constantly contested. In fact, some of the movements contesting emissions trading, the CDM and the voluntary carbon markets, have grown out of the anti-globalization movement, resisting neoliberal globalization, and identifying the similarities between the development of carbon markets and the more general operation of finance-led, market-fetishizing neoliberalism. Indeed the current financial crisis of 2008–9 has led many critics of carbon markets to draw parallels with the lack of regulation of the financial system and its consequences, referring to 'sub-prime carbon', 'the carbon crunch' and 'toxic carbon' for example. Protest groups like Rising Tide, Climate Justice, Carbon Trade Watch (part of the anti-neoliberal Transnational Institute), Plane Stupid!, and more loose networks of activists organizing protests such as those at The Hague Climate Summit in 2000 or the climate camp in the City of London in 2009, frequently make the connection between the weak response to climate change and the domination of the world by neoliberal capitalism. Some look at the history given above, the close link between energy use and growth, and conclude that to deal with climate change means an end to economic growth and, by extension, to the capitalist way the world is organized. To act on climate change is, for many activists, to oppose capitalism, or at least its current form.

Unsurprisingly, then, the 'climate crisis' increasingly features in broader critiques of neoliberalism, testimony to which is the profile the issue has received in European and World Social Forums. Activists have made links to unjust North–South relations, globalization and long-standing traditions of environmental justice campaigning centred on the disproportionate exposure of poorer communities to pollution. In the latter regard, groups have invoked the notion of 'climate justice' to contest their role as the 'social sinks' for the externalization of environmental costs. More generally, Pettit notes, 'By and large, the framing of "climate justice" reflects the same social and economic rights perspectives voiced by global movements on debt, trade and globalization' (2004, 103). The Durban Declaration on Carbon Trading produced by the climate justice movement, for example, makes explicit links between current attempts to turn the earth's 'carbon-cycling capacity into property to be bought and sold in a global market', and historical 'attempts to commodify land, food, labour, forests, water, genes and ideas' (CNE 2004). Groups signing up to the declaration claim, 'Through this process of creating a new commodity – carbon – the Earth's ability and capacity to support a climate conducive to life and human societies is now passing into the same corporate hands that are destroying the climate' (Durban Declaration 2004).

The groups adopting these more critical positions under the umbrella of climate justice held a summit by this name at the eighth Conference of the Parties (COP-8) in 2002 in Delhi. The event was attended by hundreds of activists from throughout India, including farmers, fisherfolk, indigenous peoples and the urban poor. The Delhi Climate Justice Declaration reveals the essence of these groups' concerns about climate change, and the current nature of policy responses to the threat:

We affirm that climate change is a rights issue – it affects our livelihoods, our health, our children and our natural resources. We will build alliances across states and borders to oppose climate change inducing patterns and advocate for and practice sustainable development. We reject the market based principles that guide the current negotiations to solve the climate crisis: Our World is Not for Sale!

(India Climate Justice Forum 2002)

Beyond the general activist critiques of the neoliberal foundations of the carbon economy, specific campaigns have been directed at the carbon offset markets, both in the CDM and in the voluntary carbon market. To the charge of 'carbon colonialism' is added that of 'climate fraud'; that many of the projects double-count emissions paid for by other clients, or that the scale of the emissions reduction is exaggerated or non-existent (Lohmann 2006). Indeed, the allocation of projects under the CDM and the popularity of carbon sink schemes have each given rise to watchdog activism aimed at scrutinizing the conduct of these carbon deals, and exposing what activists consider to be phony projects where environmental gains are unlikely to be forthcoming or the social costs high or ignored (Lohmann 2006). SinksWatch, for example, an initiative of the World Rainforest Movement set up in 2001 and implemented by FERN (Forests and the European Union Resource Network), monitors the impact of the financing and creation of sinks projects in order to highlight the threat they pose to forests and other ecosystems, to forest peoples as well as to the climate. A particular concern is the exclusion of marginalized groups from their own forest resources once they become the property of a distant carbon trader for whom they represent a valuable investment opportunity. For example, Heidi Bachram notes the case of a Norwegian company operating in Uganda that leased its lands for a sequestration project which allegedly resulted in 8,000 people in 13 villages being evicted (Bachram 2004).

Nevertheless, dilemmas of how to engage the carbon economy have divided climate activists between those who believe carbon markets can be effective if constructed within the right regulatory environment and those who oppose outright the logic of commodification and the practices that flow from it. The 'big 10' Washington-based groups such as Environmental Defense and the Natural Resources Defense Council see important potential in market mechanisms to achieve much-needed emissions reductions. They are aligned against more critical groups such as Carbon Trade Watch and Sinks Watch who view carbon markets as a distraction from the need for the largest polluters, primarily in the North, to reduce their own emissions through actions at home rather than projects sponsored in developing countries (CNE 2004). Their critique is informed by a broader position adopted by many environmental NGOs on this issue that such practices 'distract attention away from the fundamental changes urgently necessary if we are to achieve a more sustainable and just future' (CTW 2004).

This sort of activism clearly questions and contests the commodification of carbon and exposes 'fraudulent' practice in carbon markets. However, they also force advocates of market approaches to legitimize themselves by, for example, restricting the sorts of projects that can be included within the CDM, or by creating forms of private carbon governance such as the Voluntary Carbon Standard (VCS 2008) or the Gold Standard. These certification schemes set higher standards than the basic CDM rules (or simply create rules in the case of the voluntary market), enabling buyers and sellers of emissions reductions to distance themselves from the scandals and controversy that activists have created around 'climate fraud' and 'carbon colonialism'. In so doing, they clearly seek to safeguard the profits they make from such markets as well as secure a role for carbon markets as a legitimate response to climate change by deflecting or accommodating criticism of them.

CONCLUSION

In this chapter we have sought to make sense of the nature of the rapidly expanding carbon economy. We provided a brief historical overview of how the world of contemporary capitalism and climate politics became increasingly intertwined. We observed how existing actors, institutions and technologies of governance at work in the capitalist economy have been brought to bear on the problem of climate change. These have aimed, first, to render the problem manageable through enrolling a diverse range of actors in networks with distinct capacities to address the problem; by measuring emissions through accounting and disclosure (CDP); and by ensuring that market and voluntary-based over command and control measures prevail (as with emissions trading). Second, they have sought to create opportunities to make profit. This has occurred through efforts to ensure that responses are either non-threatening to, or compatible with, existing accumulation strategies, as well as through attempts to create new sites of accumulation (through offsets and emission trading). However, what is as interesting as the parallel and mutually constituting nature of neoliberalism and climate governance in historical and contemporary terms, is the latent potential for the carbon economy to develop into a larger-scale transition to 'climate capitalism' where successful accumulation strategies are to be found in decarbonizing the economy.

We have tried to show that neoliberalism has specific features which have played a key role in structuring climate capitalism. The four key elements we outlined above—its ideological fixation with markets, the dominance of finance in neoliberal capitalism, the widening global economic inequalities, and the focus on networks as a means of organizing action—have all combined to shape the character of responses to climate change. First, the fetishization of markets and market mechanisms as a means to govern the economic activities that produce climate change drove the creation of the 'flexibility mechanisms' central to the Kyoto Protocol, as well as similar initiatives at national and regional levels. They have also favoured various forms of private governance, including self-regulation by market actors, supported by a market-enabling rather than market-restricting state. Second, the extraordinary dominance of finance within different fractions of capital has favoured emissions trading and market access policies, which principally benefit traders in the markets. This also accounts for the emergence of a range of private governance arrangements, many of which are organized by financial actors. The spectacular success of carbon markets in attracting interest from finance in climate policy is precisely a condition for the possibility for decarbonizing the economy, as this bloc is necessary, politically, to sustain action on climate change. Third, we noted the economic inequalities that create opportunities for emissions savings at lower costs, which compliance and voluntary offset markets have sought to capture by globalizing carbon markets. Presenting carbon markets as a development opportunity for poorer nations has also enabled actors such as the World Bank, among the leading architects of neoliberalism, to subject climate action to the logic of broader neoliberal (environmental) reforms such as payment for ecosystem services. However, we also noted the ways in which such inequalities give rise to sites of contestation around claims of climate colonialism and demands for climate justice. Fourth, we noted the networks that have been created by a growing array of public and private actors operating across scales to produce new forms of climate and carbon governance within and beyond the market. Finally, we showed that future forms of climate governance will also be shaped, just as they have been to date, by a range of actors critiquing the equity, efficiency and effectiveness of marketized solutions in tackling climate change. This criticism is unlikely to force powerful actors to abandon such marketized governance, but it will shape the way that carbon markets are governed. Doubts will remain about the contribution of emissions trading and other facets of the carbon economy unless and until they hold out the prospect of engaging with and transforming capitalism as usual into climate capitalism: a system of wealth generation that is truly compatible with a low-carbon future.

We suggest that despite its problematic character, finance may in fact be able to drive strategies of decarbonization in the economy, extending its role beyond the creation of discrete carbon markets to broader forms of transformation. Such an outcome is far from guaranteed and has to be secured through forms of public and private regulation, coalition building and social practices, which enrol an array of actors in realizing governance through and for the market. For this reason the future of climate capitalism is open-ended even if we can anticipate a prominent role for certain key actors. This indeterminacy leaves open the possibility of various scenarios for the future direction of the carbon economy. There is potential for scenarios of unregulated, barely credible 'cowboy climate capitalism', a more regulated and state-managed 'climate Keynesianism', or a scenario in which new modes of accumulation are hugely successful, and set up positive incentives and feedback mechanisms that link finance and productive capital in ways which de-couple growth from increased emissions of greenhouse gas emissions.

It is clear that the unregulated 'cowboy' version entails very significant risks. It requires enormous faith in 'markets' to be able to reshape incentives (through carbon prices) and investment across the entire global economy to produce decarbonization—a faith that many carbon traders hold dear, but about which we are much more sceptical. It may well also produce a highly unequal form of climate capitalism, where the rich pull up the ladder, offsetting their high emissions in an eco-colonial fashion in the South, locking the latter even further into dependent and unequal relations.

The 'climate Keynesian' approach is significantly more promising, though, involving the use of state power (nationally and internationally) to direct investment, make sure carbon prices are stable, and creating meaningful incentives for consumers, producers and investors that reach those parts of the economy that carbon markets fail to reach (home energy efficiency measures are a classic problem here). There are also some signs that such an approach may be possible to pursue. There has been much recent discussion about the possibility of a 'green New Deal' in the context of the current economic crisis. In the USA, in particular, there has been talk about 'Obamanomics' (from President Barack Obama) entailing a shift towards a more state-centred approach both to the economy and to climate change specifically (although there is always more continuity in US politics than official rhetoric reveals). Finally, civil society engagement, both from those criticizing carbon markets per se, and those attempting to regulate them (for example, through certification standards and limits on which sectors and projects are subject to inclusion in the market), has already shaped carbon markets to make them more regulated than traders might want, towards a more 'Keynesian' version of climate capitalism. We expect this sort of political dynamic to continue.

Whichever version of climate capitalism emerges over the next few decades, its capacity to deliver decarbonization will be determined by the ability to direct investment into low-energy and non-carbon energy sources, while managing the legitimacy challenges that are inevitably posed by this reliance on global finance as a means to manage carbon emissions. As global climate change governance develops, both within the UNFCCC regime and beyond, the key measure of its success will be whether it manages to create an enabling environment for the transformation of the global economy into a system of climate capitalism compatible with addressing climate change, or whether carbon markets are to exist as isolated sites of accumulation in an economy whose orientation is incompatible with serious efforts to address the climate crisis.

REFERENCES

Bachram, H. (2004) 'Climate Fraud and Carbon Colonialism: The New Trade in Greenhouse Gases', *Capitalism, Nature, Socialism* 15 (4), 10–12.

Bäckstrand, K. (2008) 'Accountability of networked climate governance: The rise of transnational climate partnerships', *Global Environmental Politics* 8 (3), 74–102.

Betsill, M. and H. Bulkeley (2004) 'Transnational Networks and Global Environmental Governance: The Cities for Climate Protection Program', *International Studies Quarterly* 48, 471–93.

Betsill, M. and M. Hoffmann (2008) 'The Evolution of Emissions Trading Systems for Greenhouse Gases', paper presented at the International Studies Association Annual Conference, San Francisco, 26–29 March 2008.

Bullard, R. (2000) 'Climate Justice and People of Color,' Atlanta, GA: Environmental Justice Resource Centre, Clark Atlanta University, www.ejrc.cau.edu (accessed 18 November 2004).

Bumpus, A. and D. Liverman (2008) 'Accumulation by Decarbonization and the Governance of Carbon Offsets', *Economic Geography*, Vol. 84, No. 2, 127–55.

Castells, M. (1996) *The Rise of the Network Society*, Oxford: Blackwell.

Castree, N. (2008) 'Neo-liberalising nature 1: the logics of de- and re-regulation', *Environment and Planning A* 40, 1.

CDP (2007), www.cdproject.net (accessed 19 November 2008).

Climate Trade Watch (2005), www.tni.org/ctw (accessed 27 April 2005).

CNE (Climate Action Network Europe) (2004) 'Climate Justice Now! The Durban Declaration on Carbon Trading', Meeting of CNE, Durban, 4–7 October, www.climnet.org/resources/docs_interest.htm (accessed 19 November 2004).

CTW (Carbon Trade Watch) (2004) 'Environmentalists Cry Foul at Rock Stars Polluting Companies Carbon-Neutral Claims', press release, 6 May, www.tni.org/ctw (accessed 19 November 2004).

Durban Declaration (2004) 'Climate Justice Now! The Durban Declaration on Carbon Trading', signed 10 October 2004, Glenmore Centre, Durban, South Africa.

EJCCI (Environmental Justice and Climate Change Initiative) (2002) 'About Us', www.ejcc.org/aboutus. html, and 'Climate Change and Environmental Justice Fact Sheet', press briefing, 28 January, www.ejcc.org/releases/020128fact.html (accessed 11 November 2004).

FERN (2005) www.fern.org (accessed 27 April 2005).

Grubb, M. (1989) *The Greenhouse Effect: Negotiating Targets*, London: Royal Institute of International Affairs.

Harvey, D. (1989) *The Condition of Postmodernity*, Oxford: Blackwell.

Harvey, D. (2005) *A Brief History of Neoliberalism*, Oxford: OUP.

Heynen, N., J. McCarthy, S. Prudham and P. Robbins (eds) (2007) *Neoliberal Environments: False promises and unnatural consequences*, London: Routledge.

India Climate Justice Forum (2002) 'Delhi Climate Justice Declaration', Delhi: India Resource Centre, 28 October, www.indiaresource.org/issues/energycc/2003/delhicjdeclare.html (accessed 12 November 2004).

Kovel, J. (2002) *The Enemy of Nature: The End of Capitalism or the End of the World*, London: Zed Books.

Lohmann, L. (2005) 'Marketing and making carbon dumps: Commodification, calculation and counter-factuals in climate change mitigation', *Science as Culture* Vol. 14, No. 3, 203–35.

——(2006) 'Carbon Trading: A Critical Conversation on Climate Change, Privatisation and Power', *Development Dialogue* No. 48, September.

Lunde, L. (1991) 'Global Warming and a System of Tradeable Emissions permits: A Review of the Current Debate', *International Challenges* 11 (3), 15–28.

Mansfield, B. (ed.) (2008) *Privatization: Property and the Remaking of Nature-Society Relations*, Oxford: Blackwell.

Mol, A. (2003) *Globalization and Environmental Reform: The Ecological Modernization of the Global Economy*, Cambridge, MA: MIT Press.

Newell, P. (2005) 'Climate for Change: Civil society and the politics of global warming', in F. Holland et al. (eds), *Global Civil Society Yearbook*, London: SAGE.

——(2008a) 'Civil society, corporate accountability and the politics of climate change', *Global Environmental Politics* Vol. 8, No. 3, 124–55.

——(2008b) 'The Marketisation of Global Environmental Governance: Manifestations and Implications', in J. Park, K. Conca and M. Finger (eds), *The Crisis of*

Global Environmental Governance: Towards a New Political Economy of Sustainability, London: Routledge, 77–96.

Newell, P. and M. Paterson (1998) 'A climate for business: Global warming, the state and capital', *Review of International Political Economy* Vol. 5, No. 4, Winter, 679–704.

Newell, P., N. Jenner and L. Baker (2009) 'Governing Clean Development: A Framework for Analysis', *The Governance of Clean Development Working Paper Series* No.1 UEA, www.clean-development.com.

Pattberg, P. (2007) *Private Institutions and Global Governance: The New Politics of Environmental Sustainability*, Cheltenham: Edward Elgar.

Pearce, D., A. Markandya and E. Barbier (1989) *Blueprint for a Green Economy*, London: Earthscan.

Pettit, J. (2004) 'Climate Justice: A New Social Movement for Atmospheric Rights, *IDS Bulletin* 35 (3), 102–6.

Rising Tide (2004) 'Rising Tide: Supporting the Grassroots Movement Against Climate Change', London: Rising Tide, www.risingtide.org.uk (accessed 5 January 2005).

SinksWatch (2004) www.sinkswatch.org (accessed 19 November 2004).

——(2005) www.sinkswatch.org (accessed 6 July 2005).

Stiglitz, J. (2003) *Globalization and Its Discontents*, London: Penguin.

Streck, C. (2004) 'New partnerships in global environmental policy: The Clean Development Mechanism', *Journal of Environment and Development* Vol. 13, No. 3, September, 295–322.

van der Pijl, K. (1998) *Transnational Classes and International Relations*, London: Routledge.

VCS (2008) *Voluntary Carbon Standard Program Guidelines*, www.v-c-s.org/docs/ Voluntary%20Carbon%20Standard%20Program%20Guidelines%202007_1.pdf (accessed 18 November 2008).

Walton, J. and D. Seddon (eds) (1994) *Free Markets and Food Riots: The Politics of Global Adjustment*, Oxford: Blackwell.

Weale, A. (1992) *The New Politics of Pollution*, Manchester: Manchester University Press.

World Bank (2000) *Greening Industry: New Roles for Communities, Markets and Governments*, New York: Oxford University Press.

——(2008a) *Climate Investment Funds*, Washington, DC, www.worldbank.org/cifs.

——(2008b), *Development and Climate Change: A Strategic Framework for the World Bank Group*, report to the Development Committee, Washington, DC.

Wright, C. and A. Rwabizambuga (2006) 'Institutional pressures, corporate reputation and voluntary codes of conduct: An examination of the Equator principles', *Business and Society Review* 111 (1), 89–117.

The Politics of Adaptation Across Scales: The Implications of Additionality to Policy Choice and Development

Maria Carmen Lemos and Emily Boyd

INTRODUCTION

In the past decade, the debate over the inevitability of climate adaptation has moved from academic to policy circles. In less-developed regions, this process of mainstreaming policy—or the integration of adaptation into development—is underway in places as diverse as Bangladesh and Fiji (Agrawala 2004). The IPCC (2007) defines adaptation as the '[a]djustment in natural or *human systems* in response to actual or expected climatic stimuli or their effects, which moderates harm or exploits beneficial opportunities'. As climate adaptation becomes policy, it confronts the opportunities, limitations and capacities of complex processes that go beyond the alternatives science can propose or illuminate (Adger et al. 2009; Eakin and Lemos 2006). One source of complexity is politics—that is, the many ways actors, organizations and institutions seek to guide and influence governmental policy. Broadly, politics influence adaptation at all levels; in this chapter, we focus on how global level politics affect adaptation options at the national and local levels, especially in less-developed countries. We particularly examine how the political distribution of causes, consequences, costs and benefits of climate change at the global level shape access to adaptation funding both under the United Nations Framework Convention for Climate Change (UNFCCC), and under multilateral and bilateral overseas development assistance for adaptation.

At the root of this dilemma is a mismatch between the causes and consequences of climate change and the making of climate winners and losers. Those likely to be most vulnerable to climate change impact are both the least to blame for its causes and the least capable of responding to and recovering from its impacts. This mismatch has contributed to a political debate that has pitched developed and less-developed countries against each other. Less-developed countries (UNFCCC Annex II countries) argue that since they have not caused the problem, but are likely to be the most affected by it, they should be supported and aided in responding to, coping with and adapting to climate change negative impacts. Developed countries (UNFCCC Annex I countries), acknowledge their contribution to climate change (through historical carbon emissions), but argue that their responsibility in supporting adaptation should be limited to the problem itself, that is, adaptation action *in addition to* a baseline that developing countries would undertake in the absence of climate change. In principle, there is no contradiction between these two arguments—developed countries caused the climate problem and should pay for the unintended damage to third parties; they should pay only for the damages attributable to the problem. However, in the implementation of adaptation funding, the definition of what is fair and what is desirable/necessary underline the political struggle between Annex I and Annex II countries in setting the rules for adaptation funding.

We argue that some of the rules of access to adaptation funding, specifically additionality, may not only fail to support less-developed countries to prepare for, cope with and adapt to climate change, but can potentially place extra burden on these countries. First, in order to qualify for funding sources, developing countries, especially those with the least policy and administrative capacities, may have to spend scarce financial, human and technical resources to meet these funds' additionality requirements. Second, governments may be tempted to prioritize policies that meet the additionality requirement rather than policies that best promote the sustainability and well-being of vulnerable ecosystems and populations. Moreover, in countries where structural inequality and lack of resources critically shape vulnerability, the additionality requirement may obstruct policies that integrate climate adaptation into development policy and create positive synergies between them (Klein et al. 2007; Lemos et al. 2007). For example, in order to meet the additionality requirement, it may be easier for governments to build water storage structures or invest in drought resistant crops than to implement household income diversification policies that increase overall adaptive capacity (Agrawal 2008; Eakin 2000). While the latter may be more resilient in the long run, the former is easier to characterize as meeting the goals of additionality. We suggest that because climate change is one among many stresses that define the vulnerability of people and ecosystems in less-developed regions, it makes little sense to prioritize additionality over the need to integrate across policies to adapt to these multiple stresses (Bizikova et al. 2007; Huq et al. 2005; Jerneck and Olsson 2008; Klein et al. 2007). Through additionality, adaptation policy at the global level divides and circumscribes processes that are indivisible at the local level and, in practice, disables the opportunities for complementarities and synergies in adapting to climate change.

Historically, climate change and development have been unavoidably connected since the accumulation of CO_2 in the atmosphere relates directly to development choices (Agrawala 2004). Moreover, adaptation as a policy option intersects with development through the building of adaptive capacity—that is, by increasing the ability of vulnerable systems to respond, cope and recover from the negative impacts of climate change. Indeed many of the determinants of adaptive capacity (income, education, health, technology, knowledge, sustainability, etc.) directly overlap with development goals (Boyd et al. 2008; Lemos et al. 2007).

In the following sections, we explore these issues in detail and examine their political and policy implications and interdependencies. Section two reviews the literature focusing on climate change costs and benefits, and discusses the implications of their distribution to the design of adaptation mechanisms at the global level. Section three briefly describes these mechanisms and their implications for the design of adaptation policy in less-developed countries. Finally, we speculate about the opportunities and limitations of adaptation politics and policy across scales.

ADAPTATION FUNDING, EQUITY AND THE DISTRIBUTION OF COSTS AND BENEFITS

The distribution of costs and benefits, causes and consequences of climate change crucially influences the architecture of international funding for climate adaptation. The equity implications of adaptation action are defined by the fact that the potential costs and benefits of climate change effects are unevenly distributed, with less-developed countries and the poor in general being the most likely to be adversely affected and to accrue little or none of the potential benefits. These ethical considerations are further complicated by the fact that the developed world is mainly responsible for current global warming and potential climate change through historical emissions of CO_2 in the atmosphere. The equity question, and its social and economic consequences, influences and is influenced by politics and ultimately defines international negotiations and future national responses to the impacts of climate change (O'Brien and Leichenko 2003). From calls for more equitable policy designs to academic discussions of distributional justice, the apportioning of climate change effects has been a central issue in international negotiations and debates (for an in-depth discussion of these issues, see Adger et al. 2006). One way in which the equity question gets practical is in the design and implementation of the climate change international regime, especially the Kyoto Protocol and its mechanisms. Another is painfully evident in the inability of countries to go beyond Kyoto's clearly insufficient targets and agree on joint action to dramatically decrease emissions and collectively prepare for future negative impacts already under way (Parks and Roberts 2009) (see Chapter 7 by Parks and Roberts).

At the surface, the issue is neatly outlined by two straightforward principles: 'polluter pays' and 'unequal but shared responsibilities'. The former advocates that whoever is responsible for causing climate change through CO_2 emissions should be responsible for paying to clean it up. Under the Kyoto Protocol, the current distribution of costs and benefits is unfair because it rewards polluters by limiting the costs for developed countries, which have historically polluted much more than developing countries (Baer et al. 2000). The second principle recognizes that even if polluters agree to shoulder the responsibility of mitigating future CO_2 emissions and offsetting historical ones, their actions are likely to be insufficient to halt or reverse what has already happened or might happen, especially if developing countries increase their CO_2 emissions in their path to economic development. The growing rates of emissions from emerging economies such as the People's Republic of China and India may seriously offset the developed world's mitigation action. For example, despite Kyoto, CO_2 emissions (from both developed and developing countries) grew at a rate of 3.5% per year from 2000 to 2007 (Global Carbon Project 2008) and CO_2 concentration is projected to grow from 2005 levels of 379 parts per million (ppm) to about 440 ppm by 2030, based on estimates that CO_2 emissions in China would grow at an annual rate of between 3% and 4% a year. However, recent inventories from China found that emissions growth might actually be close to 10%–11% (Auffhammer and Carson 2008, cited in NRC 2009). Yet, instructing developing countries to develop less or more slowly has little ethical basis for justification (Baer et al. 2000). (Here, many would argue that developing less or more slowly is not really the point, rather developing countries should develop rapidly but sustainably, which raises a number of other questions concerning capacities, resources and access—of technology, financial and human resources, political capital, etc.—which are beyond the scope of this chapter.) In view of the rapid pace of global warming, unequal but shared responsibility means that the developing world should be allowed to pursue their development plans but also share the burden of offsetting the potential negative effects of their increased CO_2 emissions rates.

While mitigation has mostly dominated global negotiations and scholarly debates, the politics of adaptation remain relatively unexamined. The adaptation portion of the climate injustice debate is also defined by a simple notion: that countries which have contributed the least to climate change are likely to be the ones suffering the brunt of its negative impacts, both because their higher level of exposure to negative impacts (sea-level rise, extreme weather events, ecosystem degradation, etc.) and because of their lower adaptive capacity to respond to them (Lemos et al. 2007). The main mechanism to support adaptation within the Kyoto Protocol is the Adaptation Fund, the main source of income of which is a 2% levy on the funds generated by the Protocol's CDM programme (for more on the status of the CDM, see Boyd et al. 2009; Bozmoski et al. 2008). The adaptation fund currently yields an estimated US $200–300m. a year; Parks and Roberts (2009) point out that these funds represent 'a tiny fraction (less than one-twentieth) of the total adaptation financing needed according to most objective assessments'. In addition, there are other sources of adaptation funding (see next section for more detailed description), through both multilateral and private sources, to which less-developed countries can apply. The UNFCCC (2007) estimates that between $28 billion and $67 billion a year will be needed by 2030 to finance adaptation activities in the developing world. Oxfam puts the cost at $50 billion a year (Oxfam International 2007) and the

UNDP (2007) estimates that $86 billion a year will be needed by 2015 to prevent 'adaptation apartheid' (Parks and Roberts 2009). In this context of great need and scarce resources, additionality requirements may impose further hardships on countries trying to access into these funds. Most importantly for the discussion in this chapter, tapping into the adaptation fund may interfere with the ability of vulnerable developing countries to integrate climate adaptation policy into development, a strategy strongly advocated both by scholars and policy-makers (McGray et al. 2007; Huq et al. 2005; Klein et al. 2007; Lemos et al. 2007). In the next section, we discuss international climate adaptation funding and its implications for development policy.

ADAPTATION FUNDING

As mentioned above, adaptation is narrowly defined by the IPCC (2007) and UNFCCC as an 'adjustment in natural or human systems in response to actual or expected climatic stimuli or their effects, which moderates harm or exploits beneficial opportunities'. Articles 4.4 and 4.3 of the UNFCCC set out the mandatory provision for the transfer of resources to vulnerable countries to adapt to climate change; one of these provisions is that these resources must be new and additional (Mitchell et al. 2009).

Since the beginning of the UNFCCC negotiations, developing countries have expressed their concern with climate impacts, yet the need to adapt to these impacts remained relatively low in the Convention's agenda. The prevailing view, especially in developed countries such as the USA, was that autonomous adaptation would happen anyhow as people and communities use their resources to respond to change. The devastating effects of Hurricane Katrina in New Orleans in 2005 challenged this argument and contributed to change public perception of the vulnerability of different communities—even in rich societies—to extreme climate events (Boyd and Tompkins forthcoming 2010). In addition, around the world, but especially in developed regions, there was strong concern from groups interested in curbing carbon emissions that acknowledging the possibility of adaptation would weaken the resolve of governments and society to invest in less politically palatable mitigation (Pielke, Jr et al. 2007). Finally, has adaptation debates in the negotiations were hijacked by oil-producing countries such as Saudi Arabia complaining about the 'adverse' effects of reducing the global fossil fuel dependency on these countries. The question about how adaptation policies and measures relates to the oil-producing countries remains a contentious and unresolved issue.

Adaptation first gained traction in the Berlin Mandate (Decision 11CP/1) at the Conference of the Parties (COP-1) in 1995, which 'set in motion studies of adaptation and laid out a broad timetable over which these studies would be conducted' (Burton et al. 2007, 4). Even before that, USA-based scientists carried out many climate vulnerability country studies in Africa under the auspices of the UNFCCC and funded by the United States Country Studies Program (USCS) (see for example, Dixon et al. 2003). At COP-1 the World

Bank Global Environment Facility (GEF) was established as the financial mechanism of the UNFCCC with a mandate to support studies, assessments, capacity building and planning for adaptation in low-to-middle income countries (Ayers 2009, 227) (see Chapter 2 by Schroeder for more).

In 2001, in the Marrakesh Accords, adaptation funding gained even more attention and featured in the decision to address the adverse effects of climate change (Decision 5 CP/7) of the Accords. The release of the scientific IPCC reports in 2001 made clear that climate change was already having an effect on many parts of the world, sparking the interest among negotiators in adaptation. New funds were promised and the GEF was requested under the Marrakech Accords to establish pilot adaptation projects, thus giving rise to the Strategic Priority Adaptation (SPA) under the GEF Trust Fund (Ayers 2009, 227). In 2002, the Convention established three additional funds for adaptation purposes to be managed by the GEF—two of those under the Convention and one under the Kyoto Protocol. The funds are: 1) the Least Developed Countries Funds (LDCF) under the UNFCCC, which aims to support 49 least-developed countries to adapt to climate change and establish national adaptation plans of action (NAPA); 2) the Special Climate Change Fund (SCCF) to support a number of climate-related activities including technology transfer, mitigation and adaptation; and 3) the Adaptation Fund (AF), which aims to fund practical adaptation projects from the proceeds of a 2% tax on the Clean Development Mechanism.

Following the release of the Third Assessment Report of the IPCC in 2003, governments requested the UN Subsidiary Body for Scientific and Technological Advice (SBSTA) to commence work on the scientific, technical and socio-economic aspects of, and vulnerability and adaptation to, climate change (Decision 10/CP9) (IISD 2009a). At COP-10 in Buenos Aires in 2004, governments reached a decision (1/CP10, otherwise known as the Buenos Aires Programme of Work on Adaptation and Response Measures) which set in motion a parallel two-track approach in international adaptation policy. Track one aimed to initiate the development of a five-year programme of work on the scientific, technical and socio-economic aspects of vulnerability and adaptation to climate change under the UNFCCC SBSTA, adopted in decision 2/CP11 at the COP in 2005. Track two involved the improvement of information and methodologies, concrete adaptation activities, technology transfer and building capacity under the UNFCCC Subsidiary Body for Implementation. A window of opportunity and a 'breakthrough' success ensued in Nairobi at COP-12 (Muller 2007), where a list of activities was drawn up to be implemented under the five-year programme of work in the Nairobi Work Programme on 'Impacts, Vulnerability and Adaptation to Climate Change'. Governments agreed to a five-year international work plan on adaptation, which includes examining scientific, technical and socio-economic characteristics of impacts, vulnerability and climate change adaptation. Following the release of the IPCC Fourth Assessment Report in 2007, the gravity of climate change stresses became increasingly evident to negotiators, and at

COP-13 in Bali in the same year governments agreed on a road map for a future climate regime, which included adaptation as one of its four pillars in addition to mitigation, finance and technology. In the run-up to Copenhagen in 2009, governments continue to deliberate on how funding for adaptation will be implemented (IISD 2009a). Leading adaptation experts call for mandatory adaptation contributions in the Copenhagen package and argue that without mandatory contributions the lack of financial and institutional capacity will limit the implementation of adaptation in developing and least-developed countries (Boyd and Tompkins 2009).

In 2007, the global promised contributions to adaptation financing amounted to $180m., although only $84m. had actually been collected. It is speculated that demand for adaptation financing will exceed $10 billion to fund the most urgent adaptation projects and programmes, yet the funds actually available through international funding agencies fail to come close to this amount, suggesting that the funds available are there to provide token assistance at best (Boyd and Tompkins forthcoming 2010). Additional funding from other sources may be used to fund post-disaster reconstruction and risk reduction, and most countries have available resources through public expenditure, insurance and disaster pooling, bilateral and multilateral development assistance, and foreign direct investment. What is clear is that significant work is needed to enable the poorest countries to adapt, and it is not yet guaranteed that support or work can be funded or delivered. Of the 12 multilateral and bilateral adaptation-related funds in existence in mid-2009, the GEF has disbursed the largest total funds to adaptation (see Table 1). It also distributes funds to adaptation through its GEF Trust Fund (Climate Change focal area), which includes 591 projects costing around $2,338.7m. (www.climatefundsupdate.org).

Despite welcoming additional funding for adaptation, non-governmental organizations (NGOs) criticize these GEF-managed funds for three reasons (Ayers 2009, 227). First, the financial contributions are inadequate, especially considering that the funds are required to be in addition to ODA funds. Second, the GEF governance structure undermines ownership by developing countries; and finally, guidance on implementation is lacking and transaction costs are too high. Moreover, the GEF has a weak track record of reaching the most vulnerable and its delivery of adaptation finance appears to be targeted at countries with lower rates of poverty (Mohner and Klein 2007, cited in Mitchell et al. 2009).

A more promising model is the Adaptation Fund (AF). It is considered unique in that it is owned by developing countries (Muller 2008), and in that it allows for direct access to resources. A governing board of a majority of developing country representatives oversees the AF and its funds are independent of donor contributions, as proceeds are taken from a 2% share of the CDM Certified Emissions Reductions (CERs) (Harmeling et al. 2008). In Nairobi, the Parties decided that the AF should be based on full adaptation costs, which means that the additionality requirement is relaxed in this case. The AF was written into the Kyoto Protocol (a subsidiary document to the

UNFCCC) and it came into being in 2007. By January 2007, CERs (or CDM credits) in excess of 560,000 had been set aside the Fund (UNFCCC 2007; Huq and Alam 2008). However, in practice, given that the scale of the AF is dependent on the volume of the CDM market, it is difficult to estimate the overall value of the Fund (Flåm and Skjaerseth 2009). By mid 2009, the Fund remained non-operational as the modalities of operation were being debated by the AF Board, which is the supervisory group comprising 16 signatories to the UNFCCC from both developed and developing countries. Once operational, the purpose of the Fund is to finance concrete adaptation projects and programmes. By current estimates, the resources available from the AF amount to $11.2m. for adaptation-related activities, based on an estimated price of $20 per tonne of carbon during the Kyoto Protocol's commitment period (Huq and Alam 2008; UNFCCC 2007). It is likely that it will be some time before the AF is operationalized with real projects because the rules of procedure and project approval have to be finalized and the CDM credits will have to be sold to the emissions trading market for the funds to begin to trickle in (Flåm and Skjaerseth 2009, 111). Thus, sources of other funding for adaptation will remain important to cover the gap (Flåm and Skjaerseth 2009) (see Chapter 3 by Okereke).

Other funds for adaptation primarily include World Bank and bilateral funds from the United Nations Development Programme (UNDP), European Commission, Japan, United Kingdom and Germany. These funds are summarized in Table 2. The generic funds include both mitigation and adaptation, thus it is difficult to know to what extent they are financing concrete adaptation projects and programmes. The UNDP's MDG Achievement Fund's Environment and Climate Change thematic window has the highest number of projects and funding to date, followed by German bilateral funds under its International Climate Initiative. The consequences of adaptation funding can be seen in the light of the development experience in less-developed countries. Adaptation funding encounters problems familiar to the history of development policy and planning. For instance, funds are hampered by existing ODA accounting systems, which makes mainstreaming adaptation into development policy difficult (Klein et al. 2007). It is also well known that multilateral banks are ineffective at distributing development finance to national governments and local communities. Other hurdles include inaccessible and time-consuming procedures for project application, funding that is often both poorly regulated and has a bias towards projects rather than programmes (Mitchell et al. 2009). Bilateral organizations similarly face critiques familiar to development policy and planning. For example, there appears to exist a mismatch between the adaptive processes occurring on the ground (e.g. adaptation strategies to cope with and adapt to climate variability) and the linear tools that bilateral organizations commonly used to plan, monitor and evaluate adaptation as part of development assistance (e.g. logistical frameworks) (Boyd and Osbahr 2009). Klein and Person (2008, cited in Mitchell et al. 2008) highlight ways around these dilemmas by allowing developing country governments direct access to financial resources at low transaction costs. In addition, they suggest that adaptation funds should allow for the ownership of funding to fall under the control of the recipient countries and to align adaptation funding with the principles and procedures of the Paris Declaration on Aid Effectiveness 2005.

Parallel to the above-mentioned adaptation funds are alternative funds. One example is the case of Bangladesh, where there has been a significant amount of self-organizing around adaptation activities (Giddens 2009, 253). The National Climate Change Fund financed by the government of Bangladesh is a \$45m. fund established to build resilience to climate change in Bangladesh (Giddens 2009, 253). Funds such as these potentially open up the opportunity to step up adaptation activities beyond a small number of projects and programmes to mainstream adaptation across national sectors. However, international funds are still needed to scale up activities. Some suggest that the Bangladesh Multi Donor Trust Fund—a trust fund for long-term adaptation and mitigation—is a model that will reduce complex funding procedures (IISD 2009b). It is envisaged that the trust fund will allow unconventional access by government agencies, NGOs and the private sector. Other possible ideas that exist, yet are unlikely to be taken up soon, include a proposal for a levy on air travel (Muller and Hepburn 2006), bunker fuels or on international auctioning of Assigned Amounts Units (AAUs) from carbon trading schemes (Ayers 2009, 230).

In summary, though there are hopes that the AF will be able to deliver to the most vulnerable through direct access to the Adaptation Board, the amounts allocated are woefully small (Stern 2009, 256) and little progress has been made on the distribution of adaptation funding and financing to date. Whereas the National Adaptation Plans of Action (NAPAs) have paved the way for vulnerability assessments at the country level, the links between these assessments and the implementation of adaptation funds are yet to be fully activated in practice.

ADAPTATION AND DEVELOPMENT

In this section we explore the implications of global-level politics on adaptation policy choice in less-developed countries; we argue that by narrowly defining access to global adaptation funds, the UNFCCC rules ultimately shape the design of adaptation policy at the national level and the implementation of adaptation action at the local level. From a policy point of view, the term 'climate adaptation' refers to actions taken to adjust the consequences of climate change either before or after impacts are experienced. If these actions improve over the original conditions of affected groups and systems, then adaptation can also be defined as an opportunity for improvement. While these actions can be funded by myriad sources, the availability of international adaptation funds can be critical for less-developed countries to create opportunities to cope with climate change impacts.

At the local level, state interventions can modulate impacts, along with actions by communities, individuals, NGOs and the private sector. Adaptation is about both options and capacities, and refers to the specific actions individuals and systems take to prevent or overcome the consequences of climate impact. Examples of adaptation options include the design and construction of infrastructure (bridges, levies, dams, etc.); migration and relocation of vulnerable settlements and populations; and increased access to adaptation resources such as welfare and insurance. Options are often designed and implemented to offset vulnerabilities to specific exposure to climate events, that is building levies around settlements vulnerable to storms and hurricanes, reservoirs in regions vulnerable to drought, changing building codes in cities vulnerable to sea-level rise, or establishing specific health responses in cities vulnerable to heatwaves. Building adaptive capacity refers to increasing the ability of individuals, companies and states to respond and reduce their vulnerability not only to climate hazards but also to other stressors as well. Table 3 depicts a summary of determinants of adaptive capacity found in the literature. The list is certainly nothing new; many of these determinants have been essential elements of numerous programmes and policies to reduce poverty and build capacity to respond to different kinds of stressors such as economic crisis, natural disasters or political strife. As we have argued elsewhere (Lemos et al. 2007) the novelty is in the re-emergence of capacity building, long tauted as essential to development, in the context of climate change. Moreover, the reason for a new context is straightforward: climate change causes direct stress and accentuates indirect stress on people who are already vulnerable and the resources on which they depend. From a policy perspective, it may be both difficult and ineffectual to distinguish between these direct and indirect stresses when designing adaptation action. In this context, additionality requirements may push national and local governments to segregate climate and development projects.

Climate change will bring two potentially significant development challenges to less-developed countries. First, the nature and extent of the weather- and climate-related stressors already affecting vulnerable populations in these countries—such as crop losses, displacement, lack of access to clean water, which may lead to poverty, famine and even death—will become more severe under climate futures. Both the level of risk faced by vulnerable populations and the number of people at risk may grow if no proactive capacity building to respond to these additional stressors takes place. Second, as mentioned above, development policy will have to pay attention to specific vulnerabilities associated with the sensitivity of particular populations to climate impacts that may not have been on the agenda in the past. These include taking care of people living in coastal areas, lowlands, drought- and flood-prone regions, or people whose livelihoods directly depend on resources that are going to be negatively affected by climate change (Huq et al. 2005). While policy-makers often approach the former through risk management, addressing the underlying conditions of existing vulnerabilities—those likely to be exacerbated by climate change—it has proven to be much harder for development practitioners.

Vulnerabilities are symptoms of much deeper socio-economic and political inequalities that have historically plagued the less-developed world. In order to be effective, adaptive capacity building needs to address both the structural inequalities that create and sustain poverty and constrain access to resources and threaten vulnerable groups' long-term sustainability. Addressing inequalities may require policies that profoundly challenge the current distribution of power and assets across societies. It may require implementing deep reforms, such as income or land distribution/redistribution; fairer trade; universal access to education and health services; and the 'deepening' of democratic institutions through societal participation and accountability. In many less-developed countries, implementing such structural changes has been slow and incremental at best, and virtually impossible at worst. Yet, the magnitude and accelerated rate of climate change, and the possibility of catastrophic impacts may force political and policy systems to imagine and seek potentially transformative approaches, which include radical paradigmatic shifts towards social ecological integration and sustainability. In this context, by requiring additionality, adaptation funds would not only do little to challenge the conditions that impede such radical changes, but actually might reinforce them. In other words, by compartmentalizing climate impact from other stressors shaping vulnerability and threatening sustainability at the local level, the institutions of global adaptation funding could miss an opportunity to push policy designs that build long-term adaptive capacity.

A critical question that refers directly to additionality relates to donors' fears that climate adaptation funds would 'disappear' within inefficient and corrupt governments. The challenge seems to be the integration of development planning and climate adaptation policy in ways that avoid the pitfalls of failed development practices, while promoting positive synergies. Elsewhere, we have proposed that adaptive capacity building should be delivered through a two-tiered approach that focuses on both developing effective climate adaptation that offsets risks such as vulnerability to extreme events or climate-related health hazards, and on implementing policy reform that addresses deeper structural inequalities that are often at the heart of entrenched vulnerabilities (Lemos et al. 2007). While policy intervention to build adaptive capacity should happen at multiple levels to be effective (Adger et al. 2005; Jerneck and Olsson 2008), local-level interventions can often produce the most effective synergies between, for example, disaster risk management and structural reform aimed at addressing inequalities (Lemos and Tompkins 2008; Tompkins et al. 2008). The development community can clearly guide the adaptation community in building the best capacity, and the adaptation community can contribute its understanding of the unique stresses associated with climate change to the development community. This symbiotic relationship can profit from empirical research that systematically and purposefully identifies the markers of success within development programmes across different policy systems, climates and geographies, to avoid making the mistakes made by development programmes in the past. For example, empirical research shows that investments in 'good' governance such as participatory development, investment in social networks, and provision of information, technologies and new institutions for resource management, often fail if they do not redress the fundamental structural problems that are at the root of poverty (Blair 2000; Cleaver 1999; Kumar 2002; Wester et al. 2003).

However, mainstreaming climate adaptation into development can be constrained by several factors, including mismatches between 1) immediate development goals and future climate change scenarios; 2) special adaptation plans and development agendas, now that several development and special adaptation plans are already underway; and 3) donors' goals and developing countries' development agendas (Agrawala 2004; Klein et al. 2007). In addition, other factors such as lack of financial and human resources, unclear distribution of costs and benefits, fragmented management, mismatches in scale of governance and implementation, lack and unequal distribution of climate information, and trade-offs with other priorities also impose limitations to the smooth mainstreaming of climate adaptation action into development (Agrawala and van Aalst 2006; Bizikova et al. 2007; Eakin and Lemos 2006; Kok et al. 2008; Metz and Kok 2008). Current configurations of adaptation funds do little to alleviate these constraints.

To face these and other challenges, it is time to bring the development and adaptation communities together in a constructive engagement of mutual learning and practice, and to realize that the process of adaptation to climate change does not need to start from scratch. Given the urgency of climate change and the high likelihood that it will seriously affect developing countries, new forms of governance are needed at local and national levels to address disaster risk management and structural reform. Formulating systems of governance to address and build adaptive capacity among states, businesses, scientists and individuals can constructively draw from the vast development experience of building capacity for people and communities coupled with new knowledge about climate change and its impacts.

In conclusion, in less-developed regions of the world, a sustainable and fair adaptation agenda can only be realized through massive investment of new resources, in part coming from the UNFCCC Adaptation Fund and other adaptation multilateral funds. In this context, it is vital that access to these funds is operationalized in a way that not only enables less-developed regions to invest in their most urgent climate adaptation needs, but also extracts positive synergies between these investments and their development goals. At the very least, access to adaptation funds should not further the existing climate change burden on developing countries and limit the already scarce human and policy capacities. While accountability from developing countries is essential for the success of adaptation policy, additionality might not be the best mechanism to implement it.

REFERENCES

Adger, N., J. Paavola, S. Huq and M.J. Mace (2006) *Fairness in Adaptation to Climate Change*, Cambridge, MA: MIT Press.

Adger, N.W., N.W. Arnell and E. L. Tompkins (2005) 'Successful adaptation to climate change across scales', *Global Environmental Change* 15, 77–86.

Adger, W.N., S. Dessai, M. Goulden, M. Hulme, I. Lorenzoni, D.R. Nelson, L.O. Naess, J. Wolf and A. Wreford (2009) 'Are there social limits to adaptation to climate change?' *Climatic Change* 93, 335–54.

Agrawal, A. (2008) 'The Role of Local Institutions in Livelihoods Adaptation to Climate Change', in *Social Dimensions of Climate Change*, Washington, DC: Social Development Department, The World Bank.

Agrawala, S. (2004) 'Adaptation, development assistance and planning: Challenges and opportunities', *Ids Bulletin-Institute of Development Studies* 35, 50–.

Agrawala, S. and M. van Aalst (2006) 'Adapting development cooperation to adapt to climate change', *Workshop on Development and Climate*, Paris, France.

Ayers, J. (2009) 'International funding to support urban adaptation to climate change', *Environment and Urbanization* 21 (1), 225–40.

Baer, P., J. Harte, B. Haya, A.V. Herzog, J. Holdren, N.E. Hultman, D.M. Kammen, R.B. Norgaard and L. Raymond (2000) 'Climate Change: Equity and Greenhouse Gas Responsibility', *Science* 289, 2,287.

Bizikova, L., J. Robinson and S. Cohen (2007) 'Linking climate change and sustainable development at the local level', *Climate Policy* 7, 271–77.

Blair, H. (2000) 'Participation and Accountability at the Periphery: Democratic Local Governance in Six Countries', *World Development* 28, 21–39.

Boyd, E., N. Hultman, T.J. Roberts and E. Corbera (2009) 'Reforming CDM for sustainable development', *Environmental Science and Policy* (forthcoming).

Boyd, E. and H. Osbahr (2009) 'Resilient responses to climate change: Reflexive learning across internationally networked organizations for development (Practical Action, Oxfam, DFID and FCO)', paper presented at 7th International Conference on the Human Dimensions of Global Environmental Change, Bonn, 26–30 April.

Boyd, E., H. Osbahr, P.J. Ericksen, E.L. Tompkins, M.C. Lemos and F. Miller (2008) 'Resilience and "Climatizing" Development: Examples and policy implications', *Development* 5, 390–96.

Boyd, E. and E.L. Tompkins (forthcoming 2010) *A Beginners Guide to Living with Climate Change*, Oxford: OneWorld.

Bozmoski, A., M.C. Lemos and E. Boyd (2008) 'Prosperous Negligence: Governing the Clean Development Mechanism for markets & development', *Environment* 50.

Burton, I., L. Bizikova, T. Dickinson and Y. Howard (2007) 'Integrating adaptation into policy: upscaling evidence from local to global', *Climate Policy* 7, 371–76.

Cleaver, F. (1999) 'Paradoxes of participation: questioning participatory approaches to development', *Journal of International Development* 11, 597–612.

ClimateFundsUpdate (2009) *Current Climate Funds List*, London: Overseas Development Institute and Heinrich Böll Foundation, www.climatefundsupdate.org (accessed June 2009).

Dixon, R. K., J. Smith and S. Guill (2003) 'Life on the Edge: Vulnerability and Adaptation of African Ecosystems to Global Climate Change', *Mitigation and Adaptation Strategies for Global Change* 8, 93–113.

Eakin, H. (2000) 'Smallholder Maize Production and Climatic Risk: A Case Study from Mexico', *Climatic Change* 45, 19–36.

Eakin, H. and M.C. Lemos (2006) 'Adaptation and the state: Latin America and the challenge of capacity-building under globalization', *Global Environmental Change* 16, 7–18.

Flåm, K.H. and J.B. Skjaerseth (2009) 'Does adequate financing exist for adaptation in developing countries?', *Climate Policy* 9, 109–14.

Giddens, A. (2009) *Politics of Climate Change*, Polity Press.

Global Carbon Project (2008) 'Carbon Budget and Trends 2007', www.globalcarbonp roject.org.

Harmeling, S., H. Bals, M. Windfuhr and T. Hirsch (2008) 'Making the Adaptation Fund Work for the Most Vulnerable People', Brot fuer die Welt and German Watch.

Huq, S. and M. Alam (2008) *Climate change adaptation in post-2012 architecture*, London: Progressive Governance.

Huq, S., F. Yamin, A. Rahman, A. Chatterjee, X. Yang, S. Wade, V. Orindi and J. Chigwada (2005) 'Linking climate adaptation and development: A synthesis of six case studies from Asia and Africa', *IDS Bulletin, Institute of Development Studies* 36(4), 117–122.

IISD (2009a) 'A Summary of the Third International Workshop on Community-Based Adaptation to Climate Change', *Community-Based Adaptation to Climate Change Bulletin* 135.

——(2009b) 'Briefing Note on Financing the Climate Agenda'.

IPCC (2007) 'Summary for Policymakers', in M.L. Parry, O.F. Canziani, J.P. Palutikof, P.J. v.d. Linden and C.E. Hanson, *Climate Change 2007: Impacts, Adaptation and Vulnerability. Contribution of Working Group II to the Fourth Assessment Report of the Intergovernmental Panel on Climate Change*, Cambridge: Cambridge University Press, 7–22.

Jerneck, A. and L. Olsson (2008) 'Adaptation and the poor: development, resilience and transition', *Climate Policy* 8, 170–82.

Klein, R.J.T., S.E.H. Eriksen, L.O. Naess, A. Hammill, T.M. Tanner, C. Robledo and K.L. O'Brien (2007) 'Portfolio screening to support the mainstreaming of adaptation to climate change into development assistance', *Climatic Change* 84, 23–44.

Kok, M., B. Metz, J. Verhagen and S. van Rooijen (2008) 'Integrating development and climate policies: National and international benefits', *Climate Policy* 8, 103–18.

Kumar, S. (2002) 'Does "Participation" in Common Pool Resource Management Help the Poor? A Social Cost-Benefit Analysis of Joint Forest Management in Jharkhand, India', *World Development* 30, 763–82.

Lemos, M.C., E. Boyd, E.L. Tompkins, H. Osbahr and D. Liverman (2007) 'Developing Adaptation and Adapting Development', *Ecology and Society* 12.

Lemos, M.C. and E.L. Tompkins (2008) 'Creating Less Disastrous Disasters', *Ids Bulletin-Institute of Development Studies* 39, 60–.

McGray, H., A. Hammill and R. Bradley (2007) 'Weathering the Storm: Options for Framing Adaptation and Development', *WRI Reports*, World Resources Institute.

Metz, B. and M. Kok (2008) 'Integrating development and climate policies', *Climate Policy* 8, 99–102.

Mitchell, T., S. Anderson and S. Huq (2008) 'Principles for Delivering Adaptation Finance', *IDS Briefing* 1–6.

Muller, B. (2007) 'The Nairobi Climate Change Conference: A breakthrough for adaptation funding', *Oxford Energy and Environment Comment*.

——(2008) 'International adaptation finance: the need for an innovative strategic approach', background policy paper for the Climate Strategies Project on Post-2012 Policy Framework: Options for the Tokyo G8 Summit, Oxford: Oxford Institute for Energy Studies.

Muller, B. and C. Hepburn (2006) 'IATAL – An International Air Travel Adapation Levy', Oxford, UK: European Capacity Building Initiative.

NRC (2009) 'Restructuring Federal Climate Reserch to Meet the Challenges of Climate Change', Washington, DC: National Research Council.

O'Brien, K. and R.M. Leichenko (2003) 'Winners and Losers in the Context of Global Change', *Annals of the Association of American Geographers* 93 (1), 89–103.

Oxfam International (2007) 'Adapting to climate change', Oxfam Briefing Paper 104, Oxfam International.

Parks, B.C. and J.T. Roberts (2009) 'The Elusive Quest for a Fair and Effective Global Climate Agreement: A Call for Theoretical Synthesis and "Hybrid Justice" Policy Proposals', *Theory, Culture and Society*, (forthcoming).

Pielke, Jr, R., G. Prins, S. Rayner and D. Sarewitz (2007) 'Lifting the taboo on adaptation', *Nature* 445, 597–98.

Stern, N. (2009) *Blueprint for a Safer Planet: How to Manage Climate Change and Create a New Era of Progress and Prosperity*, The Bodley Head Ltd.

Tompkins, E. L., M.C. Lemos and E. Boyd (2008) 'A less disastrous disaster: Managing response to climate-driven hazards in the Cayman Islands and NE Brazil', *Global Environmental Change-Human and Policy Dimensions* 18, 736–45.

UNDP (2007) *Fighting climate change: Human solidarity in a divided world. Human Development Report 2007/2008*, New York: United Nations Development Programme.

UNFCCC (2007) 'Uniting on Climate Change: A Guide to the Climate Change Convention and the Kyoto Protocol', United Nations Framework Convention on Climate Change.

Wester, P., D.J. Merrey and M. Delange (2003) 'Boundaries of consent: Stakeholder representation in river basin management in Mexico and South Africa', *World Development* 31, 797–812.

Addressing Inequality and Building Trust to Secure a Post-2012 Global Climate Deal

BRADLEY C. PARKS AND J. TIMMONS ROBERTS

INTRODUCTION

The absence of an effective global climate treaty 20 years after the problem was identified—in the face of increasingly dire scientific evidence that we are spoiling our nest—raises broader questions about the factors that shape international environmental co-operation. Scholars and policy analysts have identified a broad range of factors that seem to influence outcomes in international environmental politics: material self-interest; bargaining power; international rules, norms and decision-making procedures; non-state actors, such as epistemic communities, non-governmental organizations (NGOs) and corporations; crises; political leadership; and domestic political institutions (Sprinz and Vaahtoranta 1994; Victor 2001; Young 1994; Wapner 1995; Haas 1990; Keck and Sikkink 1998; Levy and Kolk 2002; Meyer et al. 1997; Roberts and Parks 2007). Yet interestingly, one of the variables often singled out by policy-makers from developing countries as a major impediment to co-operation—global inequality—has not received a great detail of scholarly attention.[1]

In this chapter, we argue that inequality dampens utility-enhancing co-operative efforts by reinforcing 'structuralist' world views and causal beliefs, polarizing policy preferences, making it difficult to coalesce around a socially shared understanding of what is 'fair', eroding conditions of trust, generating divergent and unstable expectations about future behaviour, and creating incentives for zero-sum and negative-sum behaviour. We briefly review three main sources of inequality in the greenhouse—responsibility for the problem, vulnerability to climate-related shocks and stresses, and uneven participation in global efforts to solve the problem—and examine some of the different channels through which inequality may negatively influence the prospects for North–South co-operation. We conclude by exploring several policy options and providing historical examples that illustrate how countries with highly disparate world views, causal beliefs, principled beliefs and policy positions have resolved their differences and co-operated on issues of mutual interest.

ONGOING EFFORTS TO NEGOTIATE A POST-2012 GLOBAL
CLIMATE DEAL

In December 2008, 11,000 representatives from developed and developing countries, intergovernmental organizations, environmental advocacy groups, research institutes and media outlets descended upon Poznań, Poland for the 14th Conference of the Parties (COP-14) of the UN Framework Convention on Climate Change (UNFCCC). The objective of the summit was to lay the groundwork for the negotiation of an ambitious 'post-2012' global climate pact in December 2009 at COP-15 in Copenhagen, Denmark.

With the first commitment period under the Kyoto Protocol set to expire in 2012 and the release of grim new scientific findings by the Intergovernmental Panel on Climate Change (IPCC) in mid-2007,[2] there was a sense of renewed urgency at the COP-13 negotiations in Bali, Indonesia, and in the run-up to COP-14 in Poznań. There was also a broad consensus about the central task at hand: enlisting the active participation of developing countries in a post-2012 global climate regime. Although the first round of commitments under the Kyoto Protocol was a useful political exercise, it required emission reduction commitments from a group of wealthy countries that account for less than one-fifth of global carbon emissions and will likely have a minimal impact on atmospheric stability. In fact, during the first half of Kyoto's first commitment period, global carbon emissions rose sharply—from roughly 6 billion tons of carbon equivalent (GtC) per year to 7 billion GtC between 1996 and 2004 (Baumert 2002). Climate scientists warn that to avoid 'dangerous anthropogenic interference with the climate system', atmospheric CO_2 concentrations should be capped somewhere between 450 and 550 parts per million (ppm), or at approximately 9.4 billion GtC per year.[3] In short, significant emissions reductions are urgently needed within a very short period of time.

This poses a major political dilemma. The current accumulated stock of CO_2 in the atmosphere is largely the responsibility of rich, industrialized countries, but growth in future emissions is expected to primarily take place in the developing world. By 2030, developing country emissions are expected to skyrocket to 60% of total global emissions.[4] It is, then, difficult to envision a scenario in which climate stabilization does not demand 'the South [...] accept the necessity of serious, costly mitigation, and immediately embark on a low-carbon development path' (Wheeler and Ummel 2007, 10). However, the unforgiving science of future emission projections has not made the politics of negotiating a global North–South deal any less contentious. Most developing countries continue to strongly resist any binding limits on their emissions, pointing out that wealthy nations fuelled their own economic development with dirty, climate-altering energy sources and appropriated a disproportionate amount of 'atmospheric space'. As a result, they argue that the North should focus on substantially reducing its own emissions in order to free up atmospheric space for developing countries to achieve higher living standards.

As we will describe in this chapter, North–South relations are characterized by widely divergent perceived self-interests, principled beliefs, expectations of would-be co-operators, and negotiating positions. We here argue that this impasse was nearly predetermined by the profound inequality in the global system. During the COP-14 Poznań negotiations, the Republic of Korea's (South Korea) lead negotiator noted that 'the current culture is [one] of mistrust and finger-pointing', and called on developed and developing countries to begin implementing confidence-building measures.[5] South Africa's environment minister similarly argued that an effective agreement would hinge on the extent to which developed and developing countries were able to make meaningful and credible commitments. 'At what level', he asked, 'do they feel we are doing enough, and at what level do we feel they are doing enough?'[6] The *Christian Science Monitor* reported that 'industrialized and developing countries bring different expectations to the talks—and the need to build trust between the two will be vital'.[7]

Poznań was both a disappointment and a lost opportunity. After the negotiation of an ambitious and upbeat-sounding 'Bali Roadmap' at COP-13 in December 2007, several lower-middle and upper-middle income country representatives came to Poznań with concrete proposals in hand and expressed a genuine desire to begin working towards a post-2012 global deal.[8] However, the same issues that bedeviled previous rounds of climate negotiations—widely divergent policy positions, disagreements about the fairness principles that should guide and shape a future agreement, and deep-seated mistrust—also plagued COP-14. Delegations from the developing world expressed profound frustration and disappointment. The Director-General of Brazil's Forest Service asked: 'If we can talk about decreasing [emissions] 50 percent by 2018, which is in 10 years, why can't the industrialized countries commit themselves to decreasing 80 percent by 2050, which is in 50 years?'[9] At the end of the COP-14 negotiations, a representative of the European think tank, Third Generation Environmentalism (E3G) reported that 'if we wait until everybody looks at each other and sees what everybody exactly is going to do, we will never solve this issue [… W]hat is required is for [developed] countries […] to come here and put something […] on the table to build trust with the developing countries so that they believe that the North is actually going to act. We need developed countries to respond substantially to the proposals the G-77 and China have put on the table. We are hearing not only disappointment […] but anger from developing countries who have worked hard to come here to actually discuss substance, and yet […] have not had their proposals responded to.'[10]

THE CORROSIVE IMPACT OF INEQUALITY

There are three broad types of inequality: climate-related inequality, inequality in international environmental politics, and inequality in international economic regimes, which all substantially influence climate change negotiations.

Inequality in responsibility for climate change

An egalitarian might think that the best way to resolve the issue of responsibility for climate change would be to give all humans equal atmospheric rights and assign responsibility to individuals based on how much 'environmental space' they use. This is a basic rule of civil justice and kindergarten ethics: those who created a mess should be responsible for cleaning up their fair share. However, in international politics things are not so simple.

With only 4% of the world's population, the USA is responsible for over 20% of all global emissions. That can be compared with 136 developing countries that together are only responsible for 24% of global emissions (Roberts and Parks 2007). Poor countries, then, remain far behind wealthy countries in terms of emissions per person. Overall, the richest 20% of the world's population is responsible for over 60% of its current emissions of greenhouse gases. That figure surpasses 80% if historical contributions to the problem are considered, and they probably should be, as carbon dioxide, the main contributor to the greenhouse effect, remains in the atmosphere for over 100 years (IPCC 2007).

However, there are many ways to understand emissions inequality and responsibility for climate change, and each approach represents a different social understanding of fairness. 'Grandfathering' (the basis of the Kyoto Protocol, that countries should reduce from a baseline year like 1990) falls in line with the entitlement principle that individuals are entitled to what they have or have produced. The carbon intensity approach, which is usually associated with a measure of CO_2 emissions per unit of gross domestic product (GDP), represents the utilitarian principle that inefficient solutions are also unjust, as everyone is worse off in the absence of joint gains. Accounting for the historical responsibility of countries for the stock of greenhouse gases in the atmosphere represents the 'polluter pays' principle. Finally, the equal emissions rights per capita approach is consistent with the egalitarian principle that every human should have equal rights to global public goods, such as atmospheric stability. These different perceptions of fairness are to a large extent shaped by the highly disparate positions that countries occupy in the global hierarchy of economic and political power.[11] In this way, we argue that inequality has a dampening effect on co-operation by polarizing policy preferences and making it difficult for countries to arrive at a socially-shared understanding of what is 'fair'.

Inequality in vulnerability to climate change

Rising carbon emissions have created—and will continue to create—a warmer and wetter atmosphere, thereby increasing flooding, hurricanes, forest fires, winter storms and drought in arid and semi-arid regions. Climatologists have observed a sharp upswing in the frequency, magnitude and intensity of hydrometeorological disasters over the past two decades—the five warmest years on historical record were 1998, 2002, 2003, 2005 and 2007—and hydrometeorological disasters have more than doubled since 1996 (Goddard Institute for Space Studies 2008).

Although climate change is often characterized as 'everybody's problem' or the under-provision of a global public good, hydrometeorological impacts are socially distributed across human populations (Kaul et al. 1999). Some countries and communities will suffer more immediately and profoundly, and they are generally not those most responsible for creating the problem. According to the latest predictions of the IPCC, rapidly expanding popula-tions in Africa, Asia and Latin America are suffering disproportionately from more frequent and dangerous droughts, floods and storms (IPCC 2007). The World Bank reports that '[b]etween 1990 and 1998, 94 per cent of the world's disasters and 97 per cent of all natural-disaster-related deaths occurred in developing countries' (Mathur et al. 2004, 6).

There are competing ideas about how uneven vulnerability to climate change impacts will influence the prospects for North–South co-operation. On one hand, poor countries suffering from rising sea levels, devastating droughts and storms, lower agricultural yields and increased disease burdens are unlikely to be enthusiastic about cleaning up an environmental problem that the industrialized world created in the first place. On the other hand, some rational choice scholars have argued that self-interest may make vul-nerable countries *more* likely to join global efforts to curb greenhouse gas emissions (Sprinz and Vaahtoranta 1994).[12]

The weight of the evidence from the last 20 years of climate negotiations seems to provide more support for the former view than the latter. Stark inequalities in vulnerability have in fact poisoned the negotiating atmosphere and created feelings of marginalization, frustration, anger and bitterness. There is also some evidence that such feelings have led to retaliatory attitudes and negative-sum behaviour.[13] At COP-1 in Berlin in 1995, Bangladeshi Atiq Rahman declared that 'if climate change makes our country uninhabitable, we will march with our wet feet into your living rooms' (Athanasiou and Baer 2002, 23). More recently, in an April 2007 speech to the UN Security Coun-cil, the British Foreign Secretary noted that President Museveni of Uganda characterizes climate change as 'an act of aggression by the rich against the poor' (Green 2008). Although some climate policy analysts dismiss this type of rhetoric as mere posturing, a recent European Union (EU) report warns that '[c]limate change impacts will fuel the politics of resentment between those most responsible for climate change and those most affected by it' (European Union 2008, 5).[14]

Inequality in (expected) clean-up

There are also stark inequalities in who is currently doing something to reduce greenhouse gas emissions and which countries will likely bear the greatest burden of atmospheric clean-up in the future. Although northern governments are trying to convince the southern governments that they need to rein in their greenhouse gas emissions, most of them are not doing so in their own countries. Under the Kyoto Protocol, 'Annex I' (developed) countries committed to a 5.2% (average) reduction in greenhouse gas emissions (below 1990 levels) by 2012. However, with the exception of several European countries, greenhouse gas emissions have risen significantly throughout the industrialized world since 1990. Simply stated, the 'demandeurs' of global climate protection face a credibility problem: they need to demonstrate that they are willing to make difficult choices at home before they can enlist the support of developing countries.

Many industrialized countries have indicated that rather than making cuts at home, they would prefer to achieve their emission reduction commitments by funding activities in developing countries.[15] From a cost efficiency perspective, this makes good sense: the greatest opportunities for low-cost emissions reductions exist in the developing world (Stavins and Olmstead 2006). For example, Stavins (2004, 8) argues that 'the simple reality is that developing countries provide the greatest opportunities now for relatively low cost emissions reductions. Hence, it would be excessively and unnecessarily costly to focus emissions-reductions activities exclusively in the developed world'. However, there are a multitude of moral and practical problems associated with the North simply paying the South to clean up the atmosphere on their behalf (Hultman et al. 2009). If nothing else, the last 35 years of global environmental negotiations have highlighted the fact that developing countries have deeply-held distributional concerns, which can be a significant impediment to international environmental co-operation if left unaddressed. Najam (2004, 128) writes that 'as a self-professed collective of the weak, the G-77 is inherently risk-averse and seeks to minimize its losses rather than to maximize its gains; [... I]ts unity is based on a sense of shared vulnerability and a shared distrust of the prevailing world order [... and] because of its self-perception of weakness [it] has very low expectations'. Joanna Depledge (2002), a former UNFCCC Secretariat staff member, has similarly reported that many non-Annex I (developing) countries fear efforts to curb carbon emissions in the developing world will effectively place a 'cap' on their economic growth.

It is also important to note that even among developed countries that appear to have reduced or stabilized their greenhouse gas emissions since 1990, there are serious questions about whether such national statistics on greenhouse gas emissions truly indicate a shift from high-carbon to low-carbon economies and lifestyles. New research suggests that many 'service-exporting' Organisation of Economic Co-operation and Development (OECD) countries, which increasingly specialize in areas like banking, tourism, advertising, sales, product design, procurement and distribution, are in many cases 'net-importers' of carbon-intensive goods coming primarily from developing countries. As such, they do not necessarily emit less; they may simply displace their emissions (Machado et al. 2001; Muradian et al. 2002; Heil and Selden 2001). This changing pattern of production and consumption has not gone unnoticed by developing countries. In 2008, Chinese Minister of Foreign Affairs, Yang Jiechi, pointed out that many of the People's Republic of China's carbon emissions are the by-product of northern demand for manufactured goods, stating 'I hope when people use high-quality yet inexpensive Chinese products, they will also remember that China is under increasing pressure of transfer emission[s]' (Economic Times 2008).

Inequality in international environmental regimes

International climate negotiations are also deeply embedded in the broader context of North–South relations. In 1972, at the first international conference on the environment in Stockholm, Sweden, there was profound disagreement between developed and developing countries on the issue of global environmental protection. 'Late-developers' feared restrictions on their economic growth, emphasized the North's profligate use of planetary resources, and pushed for a redistributive programme that would benefit them economically and hasten the transition towards industrialization. Developed countries wanted northern consumption off the negotiating table, southern population growth on the agenda, and non-binding language on issues of financial assistance and technology transfer (Haas et al. 1993). The South's confrontational approach intensified in the late 1970s under the banner of the 'New International Economic Order' (NIEO). During this period, developing countries put forth a 'series of proposals […] which included significant wealth redistribution, greater [southern] participation in the world economy, and greater Third World control over global institutions and resources' (Sebenius 1991, 128). At the same time, late developers became strident in their criticism of northern environmentalism—an environmentalism that many perceived as 'pull[ing] up the development ladder' (Najam 1995).

In future rounds of global environmental negotiations, there were calls for increased financial compensation and more equitable representation (Sell 1996; DeSombre and Kaufman 1996). Debate over the voting structure of the Global Environmental Facility, which distributes hundreds of millions of dollars of environmental aid each year, became especially conflict-ridden. Developing countries protested 'donor dominance' and the lack of transparency in decision-making, while industrialized countries insisted that only the 'incremental costs' of global environmental projects be financed (Keohane and Levy 1996). At the 1992 Rio Earth Summit, developed countries agreed to underwrite the participation of less-developed countries in global environmental accords. However, for a variety of reasons, wealthy nations ultimately failed to honour their policy commitments (Hicks et al. 2008).

In the mid-1990s, developing countries also sought to strengthen the 'sustainable development' agenda by linking the issues of climate change, forests and biodiversity to issues of trade, investment, finance and intellectual property rights. But this was flatly rejected by rich nations (Sandbrook 1997). Finally, at the COP-6 climate negotiations, the G-77 and China charged that many of the important decisions affecting developing countries were being made in nontransparent 'Green Room' meetings, attended only by powerful countries. This set the stage for the 2002 World Summit on Sustainable Development (WSSD), where one observer noted that 'effective governance is not possible under the prevailing conditions of deep distrust' (Najam 2003, 370).

Inequality in international economic regimes

International climate negotiations are also wound up with North–South economic relations. Stephen Krasner once said that there are 'makers, breakers, and takers' in international relations, and there is little question that developing countries are generally 'takers' in international economic regimes (Krasner 1978). '[T]he "price" of multilateral rules', explains Shadlen, 'is that [the least developed countries] must accept rules written by—and usually for—the more developed countries' (Shadlen 2004, 6). Gruber (2000, 8) argues that powerful states—particularly those with large markets—possess 'go-it-alone power' in that they can unilaterally eliminate the previous status quo and proceed gainfully with or without the participation of weaker parties.

Wade (2003, 622) describes a 'shrinking of development space' and argues that 'the rules being written into multilateral and bilateral agreements actively prevent developing countries from pursuing the kinds of industrial and technology policies adopted by the newly developed countries of East Asia and by the older developed countries when they were developing'. Similarly, Birdsall et al. (2005) explain how the callous—and at times opportunistic—actions of Western governments have made upward mobility in the international division of labour difficult. Other scholars of international political economy have highlighted the fact that the governance structures of international financial institutions, like the International Monetary Fund and World Bank, prevent the institutions' main clients (developing countries) from having any significant voting power (Woods 1999; Wade 2003).

These inequalities of opportunity have an indirect, but important, impact on how developing countries approach global environmental negotiations. In 1991, Porter and Brown concluded that 'developing states' perceptions of the global economic structure as inequitable has long been a factor in their policy responses to global environmental issues' (1991, 124; see also Chasek et al. 2006). Similarly, Gupta (1997) reportes that '[southern] negotiators tend to see issues holistically and link the issue to all other international issues. Thus linkages are made to international debt, trade and other environmental issues such as desertification'. As we have argued elsewhere (e.g. Roberts and Parks 2007), when powerful states disregard weaker states' positions in the international division of labour in areas where they possess structural power (as in international economic regimes), they run a high risk of weaker states 'reciprocating' in policy areas where they possess more bargaining leverage (as in international environmental regimes).[16]

HOW GLOBAL INEQUALITY INFLUENCES INTERNATIONAL CLIMATE NEGOTIATIONS

In this section, we explore some of the causal mechanisms through which inequality—in opportunity, political power and distributional outcomes—may influence global climate negotiations. We argue that global inequality makes it more difficult for rich and poor nations to identify socially-shared understandings of 'fair' solutions. Even when countries of vastly different means can agree on general fairness principles, the heterogeneity in preferences generated by global inequality aggravates disagreements about how to make those principles operational. Global inequality also contributes to conditions of generalized mistrust, which in turn makes developing countries less trusting of would-be co-operators and more inclined to pursue self-damaging policies.

Structuralist world views and causal beliefs

One of the most important causal pathways through which global inequality can impede co-operation is by promoting 'structuralist' world views and causal beliefs. Goldstein and Keohane define world views as ideas that 'define the universe of possibilities for action' (1993, 9). For example, culture, religion, rationality, emotion, ethnicity, race, class, gender and identity all shape the way that humans (including policy-makers) perceive the opportunities and challenges facing them. As such, having a world view implies '[limited] choice because it logically excludes other interpretations of reality, or at least suggests that such interpretations are not worthy of sustained exploration' (Goldstein and Keohane 1993, 12). By limiting one's menu of available options, world views and causal beliefs have an instrumental impact on how cost-benefit calculations are conducted.[17] They also influence the very way in which actors come up with their own policy agendas.

For example, depending on one's position in the international system, states may seek to maximize absolute gains, relative gains, social (fairness) preferences or emotional utility. Highly risk-averse governments may want to freeze the status quo (Shadlen 2004; Gruber 2000; Abbott and Snidal 2000). Leaders who feel cheated by others may seek to punish their enemies or strengthen their relative power, regardless of the efficiency implications.[18] Those who see themselves as marginalized by social structures may seek to overturn regimes, rather than make changes within them (Ruggie 1983; Krasner 1985). Weak states that look down the 'decision tree' and anticipate being exploited at the discretion of powerful states may even take self-damaging steps to promote their principled beliefs (Barrett 2003). Whatever the particular course of action, ideas about how the world works 'put blinders on people' and '[reduce] the number of conceivable alternatives' from which they choose (Goldstein and Keohane 1993, 12). World views and causal beliefs, in this sense, influence issue definition, expectations, perceived interests, principled beliefs and, ultimately, the prospects for mutually-beneficial co-operation.

In the developing world, we argue that 'structuralist' ideas about the origins and persistence of global inequality form the central world view of most developing country leaders, including how they have viewed the issue of climate change.[19] The vast majority of goals developing country leaders sought since the end of the Second World War have remained elusive, and this we believe has shaped developing countries' perceptions of the world as fundamentally unequal and unjust. More than 20 years ago, Krasner (1985) argued that ideas about 'dependency' affected how many LDC decision makers viewed the world, their identity in relation to other states, their goals and how such goals could be most effectively realized. 'The [dependency perspective] embraced by developing countries', Krasner argued, '[is] not merely a rationalization. It [is] the subjective complement to the objective condition of domestic and international weakness' (Krasner 1985, 90). Najam puts it this way: 'The self-definition of the South [...] is a definition of exclusion: these countries believe that they have been bypassed and view themselves as existing on the periphery' (Najam 2004, 226).

There are several widely-held structuralist ideas related to international environmental issues, which we have argued obstruct North–South efforts to protect the climate: the idea that global environmental problems are only attributable to patterns of northern consumption and production, the idea that a nation's ability to implement environmental reform depends upon its position in the international division of labour, and the idea that the North is using environmental issues as a ruse to thwart poor countries' economic development (Roberts and Parks 2007).[20] These beliefs can be seen in both the terminology used and the arguments made by developing countries. Although wealthy, industrialized countries often dismiss claims of 'environmental imperialism', 'ecological debt', 'ecologically unequal exchange', and 'environmental load displacement' as empty and distracting rhetoric, the fact of the matter is that southern governments view their interests according to their world views and causal beliefs and this appears to be impeding international environmental co-operation. As we describe in greater detail below, the 'structuralist' way of making sense of the world has promoted generalized mistrust among rich and poor nations, which in turn has suppressed diffuse reciprocity, and led to divergent and unstable expectations about future behaviour. Structuralist ideas have also promoted particularistic notions of fairness, a victim mentality and, in some cases, zero-sum or negative-sum behaviour.

Principled beliefs

The second way in which we argue global inequality influences the prospects for North–South co-operation is through its impact on 'principled beliefs'. Goldstein and Keohane define principled beliefs as 'normative ideas that specify criteria for distinguishing right from wrong and just from unjust' (Goldstein and Keohane 1993, 9). Such ideas can facilitate co-operation if they are widely shared by providing a so-called 'focal point' that reduces the costs of negotiating and bargaining, making agreements more palatable to domestic audiences (who frequently possess an indirect veto power over ratification and implementation), and realigning the incentives of rich and poor nations to create fewer opportunities for shirking, defection and other types of opportunistic behaviour (Roberts and Parks 2007; Wiegandt 2001).

First, fairness principles can reduce the costs associated with negotiating international agreements. Shared understandings of fairness provide what game theorists call 'focal points'. By isolating one point along the contract curve that every party would prefer over a non-co-operative outcome, states can stabilize expectations for future behaviour and reduce the costs of arriving at a mutually acceptable agreement (Keohane 2001; Müller 1999). The Montréal Protocol is a good example of an agreement that was guided by a fairness focal point. During the early negotiations, developed and developing countries staked out very different policy positions regarding what would constitute a 'fair' approach to combating ozone depletion (Sell 1996; DeSombre and Kauffman 1996), but all parties eventually agreed to allow the principle of 'compensatory justice' to guide the negotiations (Albin 2001; Mitchell and Keilbach 2001).

Fairness principles can also influence the costs of monitoring and enforcing agreements. Due to the public good attributes of a stable climate (i.e. non-excludability and non-rivalry) and the fact that asymmetric information reduces the 'observability' of deviant behaviour, states may face strong incentives to free ride on the climate stabilization efforts of others. In a sense, it is in every state's self-interest to misrepresent their level of contribution to the collective good. Demandeurs must, therefore, make compliance economically rational for more reluctant participants through financial compensation schemes, issue linkage and other forms of incentive restructuring, which can reduce the likelihood of cheating and defection (Krasner 1985; Abbott and Snidal 2000; Young 1994).[21]

Finally, norms and principles of fairness can help cement a collaborative equilibrium and reduce monitoring and enforcement costs through their impact on the domestic ratification process. Müller (1999, 10–12) lays much emphasis on this point: 'It would be foolish to assume, however, that bodies such as the US Congress or the Indian Lok Sabha could be [...] bullied into ratifying an agreement [... because] parties may refuse to ratify an agreement if they feel it deviates unacceptably from what they perceive to be the just solution'.

However, as we will argue at greater length below, norms of fairness are extremely elastic and subject to political manipulation, and fairness focal points rarely emerge spontaneously. Therefore, a truly global consensus on climate change will likely require a 'hybrid justice' solution that accommodates the different circumstances and principled beliefs of many parties.

Generalized mistrust

Long-standing patterns of inequality and opportunism have fostered mistrust in North–South relations, which has proven to be a major obstacle to co-operation.

Inequality makes it harder for developing countries and developed countries to trust each other and establish mutually acceptable 'rules of the game'. Such rules are important to would-be co-operators because they reduce uncertainty, stabilize expectations, constrain opportunism and increase the credibility of state commitments.

Although few scholars have explored the causal impact of social trust in international environmental politics, there is a large literature in economics, sociology and political science on the relationship between trust and co-operation (Putnam 1993; Keohane 1984, 2001; Stein 1990; Kydd 2000). By fostering norms of reciprocity, trust increases communication and information, reduces uncertainty and transaction costs, enhances the credibility of commitments, makes defection more costly, creates stable expectations and ultimately promotes co-operation (Durkheim 1933 [1893]; Putnam 1993). Trust, in effect, allows would-be co-operators to bank on promises to honour policy commitments. Social inequality is strongly associated with lower levels of trust, lower levels of public good provision (a proxy for co-operation), and higher levels of crime and other types of socially-destructive behaviour (Putnam 1993; Knack and Keefer 1997; Easterly 2001).

In a domestic setting, the state has a 'monopoly of violence' and can enforce contracts and 'coerce trust' on behalf of its citizens (Putnam 1993, 165); but states do not have the luxury of third-party enforcement in international relations; contracting takes place under conditions of anarchy (Waltz 1979; Keohane 1984). Countries must 'decide whom to make agreements with, and on what terms, largely on the basis of their expectations about their partners' willingness and ability to keep their commitments' (Keohane 1984, 105). As a result, states seeking to promote international public good provision must develop so-called 'self-enforcing' agreements (Barrett 2003).

International relations scholarship has shed much light on how governments can convince potential partners that they will honour their commitments (Mearsheimer 1994; Stein 1990). We highlight three ways in which states may seek to enhance relations of trust: specific reciprocity, diffuse reciprocity and costly signals. Specific reciprocity refers to an 'exchange of items of equivalent value in a strictly delimited sequence' (Keohane 1986, 4). For example, the Organization of the Petroleum Exporting Countries (OPEC) and non-OPEC nations periodically agree to cut oil production at the same time in order to maximize their impact on oil prices; but this type of strategy has significant disadvantages: unequal partners often find it difficult to reciprocate equally, contingencies may unexpectedly affect an actors' ability to reciprocate, and different interpretations and measurements can degenerate into situations of mutual recrimination. An accumulated stock of 'diffuse reciprocity' is much more valuable. Diffuse reciprocity does not require that all aspects of a contract be specified *ex ante*. Rather, it requires that states make deposits at the 'favour bank' when they can in order to build conditions of trust and stabilize expectations for future co-operative efforts (Putnam 2000, 20; Keohane 1984).[22]

When inter-state relationships are characterized by mutual suspicion and deep distrust, conditions of diffuse reciprocity can be particularly difficult to build. As such, states actively seeking to foster diffuse reciprocity and build conditions of trust may need to send 'costly signals' of reassurance to would-be co-operators. Such signals 'serve to separate the trustworthy types from the untrustworthy types; trustworthy types will send them, untrustworthy types will find them too risky to send' (Kydd 2000, 326). This has special relevance to international environmental politics; while Western countries have a long history of co-operating across a wide range of policy areas and arriving at new self-enforcing contracts, no such history exists between developed and developing countries. North–South environmental relations are characterized by high levels of mistrust and significant power asymmetries. There are many ways in which rich countries can send special signals of reassurance to developing countries—e.g. by taking the lead by making deep emission cuts at home, promoting issue linkage and exercising self-restraint when the short-term return on opportunistic behaviour is high. However, regardless of the tactics chosen, the overriding goal should be to clearly signal a desire to address the 'structural' obstacles facing developing countries and reverse long-standing patterns of global inequality.

CONCLUSION

Our research suggests that global inequality is a central, but under-appreciated, impediment to North–South environmental co-operation (Roberts and Parks 2007). Therefore, we argue that crafting an effective post-2012 global climate regime will require unconventional—and perhaps even heterodox—policy interventions. To date, countries have proposed different yardsticks for measuring atmospheric clean-up responsibilities based on par-ticularistic notions of justice. However, high levels of inequality make it very unlikely that a North–South consensus will spontaneously emerge on the basis of a single fairness principle. Consequently, we believe a truly global consensus on climate change will almost certainly require a 'hybrid justice' solution that accommodates the different circumstances and principled beliefs of many parties. To break through the cycle of mistrust that plagues North–South relations, we also argue that the North needs to offer the South a new global bargain on environment and development and signal its commitment to this new 'shared thinking' through a series of confidence-building measures. Drawing upon insights from the 'strategic reassurance' literature, we argue that a series of 'costly signals' can foster mutual trust between developed and developing countries and provide a basis for long-term co-operation to stabi-lize the climate. These measures should offer a new vision of global environ-mental co-operation, provide opportunities for developing countries to transition towards less carbon-intensive development pathways, and clearly signal a desire to address the 'structural' obstacles facing developing countries and reverse long-standing patterns of global inequality. Finally, we emphasize the central importance of exercising self-restraint when the short-term payoff on opportunistic behaviour is high. When powerful states consistently treat weaker states like second-class citizens, they run the risk of weaker states 'reciprocating' in policy domains where they possess greater bargaining leverage.

Moving towards 'hybrid justice'

Earlier, we described four very different proposed yardsticks for measuring atmospheric clean-up responsibilities based on particularistic notions of justice: the grandfathering approach, which relies on entitlement principles of justice; the carbon intensity approach, which rests on utilitarian principles of justice; the historical responsibility approach, which operationalizes the 'polluter-pays' principle; and the egalitarian per capita approach. Each of these notions of justice is closely associated with where countries sit in the global hierarchy of economic and political power. It is, then, very unlikely that a North–South fairness consensus will spontaneously emerge on the basis of one of these principles. Instead, a moral compromise, or 'negotiated justice' settlement, will most likely be necessary; countries will need to be willing to reconsider and negotiate their own beliefs about what is fair.[23] As Müller (1999, 3) puts it, 'we merely need a solution which is commonly regarded as sufficiently fair to remain acceptable'.

There are already a significant number of proposals in the public domain that comport this notion of 'moral compromise'. Bartsch and Müller (2000) have proposed a 'preference score' method, which combines the grand-fathering and per capita approach through a voting system. The Pew Center for Global Climate Change has developed a hybrid proposal that assigns responsibility based on past and present emissions, carbon intensity and countries' ability to pay (e.g. per capita GDP) and separates the world into three groups: those that 'must act now', those that 'could act now' and those that 'should act now, but differently' (Claussen and McNeilly 1998). The Climate Action Network International has put forward a three-track propo-sal, with the wealthy countries moving forward on a 'Kyoto track' of com-mitments to reduce absolute emissions, the poorest focused nearly entirely on adaptation, and the rapidly developing nations focused on 'decarbonisation'. Others have focused on more per capita proposals that provide for 'national circumstances', or allowance factors, like geography, climate, energy supply and domestic economic structure, as well as 'soft landing scenarios' (e.g. Gupta and Bhandari 1999; Ybema et al. 2000; Torvanger and Godal 2004; Groenenberg et al. 2001).

Most recently, EcoEquity with support from the Heinrich Böll Foundation, Christian Aid and the Stockholm Environment Institute have developed a 'Greenhouse Development Rights' framework as a point of reference to evaluate proposals for the post-2012 commitment period (Baer et al. 2008). They propose that countries below a 'global middle class' income of $9,000 per capita should be assured that they will not be asked to make binding limits until they approach that level, while countries above that level should be responsible for rapid emissions reductions and payments to assist those below the line in improving their social and economic status while adjusting to a less carbon-intensive path of development. Funds raised in wealthy countries in reducing emissions are also used to help poor countries adapt and develop in more climate-friendly ways. We believe these hybrid proposals are among the most promising solutions to break the North–South stalemate.

Building trust through costly signals and creating a 'shared vision' of long-term co-operative action

At the same time, we recognize that simply asserting the importance of 'negotiated justice' settlement avoids the more central question of whether and to what extent a future agreement must favour rich or poor nations. Divergent principled beliefs are a consequence of more fundamental root causes: persistent global inequality, incongruent world views and causal beliefs, and an enduring trust deficit (Roberts and Parks 2007). Therefore, along with developing a workable and fair 'hybrid justice' proposal, we believe policy-makers must redouble their efforts to allay the fears and suspicions of developing countries, rebuild conditions of generalized trust, and work towards a new 'shared vision' of long-term co-operation across multiple issue areas.

Kydd (2000) has shown that a strategy of reassurance through costly signals can foster mutual trust between countries that do not have a long history of co-operation. He defines costly signals as 'signals designed to persuade the other side that one is trustworthy by virtue of the fact that they are so costly that one would hesitate to send them if one were untrustworthy' (Kydd 2000, 326). Based on an analysis of US–Soviet relations in the run-up to the end of the Cold War, he notes that '[we] can observe a series of costly signals leading to mutual trust between former adversaries. The attitudes of Western leaders, press, and publics toward the Soviet Union all underwent a substantial transformation. Soviet military and geopolitical concessions, particularly the [Intermediate-range Nuclear Forces] treaty, the withdrawal from Afghanistan, the December 1988 conventional arms initiative, and the withdrawal from Eastern Europe were decisive in changing overall Western opinion about the Soviet Union. By 1990 most observers viewed the Soviet Union as a state that had abandoned its hegemonic ambitions and could be trusted to abide by reasonably verified arms control agreements and play a constructive role in world politics'. (Kydd 2000, 350). Kydd's research also suggests that the more noticeable, irreversible, unconditional and costly the signal from a 'sending state', the more trust it can foster with a 'receiving state'.

We believe that the conditions of mistrust which currently plague North–South environmental relations can be understood as the product of a 'failed reassurance strategy'. In the early 1990s, the North sought to assure poorer nations that they would 'take the lead' in stabilizing the climate, but the lack of progress by the USA and other industrialized countries in meeting their own emission reduction targets provided developing nations with a ready excuse for not seriously contemplating low-carbon alternatives. As Baumert and Kete (2002, 6) put it, '[m]any developing countries believe that the industrialized countries lack credibility on the issue of international coopera- tion to curb greenhouse gas emissions, having done little to address a problem largely of their own making'.

To be sure, there are some examples of (modestly) successful trust-building efforts in global environmental politics. The Multilateral Ozone Fund enshrined the 'compensatory justice' principle and gave developing countries a greater stake in the decision-making process governing the allocation of environmental aid (Woods 1999; Hicks et al. 2008). The Montréal Protocol also gave developing countries a 10-year window to pursue 'cheap' economic development before making serious chlorofluorocarbon reductions. Rich nations have also made some important concessions in the context of climate negotiations. For example, developing countries were invited to participate in the Kyoto Protocol's 'Compliance Committee' (despite avoiding scheduled emission reduction commitments themselves) and treated as 'equal' partners through the double-majority voting mechanism.

However, the development and implementation of a thoughtful, focused trust-building strategy does not appear to enjoy broad support. In fact, the very idea of incremental trust-building through costly signals is flatly rejected by some respected negotiators from industrialized countries. Former US envir- onmental treaty negotiator Richard Benedick (2001) has described himself as being mystified as to why rich nations would ever include developing countries in the Kyoto Protocol's monitoring and compliance system. 'A major and dubious concession to the South', he noted, 'was an agreement to grant developing nations, who have no commitments, a decisive role in the protocol's compliance system, assessing and enforcing the commitments of industrialized coun- tries'.[24] We take a different view. Mark Twain famously said that 'the princi- ple of diplomacy [is to] give one and take ten', but we believe that developing a workable and truly global climate pact will require that Western negotiators transcend this cynical approach. Human psychology research has shown that when people feel taken advantage of, marginalized, powerless, angry, envious and spiteful, they are less likely to co-operate and more likely to engage in self-damaging behaviour. Political scientists have only recently begun to come to grips with the fact that inter-state relations may not be all that different. As Keohane (2001, 6) notes, '[c]ool practitioners of self-interest, known to be such, may be less able to cooperate productively than individuals who are governed by emotions that send reliable signals, such as love or reliability'.

We believe that rich countries need to build conditions of diffuse reciprocity and trust with poor countries before asking them to make costly policy com- mitments, and that the best way for them to do this is by launching a reassurance strategy through costly signals. Baer et al. (2008, 24) similarly suggest that 'there is only one alternative to continued impasse: a brief but relatively formal trust-building period [...] Regarding the North, anything less than explicit and legally-binding commitments—both to ambitiously pursue domestic reductions and to greatly scale up support for mitigation and adaptation in developing countries—would be seen as a failure to seriously invest in repairing the trust deficit'. We share this view and would add that during the early stages of a trust-building strategy it makes little sense to demand that the South adopt binding limits on their emissions. A more constructive approach would be to focus on so-called 'no-regrets' options and provide substantial financial assistance for voluntary mitigation efforts that are consistent with local development priorities. Policy 'sticks' like trade sanctions are also probably not the best way to build confidence in the early stages.[25]

Another costly signal would be the provision of adaptation assistance on a scale that is responsive to objective assessments of need.[26] Many negotiators and rational choice scholars believe that the wealthy countries should use environmental aid to either reward countries that demonstrate a credible commitment to reducing greenhouse gas emissions or provide an inducement for future co-operation. However, we would argue that this kind of textbook rational choice institutionalism, which assumes away weak conditions of reciprocity, generalized mistrust, and divergent world views and causal beliefs, is misguided. Environmental aid should also be used to build trust; signal confidence, solidarity, empathy and kindness to developing countries; and offer an attractive 'new thinking' about global environmental co-operation. While critics might dismiss adaptation aid as a mere palliative, or an irrational diversion of scarce resources needed to combat climate change, we would caution against making hard and fast distinctions between these two types of environmental aid. While mitigation assistance might have a direct impact on climate change, it does relatively little to address global inequality's longer-term corrosive effect on North–South environmental relations. Adaptation assistance will likely foster civic and co-operative norms and thus increase the willingness of poor countries to participate in a global climate accord.

Additionally, investments in and the dissemination of 'win-win' technologies that address local environmental issues and reduce greenhouse gas emissions would send a strong signal that, while solutions to climate change are urgently needed, wealthy, industrialized countries care about the social and economic circumstances of less developed countries. For example, and modestly, a large-scale plan to distribute clean stove technologies would help 'Annex I' countries demonstrate that climate change can be addressed while also tackling urgent human health issues in developing countries.[27] Investments in other 'brown' environmental issues, like clean water, sanitation, land degradation and urban air pollution, would also exert a positive impact on conditions of mutual trust.[28]

Finally, as we have argued elsewhere, sometimes trust-building is also about exercising strategic restraint (Roberts and Parks 2007). One of the most important ways in which wealthy, industrialized countries could build trust with the global South would be to explicitly signal their concern for the 'structural obstacles' facing developing countries and aggressively support their interests and priorities across multiple international economic regimes. This type of strategy could be pursued by reining in Western agricultural subsidies, tariff escalation practices and the ongoing 'deep integration' and anti-industrial policy crusade, which collectively reinforce the structuralist perception that rich countries do not want poor countries to get rich the same way they did; creating a commodity support fund or some other institutional mechanism to insulate natural resource-reliant countries from exogenous shocks; abandoning international economic regimes that threaten the long-term interests of developing countries; and giving developing countries a greater stake in the governance structures of international financial institutions. In this final analysis, this type of trust-building strategy could prove more important than the actual design features of a future climate agreement (e.g. banking and borrowing provisions, safety valves, linkages to trade policy, a reformed CDM).[29]

To conclude, climate change is fundamentally an issue of inequality and its resolution will likely demand an unconventional policy approach. We need a global and just transition built on diffuse reciprocity, a climate of trust, negotiated justice and a shared vision of truly long-term co-operative action.

NOTES

1 There are, of course, a few noteworthy exceptions (see Chasek et al. 2006; Najam 2004; Müller 1999).

2 The IPCC 2007 report reflected some startling evidence that global average temperatures were increasing more quickly than earlier reports had concluded, and that several new worrisome vicious cycles were taking off sooner than expected. These included melting Arctic ice packs, which then allow more solar radiation to be absorbed than in the past, and melting permafrost, which releases huge amounts of methane and carbon dioxide.

3 The atmospheric concentration of carbon dioxide has already increased by almost 100 ppm—to roughly 385 ppm—over the 'pre-industrial' level (IPCC 2007).

4 Much of this growth is expected to occur among the so-called 'BRICs' (e.g. Brazil, Russia, India and China).

5 Juliet Eilperin, 'Developing Nations Plan Emission Cuts; Shift Seen as Crucial to New Climate Pact', *Washington Post*, 12 December 2008, A10.

6 Ibid.

7 Peter N. Spotts, 'Trust tops global climate agenda', *Christian Science Monitor*, 1 December 2008.

8 The 'Bali Roadmap' identified a series of steps that might be taken to break the North–South impasse and avoid a 'gap' in the functioning of the Kyoto Protocol. In particular, a process under an Ad Hoc Working Group for Long-Term Cooperative Action under the Convention (AWG-LCA) was tasked with breaking the deadlock over who should act in cleaning up the atmosphere, and how. The answer, according to the Roadmap, was that developed and developing countries would move forward with 'a shared vision for long-term cooperative action, including a long-term global goal for emissions reductions, to achieve the ultimate objective of the Convention [avoiding dangerous climate change]'.

9 Juliet Eilperin, 'Developing Nations Plan Emission Cuts; Shift Seen as Crucial to New Climate Pact', *Washington Post*, 12 December 2008, A10. We would point out that rather than 50 it is 40 years from now until 2050, but the point holds.

10 www.boxxet.com/Climate_change/On:UNFCCC. Among the many proposals that developing country representatives brought to Poznań, Brazil indicated that it would be willing to reduce its annual deforestation rate by 70% within 10 years and South Africa floated a plan to cap emissions by 2025 and substantially reduce emissions by 2035.

11 The 'grandfathering' approach enjoyed the support of most developed countries that agreed to binding limits on their emissions under the Kyoto Protocol. The carbon intensity approach, introduced by the World Resources Institute, was supported by the George W. Bush Administration in the USA. Finally, Brazil has long advocated the 'historical responsibility' approach, while India, the People's Republic of China and much of the rest of the developing world support a per capita approach.

12 As Sprinz and Vaahtoranta (1994, 79) note, one obvious implication of rational choice theory is that 'the worse the state of the environment, the greater the incentives to reduce the ecological vulnerability of the state'. Also see Roberts et al. 2004.

13 Najam 1995, 2004. During the COP-14 negotiations, a member of the Prime Minister of India's Council on Climate Change noted that '[e]ven now, millions of poor people in developing countries are losing their homes, their livelihoods, and their lives from impacts of climate change [...] In the face of the unbearable human tragedy that we in developing countries see unfolding every day, we see callousness, strategizing and obfuscation'. See Ramesh Jaura, 'Climate Change: Poznan Produces a "Vision Gap"', *IPS News*, 13 December 2008, ipsnews.net/print.asp?idnews = 45103.

14 These concerns about the knock-on effects of perceived marginalization and anger are not new. Some 15 years ago, Young noted that '[s]ome northerners may doubt the credibility of [threats from southern nations to damage the global climate] and advocate a bargaining strategy that offers few concessions to the developing countries. But such a strategy is exceedingly risky. Many of those located in developing countries are increasingly angry and desperate [...] Faced with this prospect, northerners will ignore the demands of the South regarding climate change at their peril' (Young 1994, 50).

15 The most prominent example of this is support for Clean Development Mechanism (CDM) projects, which allow industrialized countries to meet their commitments under the Kyoto Protocol by bankrolling emission-reducing activities in developing countries.

16 Baer et al. (2008, 24) point out that 'the South's distrust is rooted in the North's repeated failure to meet its UNFCCC and Kyoto commitments to provide technological and financial support for both mitigation and adaptation, and beyond these, its protracted history of bad-faith negotiations in all sorts of other multilateral regimes (the trade and intellectual property negotiations come particularly to mind)'.

17 Causal beliefs are 'beliefs about cause-effect relationships which derive authority from the shared consensus of recognized elites' (Goldstein and Keohane 1993, 9–10).

18 Najam 1995, 2004.

19 Through the lens of a structuralist, the international system is characterized by a division of labour. There is a global stratification system that places nations on the top, in the middle or on the bottom, and only a few manage to move up. Nations can move up or down the hierarchy, but the structure largely remains unchanged (Roberts and Parks 2007).

20 Najam 1995, 258; Porter et al. 2000; Baumert et al. (2003: 21) rightly note that 'achieving an internationally acceptable differentiation of greenhouse gas

commitments is not just a matter of agreeing on equity principles. Countries may hold fundamentally different world views on climate change encompassing very different notions about the urgency of climate protection and the nature of appropriate management strategies'.

21 Raúl Estrada-Oyuela, one of the leading climate negotiators at Kyoto, noted that 'equity is the fundamental condition to ensure compliance of any international agreement' (Estrada-Oyuela 2002, 37).

22 The standard narrative about trust and co-operation among rational choice scholars is that rational individuals value trust for its instrumental worth. Therefore, building trust is only a means to an end. However, this 'strategic trust' narrative seriously underestimates the importance of 'moralistic trust'. As Uslaner (2003, 2) explains, '[t]rust in other people is based upon a fundamental *ethical* assumption: that other people share your fundamental values. They don't necessarily agree with you politically or religiously. But at some fundamental level, people accept the argument that they have common bonds that make cooperation vital'. For more on the contested social capital literature, see Fine 2001; Fox 1997; Swain 2003.

23 This point is increasingly recognized by scholars and policy-makers. Blanchard et al. note that 'any future burden-sharing agreement involving developing countries will probably be based on a complex differentiation scheme combining different basic rules' (Blanchard et al. 2003, 286).

24 Benedick 2001. On the Kyoto Protocol's 'compliance committee', see Ott 2001.

25 During the COP-13 negotiations in Bali, the G-77 Chair reported that several industrialized countries had threatened trade sanctions if developing countries were unwilling to take on commitments to reduce their emissions. Not surprisingly, this approach elicited a negative response and reinforced the perception that the global North is more interested in limiting the South's economic development than reducing global greenhouse gas emissions. See www.opendemocracy.net/global_deal/g77_threats.

26 According to the latest UNFCCC estimates, by 2030, $100 billion a year will be needed to finance mitigation activities and $28–$67 billion a year to finance adaptation activities in the developing world. Oxfam has put the cost at $50 billion a year and created an 'Adaptation Financing Index' to provide a rough sense of who should pay how much based on the 'common but differentiated responsibilities and respective capabilities' principle. See www.oxfam.org/files/adapting%20to%20climate%20change.pdf.

27 Household use of solid fuels is a leading cause of mortality and morbidity in the developing world. Every year, approximately 2m. people die unnecessarily from exposure to stove smoke inside their home. With modest investments, such diseases are preventable (Hicks et al. 2008). Widespread dissemination of clean stove technologies would also have a significant impact on global greenhouse gas emissions. As Jorgenson (2006) points out, 'methane emissions are the second largest overall human generated contributor to global warming, and [… w]hile atmospheric carbon dioxide is two hundred times more plentiful than atmospheric methane, molecule-for-molecule methane is ten times more effective at absorbing and reradiating infrared energy and heat back to the earth's surface, which impacts global warming'.

28 Typically, developing countries are more interested in addressing local environmental issues than the regional and global problems that wealthy donor countries want them to address. Rich donor countries are, then, often in the difficult business of 'persuad[ing] recipient countries […] to take the environmental actions of [lowest] priority to them' (Connolly 1996, 330; see Hicks et al. 2008). As we describe in greater detail in Roberts and Parks (2007), this overriding concern for 'First World environmental issues' has proven rather costly. Specifically, it has limited the North's ability to signal solidarity, empathy and kindness, and rebuild conditions of mutual trust.

29 According to seasoned analyst Herman Ott and others, 'it became clear [at COP-8 in New Delhi] that developing countries would not give up their "right" for increasing emissions without serious concessions in other fields of the development agenda which satisfy the demand for global equity and poverty reduction' (Ott et al. 2004, 261).

REFERENCES

Abbott, K. and D. Snidal (2000) 'Hard and soft law in international governance', *International Organization* 54:3, 421–56.

Albin, C. (2001) *Justice and Fairness in International Negotiation*, Cambridge: Cambridge University Press.

Athanasiou, T. and P. Baer (2002) *Dead heat: global justice and global warming*, New York: Seven Stories Press.

Baer, P., T. Athanasiou, S. Kartha and E. Kemp-Benedict (2008) 'The Greenhouse Development Rights Framework: The right to development in a climate constrained world', revised second edn, Berlin: Heinrich Böll Foundation, Christian Aid, EcoEquity and the Stockholm Environment Institute.

Barrett, S. (2003) *Environment and Statecraft: the Strategy of Environmental Treaty-Making*, Oxford: Oxford University Press.

Bartsch, U. and B. Müller (2000) *Fossil fuels in a changing climate: impacts of the Kyoto Protocol and developing country participation*, Oxford: Oxford University Press.

Baumert, K.A. (ed.) (2002) *Building on the Kyoto Protocol: Options for Protecting the Climate*, Washington, DC: World Resources Institute.

Baumert, K.A. and N. Kete (2002) 'An architecture for climate protection', in Kevin Baumert (ed.) *Building on the Kyoto Protocol: options for protecting the climate*, Washington, DC: World Resources Institute, 1–30.

Baumert, K.A., J.F. Perkaus and N. Kete (2003) 'Great expectations: can international emissions trading deliver an equitable climate regime?', *Climate Policy* 3 (2), 137–48.

Benedick, R. E. (2001) 'Striking a New Deal on Climate Change', *Issues in Science and Technology Online* (Fall), 71–76.

Birdsall, N., D. Rodrik and A. Subramanian (2005) 'If rich governments really cared about development', Working Paper, International Centre for Trade and Sustainable Development, Geneva.

Blanchard O., P. Criqui, A. Kitous and L. Viguier (2003) 'Combining Efficiency With Equity: A Pragmatic Approach', in I. Kaul, P. Conceicao, K.I. Le Goulven and R. U. Mendoza (eds), *Providing Global Public Goods: Managing Globalization*, New York, NY: Oxford University Press.

Carraro, C. and D. Siniscalco (1993) 'Strategies for the international protection of the environment', *Journal of Public Economics* 52:3, 309–28.

Chasek, P., D. Downie and J. Welsh Brown (2006) *Global environmental politics*, 4th edn, Boulder, CO: Westview Press.

Claussen, E. and L. McNeilly (1998) *Equity and global climate change: the complex elements of fairness*, Arlington, VA: Pew Center on Climate Change.

Connolly, B. (1996) 'Increments for the Earth: The Politics of Environmental Aid', in R.O. Keohane and M.A. Levy (eds), *Institutions for Environmental Aid*, Cambridge, MA: MIT Press, 327–65.

Depledge, J. (2002) 'Continuing Kyoto: extending absolute emission caps to developing countries', in Kevin Baumert (ed.) *Building on the Kyoto Protocol: options for protecting the climate*, Washington, DC: World Resources Institute, 31–60.

DeSombre, E.R. and J. Kaufman (1996) 'The Montreal Protocol Multilateral Fund: partial success story', in R.O. Keohane and M.A. Levy (eds), *Institutions for environmental aid: pitfalls and promise*, Cambridge, MA: MIT Press, 89–126.

Durkheim, E. (1933 [1893]) *On the Division of Labor in Society*, translated by G. Simpson, New York: Macmillan.

Easterly, W. (2001) 'The middle class consensus and economic development', *Journal of Economic Growth* 6:4, 317–35.

Economic Times (2008) 'China tells developed world to go on climate change "diet"', 12 March.

Estrada-Oyuela, R.A. (2002) 'Equity and climate change', in L. Pinguelli-Rosa and M. Munasinghe (eds), *Ethics, Equity and International Negotiations on Climate Change*, Cheltenham: Edward Elgar Publishing, 36–46.

European Union (2008) 'Climate change and international security', paper from the High Representative and the European Commission to the European Council, Brussels, 14 March 2008.

Fine, B. (2001) *Social Capital versus Social Theory: Political Economy and Social Science at the Turn of the Millennium*, London: Routledge.

Ford, P. (2007) 'China balks at emissions caps', *The Christian Science Monitor* 5 June.

Fox, J. A. (1997) 'The World Bank and Social Capital: Contesting the Concept in Practice', *Journal of International Development* 9 (7), 963–71.

Goddard Institute for Space Studies (2008) 'Global temperature anomalies in .01 C', data.giss.nasa.gov/gistemp/tabledata/GLB.Ts.txt (accessed 10 July 2008).

Goldstein, J. and R. Keohane (eds) (1993) *Ideas and foreign policy: beliefs, institutions, and political change*, Ithaca, NY: Cornell University Press.

Graham, E.M. (1996) 'Direct Investment and the Future Agenda of the World Trade Organization', in J.J. Schott (ed.), *The World Trading System: Challenges Ahead*, Washington, DC: Institute for International Economics, 205–17.

Green, D. (2008) *From Poverty to Power: How Active Citizens and Effective States Can Change the World*, Oxford: Oxfam International.

Groenenberg, H., D. Phylipsen and K. Blok (2001) 'Differentiating commitments world wide: global differentiation of GHG emissions reductions based on the Triptych approach-a preliminary assessment', *Energy Policy* 29:12, 1,007–30.

Gruber, L. (2000) *Ruling the world: power politics and the rise of supranational institutions*, Princeton, NJ: Princeton University Press.

Gupta, J. (1997) *The Climate Change Convention and Developing Countries: From Conflict to Consensus?*, Dordrecht, Netherlands: Kluwer Academic Publishers.

——(2000) *'On behalf of my delegation … ': a survival guide for developing country climate negotiators*, Washington, DC: Center for Sustainable Development in the Americas.

Gupta, S. and P.M. Bhandari (1999) 'An effective allocation criterion for CO_2 emissions', *Energy Policy* 27:12, 727–36.

Haas, P.M. (1990) *Saving the Mediterranean: The Politics of International Environmental Cooperation*, New York: Columbia University Press.

Haas, P.M., R.O. Keohane and M.A. Levy (eds) (1993) *Institutions for the Earth: Sources of Effective International Environmental Protection*, Cambridge, MA: The MIT Press.

Heil, M.T. and T.M. Selden (2001) 'International trade intensity and carbon emissions: a cross-country econometric analysis', *Journal of Environment and Development* 10:1, 35–49.

Hicks, R.L., Bradley C. Parks, J. Timmons Roberts and M.J. Tierney (2008) *Greening aid? Understanding the environmental impact of development assistance*, Oxford: Oxford University Press.

Hultman, N.E., E. Boyd, E. Corbera, D. Liverman, J. Ebeling and K. Brown (2009) 'How can the Clean Development Mechanism better contribute to sustainable development?' *Ambio* 38(2), 120–22.

IPCC (2007) *Climate change 2007: fourth assessment report of the Intergovernmental Panel on Climate Change*, Cambridge: Cambridge University Press.

Jorgenson, A.K. (2006) 'Global Warming and the Neglected Greenhouse Gas: A Cross-National Study of Methane Emissions Intensity, 1995', *Social Forces* 84, 1,777–96.

Kaul, I., I. Grunberg and M. Stern (1999) 'Defining global public goods', in I. Kaul, I. Grunberg and M. Stern (eds), *Global public goods: international cooperation in the 21st century*, Oxford: Oxford University Press, 2–19.

Keck, M. and K. Sikkink (1998) *Activists Beyond Borders: Advocacy Networks in International Politics*, Ithaca, NY: Cornell University Press.

Keohane, Robert (1984) *After hegemony: cooperation and discord in the world political economy*, Princeton, NJ: Princeton University Press.

——(1986) 'Reciprocity in International Relations', *International Organization* 40 (1), 1–27.

——(2001) 'Governance in a partially globalized world', *American Political Science Review* 95:1, 1–13.

Keohane, R. and M.A. Levy (eds) (1996) *Institutions for environmental aid: pitfalls and promise*, Cambridge, MA: MIT Press.

Knack, S. and P. Keefer (1997) 'Does social capital have an economic payoff? A cross-country investigation', *Quarterly Journal of Economics* 112:4, 1,251–88.

Knight, D. (1998) 'Environment: In Defence of Developing Nations', *IPS News*, 27 October, www.sunsonline.org/trade/process/followup/1998/10270498.htm.

Krasner, S. (1978) 'United States commercial and monetary policy: unraveling the paradox of external strength and internal weakness', in P.J. Katzenstein (ed.), *Between power and plenty: foreign economic policies of advanced industrial states*, Madison, WI: University of Wisconsin Press, 51–87.

——(1985) *Structural conflict: the third world against global liberalism*, Berkeley, CA: University of California Press.

Kydd, A. (2000) 'Trust, reassurance, and cooperation', *International Organization* 54:2, 325–57.

Levy, D.L. and A. Kolk (2002) 'Strategic Responses to Global Climate Change: Conflicting Pressures on Multinationals in the Oil Industry', *Business and Politics* 4 (3), 275–300.

Machado, G., R. Schaeffer and E. Worrell (2001) 'Energy and carbon embodied in the international trade of Brazil: an input-output approach', *Ecological Economics* 39:3, 409–24.

Mathur, A., I. Burton and M. van Aalst (eds) (2004) *An adaptation mosaic: a sample of the emerging World Bank work in climate change adaptation*, Washington, DC: World Bank.

Mearsheimer, J.J. (1994/95) 'The false promise of international institutions', *International Security* 19:3, 5–49.

Meyer, J.W., D. J. Frank, A. Hironaka, E. Schofer and N. Brandon Tuma (1997) 'The Structuring of a World Environmental Regime, 1870–1990', *International Organization* 51 (4), 623–29.

Mitchell, R. and P.M. Keilbach (2001) 'Situation structure and institutional design: Reciprocity, coercion, and exchange', *International Organization* 55 (4), 891–917.

Müller, B. (1999) *Justice in global warming negotiations: how to obtain a procedurally fair compromise*, Oxford: Oxford Institute for Energy Studies.

——(2001) 'Fair compromise in a morally complex world', paper presented at Pew Equity Conference, Washington, DC, 17–18 April.

Muradian, Roldan, Martin O'Connor and Joan Martinez-Alier (2002) 'Embodied pollution in trade: estimating the "environmental load displacement" of industrialized countries', *Ecological Economics* 41:1, 51–67.

Najam, A. (1995) 'International environmental negotiations: a strategy for the South', *International Environmental Affairs* 7:2, 249–87.

——(2003) 'The Case Against a New International Environmental Organization', *Global Governance* 9, 367–84.

——(2004) 'The view from the South: developing countries in global environmental politics', in Regina Axelrod, David Downie and Norman Vig (eds), *The global environment: institutions, law, and policy*, 2nd edn, Washington, DC: CQ Press, 225–43.

Ott, H.E. (2001) 'The Bonn Agreement to the Kyoto Protocol – Paving the Way for Ratification', *International Environmental Agreements: Politics, Law and Economics* 1 (4), 469–76.

——(2004) 'Global climate', in *Yearbook of international environmental law* 12, 261–70.

Porter, G. and J.W. Brown (1991) *Global environmental politics*, Boulder, CO: Westview Press.

Porter, G., J. Welsh Brown and P. Chasek (2000) *Global Environmental Politics*, Boulder, CO: Westview Press.

Putnam, R.D. (1993) *Making democracy work*, Princeton, NJ: Princeton University Press.

——(2000) *Bowling Alone: The Collapse and Revival of American Community*, New York: Simon and Schuster.

Ringus, L., A. Torvanger and A. Underdal (2002) 'Burden sharing and fairness principles in international climate policy', *International Environmental Agreements: Politics, Law and Economics* 2:1, 1–22.

Roberts, J. Timmons and B.C. Parks (2007) *A climate of injustice: global inequality, North–South politics, and climate policy*, Cambridge, MA: MIT Press.

Roberts, J. Timmons, B.C. Parks and A.A. Vásquez (2004) 'Who Ratifies Environmental Treaties and Why? Institutionalism, Structuralism and Participation by 192 Nations in 22 Treaties', *Global Environmental Politics* 4:3, 22–64.

Ruggie, J.G. (1983) 'Political Structure and Change in the International Economic Order: The North–South Dimension', in John Gerard Ruggie (ed.), *The Antinomies of Interdependence*, New York: Columbia University Press, 423–87.

Sandbrook, R. (1997) 'UNGASS has run out of steam', *International Affairs* 73, 641–54.

Sari, A. (2003) 'CoP-9 in Milan: a fashionable trend for climate agreements', Centre for Science and Environment, www.cseindia.org/campaign/ew/agreements.htm (accessed 10 July 2008).

Sebenius, J.K. (1991) 'Designing Negotiations Towards a New Regime: The Case of Global Warming', *International Security* 15:4, 110–48.

Sell, S. (1996) 'North-South environmental bargaining: ozone, climate change, and biodiversity', *Global Governance* 2:1, 97–118.

Shadlen, K. (2004) 'Patents and pills, power and procedure: the North–South politics of public health in the WTO', *Studies in Comparative International Development* 39:3, 76–108.

Sijm, J.P.M., J.C. Jansen, J.J. Battjes, C.H. Volkers and J.R. Ybema (2000) *The multi-sector convergence approach of burden sharing: an analysis of its cost implications*, Oslo: Center for International Climate and Environmental Research.

Sprinz, D. and T. Vaahtoranta (1994) 'The interest-based explanation of international environmental policy', *International Organization* 48:1, 77–105.

Stavins, R. (2004) *Can an Effective Global Climate Treaty be Based Upon Sound Science, Rational Economics, and Pragmatic Politics?* Cambridge, MA: KSG Faculty Research Working Paper Series RWP04–020.

Stavins, R. and S. M. Olmstead (2006) 'An international policy architecture for the post-Kyoto era', *American Economic Review Papers and Proceedings* 96:2, 35–38.

Stein, A. (1990) *Why nations cooperate: circumstance and choice in international relations*, Ithaca, NY: Cornell University Press.

Swain, N. (2003) 'Social Capital and its Uses', *Archives Européennes de Sociologie* 44 (2), 185–212.

Torvanger, A. and O. Godal (2004) 'An evaluation of pre-Kyoto differentiation proposals for national greenhouse gas abatement targets', *International Environmental Agreements: Politics, Law and Economics* 4:1, 65–91.

UNFCCC (1992) 'United Nations Framework Convention on Climate Change', New York: United Nations, unfccc.int/resource/docs/convkp/conveng.pdf (accessed 10 July 2008).

Uslaner, Eric (2003) *The Moral Foundations of Trust*, Cambridge: Cambridge University Press.

Victor, D. (2001) *The collapse of the Kyoto protocol and the struggle to slow global warming*, Princeton, NJ: Princeton University Press.

Wade, R. (2003) 'What strategies are viable for developing countries today? The World Trade Organization and the shrinking of development space', *Review of International Political Economy* 10:4, 627–44.

Waltz, K. (1979) *Theory of international politics*, New York: Random House.

Wapner, Paul (1995) 'Politics Beyond the State: Environmental Activism and World Civic Politics', *World Politics* 47 (April), 311–40.

Wheeler, D. and K. Ummel (2007) 'Another inconvenient truth: a carbon-intensive South faces environmental disaster no matter what the North does', Working Paper Number 134, Washington, DC: Center for Global Development.

Wiegandt, E. (2001) 'Climate change, equity, and international negotiations', in U. Luterbacher Detlef Sprinz (ed.), *International Relations and Global Climate Change*, Cambridge: MIT Press, 127–50.

Woods, N. (1999) 'Good governance in international organizations', *Global Governance* 5:1, 36–61.

Ybema, J.R., J. J. Battjes, Jaap C. Jansen and Frank Ormel (2000) *Burden differentiation: GHG emissions, undercurrents and mitigation costs*, Oslo: Center for International Climate and Environmental Research.

Young, O.R. (1994) *International governance: protecting the environment in a stateless society*, Ithaca, NY: Cornell University Press.

Cultural Politics of Climate Change: Interactions in Everyday Spaces

MAXWELL T. BOYKOFF, MICHAEL K. GOODMAN
AND IAN CURTIS

INTRODUCTION

In this chapter, we connect the more formal spaces of climate science, policy and politics operating at multiple scales to those of the spaces of the 'everyday'. Climate change is a high-stakes, high-profile and highly politicized issue that relates—often in messy, non-linear and diffuse ways—to people's everyday lives, lifestyles and livelihoods. It is no longer thought of merely as scientific issue; rather, the 'climate question' is considered one that now, more than ever, permeates our individual, as well as shared, economic, political, cultural and social lives. Through a brief accounting of these interactions, we explore some interesting and notable spaces comprising what we see as the emerging *cultural politics of climate change* at the scale of the everyday discourses, representations and 'popular' cultures that work to engage society.

By cultural politics we mean those oft-contested and politicized processes by which meaning is constructed and negotiated across space, place and at various scales. This involves not only the representations and messages that gain traction in discourses, but also those that are absent from them or silenced (Derrida 1978; Dalby 2007). In these spaces, discourses are tethered to positionalities, material realities and social practices (Hall 1997). As David Harvey has commented, '*struggles over representation* are as fundamental to the activities of place construction as bricks and mortar' (1990, 422, emphasis added). By examining these features as manifestations of ongoing and contested processes, we can consider questions regarding how power flows through the capillaries of our shared social, cultural and political body, constructing knowledge, norms, conventions, truths and untruths (Foucault 1980). Such dynamic interactions form nexuses of power-knowledge that shape how we come to understand things *as* 'truth' and 'reality' and, in turn, contribute to managing the conditions and tactics of our social lives (de Certeau 1984). However, rather than brash imposition of law or direct disciplinary techniques, we consider how more subtle power-knowledge regimes in, for example, the likes of the arts, sports and celebrities, permeate and create what becomes 'permissible' and 'normal' as well as 'desired' in everyday discourses, practices and institutional processes (Foucault 1977).

Specifically here, the discursive and material elements comprising a cultural politics of climate change are inextricably shaped by ongoing environmental processes and those of the science of climate change. This has been described as the inseparable dialectic of nature and culture (Cosgrove 1983). Nature is not a backdrop upon which heterogeneous human actors contest and battle for epistemological and material successes. Rather, (scientific) meaning is constructed, maintained and contested through intertwined socio-political and bio-physical processes (Blaikie 1985; Whatmore 2002). Meaning is con-structed and manifested through *both* the ontological conditions of nature and contingent social and political processes involved in interpretations of this nature in the processes and politics of science (Robbins 2004). Approaching these spaces of the cultural politics of climate change in this way helps to interrogate 'how social and political framings are woven into both the formulation of scientific explanations of environmental problems, and the solutions proposed to reduce them' (Forsyth 2003, 1). These 'framings', then, are inherent to cognition, and effectively contextualize as well as 'fix' inter-pretive categories in order to help explain and describe the complex environ-mental processes of climate change (e.g. Robbins 2001). Thus, particular framings serve to assemble and privilege certain interpretations and under-standings over others (Goffman 1974; Entman 1993) and this has certainly been the case with the highly-charged discourses surrounding climate change.

Given the increasingly obvious societal attention to the urgencies of climate change, it might not be a surprise that the discourses and associated praxis of 'dealing' with climate change have so rapidly filtered into the spaces of the everyday. Rather, what is surprising is how widespread and indeed 'main-streamed' the discourses of climate change are at this particular moment. Indeed, through all sorts of media forms—from newspapers and books, to television and films, to radio and the internet—a diverse groundswell of actors and institutions are bringing climate change 'home' (Slocum 2004) by encouraging us to change and improve daily routines, practices and lifestyles that impact the global climate. The Live Earth slogan of 'One world, One climate, Be the change' has at its base the desire to primarily motivate *indi-viduals* to do 'something' for the climate in their daily lives. Here, the instal-lation of compact-fluorescent light bulbs in one's house or at work has become *the* most iconic of 'somethings' to do (see Hobson 2006; Slocum 2004); this is taken up further below.

Many climate change campaigns see the everyday much as it perhaps should be seen: 'there is nothing "natural" or "inevitable" about everyday life [...] it reveals itself as complex and processual rather than simple and reified' (Paterson 2006, 7). Indeed, it might be argued that this is *precisely* why these campaigns have focused on the spaces and praxis of the everyday and, in combination, why they have moved so heavily into the realms of popular culture like MTV, which are predominantly designed to shift consumer con-sumption behaviours towards more sustainable ends. In regards to ethical consumption—a subset of the broader category of sustainable consumption

(Hinton and Goodman, forthcoming)—Clarke et al. have commented, '[e]thical consumption campaigning redefines everyday consumption as a realm through which consumers can express a wide range of concerns and engage in a broad set of projects, including social justice, human rights, development or environmental sustainability' (2007, 241). Yet, several critical issues stand out—*especially* with respect to climate change—in not only what gets defined and constructed as the 'right' or 'moral' actions to take or the scale at which they are pitched, but in how these campaigns are put together and enter the public realms of cultural politics.

As above, these discourses construct their own power-knowledge regimes that can, perhaps, be critically assessed: Why the massive focus on switching over light bulbs rather than some other activity? Why not no/less consumption rather than different consumption in its green/ethical forms? For example, why not *no* car instead of a hybrid car? More generally, why is consumption elevated and entrenched—now, in academic work as much as any other media—as the axis of engagement concerning climate change for civil society? Where might more fundamental structural changes lie in this and other discourses and narratives on sustainable and ethical consumption? In short, there is theoretical/conceptual as well as empirical/material need to consider the political economic realities that not only construct people's everyday lives through (very often unequal) material and structural relationships, but, in particular here, the 'everyday' inequalities many experience in their access, understanding and abilities to respond to climate change campaigns.

If anything, the cultural politics of climate change are rife with ambiguities and ambivalences, conflicts and contradictions that complicate not only their actual material and 'real' effectiveness, but their role in doing that 'something' for the climate. For instance, communicating climate change through popular culture—celebrities, movies, popular music—can easily work to sensationalize the issues and act as distractions as much as it can bring in new 'eyes' and 'ears' to the salient issues. Making climate change an everyday, individualized issue—e.g. 'Be the change'—can, on the one hand, empower individuals and create and foster emergent movements through these 'singularities' (Clarke et al. 2007), but at the same time it can work to unfairly 'responsibilize' (Guthman 2007) and socialize climate change problems and solutions at the level of the individual and consumers at the expense of holding states, institutions and corporations accountable. Individualization can work to simultaneously atomize social, economic and environmental changes and movements at the same time it might open up space for the development of a more 'cosmopolitan ethic' (Popke 2006, 2009) by suggesting that by 'being the change', individuals/consumers are connecting to and creating a 'better' planet. Given that shifting to more 'climate neutral' consumption—e.g. 'low carbon'/meatless diets, hybrid cars, the purchase and installation of fluorescent light bulbs—is what is very often recommended, it is argued that it is through these acts of more sustainable consumption choice that this cosmopolitanism and/or 'ecological citizenship' can be enacted on an everyday basis (i.e. Seyfang

2005; see also Sassatelli 2006). Thus, for better or worse, the figure of the globalized climate change 'consumer-citizen' can seemingly be created, fostered and furthered through a simple trip to the shopping mall, local store and/or supermarket, attendance at a football game, or by just flicking off (or on as the case may be) the television.

Below we explore how, in the development of the cultural politics of climate change, the spaces, places and processes of the everyday are increasingly powerful and transgressive—yet also fundamentally ambiguous and problematic—in the discourses and materialities that surround climate change and its highly politicized amelioration. We first touch on some contemporary turns in the realms of businesses and environmental non-governmental organizations (ENGOs). We then address the burgeoning arenas where popular culture—particularly through the arts, music, film and sport—has taken up climate challenges and opportunities for engagement with much wider 'audiences' than heretofore. Given the confined spaces of this book chapter, we have limited ourselves to select examples that we find help illuminate how cultural politics are engaging with climate change politics in a range of interactive, uncertain and potentially fraught ways.

WHO SPEAKS FOR THE CLIMATE, NOW?

The cultural politics of climate change construct and exist in a multitude of rapidly expanding spaces. A prominent link between these spaces is mass media, from entertainment to news, the representations of climate change shaping perceptions and considerations for action. In the last decade, there has been a significant expansion from consumption of traditional mass media—broadcast television, newspapers, radio—into consumption of 'new media', such as the internet and mobile phone communications. This movement has signalled substantive changes in how people access and interact with information, who has access, and who these '"authorized definers" of climate change' are (Carvalho 2007, 232). In tandem with technological advances, these communications are seen to be a fundamental shift from 'one to many' (i.e. one-way) communications to 'many to many' (i.e. more interactive webs of communications). Together, these media are constituted by a diverse and dynamic set of institutions, processes and practices that together serve as 'mediating' forces between communities such as science, policy and public citizens. Members of the communications industry and profession—publishers, editors, journalists and others—produce, interpret and communicate images, information and imaginaries for varied forms of media consumption. Thus, the reporting and communication of climate change science and policy, *in particular*, is not just the innocent reporting of scientific 'facts' and 'truths' (Boykoff and Boykoff 2004; McChesney 2008).

By way of numerous tributaries (outlined by Heike Schroeder, Chapter 2), climate science and governance has flowed into public view with significant attention through mass media since the 1980s (Carvalho and Burgess 2005).

A number of key factors contributed to this trend. Amongst them was NASA scientist James Hansen's testimony to the US Congress in the summer of 1988, during the time of an intense heatwave and drought across North America. Also, in the United Kingdom, Prime Minister Margaret Thatcher spoke to the Royal Society in what became known as her 'green speech' on the dangers of climate change. Meanwhile, early climate governance became operational as a 46-country climate conference took place in Toronto, Canada and the United Nations Intergovernmental Panel on Climate Change (IPCC) began its work. These high-profile interventions-turned-spectacles generated substantial attention and became emblems for newfound public concern on the issue (Boykoff and Boykoff 2007). As this issue first unfolded in the public sphere, climate scientists were widely canvassed as the pre-dominant 'claims makers'. Yet, in addition to climate science 'speaking' on behalf of the climate, carbon-based business and industry interests and ENGOs grappled for their particular discursive and material 'locations' from which to address climate challenges. Many of the struggles to represent climate change in the 1980s and 1990s were dominated by carbon-based energy businesses and ENGOs (Gottlieb 2002). Here, then, in the process of understanding changes in the climate, many entities, organizations, interests and individuals battled to shape not only the science but fundamentally the awareness, engagement and possible actions around the climate agenda. Indeed, as John Street (2004, 445) has commented on the growing connections between politics and popular culture, '[re]presentation, whatever the principles or ethical values informing it, does not reflect the world so much as organize knowledge about it', and, as we might add here, it does so in very politicized and politicizing ways.

From early on, the variously embattled efforts to define the 'climate ques-tion' and frame the problems, predicaments and possibilities have expanded to today's tremendous variety of 'actors', (everyday) actions and numerous media forms. Subsequent to the 18th-century English-led Industrial Revolu-tion and its 'dark satanic mills', 'progress' has often been defined by the carbon-based technological advancements driven by the engines of coal, oil and natural gas. Yet, beginning even in the late 1800s, scientists such as Svante Arrhenius, G.S. Callendar, Gilbert Plass and others began making links between greenhouse gas (GHG) emissions from energy production and increases in atmospheric temperature as well as other climatic changes (Weart 2003). As further and extensive scientific work coalesced on basic points that the climate was changing and that humans played a part in such changes, early actors responded to these findings. In terms of business, some adapted and changed practices, while others called such research into question. Meanwhile, many ENGOs—such as Greenpeace, Friends of the Earth, Oxfam and the Natural Resources Defense Council—sought to raise public awareness and policy-actor concern regarding 'negative externalities' of environmental damage and risk from climate change. On this dynamic battle-field of competing knowledges and representations, predominantly US-based think tanks influenced by conservative ideologies—and often funded by the carbon-based industry–amplified uncertainties regarding various aspects of climate science, de-emphasized the human contribution to climate change, and called attention to the costs of action, such as mode-switching to renewable energy sources. These messages were repeated in multifarious ways, through subtle scientific 'certainty' argumentation methods (Freudenburg et al. 2008) to more deliberate politics of manipulation (McCright and Dunlap 2003; Oreskes et al. 2008) to overtly deceptive disinformation campaigns and initiatives (Gelbspan 1998; Beder 2002). In turn, these controversial narratives and media campaigns have been found to not only dampen social movements for change (e.g. Norgaard 2006), but to also inspire and catalyze (e.g. Moser and Dilling 2007) action in the realms of environmental politics and movements, from the more 'mainstream' efforts of large ENGOs to more grassroots, direct-action efforts such as the 'performance spaces' of Climate Camp based in the United Kingdom (see climatecamp.org.uk) (see also Moser in Chapter 9).

In the last decade or so, questions raised across this spectrum have largely moved away from 'is the climate changing?' and 'do humans play a role in climate change?', to more textured considerations of how to effectively govern the mitigation and adaptation alternatives. While these newfound challenges have enrolled actors from other spaces such as popular culture, business groups, ideologically-driven think tanks and ENGOs have continued to vigorously debate and discuss associated features and consequences of climate mitigation. For example, as businesses have touted 'carbon neutrality' in their practices, some ENGOs have praised such activities as a first awareness-raising step towards ongoing decarbonization of industrial practices, while others have fiercely critiqued these claims as 'greenwashing' business-as-usual actions. Similar debates also hold for questions regarding 'voluntary carbon offsets' for carbon-unfriendly travel, carbon labelling of food and household products, movements towards 'low carbon diets' by purchasing local goods and the inherent paradoxes of calling on 'clean coal' technologies to reduce GHG emissions.

While these various initiatives and plans have gained traction in recent years in the everyday lives of many, important critiques have emerged regarding the dangers of an emergent 'carbon capitalism' associated with commodifying the atmosphere, and the fixation with market mechanisms as primary tools to 'answer' climate questions (Newell and Paterson, in Chapter 5). Indeed, these solutions have been deemed problematic to the extent that, at their core, these activities 'render the messy materiality of life legible as discrete entities, individuated and abstracted from the complex social and ecological integuments' (Prudham 2007, 414). Thus, in the rapidly-expanding, dominant market-oriented approaches of carbon capitalism (Bumpus and Liverman 2008), decarbonization is seemingly reduced to the simple matter of neoliberal (political) economy that, now more often than not, is defined by shifts in consumer choice and activism.

While carbon-based industry interests have consistently been pilloried for defending their political economic interests over social and environmental concerns, these landscapes have certainly become more nuanced in recent years across a range of scales and spaces. Examples include large-scale co-operative efforts such as the World Business Council for Sustainable Development, to more local initiatives such as the Energy4All wind farm co-operative in the United Kingdom. Another example of a local project is the Eco-Renovation initiative in Oxfordshire, England, which is a cross-sectoral community-based enterprise to promote significant low carbon refurbishment of local homes. Participants open their homes to the public on designated weekends to exhibit these re-designs, and thus demonstrate how local suppliers and installers have worked to reduce GHG emissions at the household level. This project links into a burgeoning array of organizations and initiatives throughout the region and illustrates the rapidly expanding engagement in the public sphere with climate change mitigation challenges.

While scientists, businesses and environmental groups have populated the discursive spaces of the climate change issue through mass media since the 1980s, there has emerged a broader spectrum of voices in recent years. This does not mean that scientists and others have 'stopped' speaking; rather, in the public sphere within which climate science and politics find meaning in our everyday lives, the boundaries between who constitutes an 'authorized' speaker (and who does not) has expanded (e.g. Gieryn 1999; Eden et al. 2006). In so doing, these spaces have been increasingly infiltrated by new 'actors' in the Shakespearian global stage; these influences have changed the architecture and processes propping up and perpetuating a cultural politics of climate change.

THE CLIMATE CHANGE CULTURE INDUSTRY

Sculpting, Crooning and Blogging for Change: Art, Movies, Music and the Web in Climate Change Debates

While some of the spaces comprising popular culture have been dismissed as mere distraction (e.g. Weiskel 2005), these can in fact be potent yet also fraught opportunities to reach places where many citizens reside, discursively, materially and cognitively. Herein lays the contested nature of these expanded interactions. As an example of these conflicts, at the November 2008 launch of his 'culture strategy', conservative London Mayor Boris Johnson embodied the promises and perils of such boundary work. In his remarks, Johnson argued that, 'arts chiefs must stop dumbing down culture for young people'. According to reporter Ian Drury (2008), 'the mayor of London pledged to stop targeting [young people] with hip-hop music and movies, and instead encourage them to enjoy opera and ballet'. Importantly, this raises questions regarding whether such channels of communication might reach people where they *are* or where others think they *should be*. Yet, more fundamentally, Johnson's comments highlight how political actors are prepared to wield and negotiate the contours of (popular) culture as a key means to various cultural and political economic ends, in this case to try to foster greater cultural awareness in the lead up to the London 2012 Olympics.

Today, many musicians, artists, athletes and actors are increasingly involved in climate change initiatives. Some have focused their energies in what has traditionally been characterized as 'high culture'. For example, London choreographer Siobhan Davies has developed the performance *Endangered Species* where semi-human forms perform inside museum display cases to evoke notions of fragility and survival. Similarly, British sculptor Antony Gormley worked with human images in ice to demonstrate the ephemeral nature of human existence as part of a Cape Farewell project and expedition. These activities have been associated with a wider project begun in 2005 entitled 'TippingPoints: A climate scientist and artist's encounter'. The TippingPoint initiative arose amongst practising artists, automotive designers and engineering academics. While these endeavours have met a great deal of critical acclaim, others have argued that they enjoy a relatively limited reach beyond 'high culture' and the traditional art form.

Other engagements in the cultural and political landscapes of climate change include those through more 'popular' forms of mass media. In particular, the 2006 release and success of the powerpoint-turned-documentary film 'An Inconvenient Truth' (hereafter AIT) featuring Al Gore has been an illustrative watershed moment in the shifting politics of climate change as they meet popular culture (cf. Luke 2008). Mass media around the planet analysed, commented on and reported various facets of the film, from the content and substantive issues the film raised, to its 'celebrity-meets-science' spectacle. In so doing, stories spanned straight news reporting to entertainment culture 'buzz' (Seabrook 2000), thereby further expanding the climate question into other transgressive spaces and places. For instance, in the *Washington Post*'s major coverage of the movie, a substantial article was produced for the Style section of the newspaper that reported on the red-carpet premiere in the USA without even a touch of irony or deviation from other movie premiere event reporting. Interestingly, movie-goer Jessica Simpson's 'black pantsuit, pearl earrings [and] hair tucked conservatively in a loose bun' (Argetsinger and Roberts 2006, C3) was elevated to a level of relevance on par with the film's depiction of the potentially cataclysmic environmental outcomes of climate change. Such past and current mass-media cross-pollenization contributed to the claim by 89% of AIT filmgoers that they became more aware of climate change causes and consequences, while 74% of this same group claimed they were taking action to address climate change as a direct result of viewing the movie (AC Nielsen 2007).

Further engagements are taking place in the 'convergence cultures' (Jenkins 2006) of music, television and the internet. Begun in earnest through the Al Gore-sponsored Live Earth concerts of 2007, musicians have begun to incorporate climate change-themed lyrics and images into their songs and videos. One of the most prominent in this regard would be Madonna, who not only released her single 'Hey You' to coincide with the Live Earth climate change 'event', but has continued on this theme with '4 Minutes to Save the World' which includes contributions by the enormously popular Justin Timberlake and Timbaland.

More specifically, Madonna's songs contribute directly to some of the ambiguities circulating in these everyday discourses and representations of climate change. On the one hand, both work to inscribe the individualism, personalization and responsibilism of much of the climate change discourse into the lyrics: 'Hey You' is peppered with the refrains (amongst others) of:

Hey you, don't you give up
It's not so bad, there's still a chance for us ...
Hey you, open your heart
It's not so strange,
You've got to change this time.

The song—spliced with the performers jumping in and out of old cars surrounded by supermarket shelves and a clock ticking down in the background—continues with:

We only got four minutes, huh, four minutes,
So keep it up, keep it up, don't be afraid,
You gotta get 'em a heart,
Tick tock tick tock tick tock'.

Both sets of lyrics seem to open up space for 'us' to do our own personally transformative 'somethings'—from being persistent and brave, to compassionate and hopeful—about the apparently disconnected, depressing and overwhelming problems of global climate change.

On the other hand, the video for 'Hey You', sends a slightly different message; it directly intersperses images of climate-based environmental catastrophe and poverty with those of world leaders such as Gordon Brown and George W. Bush, who have the lyric 'hey you!' juxtaposed over their images. Here the 'you' being referred to in the song might not only be these specific individuals, but might also be a way of imploring 'us' to hold these powerful leaders accountable through more traditionally political or direct-action means. Yet, both interpretations of Madonna's engagements with climate change politics are somewhat contradicted by the fact that she herself has been called a 'climate-change catastrophe' given the large amount of carbon emissions associated with her personal and professional life (hippyshopper. com 2008).

Different musicians have engaged in yet other ways. Thom Yorke, the lead singer of Radiohead, was not only the face of the Big Ask—Friends of the Earth's campaign to get the United Kingdom Government to change its climate policy—but has pledged to reduce the carbon footprint of the band by shipping tour equipment on boats and reducing the band's touring schedule. Both Coldplay and Pearl Jam have pledged to be 'carbon neutral' on their various tours and albums by purchasing offsets to reduce their carbon footprint. At the same time, all three work to organize fans by having booths from environmental campaigns on tour, as well as speaking on climate-related issues in the mass media and to fans. Also engaged in this area is a London-based ENGO known as Julie's Bicycle which, since 2007, has deliberately worked 'backstage' to build capacity and motivation amongst music industry players. Formed by a group wanting to find ways to reduce the carbon foot-print of the British music industry, the organization has sought to be an example to other entertainment sectors as well as in other countries. Key features of Julie's Bicycle (as with TippingPoint) are the direct links it has forged with climate and environmental scientists. These elements seek to emphasize and cement the scientific foundations of the organization, rather than place a focus on explicit climate campaigning.

In still other media arenas and working across myriad mass media forms—from the internet and user-generated message boards, to music, television and celebrity spokespeople—the United Kingdom ENGO Global Cool has taken to popular culture in order to raise awareness amongst younger generations and offer them 'practical solutions' to climate change. As they put it:

> Global Cool is the climate change charity to get you inspired. We want you to feel good about doing good. [...] Global Cool will show you that saving the planet isn't just for the people who like to think of them-selves as 'green'. We give you practical advice on the things you can do that will make a positive difference. [...] And we're not going to preach. We won't lecture you on melting ice caps. We're not asking you to live in a cave or give up all the good things in life. We're here to show you that you can lead a fun, exciting life and do your bit for the environment, with a few tweaks to your lifestyle and a little help from our celebrity friends.
>
> (Global Cool 2009)

One of the more unique efforts by Global Cool was to get the DJ Erik Prydz to help with a music video entitled 'Proper Education' featuring a remix of Pink Floyd's 'Another Brick in the Wall' paired with school kids on a public-housing estate secretly installing compact fluorescent bulbs into unaware residents' flats. At the end of the video, there appears a tag-line reading '*you don't need a proper education to save the planet*'. Speaking about the project, Prydz explains:

> There was a lot of anticipation around this video and I was really keen to do something a bit different. [...] Pink Floyd would always use their videos to get a message across and I really wanted to carry on this spirit. I'd been reading so much in the press about climate change and global warming recently and felt it would be great to try and empower people to do something about it. It's not making a grand statement. It's just simply saying everyone can do a little and it will make a difference.
>
> (The Inspiration Room 2009a)

A wider description of the project states that:

> The video, directed by Marcus Adams, saw Prydz consult with climate change charity Global Cool. Global Cool believes that the solution to defeating global warming lies within the power of the individual, empowering them to take personal action to make a valuable difference. Global Cool spokesman, Dan Morrell said, 'The message is clear, climate change is happening but collectively, given the tools and the knowledge to actively reduce CO2 emissions, and to encourage others to do the same, we can collectively push the climatic tipping point long into the future'.
>
> (The Inspiration Room 2009a)

Indeed, in the cultural politics of climate change—seen here, and in other examples in the chapter—there is the problematic tendency to lionize and entrench the acts of individuals *primarily as consumers* at the expense of more critical considerations of citizenship, amid powerful carbon-based political economies. Here, although Global Cool works to open space for individuals to do something about climate change, through these methods they elevate voluntaristic and individualized forms of engagement and climate change problem-solving.

Finally, MTV has also got into the climate change 'act' through its 'MTV Switch' campaign. Similar to Global Cool's multimedia approach, but based much more around its television empire, MTV Switch operates through 'public service announcements' (PSAs) that work 'to promote environmentally-friendly lifestyle choices amongst youth in order to reduce the carbon emissions that contribute to climate change' (MTV 2009). Centred on celebrity shorts from, for example, the likes of Cameron Diaz and video feature spots developed by some of the world's leading-edge marketing firms (who did the work *pro bono*), the main hub of the campaign is the website (www.mtvswitch.org) which contains access to the videos, has a user-generated weblog (or blog), news, downloads and a carbon footprint calculator hosted at the Global Cool website. Not surprisingly, the focus, *again*, is on shifting individuals towards 'simple climate conscious acts' much like the Global Cool campaign:

> Everyone, no matter what age or where they live, can take action to reduce their carbon footprint. The MTV SWITCH PSAs seek to entertain, intrigue and inspire viewers to take on simple climate conscience acts such as unplugging mobile chargers and turning the thermostat down one degree.
>
> (MTV 2009)

Further, much like not needing a 'proper education' to do something for the climate, one PSA in particular—the aptly named 'Green Song' (The Inspiration Room 2009b)—argues that 'greenwashing' is so prevalent that one shouldn't (have to) be 'green' to be 'green':

Politicians feed us crap, celebrities are the same,
It's all about how green they are and who deserves the blame;
How green you are not how much you give,
How loved you are is how you live,
So know your greens and think a bit,
Because you don't have to be green to be green.

That MTV is airing videos arguing we shouldn't trust 'green' celebrities, many of whom are the very face of MTV Switch itself, is not only deeply ironic—if not passing straight into parody and, indeed, absurdity—but it should tell us that, at the least, this 'celebritization' of climate change (see Boykoff and Goodman 2009) *thoroughly* delineates the mainstream of the contemporary cultural politics of the environment. While we address this overt 'spectacle-ization' of climate change much more below, we now turn to look at the growing connections between sport and climate change mitigation.

Sport

In recent years, many climate change initiatives have developed in the realms of sport with many organizations, institutions and individuals increasingly addressing various aspects of the climate question. The majority of the activities have focused on climate mitigation, but an increasing number of endeavours are addressing adaptation questions, such as those involving how various sporting activities can continue in a changing climate. Many of these programmes to date have been taking place in Europe. At the 2006 World Cup in Germany, there were a number of Fédération Internationale de Football Association (FIFA) initiatives aimed at reducing emissions related to the tournament, from generating energy for the stadium in Hamburg from renewable biogas to reduced fares on the German Railway—called 'World Champion Tickets'—for taking public instead of private transport to the various matches around the country. Furthermore, over the 2007–8 English Football Association (FA) Cup Tournament, the league sponsored a voluntary initiative that they called 'Carbon Footyprint'. In this initiative, supporters were to pledge to reduce their GHG emissions as they travelled to FA Cup matches, and to reduce emissions in other aspects of their daily lives. As they did so, if they documented these actions through the FA website, they would push their favourite club up the Footyprint table. In addition, Ipswich Town FC became the first United Kingdom football club to go 'carbon neutral' through a variety of initiatives such as supporter carbon off-setting and greater energy efficiency (Holt 2007). Individuals such as England and Portsmouth FC goalkeeper David James have spoken out about issues of transport, renewables and climate change; James, in particular, has personally converted his automobile fleet to be fully bio-fuel (James 2006), while Manchester United FC manager Sir Alex Ferguson garnered a wave of media attention when he took part in an Al Gore-run climate leadership training session at the University of Cambridge in 2007 (Adam 2007).

In North America, a significant moment addressing climate change through sport came in the form of a *Sports Illustrated* special issue in March 2007 entitled 'Sports and Global Warming: as the planet changes, so do the games we play – time to pay attention'. The cover story focused on adaptation to climate change and began with the following warning:

> As global warming changes the planet, it is changing the sports world. To counter the looming environmental crisis, surprising and innovative ideas are already helping sports adapt.
>
> (Wolff 2007, 36)

In terms of mitigation, many North American sports are developing their own initiatives. Through purchasing carbon offsets, the National Football League staged a 'Carbon Neutral Superbowl' in 2007 (Davidson 2007) and Major League Baseball announced—in co-ordination with the National Resources Defense Council—that it was 'going green' through various activities and programmes (Bowen 2007). Similarly, in March 2008 Japanese Baseball announced plans to 'green' the sport by shortening the time of games by 6% (or 12 minutes) in order to save energy from lighting (Associated Press 2008).

These various activities have developed, interacted and gained greater co-ordination in recent years. Prominently, a United Nations Environment Programme (UNEP) initiative has organized conferences on the theme of sport and the environment since 2001. Called the 'Global Forum for Sport and the Environment' (G-ForSE), the fifth meeting was held in Alicante, Spain in October 2008 with a focus on climate change. Also, at the 14th United Nations Conference of the Parties meeting (COP-14) in Poznań, Poland in December 2008, top Olympic snow skiers presented a petition to negotiators which read, '[i]ce and snow are particularly vulnerable to the impacts of global warming, and as avid skiers and snowboarders we see our beloved sports endangered' (Roddy 2008). However, it is worth noting that not all sports activities will necessarily 'lose' from anticipated climate changes. In particular, a 2006 study from the *Journal of Leisure Research* concluded that the typical golfer in Toronto, Ontario will play in climate conditions like they are in Columbus, Ohio by the year 2080 (Scott and Jones 2006). Irrespective of rainfall extremes and sea-level rise, perhaps mogul Donald Trump has made a sagacious move in the golfing world by investing in a course back in golf's birthplace of Scotland, where year-round play might just become the norm by 2100!

Glamorous Politics?: The Celebritization of Climate Change

The preceding discussion can be connected and taken further through an analysis of how *a range of celebrities*—the new 'charismatic megafauna' in climate change debates—are populating the discourses on possibilities for

climate governance and everyday mitigation/adaptation action. In contemporary society, celebrities undoubtedly have amplified voices and garner
increased attention in the public purview (Marshall 1997; Street 2004). Constituted by interacting and interactive media representations (Littler 2008),
celebrities have become the 'intimate strangers' (Schickel 2000) we wish (and
are told) to know—and know everything about—at media-ted distances. To
capitalize on this 'star power' with respect to a range of environmental issues,
discrete organizations—such as the Science and Entertainment Exchange
(Lieberman 2009)—have moved to support and improve interactions among
celebrities and science, environment and conservation (Brockington 2008).

In efforts to understand and catalogue the growing role of celebrities in
connection to climate change, Boykoff and Goodman have developed a 'tax-
onomy of climate celebrities' (2009). Thus, celebrity voices are defined by six
main types of political or social determinants that shape their actions: actors,
politicians, sports figures/athletes, business people, musicians and public
intellectuals (Boykoff and Goodman 2009). Specific examples include many of
the individuals already mentioned, but also Sienna Miller working with
Global Cool, Oprah Winfrey through guests and themes on her talk show,
Richard Branson as head of the self-proclaimed 'environmentally-conscious'
Virgin business empire, and George Monbiot, an activist-journalist who
writes and speaks about climate change in the United Kingdom. As Bono,
U2 front man and politicized celebrity *extraordinaire*, has put it in the pages
of *Vogue*, 'celebrity is a bit silly, but it's currency of a kind'. Indeed, it is a
currency that spends (overly) well in the neoliberal spaces carved out by the
increasingly marketized, privatized, voluntary and individualized ways of
addressing climate questions.

Divergent and ambivalent perspectives on the roles of celebrity—analytical,
descriptive and normative—have raised deep-rooted and fundamental concerns about the processes and functions of celebrity, as well as the nature of
their influence (Littler 2008; Redmond and Holmes 2007). It is important to
ask, can these 'celebrity effects' inspire and foster grassroots, democratic
movements and responses to climate change by and for 'the people', or are
they plutocratic, unique and extraordinary elite behaviours of distraction that
work to build up the celebrity environmental 'brand'? Furthermore, as these
questions relate to climate governance and everyday practices, they are arguably as important now as ever before inasmuch as they also lead us to better
understand the broader contemporary expansion of celebrities into environmental politics and other realms such as development (e.g. Goodman, forthcoming; Richey and Ponte 2008). Indeed, as Gore optimistically put it
speaking to an international climate change conference in 2008:

> We have to overcome the paralysis that has prevented us from acting [to
> address climate change] and focus unblinkingly on this crisis as opposed
> to spending so much time on OJ Simpson and Paris Hilton and Anna
> Nicole Smith.

In uttering this statement, Gore failed to recognize the role of *his own type* of celebrity, which surely allowed his commentary to pass from the confined spaces of the conference to much beyond the eyes and ears of the delegates and, through the processes of the mass media, into the public realm in a set of discursive pathways reserved for very few individuals engaged in climate change debates. These, perhaps, *differing* celebrity effects and their shifting contexts, then, beg the following question: When working towards climate change mitigation, is it *more effective* to plant celebrities than to plant trees? Very much more than a silly glib quip, we feel that this question, in addition to the others exploring the growing connections between climate change and popular culture, should perhaps be one of the fundamental considerations concerning the 'effectiveness' of the current tactics that have and continue to form the contemporary cultural politics of climate change.

CONCLUSION

In this chapter, we have sought to provide some lines of connectivity amongst the book's contributions by exploring how mitigation and adaptation initiatives as well as arenas of expertise translate into the 'everyday' media spaces of potential citizen awareness and engagement. At a minimum, 'public' space is dynamic and heterogeneous, where 'mainstreaming' processes face a range of responses amongst varied social groupings. In this sense, connections between formal climate policy initiatives and potential behavioural changes are not straightforward: engagement does not merely stem from glamour-oriented messaging, but possibilities for actions are shaped by a range of cultural and political factors. For our purposes here, we see these as places and spaces where meaning, value, power and rhetoric are negotiated through various popular media and mediums and more broadly through cultural politics—what Alvarez et al. (1998, 7) refer to as that bundle of processes 'enacted when sets of social actors shaped by, and embodying, different cultural meanings and practices come into conflict with each other'.

Further, the many 'actors' in this theatre of discursive and material structuration—from climate scientists, business industry interests and ENGO activists, to artists, television and movie stars—are ultimately all members of the 'public citizenry'. So, responses to media messaging thereby feed back to varying degrees into ongoing environmental science and policy formulations. In other words, the cultural politics of climate change are situated, power-laden, media-ted *and* recursive, and should be conceptualized as such. Much like many of the growing list of 'climate change celebrities', those who have power, access and influence are those who have the advantage in this battle-field of knowledges, understandings and interpretations. Here, mass media representations of climate change actors, action, predicaments and progress remain key influences that shape discourses and bounding considerations for possible climate action. These elements may be as important as formal climate governance architectures—such as those currently being constructed in the lead up to COP-15 in Copenhagen—to the long-term success or failure of efforts to take carbon out of the atmosphere, or keep it out. To the extent that we fail to examine how these representations and symbols are negotiated through relations of dominance, subordination, and inequalities of access and resources, we miss out on important components of the 'scope of [climate] politics' (Rosati 2007, 996) or the full spectrum of possibilities for future climate mitigation and adaptation action.

The efforts described here focused towards the reconfiguration (or reorganization) of discourses might open up new possibilities for climate change negotiation and action (cf. Swyngeduow 2007). Still, as this chapter has illustrated, these spaces can be as contradictory and problematic as they are complimentary and transgressive. To the extent that Brad Pitt garners interest in green building and energy conservation for readers of *Us Weekly* in ways that many others—including scientists and sustainability campaigners—likely cannot achieve, we suggest that awareness-raising is a short-term gain. However, voluntaristic and individualized responsibilism by citizens and consumers—and considerations of how *shifting consumption patterns* may influence climate causes and effects—remains a rather awkward and problematic facet of movements for climate mitigation/adaptation action. How these movements in the cultural politics of climate change will engage with topics such as food choices (e.g. meat consumption) and links to climate change (e.g. through land use) over the medium and long term remain open questions worthy of vigorous discussion. Through the comments on offer here, we aim to provide greater context and insights to facilitate these ongoing dialogues, with a critical eye on what we may expect in the next years in the cultural politics of climate change, and related interactions in the spaces of the everyday. We ignore or dismiss the influence of popular culture in shaping climate politics at our collective peril.

REFERENCES

AC Nielsen (2007) *Global Omnibus Survey*, Oxford: AC Nielsen.

Adam, D. (2007) 'The persuaders: Sir Alex Ferguson joins Gore's climate A-team', *Guardian* 29 March, 11.

Alvarez, S.E., E. Dagnino and A. Escobar (eds) (1998) *Cultures of Politics and Politics of Cultures: Re-visioningLatin American Social Movements*, Boulder, CO: Westview Press.

Argetsinger, A. and R. Roberts (2006) 'The reliable source', *Washington Post*, C3.

Associated Press (2008) 'Japan baseball looking to fight global warming with shorter games', *Associated Press*, 18 March.

Beder, S. (2002) *Global Spin: The Corporate Assault on Environmentalism*, White River Junction, VT: Chelsea Green Publishing Company.

Blaikie, P. (1985) *The political ecology of soil erosion in developing countries*, London: Longman Scientific and Technical.

Bowen, T.S. (2007) 'Red Sox turn green', *Business Week*, 26 October.

Boykoff, M.T. and J.M. Boykoff (2004) 'Bias as Balance: Global Warming and the U.S. Prestige Press', *Global Environmental Change* 14 (2), 125–36.

——(2007) 'Climate Change and Journalistic Norms: A Case Study of U.S. Mass-Media Coverage', *Geoforum* 38 (6), 1,190–204.

Boykoff, M.T. and M.K. Goodman (2009) 'Conspicuous redemption? Reflections on the promises and perils of the "celebritization" of climate change', *Geoforum* 40, 395–406.

Brenner, N. and N. Theodore (2002) 'Cities and the geographies of actually existing neoliberalisms', *Antipode* 34 (3), 349–79.

Brockington, D. (2008) 'Powerful environmentalisms: Conservation, celebrity and capitalism', *Media, Culture and Society* 30 (4), 551–68.

Bumpus, A. and D. Liverman (2008) 'Accumulation by decarbonisation and the governance of carbon offsets', *Economic Geography* 84 (2), 127–55.

Carvalho, A. (2007) 'Ideological cultures and media discourses on scientific knowledge: re-reading news on climate change', *Public Understanding of Science* 16, 223–43.

Carvalho, A. and J. Burgess (2005) 'Cultural circuits of climate change in UK broadsheet newspapers, 1985–2003', *Risk Analysis* 25 (6), 1,457–69.

Clarke, N., C. Barnett, P. Cloke and A. Malpass (2007) 'Globalising the consumer: Doing politics in an ethical register', *Political Geography* 26, 231–49.

Cosgrove, D.E. (1983) 'Towards a radical cultural geography: problems of theory', *Antipode* 15, 1–11.

Dalby, S. (2007) 'Anthropocene Geopolitics: Globalisation, Empire, Environment and Critique', *Geography Compass* 1, 1–16.

Davidson, A. (2007) 'Greening the Superbowl', *Forbes Magazine*, 19 January.

de Certeau, M. (1984) *The practice of everyday life*, translated by S. Rendall, Berkeley, CA: University of California Press.

Derrida, J. (1978) 'Structure, sign, and play in the discourse of the human sciences', in Writing and Difference, translated by Alan Bass, University of Chicago Press, 278–93.

Drury, I. (2008) 'Boris orders arts chiefs to stop "dumbing down" culture for young people', *Mail on Sunday Online*, 24 November, www.mailonsunday.co.uk/news/article-1088956/Boris-orders-arts-chiefs-stop-dumbing-culture-young-people.html (accessed 15 December 2008).

Eden, S., A. Donaldson and G. Walker (2006) 'Green groups and grey areas: Scientific boundary-work, nongovernmental organizations and environmental knowledge', *Environment and Planning A* 38, 1,061–76.

Entman, R. M. (1993) 'Framing: Toward Clarification of a Fractured Paradigm', *Journal of Communication* 43 (4), 51–58.

Forsyth, T. (2003) *Critical Political Ecology: The Politics of Environmental Science*, London: Routledge.

Foucault, M. (1977) *Discipline and punish*, translated by A. Sheridan, New York: Pantheon.
——(1980) *Power/knowledge*, translated by A. Sheridan, New York: Pantheon.

Freudenburg, W.R., R. Gramling and D.J. Davidson (2008) 'Scientific certainty argumentation methods (SCAMs): Science and the politics of doubt', *Sociological Inquiry* 78 (1), 2–38.

Gelbspan, R. (1998) *The Heat is On: The Climate Crisis, the Cover-up, the Prescription*, Boston: Perseus Press.

Gieryn, T. (1999) *Cultural boundaries of science: Credibility on the line*, Chicago, IL: University of Chicago Press.

Global Cool (2009) 'About us', www.globalcool.org/about.

Goffman, E. (1974) *Frame Analysis: An Essay on the Organization of Experience*, Cambridge, MA: Harvard University Press.

Goodman, M. (forthcoming) 'The mirror of consumption: Celebritisation, developmental consumption and the shifting cultural politics of fair trade', *Geoforum*.

Gottlieb, R. (2002) *Environmentalism unbound: exploring new pathways for change*, Cambridge, MA: MIT Press.

Guthman, J. (2007) 'The Polyanyian way?: Voluntary food labels and neoliberal governance', *Antipode* 39, 456–78.

Hall, S. (ed.) (1997) *Representation: cultural representation and signifying practices*, Thousand Oaks, CA: Sage.

Harvey, D. (1990) 'Between space and time: reflections on the geographical imagination', *Annals of the Association of American Geographers* 80, 418–34.

Hinton, E. and M. Goodman (forthcoming) 'Sustainable consumption: Developments, considerations and new directions', in G. Woodgate and M. Redclift (eds), *International handbook of environmental sociology*, 2nd edn, London: Edward Elgar.

hippyshopper.com (2008) 'Madonna on cover of green vanity fair. But why?', www. hippyshopper.com/2008/03/madonna_on_cover_of_green_vanity_fair_but_why.html.

Hobson, K. (2006) 'Bins, bulbs and shower timers: On the "techno-ethics" of sustainable living', *Ethics, Environment, and Place* 3, 317–36.

Holt, S. (2007) 'Can football save the planet?', *BBC News online*, news.bbc.co.uk/sport1/low/football/6908507.stm (accessed 21 December 2008).

The Inspiration Room (2009a) 'Eric Prydz vs Floyd Proper Education', theinspirationroom.com/daily/2007/eric-prydz-vs-floyd-proper-education.

——(2009b) 'The MTV Switch Green Song', theinspirationroom.com/daily/2008/mtv-switch-green-song.

James, D. (2006) 'Forget Joey's arse – it's wind turbines that matter', *Guardian*, 3 December, 30.

Jenkins, H. (2006) *Convergence culture: Where old and new media collide*, New York: New York University Press.

Lieberman, B. (2009) 'Hollywood to the aid of serious science: pairing entertainment and drama with education', *Yale Forum on Climate Change and the Media*, 23 April.

Littler, J. (2008) '"I feel your pain": Cosmopolitan charity and the public fashioning of the celebrity soul', *Social Semiotics* 18 (2), 237–51.

Luke, T. (2008) 'The politics of true convenience or inconvenient truth: struggles over how to sustain capitalism, democracy, and ecology in the 21st century', *Environment and Planning A* 40, 1,811–44.

McChesney, R. (2008) *The political economy of media: Enduring issues, emerging dilemmas*, New York: Monthly Review Press.

McCright, A.M. and R.E. Dunlap (2003) 'Defeating Kyoto: the conservative movement's impact on U.S. climate change policy', *Social Problems* 50 (3), 348–73.

Marshall, P. D. (1997) *Celebrity and power: Fame in contemporary culture*, Minneapolis, MN: University of Minnesota Press.

Moser, S. and L. Dilling (eds) (2007) *Creating a climate for change: communicating climate change and facilitating social change*, Cambridge: Cambridge University Press.

MTV (2009) 'MTV networks international launches first youth-focused, global, multi-platform climate change campaign', MTV switch, www.mtvnetworks.co.uk/mtvswitch.

Norgaard, K.M. (2006) '"People want to protect themselves a little bit": emotions, denial and social movement nonparticipation', *Sociological Inquiry* 76 (3), 372–96.

Oreskes, N., E.M. Conway and M. Shindell (2008) 'From Chicken Little to Dr. Pangloss: William Nierenberg, global warming, and the social deconstruction of scientific knowledge', *Historical Studies in the Natural Sciences* 38 (1), 109–52.

Paterson, M. (2006) *Consumption and everyday life*, London: Routledge.

Popke, J. (2006) Geography and ethics: Everyday mediations through care and consumption, *Progress in Human Geography* 30 (4), 504–12.

——(2009) 'Geography and ethics: non-representational encounters, collective responsibility and economic difference', *Progress in Human Geography* 33 (1), 81–90.

Prudham, S. (2007) 'The fictions of autonomous invention: accumulation by dispossession, commodification, and life patents in Canada', Antipode 39 (3), 406–29.

Redmond, S. and S. Holmes (2007) *Stardom and celebrity: A reader*, London: Sage.

Richey, L. and S. Ponte (2008) 'Better (RED)™ than dead: Celebrities, consumption and international aid', *Third World Quarterly* 29 (4), 711–29.

Robbins, P. (2001) 'Fixed categories in portable landscape: The causes and consequences of land cover categorization', *Environment and Planning A* 33 (1), 161–79.

——(2004) *Political Ecology: A Critical Introduction*, London: Blackwell Publishers.

Roddy, M. (2008) 'Skiers tell UN climate talks "save our snows"', *Reuters*, 5 December, www.reuters.com/article/latestCrisis/idUSL5419888 (accessed 20 December 2008).

Rosati, C. (2007) 'Media geographies; uncovering the spatial politics of images', *Geography Compass* 1 (5), 995–1,014.

Sassatelli, R. (2006) 'Virtue, responsibility and consumer choice: Framing critical consumerism', in J. Brewer and F. Trentmann (eds), *Consuming cultures, global perspectives: Historical trajectories, transnational exchanges*, London: Berg, 219–50.

Schickel, R. (2000) *Intimate strangers: The culture of celebrity in America*, Chicago, IL: Ivan R. Dee.

Scott, D. and B. Jones (2006) 'The impact of climate change on golf participation in the Greater Toronto Area (GTA): a case study', *Journal of Leisure Research* 38 (3), 363–80.

Seabrook, J. (2000) *Nobrow: The culture of marketing and the marketing of culture*, New York: Vintage.

Seyfang, G. (2005) 'Shopping for sustainability: Can sustainable consumption promote ecological citizenship?', *Environmental Politics* 14 (2), 290–306.

Singer, S. (2002) 'Warrior One', *Vogue*, October.

Slocum, R. (2004) 'Polar bears and energy-efficient lightbulbs: Strategies to bring climate change home', *Environment and Planning D: Society and Space* 22, 413–38.

Street, J. (2004) 'Celebrity politicians: popular culture and political representation', *The British Journal of Politics and International Relations* 6 (4), 435–52.

Swyngeduow, E. (2007) 'Impossible sustainability and the post-political condition', in *The sustainable development paradox: urban political economy in the United States and Europe*, New York: Guildford Press, 13–40.

Weart, S. (2003) *The discovery of global warming*, Cambridge, MA: Harvard University Press.

Weiskel, T. (2005) 'From sidekick to sideshow: Celebrity, entertainment, and the politics of distraction', *American Behavioral Scientist* 49 (3), 393–409.

Whatmore, S. (2002) *Hybrid geographies: Natures, cultures, spaces*, London: Sage.

Wolff, A. (2007) 'Sports and global warming: as the planet changes, so do the games we play – time to pay attention', *Sports Illustrated*, 12 March, 36–45.

Costly Knowledge— Unaffordable Denial: The Politics of Public Understanding and Engagement on Climate Change

SUSANNE C. MOSER

WHICH FUTURE WORLD?

It is the year 2050, two years into the presidency of a newly elected US President. Asian and European leaders are meeting with their North American counterparts at the 56th Conference of the Parties to discuss anew adaptation aid for developing nations. Tensions run high as monetary aid is much needed in the poorest nations of the world to deal with the consequences of climate change, yet developed nations are hardly in a position to assist their less developed neighbours. With global greenhouse gas emissions reduced more than 80% below 2000 levels and carbon markets generating only small revenues now to maintain the Adaptation Fund, the hardest hit nations are demanding new funding mechanisms to support their adaptation and coping needs. Developed nations in turn have trouble financing their own adaptation projects, as cities have to be protected from rapidly rising seas, water supplies are limited and food production is declining. Research cannot keep pace with the newly emerging public health challenges. The remarkable transformation of the energy and transportation sectors has stimulated enormous economic growth, but the loss of biodiversity and ecosystem services require massive compensatory programmes and interventions. The world that has made good on its policy promises in the early years of the 21st century has indeed averted more catastrophic increases in greenhouse gas concentrations and temperatures, yet adaptation is a persistent and expensive 'industry'.

This fictitious snapshot of the politics in the world of 2050 presents, alarming as that may be, an optimistic image. In a January 2009 hearing in the US Senate's Foreign Relations Committee, Democratic Chairman, Senator John Kerry, made that abundantly clear in his opening remarks. He stated:

A partnership led by the University of Pennsylvania, MIT [Massachusetts Institute of Technology], and the Heinz Center recently aggregated the impact of all the domestic policy proposals that every country currently talking about doing something [about their greenhouse gas emissions] has laid out, including President Obama's aggressive goal of 80% reductions by 2050. What they found was sobering. If every nation were to make good on its existing promises – *if* they were able to; there is no indication yet that we are – we would still see atmospheric carbon dioxide levels well above 600 parts per million, 50% above where we are today. This translates into global average temperatures at least 4 degrees Celsius above pre-industrial levels and no one in the scientific community disputes that this would be catastrophic. That is why we need more than just a policy shift. We need a transformation in public policy thinking to embrace the reality of what science is telling us. We must accept its implications and then act in accordance to the full scope and urgency of the problem.

(Kerry 2009)

The imagined policy challenge in 2050 described at the opening of this chapter thus emerges as the comparatively 'easy' world that policy-makers, resource managers and individuals get to navigate if the dramatic policy transformation invoked by Senator Kerry will have occurred in the early years of the 21st century. The *realpolitik* of our times demands, however, that we also imagine a far darker alternative—a world that did not manage to achieve such substantial emissions reductions, a world facing the impacts of a frightfully warmer world, with catastrophic, economy-crippling consequences, where coastal cities are abandoned or relocated inland, where hunger and drought are widespread, even in formerly rich, mid-latitudinal countries, where old and new diseases are rampant, and where tensions between nations vying for limited essential resources frequently erupt. Living from catastrophe to catastrophe may become a phenomenon not just common in poor nations.

Whatever the reality will be in just one or two generations from now, climate change is likely to manifest far more clearly in our lives than at present, especially in some regions of the world (such as the polar and dry, subtropical regions), for some sectors, and for those most vulnerable to climate variability and extremes. Whether the world of 2050 is a hugely transformed one with moderate adaptation needs or one trying to survive one crisis after another, one may legitimately ask: How did we get to this future world?

THE POLITICS OF PUBLIC UNDERSTANDING AND ENGAGEMENT ON CLIMATE CHANGE

This chapter attempts to answer this question from the standpoint of public understanding and engagement on climate change. It rests on the basic assumption that no matter which international climate treaties will be signed, no matter which national policy mechanisms are chosen to realize these multi-lateral commitments, political support and engagement of the public will be required for any political leader to realize them. In democratic societies, advocacy groups and voting individuals must actively advocate, shape and support, vote for, or at least quietly acquiesce to any proposed policy. Societies and their individual members must also engage practically by adopting into their daily lives the changes, policies, technologies, and shifting consumer and travel choices which policies and markets have set in motion. Thus, both political pragmatism and normative arguments suggest that the future world is unavoidably dependent on the degree to which the public is engaged on the issue of climate change (Moser 2008; see also Halpern and Bates 2004). This basic assumption does not imply that such democratic engagement is efficient in the short run or that it can guarantee ecological survival and the socially most desirable results, certainly not for everyone. On the other hand, the counterfactual—a technocratic or ecofascist world in which democracy and public engagement are ignored—may well produce significant resistance, defiance and obstinate refusal to change that would make it even less likely to achieve rapid and substantial emissions reductions. I will return to this discussion of political alternatives again in the concluding section, as there is considerable discussion in the literature and important considerations follow from it for the politics of public understanding and engagement (see, for example, the review in Ockwell et al. 2009; or Bartels 2001). The challenge before policy-makers today thus is not only to produce viable and effective international policy solutions involving technological and economic means (as discussed, for example, in the chapters by Newell and Paterson, Okereke, and Schroeder in this volume), but to educate, bring along, gain the support of, and actively engage their various publics.

By public 'engagement' I mean more than a level of awareness or even a high rating of the issue's importance in public opinion surveys. Engagement is defined here similarly as in Lorenzoni et al. (2007), who identified three dimensions of people's connection to the issue: 1) a cognitive dimension (related to people mentally grappling with and gaining understanding of the issue); 2) an affective dimension (reflecting an emotional response to the information and knowledge, such as interest or concern); and 3) a behavioural dimension (illustrated by people's active response through some kind of action, including pragmatic changes in climate-relevant, frequently habitual behaviour and political action) (see also Maibach et al. 2008; Nisbet and Kotcher 2009; Ockwell et al. 2009). An implicit normative assumption in Lorenzoni et al.'s (2007) definition is that such engagement will lead to climate-friendly behaviour, as opposed to activism that defends a status quo marked by heavy reliance on fossil fuels, energy-intensive economic development, wasteful modern-day conveniences and lifestyles; aims to confuse the public; or fights against climate legislation. While this chapter adopts the normative goal implied by Lorenzoni et al. (2007), it recognizes the central importance of certain actors working *against* greater public understanding that is consistent with scientific understanding and active engagement as defined above. This chapter focuses on the challenges and politics of achieving positive, climate-protective public engagement, particularly in developed nations, with an emphasis on the USA. This focus is largely determined by the greater availability of surveys and in-depth studies in developed nations, especially in the USA and the United Kingdom. While some of the challenges that will be identified below (e.g. scientific literacy, changing habitual behaviour, the contextual importance of institutions and infrastructure in determining behavioural choices) may be quite similar in other nations and beyond the developed world, caution is warranted in transferring insights from these locations to other, especially less-developed nations.

If politics are not just understood as the affairs of a state, but also as the struggle for dominance among political opinions and sympathies, attitudes and positions, and, therefore, as a matter of power struggles among members of a society who hold different beliefs and political convictions, then the politics of public understanding and engagement on climate change is a struggle over who communicates and advocates what. It is a struggle over who knows what and how much; what it means in terms of individual and common interests and stakes; and what it implies in terms of action. It reflects how members of society with their different understandings and interests enact their personal and political convictions, and how they come together to form coalitions behind different policy proposals to support the political actors who can enact or block them. In the politics of public understanding and engagement, information and knowledge become resources that can empower and enable, but also challenge and obligate people to respond in certain ways. They can also become means to disempower and overwhelm individuals. In either case, information and knowledge become strategic goods and tools to communicators—a notion maybe anathema to scientists who insist on the objectivity, policy neutrality, or sometimes self-evidence of their claims, but familiar to advocates who use them deliberately to persuade, engage, confuse, disassociate, or otherwise influence their audiences, sometimes with inadvertent consequences. To achieve public engagement, then, in the ways defined above, communicators and advocates have to overcome a variety of barriers that stand in the way of people's cognitive, affective and behavioural connection with the issue. This chapter conceptualizes overcoming these barriers as 'costs'. While the use of an economic metaphor is intentional, the notion of 'costs' is by no means limited to a matter of money, financial losses, opportunities, or gains. Instead, the 'costs' incurred in the politics of climate change communication and public engagement may be financial, but are first and foremost cognitive, psychological, behavioural, social and cultural, and are borne by the public and those who try to foster or hinder greater public understanding and engagement. As we will see in this chapter, these costs arise from the structural, institutional and economic contexts that mediate and magnify the politics of communication and engagement on climate change, and thus cannot be understood if divorced from the structural forces that shape societal interactions and responses to global environmental change.

There also quite likely are significant 'benefits' to be gained from greater understanding and engagement with climate change. These may range from personal psychological gains such as knowledgeability, satisfaction, sense of self-worth and integrity; to social gains such as being accepted, admired, or in a leadership position; to practical gains such as lower energy consumption and consequent financial savings; to the penultimate social-environmental gain of socio-economic well-being, safety, environmental protection and species preservation. These potential gains are frequently motivational for individuals, organizations or communities to engage with the climate change issue, but are rarely sufficient to overcome the barriers typically encountered (Moser and Dilling 2007b). To better understand why even high understanding, concern or other motivations do not necessarily lead to active behavioural and political engagement, it is critical to recognize the many costs involved in overcoming them.

THE STATE OF PUBLIC OPINION, UNDERSTANDING AND ENGAGEMENT

To begin to appreciate the costs of engaging on climate change, then, it is essential to establish where the public is at this time in terms of its attitudes, understanding and active involvement with climate change. Public opinion polls abound on the issue, especially in the USA and the United Kingdom, but to a lesser extent in other developed, and some in developing nations, that allow for trend analysis over time. In the USA and the United Kingdom a number of surveys have been conducted repeatedly by individual researchers and surveying organizations (such as the Pew Research Center for the People and the Press, the Gallup Poll/EOS Gallup Europe, or The PIPA/Knowledge Networks Poll, GlobeScan's Climate Change Monitor, the Eurobarometer, the BBC, Ipsos/MORI and The Nielson Company). Nisbet and Myers (2007), updated by Moser (2008), recently reviewed more than 20 years of such polling information for the USA and found consistent and perplexing trends. Brewer (2003, 2005a, 2005b) has been following changes in public attitudes internationally, and other—regionally specific—in-depth reviews and analyses are occasionally published (e.g., Leiserowitz 2007b; Brechin 2003; Lorenzoni and Pidgeon 2006). Below, some of these findings are discussed, with particular emphasis on the data-rich countries (the USA and United Kingdom).

Awareness and Understanding

The greatest gains over the past 20 or more years have been made in terms of raising public awareness of climate change—a first indicator of cognitive engagement with the issue. The generally upward trend over the last two decades has been modified only by variability in media attention to the issue. In the USA, in 2006, 90% of Americans said they had heard of the greenhouse effect or global warming, and figures have remained at this level since (Nisbet and Myers 2007, 444–47). Some US location-specific surveys have found virtually universal awareness (e.g. Semenza et al. 2008). A 2007 international comparison of attitudes in 21 countries—using a slightly different wording—found that while some European countries (France and Great Britain) showed a generally higher level of issue awareness than the USA or Canada, other European nations (e.g., Germany and some of the Mediterranean countries) did not (BBC World Service 2007). The most recent Eurobarometer did not ask this question (Directorate-General for Communication of the European Commission 2008). Moreover, such snapshots can be difficult to evaluate out of context and without a historical perspective. In a review of a range of international survey data, Brewer (2006) found, however, that awareness and concern (see below) have risen almost universally and in some instances quite dramatically (15–20% over three to five years) in the early years of the 21st century (see also Leiserowitz 2007b).

In the USA, for which the most detailed data are available, two different polls conducted in April and July 2007 found that between 72% and more than 80% of Americans believed that rising carbon dioxide levels and global temperature increases were 'real' (ABC News, Washington Post and Stanford University 2007; Leiserowitz 2007a). However, more recent audience segmentation studies of the American population show a more differentiated picture. In two repeat polls, the authors differentiated six segments of the public, three of which—the Alarmed, the Concerned and the Cautious—were somewhere between completely and mostly convinced that global warming was a reality, while the other three—the Unconcerned, the Doubtful and the Dismissive—were hardly or not at all convinced that climate change was happening (Leiserowitz et al. 2008; Maibach et al. 2009). Audience segmentation studies in the United Kingdom and in Canada show similar patterns, albeit with nationally and regionally specific variations (Angus Reid Strategies 2007a, 2007b, 2007c; Davidson et al. 2009; Downing and Ballantyne 2007).

Even less encouraging are the findings in terms of changes over time in public understanding of climate change. According to Nisbet and Myers (2007, 447) for the USA, 'Twenty years after scientists and journalists first alerted the public to the potential problem of global warming, few Americans are confident that they fully grasp the complexities of the issue, and on questions measuring actual knowledge about either the science or the policy involved, the public scores very low'. In fact, a Gallup Poll in 2008 found that only 21% of Americans say that they understand climate change 'very well' (Gallup 2008). Factual knowledge (for example, about what does and does not constitute a significant cause of climate change) remains shaky, and the percentage of people being able to give correct answers to true/false questions about climate change have not changed significantly over the past decade. In a survey published in early 2009, 44% of likely US voters believed that global warming was caused by natural, planetary trends rather than by human activity; a smaller percentage (41%) was convinced otherwise (Rasmussen

Report 2009). Just one year earlier only 34% believed climate change was an all-natural phenomenon, and that again was a few percentage points higher than in 2007—at the height of US news coverage on anthropogenic climate change (Leiserowitz 2007a).

The situation is hardly more encouraging elsewhere. Only 10 years ago, in the 1999 GlobeScan survey of 25 developed and developing nations, when respondents were asked about the 'main cause of the greenhouse effect', the depletion of the earth's ozone layer was—of course, erroneously, but almost universally across the entire set of nations—considered the number one cause of global warming (see summary and discussion in Leiserowitz 2007b).

After a decade of news reporting, online information and science education, in a 2006 survey of British citizens, 69% of respondents believed they knew 'a great deal' or a 'fair amount' about climate change, yet 41% of respondents were out of step with the IPCC conclusions, still believing that the causes of global warming are equally natural and human (Downing and Ballantyne 2007). Moreover, the number one action thought to alleviate climate change—chosen by 40% of the respondents—was (erroneously) recycling. Maybe not surprisingly, 63% of the British say they would like to have more information about climate change (Downing and Ballantyne 2007).

The most recent Eurobarometer suggests that Europe-wide, 9% feel very well informed about climate change, 47% feel fairly well informed, and the remaining more than 40% feel not very well or not at all informed about climate change. In this subjective self-assessment, Nordic and Western Europeans generally say they understand the issue better than other Europeans. Factual knowledge, though, was not tested to be able to assess what 'well informed' means (Directorate-General for Communication of the European Commission 2008). In Canada in 2007, 77% were convinced that global warming was real, and 70% believed that the science behind human-induced climate change was 'true', though detailed understanding of causes and impacts were significantly lower and more variable across segments of the population (Angus Reid Strategies 2007b).

As for Americans' perceptions of whether or not scientists agree about the reality, seriousness and causes of climate change, opinions have varied significantly over time. This variability reflects changes in science understanding, reporting practices in the media, and the efforts by conservative politicians, think tanks and fossil fuel-funded activists to spread contrarian and denialist thoughts, deliberately try to confuse the public, deliberately play on the ignorance of the lay public with scientific factoids taken out of context, and deliberately use scientific insignia and credentials to invoke a sense of credibility when they have none. The result has been to sow just enough doubt in Americans' minds to undermine confidence in scientific conclusions (Boykoff 2007a, 2007b; Boykoff and Boykoff 2004; Davidson 2008; Krosnick et al. 2000; Lahsen 2008; McCright and Dunlap 2001, 2003). In the 2008 Gallup Poll, the highest percentage of Americans ever (65%) believed that 'most scientists believe that global warming is occurring' (Gallup 2008), but again, audience segmentation suggests that Americans are quite distinctly and increasingly divided, roughly along Democratic/Republican or liberal-to-moderate/conservative lines on this question (Dunlap and McCright 2008; Leiserowitz et al. 2008). Compare this with a similar question asked in the United Kingdom: the 2008 Ipsos MORI update of British attitudes and opinions on global warming found significant uncertainty (and misperception of the actual reality) among respondents about the scientific consensus. A full 60% of the population believed that 'scientific experts still question if humans are contributing to climate change' (Downing 2008).

Concern

The level of affective connection to climate change is variably assessed, if maybe inadequately, by measuring levels of public concern or personal worry (Kahlor and Rosenthal 2009). Few opinion polls examine a wider range of affective responses to climate change (e.g. levels of interest, fear or dread, level of optimism or pessimism about the future), though anecdotal evidence (e.g. Anthes 2009) and some empirical studies (such as detailed interviews, focus group studies) have revealed a broader range of emotions (e.g. Immerwahr 1999; Leiserowitz 2006; Lowe 2006; Lowe et al. 2006; O'Neill and Nicholson-Cole 2009; Stoll-Kleemann et al. 2001). One way to assess the level of concern is the common question about whether or not individuals believe that the impacts of climate change have already begun to manifest, will soon, or will do so only in the future, if at all. The 2008 Gallup Poll suggests for the US population that a growing proportion of Americans believe global warming will pose a serious threat in their own lifetimes—now 40%, up from 35% in 2006 and 31% in 2001 (Gallup 2008). A 2006 British survey found similar figures, with 45% of respondents saying that they view climate change as 'the most serious threat' to the future well-being of the world (though a much smaller number, 19%, believed it would be so for Britain) (Downing and Ballantyne 2007). Europe-wide, in 2007 respondents believed that global warming/climate change was only second in overall seriousness to global poverty (including a lack of food and drinking water), with 62% of Europeans believing that the climate issue is the most serious issue facing the world now. When the degree of seriousness was judged on a scale from 1 (not at all serious) to 10 (extremely serious), no country had fewer than 59% ranking global warming in the top category (7–10 on the seriousness scale). Interestingly, the lowest ranking country (at 59%) was the United Kingdom, while the European average was at 75% and some of the southern and eastern European countries, which recently had experienced weather extremes such as droughts and floods, ranked highest, with more than 80% or even 90% believing that climate change is a very serious issue (Directorate-General for Communication of the European Commission 2008).

As for whether or not the impacts of climate change are already being felt, 65% of Americans—the highest percentage since the survey began asking this question in 2001—believe the effects of global warming are already manifest or will happen within a few years (Gallup 2008). Other surveys show that even if Americans believe the impacts are already beginning to manifest, pluralities still view climate change as primarily a threat to other species, to people in far-away places, or to Americans elsewhere, but far less so to their own communities or families. Many still do not view the threat as particularly severe, even for other species and the environment (Leiserowitz 2007a; Moser 2008). An in-depth review of studies and surveys undertaken in the United Kingdom suggests similarly that the threat of global warming is mostly viewed still as a distant one (Lorenzoni and Pidgeon 2006).

While the percentage of Americans saying that global warming is either 'extremely' or 'very' important to them personally has grown from 27% in 1997 to 52% in 2007, the level of people's personal 'worry' has varied considerably over time. Similar variability has been shown among Europeans (for environmental attitude surveys by Ipsos/MORI and the Eurobarometer, see www.ipsos-mori.com and ec.europa.eu/public_opinion/archives/eb_special_en.htm). In the 2006 Pew Global Attitudes Survey, when respondents from various developed and developing nations were asked about their personal worry about global warming, levels were generally lower than perceived seriousness and greatly varied across countries. Direct threats to respondents or to their families in the next 10 years produced significant numbers only among developing nations, but remained consistently below about 20% among developed nation respondents (see summary and discussion in Leiserowitz 2007b). This variability reflects reporting cycles in the news media, direct experience with the vagaries of climate, and competing worries (for example, basic needs being met or not, the economy, jobs, health care, or terrorism since 2001) (e.g. Weber 2006). In the 2008 Gallup Poll, the proportion of Americans saying they personally worried 'a great deal' about global warming declined from the previous year's high of 41% to 37%; the combined proportion of those worrying 'a great deal' and 'a fair amount' (66% in 2008) was only 3% higher than when the question was first asked in 1989 (Gallup 2008).

Over the years, climate change has consistently ranked lower than most other environmental problems on people's list of concerns and far below most non-environmental issues (e.g. Macnaghten 2003; Poortinga and Pidgeon 2003). In 2007, an unprecedented 33% of Americans in open-ended questions offered global warming for the first time as the top global environmental problem (ABC News, Washington Post and Stanford University 2007). A similarly high ranking has been reported across Europe (Directorate-General for Communication of the European Commission 2008). Since then, the issue has resumed its more common position well below other issues. For example, in a January 2009 survey, American respondents assessed 20 policy priorities, ranking energy as number six, the environment as number 16, and global warming fading far behind the economy, jobs, terrorism, or any other issue as number 20 (The Pew Research Center for the People & the Press 2009). By general comparison, in an 'economy vs. environment' importance ranking by the British population, the economy has always been more important than the environment—with exceptional years where both ranked almost the same—but in mid-2007, with the stock market collapse and economic recession in full swing, the economy surpassed the environment in relative importance by a 10:1 margin, and has not returned to historical levels since (Downing 2008). While not specific to climate change, such data suggest that climate change—conceived of as an environmental issue—also may have suffered a decline in societal importance during the recent economic crisis.

Personal Actions and Policy Support

The behavioural dimension of public engagement can be assessed by looking at different indicators of political support for particular mitigation strategies, political activism, behavioural changes and consumer choices. Since individuals do not get to vote on international or national policy proposals directly, surveys assessing categorical support must serve as proxies. Over the past two decades, surveys have revealed variable support for immediate (if unspecified) action to slow global warming. For example, in a 2007, 21-country comparison conducted by the BBC World Service, a significant majority (65%) of all respondents believed that there was a 'need for major action'. The countries with the largest majorities favouring taking major steps on climate change included Spain (91%), Italy (86%) and France (85%), as well as several Latin American countries, such as Mexico (83%), Chile (78%) and Brazil (76%) (BBC World Service 2007). While indicative of pervasive values (e.g. pro-environment, pro-social justice, precaution), such survey questions offer only limited insight into 'active engagement' as previously defined.

Similarly, in the US population, while support for policy action has generally risen in recent years (much dependent on how the questions are asked), many Americans still prefer doing more research, reflecting their general insecurity about the state of knowledge and varying perceptions of seriousness. In recent years, though, a plurality of Americans has emerged that seems to favour 'action now' versus 'wait and see' (see the review in Nisbet and Myers 2007). Support for actions has generally been lower during economic downturns, especially if actions involved economic costs, but surveys from the early years of the 21st century indicate a growing number of Americans favouring action even if it involves some costs. The low ranking of global warming in the 2009 Pew Research Center survey and political debates in the USA around economic recovery measures, however, put in question how solid the support is among Americans (and that of many members of Congress) for climate change action during crisis times and when personal interests and income are at stake.

Questions about more specific policy options, actions taken, or behavioural intentions may be more revealing (if maybe not conclusive). For example, surveys show rather consistent support among Americans for mandatory regulations imposed on industry and automobile manufacturers, as well as on utilities. Especially higher fuel efficiency standards on vehicles are consistently favoured by a majority of Americans, even if vehicle costs would increase (Nisbet and Myers 2007). Interestingly, when asked directly about the type of car Americans own or are likely to purchase, a recent survey revealed that only 21% of Americans currently own a vehicle that gets 30 miles per gallon (about 7.8 litres/100 km) or more, and while another 61% would like to buy such a vehicle, 40% believe they probably will not do so because of high costs and other reasons (Leiserowitz et al. 2009).

In terms of Americans' other energy saving behaviours—either already adopted or intended in the near future—recent research found quite optimistically that, '[o]verall roughly half of Americans say they have already made energy-efficiency improvements to their homes', although percentages varied significantly by the type and level of investment in different activities (Leiserowitz et al. 2009). Similarly, among the British there is strong support for climate-protective technologies (e.g. renewables) and related policy changes (Ipsos/MORI 2008, see Downing 2008). Moreover, 78% of the population responded in 2006 that they would be prepared to change their behaviour to help limit climate change (though only 22% felt strongly so). When asked specifically whether they had any plans to change their air travel behaviour, however, 70% intended to take 'about the same number of flights' in the next 12 months as they did previously (Downing and Ballantyne 2007). A recent review of Canadians' willingness to act on climate change and actual engagement found that 'Canadians vary in the level of action they take with respect to their global warming beliefs' (Moser 2009): 23% didn't believe in global warming and were completely opposed to action (identified by surveyors as 'skeptics'); 16% had not yet made up their mind on global warming ('agnostics') and tended not to act consciously in climate-friendly ways; another 22% (the 'converts') did not act on climate change either, but felt guilty about their lack of environmentally conscious behaviour; the 22% of Canadians identified as 'believers' were far more environmentally conscious and behaved accordingly; and a final 18% of 'activists' acted most environmentally conscious and fervently tried to convert others to do the same (Angus Reid Strategies 2007c, percentages do not add up to 100% due to rounding error). Taken together, these data suggest that 'about six out of 10 Canadians either doubt the need for action and/or do not act on their beliefs for action' (Moser 2009).

Several of the recent surveys on behavioural engagement and intention found that respondents would be interested in taking additional steps in the coming year, but cost, inconvenience, or competing priorities stand in the way (Leiserowitz et al. 2009). British respondents in addition found the lack of logistical support (such as amenities to help with recycling), lack of time, lack of interest, or an attitude that a single person's action would make no difference among the most pervasive action barriers preventing more environmentally friendly behaviour (Downing and Ballantyne 2007). These barriers to becoming more practically engaged will be discussed further below, as they speak to the range of 'costs' involved in the politics of public engagement. The findings also reflect the well-established fact—not just from survey studies but also from in-depth research of environmentally significant behaviour (e.g. Verplanken 2006; Verplanken and Aarts 1999; Verplanken and Orbell 2003; Verplanken and Wood 2006)—that habitual behaviour is particularly hard to change. The shift to more climate-friendly behaviour can be enabled and sustained, however, by pertinent economic, social and infrastructure conditions and support. The resulting new routines and habits can be equally persistent and even supportive of adopting additional green behaviours (Costanzo et al. 1986; de Young 1993; Gardner and Stern 2002; Knussen and Yule 2008; Kollmuss and Agyeman 2002; McKenzie-Mohr 2000; Prochaska 2003; Barr 2008; Tudor et al. 2008). A case in point is that relatively 'easy' energy saving actions—such as turning off unnecessary lights—are already being taken by more than nine out of 10 Americans, while only 20% always or often take public transportation, car pool, walk or cycle instead of driving (Leiserowitz et al. 2009).

In summary, surveys over the years find rather consistently that large numbers of individuals from a diverse set of nations support international policy commitments, even though factual knowledge of what they would entail is extremely limited, and probably reflect basic value commitments to fairness, leadership and equitable co-operation. Many individuals expect their governments to take proactive leadership roles in international negotiations, but most believe that everyone in society (including industry and businesses, all levels of government, civic institutions and individuals themselves) must do more to tackle climate change (e.g. Directorate-General for Communication of the European Commission 2008; Downing and Ballantyne 2007; Ipsos/MORI 2008 in Downing 2008; Leiserowitz 2007b; The Nielsen Company and Oxford University 2007). They also support mandatory policies at the national, state and local levels if they affect others or their own pocketbooks only marginally, but generally prefer incentives over taxes or regulatory approaches to support individual actions. If policies involve personal costs, support tends to decline, but recovers a little if the generated revenues are used to fight global warming, and if they are perceived as fair and applying to everyone (e.g. Brewer 2006; GfK Roper Public Affairs & Media and Yale School of Forestry & Environmental Studies 2007; Krosnick et al. 2000; Leiserowitz et al. 2008, 2009; Next 10 and Field Research Corporation 2007; Nisbet and Myers 2007).

This review also suggests that there are ample opportunities for increasing the level of cognitive, affective and behavioural engagement of individuals. At each level, untapped or insufficiently utilized potentials, frames, emotions, motivations, actors and actions are available to help people become more involved. Yet these opportunities are unlikely to be realized without equal attention to the barriers that prevent individuals from engaging more (Moser and Dilling 2007a). This would include, but certainly not be limited to, removing erroneous or misguided beliefs many individuals still appear to hold that either nothing needs to be done, nothing can be done to slow climate change, individual and collective efforts are in vain, or that they are already taking climate-protective/ emission-reducing actions, when in fact they are not (e.g. Downing and Bal-lantyne 2007; IMPACTS 2008; Leiserowitz et al. 2008). Clearly, more than 20 years of climate change on the public agenda would have offered enough opportunities to get engaged, if it just were not so costly to do.

THE COST OF INCREASING PUBLIC UNDERSTANDING AND CONCERN

From the modernist perspective of enlightenment, there is value to individuals and to society in being educated generally and knowledgeable about specific issues. Theorists of democracy and of education would argue, in fact, that such education is necessary to be an able participant in the political and civic affairs of a society (e.g. Albert Shanker Institute 2003; Dewey 1915; Freire 2008; Galston 2001). A more critical perspective might suggest that in Wes-tern, consumption-oriented, capitalist societies, there is also a value in staying (or keeping people) ignorant of certain issues. Certainly, as the US experience over the past 10–15 years with climate contrarians has shown, there are powerful forces who expend enormous resources and efforts not just on lob-bying and defending their own economic and political interests, but on actively attempting (and succeeding) in undermining Americans' conviction that climate change is happening, largely human-caused, serious, and requir-ing policy and behavioural changes throughout society (e.g. McCright 2007; McCright and Dunlap 2003). Yet, as the survey research summarized above suggested, even where climate denialists are less active and audible through mainstream media channels, the nature of climate change itself offers plenty of opportunities to deny its reality, seriousness and urgency—at least for now (Moser, forthcoming). Thus, both those who try to increase public under-standing and engagement, and those who would rather undermine it, have incentive—and real financial costs—in pursuing their respective goals. The question, then, of how to be most effective becomes a critical one. The answer requires understanding of the cognitive, psychological and other barriers that can prevent deeper public understanding.

Importantly, the forces defending the fossil fuel-heavy, energy-consumptive status quo always have an advantage over those who would try to change it given the enormous effort that has to be generated to overcome human habits, replace existing infrastructure, loosen technological and economic path dependencies, shift policy commitments, and try to change people's percep-tions of self-interest, stakes, and long-held beliefs and values. Together, these social and structural factors are at the root of the politics of public under-standing and engagement. They strongly influence 1) the cost involved in providing information, educating individuals, and attempting to increase their understanding and concern—itself a highly contested and political activity; and 2) the cost to individuals in acquiring knowledge, deepening their understanding of specific issues and the connections among them, and tolerating the cognitive and emotional impact of taking in and processing such information. These costs have cognitive, psychological, social, political and economic dimensions, and overlap with the behavioural, social, economic and institutional ones incurred in increasing practical engagement discussed below. This section explores those dimensions relevant to increasing public understanding and concern (the cognitive and affective dimensions of engagement), which make it 'costly' for individuals to understand what is at stake with global warming. As Boykoff, Goodman and Curtis (Chapter 8) show, the forces that would foster public understanding are pitched against those that would rather suppress it.

There is an increasing recognition of the range of barriers people face when encountering and processing climate change information (see reviews and discussions in Jamieson and VanderWerf 1994; Kollmuss and Agyeman 2002; Lorenzoni et al. 2007; Moser 2009; Moser and Dilling 2007b; Ockwell et al. 2009; O'Neill and Nicholson-Cole 2009). It takes significant cognitive effort to try to understand climate change, its causes, and how it is relevant to one's personal life, family, community, and economic, environmental and social context; it would take research and sorting through mounds of highly technical (and politicized) information on possible policies and technological solutions to identify what is viable, what the costs and possible risks involved are, and what the environmental or cultural consequences of adopting them may be. A growing concern in the media with 'green washing' and 'green fatigue' is indicative of the cognitive challenges individuals face in trying to make sense of the sheer amount and sometimes conflicting information about what actions and consumer choices would achieve the lowest carbon footprint and, more generally, the smallest impact on the environment in terms of pollutants, toxins and waste (e.g. Barringer 2008; Williams 2008). To the extent such information requires revision of previously held mental models or attitudes, the cognitive cost rises significantly; so much so, in fact, that individuals frequently reject the new information as 'false' (e.g. Bostrom and Lashof 2007; Dunwoody 2007). Even without trying to become a 'lay expert' on such matters, it is difficult to discern whom to trust. In the absence of technical expertise and in the face of too much and/or uncertain information, individuals tend to fall back on heuristic thinking—mental shortcuts—and other clues emerging from the framing, language, imagery and messenger to help them 'satisfice', i.e. to arrive at conclusions or decisions with limited, simplified information (e.g. Kahneman 2003; Kahneman et al. 1982; Krosnick 1991; Tversky and Kahneman 1974).

Processing climate change information can either increase or undermine the motivation to engage with the issue further. Very quickly, emotional responses arise (e.g. to images of a doom-and-gloom future) that might involve a sense of being powerless and overwhelmed; denial; numbing; feeling exempt from the threat; blaming others for the problem; wishful thinking or rationalization that the problem will be resolved by experts; displacement of attention on other problems; apathy; fatalism; or other forms of psycho-cognitive capitulation or transference (Immerwahr 1999; O'Neill and Nicholson-Cole 2009). These types of cognitive and emotional responses are particularly common in response to issues that are scary, ill-understood, difficult to control, overwhelming, and in which people are complicit, such as global climate change (Moser 2007). By contrast, images of a positive future, empowering messages and admirable, trusted opinion leaders can support further engagement (Benjamin et al. 2001; Cartwright 1959; French and Raven 1959; Meadows et al. 1992; Nisbet and Kotcher 2009; Olson 1995; Raven 1993; Stevenson 2006).

In addition, there are social barriers that not only affect people's behavioural and political engagement (see the next section), but also one's cognitive and affective engagement. As socially embedded individuals people tend to associate with 'like' individuals, with people much like themselves—a commonly observed principle called 'homophily' (Lazarsfeld and Merton 1954; McPherson et al. 2001; Rogers 2003). As McPherson et al. (2001, 415) stated in a review of the relevant literature, '[h]omophily limits people's social worlds in a way that has powerful implications for the information they receive, the attitudes they form, and the interactions they experience'. Members of one group are more likely to hear only the information, opinions and attitudes that conform with that group's social and political norms, and are attracted to similar kinds of issue framings, while discounting or even rejecting information that does not reflect the values, attitudes and opinions held by the members of one's group. People tend to communicate most frequently with people of similar socio-economic and attitudinal background, and thus are less likely to hear from others with different knowledge, attitudes and opinions. It takes work to put aside—at least temporarily—one's closely held views and explore those of others, to cross the distance to those from whom one is otherwise relatively isolated (e.g. upper- or middle-class people talking to working-class individuals; people of one racial or ethnic background talking to those of another), and to overcome the psychological resistance to thinking about or doing something that could potentially disconnect oneself from those with whom one bonds for social recognition, identity and validation. While it may be costly to build the broad issue coalitions needed to support substantial policy change, doing so tends to pay great political dividends (e.g. Agyeman et al. 2007; Sabatier and Jenkins-Smith 1993).

These personal tendencies can be exacerbated by information sources and channels as well as the communication infrastructure hindering exchange and engagement, even in the age of ubiquitous information available in the palm of one's hand. Heavy perceptual filters to prevent information overload, declining newspaper readership, reliance on 'bite-sized' television news, much reduced diversity in news sources as a result of media industry consolidation, and increasing reliance on, and high selectivity among, internet news sources can limit depth of coverage, understanding of an issue, and frequently does not offer individuals the breadth of views that may allow them to develop a well-considered opinion (The Pew Research Center for the People & the Press 2004).

In summary, the discussion of cognitive, psychological, social and other structural barriers makes clear how costly it is to reach diverse social groups and individuals, to attract and keep their attention, and invite or even compel them to mentally and emotionally engage with the complex, removed, uncertain and overwhelming issue of climate change. To increase the level of engagement, researchers and advocates have proposed a wide range of improvements, and none, probably, can be dismissed. Instead, an effective public engagement campaign is likely to require elements of all: a more sophisticated use of messengers, opinion leaders and the social influence they exert (Bagozzi and Lee 2002; Chess and Johnson 2007; Nisbet and Kotcher 2009); framing of climate change that links the issue with more persistent concerns and values (Bostrom and Lashof 2007; FrameWorks Institute 2001); the complementary use of mass media and face-to-face communication channels (Dunwoody 2007; Regan 2007); careful attention to the emotional impact of climate change communication, sending messages that prevent evoking fear or overwhelm and instead convey empowerment, positive vision and practical, enabling help (Moser 2007; O'Neill and Nicholson-Cole 2009). Maybe, counter-intuitively, communicators and advocates interested in increasing positive public engagement may even have to rethink their own commitment to the enlightenment ideal. Substantial research shows that providing information and filling knowledge gaps is at best necessary, but rarely sufficient to create active, behavioural engagement, and occasionally may even be used as a substitute for action (Kellstedt et al. 2008; Rabkin and Gershon 2007; Schultz 2002; Sturgis and Allum 2004; Tribbia 2007).

THE PRICE OF ACTIVE ENGAGEMENT

If knowledge and understanding constitute only a necessary, but typically insufficient motivation for people to actively engage with climate change, what else may be needed? It is important to recognize that different people are motivated by different things. Some will be motivated by self-interest, while others will act altruistically and prioritize communal goals and common goods; individuals may need a range of reasons to stay engaged over time. Clearly, knowledge and information can be a pathway to tapping deeper motivations. Communicators and advocates must reach these deeper levels of motivation, such as persistent beliefs, concerns, emotions, social norms, aspirations, social identities, visions of a promising future and underlying values through the messages, frames and messengers chosen to convey the need for greater engagement. Some audiences may only respond to financial incentives or higher costs; others may not act until compelled legally or unless there is political gain; and many may see the need to 'do something' only once the problems manifest in their backyards (Moser and Dilling 2007a). In the politics of public understanding and engagement, advocates for change—incurring significant cost—must motivate action long before climate change unfolds its full impacts.

An increasing number of researchers recognize that there is an even greater price tag attached to overcoming the internal resistances and external barriers that can prevent or constrain active political or behavioural engagement (e.g. DEFRA 2007; Lorenzoni et al. 2007; Moser and Dilling 2007b; Ockwell et al. 2009; O'Neill and Nicholson-Cole 2009). Internal barriers to making behavioural changes can arise from perceptions of comfort and ease (with current behaviour) and those of discomfort, loss, 'too much effort', difficulty, or helplessness vis-à-vis the novel behaviour, as well as the lack of requisite skills, knowledge of what to do, or the means to implement them, as reflected repeatedly in detailed studies of environmentally significant behaviour (e.g. Kollmuss and Agyeman 2002; Leiserowitz et al. 2009). As socially embedded individuals, individuals' adopted identities and social norms also suggest what is or is not appropriate behaviour. If, for example engaging in political action on climate change or changing one's behaviour portrays a particular social identity, produces a social stigma, or reflects social norms that are in conflict with people's desired identity and aspirations, individuals will resist engaging. If such practical engagement (e.g. writing letters to political representatives, investigating energy-efficient heaters for the home) takes 'too much' time or resources, and is inconvenient or too demanding given other daily concerns and competing obligations, even those who are sympathetic to the cause may refuse to get involved.

In addition to the psychological, mental, financial and social barriers to changing one's actions, there are also significant and sometimes ossified structural barriers that may not allow realization of one's motivation and commitment to action. There may not (yet) be a convenient or economically feasible alternative technology (e.g. widespread, affordable solar energy), the public infrastructure may not be in place e.g. mass transportation, distributed renewable energy production), path dependencies from land use and technological choices may inhibit quick and easy changes (e.g. urban sprawl and fuel-inefficient vehicles), or existing laws, regulations and associated interests may prevent or at least delay adoption of climate-friendly, energy-saving technologies and practices (e.g. fuel- and energy-efficiency standards in vehicles and appliances, building codes). It is for these reasons that communication and outreach campaigns cannot succeed without concomitant policy changes that remove barriers or provide specific assistance in overcoming them (e.g. Leiserowitz et al. 2009; Ockwell et al. 2009).

Political activism may be particularly difficult to increase. While political engagement through voting was higher in the 2008 US presidential elections than in many previous elections, only relatively small percentages of Americans engage in political and civic activism such as writing letters to the editors of newspapers, voicing their opinions personally and directly to elected officials, engaging in local town hall meetings, participating in political organizations, standing for political office, or engaging in demonstrations, civil disobedience, or other forms of protest (Lopez et al. 2006; National Conference on Citizenship 2008; Teske 1997). Reasons vary by age, gender, ethnicity and political leanings, and range from individuals being disinterested in political matters, preferring to leave political activism to others, being uneducated about political and civic actions, and/or feeling disenfranchised from the political process. Moreover, many individuals in Western and Westernized societies display a strong technological optimism, expecting or hoping that technological fixes (and associated policy and market mechanisms) will be found (e.g. Dunlap and van Liere 1984; Kirk 2007; Marx 2000; Nye 1996; Weinstein 1980). Even so, many individuals expect that technology alone will not suffice to solve the problem (Patchen 2006). Yet others may not believe that existing institutions are failing in their responsibilities, thus seeing no need for activism, or believing that they cannot change them. A related response is blaming others for the problem and/or projecting responsibility for remedial action onto them, as was found in a recent cross-national survey (IMPACTS 2008), and which also holds true at the neighbourhood or person-to-person level ('why should I ride my bike in the rain if my neighbour still drives his gas guzzler?'). Those with strongly vested interests may simply refuse to do anything different or new or use their influence on political institutions and electoral processes to delay action; for them, scientific uncertainty, time delays and perceptions of remote impacts can serve as a rationale to hold on to the status quo (e.g. Klandermans and Oegema 1987; Leighley 1995; Macnaghten and Jacobs 1997). While this dismissive segment of the population may not (need to) be persuaded, their potentially significant social influence on others (as opinion leaders or trusted spokespeople for certain segments of the population) may prevent deeper engagement and action by many others and thus deeply shape the politics of public engagement with climate change (see also Chapter 7 by Parks and Roberts).

THE UNAFFORDABILITY OF DENIAL AND INACTION

In this chapter, I have argued that the politics of public understanding and engagement is a struggle for dominance among political opinions and sympathies, attitudes and positions, and one in which members of society have to become at once more motivated to understand and act differently, and to overcome a wide range of internal and external barriers to enact their personal and political convictions. Both raising the motivation and lowering or helping to overcome the barriers to political and behavioural engagement occurs among competing interests embedded in a cultural, social, institutional, economic and political context that tends to favour the status quo, and thus makes it more difficult and costly for change agents to succeed.

Clearly, the journey toward greater public understanding and engagement emerges as an arduous, long and 'expensive' one given the many hurdles that must be overcome, only overshadowed by the prohibitively expensive alternative described in the introduction (see also Chapter 1 by Schneider and Mastrandrea). In the USA, the level of public understanding and engagement to date has suffered from unsophisticated communication and inadequate engagement campaigns, as well as persistent efforts of countervailing interests to confuse public understanding and block policy changes that could help reduce emissions or facilitate public engagement in climate-friendly behaviour. Such deliberate interference and willful denial of the need to change energy production and consumption patterns in the face of awareness and understanding of the problem has been termed 'ignore-ance' (Glantz 2003, 228), and may well lead to a future far worse than that described by Senator Kerry in the introduction.

However, a depiction of the politics of public understanding and engagement as merely a communicative or political-economic struggle between 'green' advocates and nay-saying defenders of fossil fuel interests would be incomplete, if not misleading. Rather, these politics must be placed in the structural, institutional and economic context that mediates and magnifies them, including media industry trends and reporting practices, trends in political and civic engagement, competing issues vying for attention and resources, structural forces that perpetuate habitual behaviour, and last, but not least, the nature of global climate change itself. Moreover, cognito-psychological, educational, social and cultural factors intervene in people's perception and understanding of issues, responsiveness to information, messages and frames, and expectations of themselves and others in solving this complex problem.

The question then arises whether the American public—as the citizens standing behind one indispensable international policy actor—can be rallied sufficiently and in time to help move the world toward the 'easier' climate future of 2050 rather than relegate it to a far more challenging one. Hulme (2008) argues that society's predominant answers to this question reflect a culturally deeply conditioned, modernist desire of mastery over 'something' in the face of fear of an unknown climate future. Those most pessimistic about society's capacity to engender sufficient public engagement promote geo-engineering or mastery over climate and the environment, while those hopeful about policy, market and technological solutions might favour 'political engineering', and those most optimistic (and maybe most demanding) of individuals and human nature might bank on the promise of social engineering (Hulme 2008). Some propose a combination of these approaches that would resemble the mobilization during the Second World War to get citizens and industry to fully support the war effort of the Allies against Nazism (e.g. Bartels 2001).

The politics of public understanding and engagement with climate change are interwoven by these discourses of mastery, even while deeper, alternative discourses are trying to be heard (e.g. Speth 2008). The US public is still largely ignorant of the prospects of geo-engineering, advocates and politicians display a half-hearted commitment to behaviour change (with a strong distaste of the notion of social engineering), and US leaders at this time lean toward policy, market and technological solutions that only hint at the hidden hand of government and policy orchestration. Currently debated policy solutions and the level of public engagement are unlikely to suffice to avert the spectre of an extremely challenging future. The insights and considerations in this chapter are offered to help inform strategies that democratically, actively and effectively engage individuals and their leaders on climate change, and thereby not just avoid the darker of our potential futures, but instead help create a brighter one.

REFERENCES

ABC News, Washington Post and Stanford University (2007) *Global Warming Soars to Top Slot as Greatest Environmental Threat*, Stanford, CA: Stanford University.

Agyeman, J., B. Doppelt, K. Lynn and H. Hatic (2007) 'The Climate-Justice Link: Communicating Risk with Low-Income and Minority Audiences', in S.C. Moser and L. Dilling (eds), *Creating a Climate for Change: Communicating Climate Change and Facilitating Social Change*, Cambridge: Cambridge University Press.

Albert Shanker Institute (2003) *Education for Democracy*, Washington, DC: Albert Shanker Institute.

Angus Reid Strategies (2007a) 'Angus Reid Climate Change Survey: Commit to Kyoto, but Don't Curb Car Travel, Say Canadians', www.angusreidstrategies.com/uploads/pages/pdfs/2007.04.03%20Enviro%20Policy%20Release.pdf (accessed 31 May 2009).

——(2007b) 'Angus Reid Climate Change Survey: Global Warming a Reality and a Threat, Canadians Say', www.angusreidstrategies.com/uploads/pages/pdfs/2007.03.21%20Enviro%20Press%20Release.pdf (accessed 31 May 2009).

——(2007c) 'Angus Reid Climate Change Survey: Rich and Educated Less Likely to Act Green, Today or Tomorrow', www.angusreidstrategies.com/index.cfm?fuseaction=news&newsid = 36&page = 27 (accessed 31 May 2009).

Anthes, E. (2009) 'Climate Change Takes a Mental Toll', *The Boston Globe*, www.boston.com/news/science/articles/2009/02/09/climate_change_takes_a_mental_toll (accessed 31 May 2009), 9 February.

Bagozzi, R.P. and K.-H. Lee (2002) 'Multiple Routes for Social Influence: The Role of Compliance, Internalization, and Social Identity', *Social Psychology Quarterly* Vol. 65, No. 3.

Barr, S. (2008) *Environment and Society: Sustainability, Policy and the Citizen*, Hampshire, UK: Ashgate.

Barringer, F. (2008) 'Talking Directly, and Kindly, to Believers in the Eco Life', *The New York Times*, 26 August.

Bartels, D. (2001) 'Wartime Mobilization to Counter Severe Global Climate Change', *Human Ecology* Vol. 10, Special Issue.

BBC World Service (2007) 'All Countries Need to Take Major Steps on Climate Change: Global Poll', survey conducted by GlobeScan together with the Program on International Policy Attitudes (PIPA) at the University of Maryland, www.worldpublicopinion.org/pipa/pdf/sep07/BBCClimate_Sep07_rpt.pdf (accessed 8 April 2008).

Benjamin, P., J.X. Kasperson, R.E. Kasperson, J.L. Emel and D.E. Rocheleau (2001) 'Social Visions of Future Sustainable Societies', in J.X. Kasperson and R.E. Kasperson (eds), *Global Environmental Risk*, Tokyo: UNU Press.

Bostrom, A. and D. Lashof (2007) 'Weather it's Climate Change?', in S.C. Moser and L. Dilling (eds), *Creating a Climate for Change: Communicating Climate Change and Facilitating Social Change*, Cambridge: Cambridge University Press.

Boykoff, M.T. (2007a) 'Flogging a Dead Norm? Newspaper Coverage of Anthropogenic Climate Change in the United States and United Kingdom from 2003 to 2006', *Area* Vol. 39, No. 4.

——(2007b) 'From Convergence to Contention: United States Mass Media Representations of Anthropogenic Climate Change Science', *Transactions of the Institute of British Geographers* Vol. 32, No. 4.

Boykoff, M.T. and J.M. Boykoff (2004) 'Balance as Bias: Global Warming and the US Prestige Press', *Global Environmental Change* Vol. 14, No. 2.

Brechin, S.R. (2003) 'Comparative Public Opinion and Knowledge on Global Climatic Change and the Kyoto Protocol: The US Versus the Rest of the World?', *International Journal of Sociology and Social Policy* Vol. 23, No. 10.

Brewer, T.L. (2003) 'Seeds of Change in the US: Public Opinion Ahead of Politicians on Climate Change', *New Economy* Vol. 10, No. 3.

——(2005a) 'US Public Opinion on Climate Change Issues: Implications for Consensus-Building and Policymaking', *Climate Policy* Vol. 4, No.1.

——(2005b) U.S. Public Opinion on Climate Change Issues: Update for 2005, *Climate Policy* Vol. 5, No. 4.

——(2006) 'Public Opinion on Climate Change Issues in the G-8 and G-5 Countries', www.usclimatechange.com (accessed 14 July 2006).

Cartwright, D. (ed.) (1959) *Studies in Social Power*, Ann Arbor, MI: University of Michigan, Research Center for Group Dynamics, Institute for Social Research.

Chess, C. and B.B. Johnson (2007) 'Information is Not Enough', in S.C. Moser and L. Dilling (eds), *Creating a Climate for Change: Communicating Climate Change and Facilitating Social Change*, Cambridge: Cambridge University Press.

Costanzo, M., D. Archer and E. Aronson (1986) 'Energy Conservation Behavior: The Difficult Path from Information to Action', *American Psychologist* Vol. 41, No. 5.

Davidson, M.D. (2008) 'Parallels in Reactionary Argumentation in the US Congressional Debates on the Abolition of Slavery and the Kyoto Protocol', *Climatic Change* Vol. 86.

Davidson, S., C. Martin and S. Treanor (2009) 'Scottish Environmental Attitudes and Behaviours Survey 2008', Edinburgh: Ipsos/MORI.

DEFRA (2007) *2007 Survey of Public Attitudes and Behaviours Toward the Environment*, London: Department of the Environment, Food and Rural Affairs.

de Young, R. (1993) 'Changing Behavior and Making it Stick: The Conceptualization and Management of Conservation Behavior', *Environment and Behavior* Vol. 25.

Dewey, J. (1915) *Democracy and Education: An Introduction to the Philosophy of Education*, New York: The Macmillan Company.

Directorate-General for Communication of the European Commission (2008) 'Europeans' Attitudes Towards Climate Change', *Special Eurobarometer* 300. Brussels, Belgium: European Commission.

Downing, P. (2008) *Public Attitudes to Climate Change, 2008: Concerned But Still Unconvinced*, London: Ipsos/MORI.

Downing, P. and J. Ballantyne (2007) *Tipping Point or Turning Point? Social Marketing & Climate Change*, London: Ipsos/MORI Social Research Institute.

Dunlap, R.E. and A.M. McCright (2008) 'A Widening Gap: Republican and Democratic Views on Climate Change', *Environment* Vol. 50.

Dunlap, R.E. and K.D. van Liere (1984) 'Commitment to the Dominant Social Paradigm and Concern for Environmental Quality', *Social Science Quarterly* Vol. 65, No. 44.

Dunwoody, S. (2007) 'The Challenge of Trying to Make a Difference Using Media Messages', in S.C. Moser and L. Dilling (eds), *Creating a Climate for Change: Communicating Climate Change and Facilitating Social Change*, Cambridge: Cambridge University Press.

FrameWorks Institute (2001) *Talking Global Warming (Summary of Research Findings)*, Washington, DC: FrameWorks Institute.

Freire, P. (2008) *Pedagogy of the Oppressed*, 30th Anniversary edn, New York, London: Continuum.

French, Jr, J.R.P. and B.H. Raven (1959) 'The Bases of Social Power', in D. Cartwright (ed.), *Studies in Social Power*, Ann Arbor, MI: University of Michigan, Research Center for Group Dynamics, Institute for Social Research.

Gallup (2008) 'Gallup's Pulse of Democracy: Environment', in *The Gallup Poll*, Princeton, NJ: Gallup.

Galston, W.A. (2001) 'Political Knowledge, Political Engagement, and Civic Education', *Annual Review of Political Science* Vol. 44, No. 1.

Gardner, G.T. and P.C. Stern (2002) *Environmental Problems and Human Behavior*, Boston, MA: Pearson Custom Publishing.

GfK Roper Public Affairs & Media and Yale School of Forestry & Environmental Studies (2007) 'The GfK Roper Yale Survey on Environmental Issues: Fall, 2007: American Support for Local Action on Global Warming', New Haven, CT: Yale University.

Glantz, M.H. (2003) *Climate Affairs: A Primer*, Washington, DC: Island Press.

Halpern, D. and C. Bates (2004) *Personal Responsibility and Changing Behaviour: The State of Knowledge and Its Implications for Public Policy*, London: UK Prime Minister's Strategy Unit.

Hulme, M. (2008) 'The Conquering of Climate: Discourses of Fear and their Dissolution', *The Geographical Journal* Vol. 174, No. 1.

Immerwahr, J. (1999) *Waiting for a Signal: Public Attitudes Toward Global Warming, the Environment and Geophysical Research*, Washington, DC: American Geophysical Union.

IMPACTS (2008) 'Public Awareness, Attitudes and Behaviors Concerning Global Climate Change: Prepared for the Monterey Bay Aquarium: Selected Findings from a Collaborative Project of The Ocean Project, the Monterey Bay Aquarium, and the National Aquarium in Baltimore', Providence RI: The Ocean Project.

Jamieson, D. and K. VanderWerf (1994) 'Societal Response to Creeping Environmental Phenomena: Some Cultural Barriers', in M. Glantz (ed.), *Creeping Environmental Phenomena and Societal Responses to Them: Workshop Report*, Boulder, CO: National Center for Atmospheric Research, Environmental and Societal Impacts Group.

Kahlor, L. and S. Rosenthal (2009) 'If We Seek, Do We Learn? Predicting Knowledge of Global Warming', *Science Communication* Vol. 30, No. 3.

Kahneman, D. (2003) 'Maps of Bounded Rationality: Psychology for Behavioral Economics', *The American Economic Review* Vol. 93, No. 5.

Kahneman, D., P. Slovic and A. Tversky (eds) (1982) *Judgment Under Uncertainty: Heuristics and Biases*, New York: Cambridge University Press.

Kellstedt, P.M., S. Zahran and A. Vedlitz (2008) 'Personal Efficacy, the Information Environment, and Attitudes Toward Global Warming and Climate Change in the United States', *Risk Analysis* Vol. 28, No. 1.

Kerry, J. (2009) 'Opening Remarks, Senate Foreign Relations Committee Hearing with Former US Vice-President, Al Gore, on January 28, 2009', transcribed from www.c-span.com (accessed 3 February 2009).

Kirk, A.G. (2007) *Counterculture Green: The Whole Earth Catalog and American Environmentalism*, Lawrence, KS: University Press of Kansas.

Klandermans, B. and D. Oegema (1987) 'Potentials, Networks, Motivations, and Barriers: Steps Towards Participation in Social Movements', *American Sociological Review* Vol. 52, No. 4.

Knussen, C. and F. Yule (2008) '"I'm Not in the Habit of Recycling": The Role of Habitual Behavior in the Disposal of Household Waste', *Environment and Behavior* Vol. 40, No. 5.

Kollmuss, A. and J. Agyeman (2002) 'Mind the Gap: Why Do People Act Environmentally and What Are the Barriers to Pro-Environmental Behavior?', *Environmental Education Review* Vol. 8, No. 3.

Krosnick, J.A. (1991) 'Response Strategies for Coping with the Cognitive Demands of Attitude Measures in Surveys', *Applied Cognitive Psychology* Vol. 5.

Krosnick, J.A., A.L. Holbrook and P.S. Visser (2000) 'The Impact of the Fall 1997 Debate about Global Warming on American Public Opinion', *Public Understanding of Science* Vol. 9, No. 3.

Lahsen, M. (2008) 'Experiences of Modernity in the Greenhouse: A Cultural Analysis of a Physicist "Trio" Supporting the Backlash Against Global Warming', *Global Environmental Change* Vol. 18, No. 1.

Lazarsfeld, P. and R.K. Merton (1954) 'Friendship as a Social Process: A Substantive and Methodological Analysis', in M. Berger, T. Abel and C. H. Page (eds), *Freedom and Control in Modern Society*, New York: Van Nostrand.

Leighley, J.E. (1995) 'Attitudes, Opportunities and Incentives: A Field Essay on Political Participation', *Political Research Quarterly* Vol. 48, No. 1.

Leiserowitz, A. (2006) 'Climate Change Risk Perception and Policy Preferences: The Role of Affect, Imagery, and Values', *Climatic Change* Vol. 77, NO. 1.

——(2007a) *American Opinions on Global Warming*, New Haven, CT: Yale University.

——(2007b) *International Public Opinion, Perception, and Understanding of Global Climate Change*, New Haven, CT: Yale University.

Leiserowitz, A., E. Maibach and C. Roser-Renouf (2008) *Global Warming's "Six Americas": An Audience Segmentation*, New Haven, CT: Yale University, Yale Project of Climate Change, Yale School of Forestry & Environmental Studies / Fairfax, VA: George Mason University, Center for Climate Change Communication.

——(2009) *Saving Energy at Home and on the Road: A Survey of Americans' Energy Saving Behaviors, Intentions, Motivations, and Barriers*, New Haven, CT: Yale Project of Climate Change, Yale School of Forestry & Environmental Studies / Fairfax, VA: George Mason University, Center for Climate Change Communication.

Lopez, M.H. et al. (2006) *The 2006 Civic and Political Health of the Nation: A Detailed Look at How Youth Participate in Politics and Communities*, College Park, MD: Center for Information and Research on Civic Learning and Engagement.

Lorenzoni, I., S. Nicholson-Cole and L. Whitmarsh (2007) 'Barriers Perceived to Engaging with Climate Change Among the UK Public and Their Policy Implications', *Global Environmental Change* Vol. 17, Nos 3–4.

Lorenzoni, I. and N.F. Pidgeon (2006) 'Public Views on Climate Change: European and USA Perspectives', *Climatic Change* Vol. 77, Nos 1–2.

Lowe, D.C. (2006) 'Vicarious Experiences vs. Scientific Information in Climate Change Risk Perception and Behaviour: A Case Study of Undergraduate Students in Norwich, UK, *Technical Report* 43, Norwich, UK: Tyndall Centre for Climate Change Research.

Lowe, T., K. Brown, S. Dessai, M. Doria, K. Haynes and K. Vincent (2006) 'Does Tomorrow Ever Come? Disaster Narrative and Public Perceptions of Climate Change', *Public Understanding of Science* Vol. 15, No. 4.

McCright, A.M. (2007) 'Dealing with Climate Change Contrarians', in S.C. Moser and L. Dilling (eds), *Creating a Climate for Change: Communicating Climate Change and Facilitating Social Change*, Cambridge: Cambridge University Press.

McCright, A.M. and R.E. Dunlap (2001) 'Challenging Global Warming as a Social Problem: An Analysis of the Conservative Movement's Counter-Claims', *Social Problems* Vol. 47, No. 4.

——(2003) 'Defeating Kyoto: The Conservative Movement's Impact on US Climate Change Policy', *Social Problems* Vol. 50, No. 3.

McKenzie-Mohr, D. (2000) 'New Ways to Promote Proenvironmental Behavior: Promoting Sustainable Behavior: An Introduction to Community-Based Social Marketing', *Journal of Social Issues* Vol. 56, No. 3.

Macnaghten, P. (2003) 'Embodying the Environment in Everyday Life Practices', *The Sociological Review* Vol. 51, No. 1.

Macnaghten, P. and M. Jacobs (1997) 'Public Identification with Sustainable Development: Investigating Cultural Barriers to Participation', *Global Environmental Change* Vol. 7, No. 1.

McPherson, M., L. Smith-Lovin and J. Cook (2001) 'Birds of a Feather: Homophily in Social Networks', *Annual Review of Sociology* Vol. 27, No. 1.

Maibach, E., C. Roser-Renouf and A. Leiserowitz (2009) 'Global Warming's Six Americas 2009: An Audience Segmentation Analysis', New Haven, CT: Yale Project on Climate Change, School of Forestry and Environmental Studies, Yale University / Fairfax, VA: Center for Climate Change Communication, Department of Communication, George Mason University.

Maibach, E., C. Roser-Renouf, D. Weber and M. Taylor (2008) *What Are Americans Thinking and Doing about Global Warming? Results of a National Household Survey*, Washington, DC: Porter Novelli / Fairfax, VA: George Mason University, Center of Excellence in Climate Change Communication Research.

Marx, L. (2000) *The Machine in the Garden: Technology and the Pastoral Ideal in America*, Oxford: Oxford University Press.

Meadows, D.H., D.L. Meadows and J. Randers (1992) *Beyond the Limits to Growth: Confronting Global Collapse, Envisioning a Sustainable Future*, White River Junction, VT: Chelsea Green Publishing.

Moser, S.C. (2007) 'More Bad News: The Risk of Neglecting Emotional Responses to Climate Change Information', in S.C. Moser and L. Dilling (eds), *Creating a Climate for Change: Communicating Climate Change and Facilitating Social Change*, Cambridge: Cambridge University Press.

——(2008) 'Toward a Deeper Engagement of the US Public on Climate Change: An Open Letter to the 44th President of the United States of America', *International Journal for Sustainability Communication* Vol. 3.

——(2009) 'Communicating Climate Change and Motivating Civic Action: Renewing, Activating, and Building Democracies', in H. Selin and S.D. VanDeveer (eds), *Changing Climates in North American Politics: Institutions, Policymaking and Multilevel Governance*, Cambridge, MA: MIT Press.

——(forthcoming) 'Communicating Climate Change: History, Challenges, Process and Future Directions', *Wiley Interdisciplinary Reviews (WIRE) – Climate Change*, accepted for publication.

Moser, S.C. and L. Dilling (2007a) 'Toward the Social Tipping Point: Conclusions', in S.C. Moser and L. Dilling (eds), *Creating a Climate for Change: Communicating Climate Change and Facilitating Social Change*, Cambridge: Cambridge University Press.

——(eds) (2007b) *Creating a Climate for Change: Communicating Climate Change and Facilitating Social Change*, Cambridge: Cambridge University Press.

National Conference on Citizenship (2008) *America's 2008 Civic Health Index: Beyond the Vote*, Washington, DC: National Conference on Citizenship.

Next 10 and Field Research Corporation (2007) *California Opinion Index: A Digest Summarizing the California Public's Views About Global Warming*, Palo Alto, CA: Next 10 / San Francisco, CA: Field Research Corporation.

The Nielsen Company and Oxford University (2007) 'Global Nielsen Survey: Consumers Look to Governments to Act on Climate Change', *Breaking News*, June 2007, Oxford: The Nielsen Company and Oxford University Environmental Change Institute.

Nisbet, M.C. and J.E. Kotcher (2009) 'A Two-Step Flow of Influence?: Opinion-Leader Campaigns on Climate Change', *Science Communication* Vol. 30, No. 3.

Nisbet, M.C. and T. Myers (2007) 'Twenty Years of Public Opinion About Global Warming', *Public Opinion Quarterly* Vol. 71, No. 3.

Nye, D.E. (1996) *American Technological Sublime*, Cambridge, MA: MIT Press.

Ockwell, D., L. Whitmarsh and. S. O'Neill (2009) 'Reorienting Climate Change Communication for Effective Mitigation: Forcing People to Be Green or Fostering Grass-Roots Engagement?', *Science Communication* Vol. 30, No. 3.

Olson, R.L. (1995) 'Sustainability as a Social Vision', *Journal of Social Issues* Vol. 51, No. 4.

O'Neill, S. and S. Nicholson-Cole (2009) '"Fear Won't Do It": Promoting Positive Engagement with Climate Change Through Visual and Iconic Representations', *Science Communication* Vol. 30, No. 3.

Patchen, M. (2006) 'Public Attitudes and Behavior about Climate Change: What Shapes Them and How to Influence Them', *PCCRC Outreach Publication No. 0601,* West Lafayette, IN: Purdue University, Purdue Climate Change Research Center.

The Pew Research Center for The People & the Press (2004) 'News Audiences Increasingly Politicized: Pew Research Center Biennial News Consumption Survey', released 8 June 2004, Washington, DC: The Pew Research Center for the People & the Press.

——(2009) 'Economy, Jobs Trump All Other Policy Priorities in 2009: Environment, Immigration, Health Care Slip Down the List', Washington, DC: The Pew Research Center for the People & the Press.

Poortinga, W. and N. Pidgeon (2003) *Public Perceptions of Risk, Science and Governance: Main Findings of a British Survey of Five Risk Cases*, Centre for Environmental Risk, University of East Anglia.

Prochaska, J.O. (2003) 'Changing for Good: Applying Theories of Behavioral Change to Environmental Action', presentation given on 16 April 2003, New England Aquarium, Boston, MA.

Rabkin, S. and D. Gershon (2007) 'Changing the World One Household at a Time: Portland's 30-Day Program to Lose 5000 Pounds', in S.C. Moser and L. Dilling (eds), *Creating a Climate for Change: Communicating Climate Change and Facilitating Social Change*, Cambridge: Cambridge University Press.

Rasmussen Report (2009) '44% Say Global Warming Due to Planetary Trends, Not People', *Rasmussen Report*, 19 January.

Raven, B.H. (1993) 'The Bases of Power: Origins and Recent Developments', *Journal of Social Issues* Vol. 49, No. 4.

Regan, K. (2007) 'A Role for Dialogue in Communication about Climate Change', in S.C. Moser and L. Dilling (eds), *Creating a Climate for Change: Communicating Climate Change and Facilitating Social Change*, Cambridge: Cambridge University Press.

Rogers, E.M. (2003) *Diffusion of Innovations*, 5th edn [1962], New York: Free Press.

Sabatier, P.A. and H.C. Jenkins-Smith (1993) *Policy Change and Learning: An Advocacy Coalition Approach*, Boulder, CO: Westview Press.

Schultz, P.W. (2002) 'Knowledge, Information, and Household Recycling: Examining the Knowledge-Deficit Model of Behavior Change', in T. Dietz and P.C. Stern (eds), *New Tools for Environmental Protection: Education, Information, and Voluntary Measures*, Washington, DC: National Academy Press.

Semenza, J.C., D.E. Hall, D.J. Wilsond, B.D. Bontempo, D.J. Sailor and L.A. George (2008) 'Public Perception of Climate Change: Voluntary Mitigation and Barriers to Behavior Change', *American Journal of Preventive Medicine* Vol. 35, No. 5.

Speth, J.G. (2008) 'Toward a New Consciousness: Values to Sustain Human and Natural Communities', *The Leopold Outlook* Vol. 8, No. 2.

Stevenson, T. (2006) 'From Vision into Action', *Futures* Vol. 38, No. 6.

Stoll-Kleemann, S., T. O'Riordan and C.C. Jaeger (2001) 'The Psychology of Denial Concerning Climate Mitigation Measures: Evidence from Swiss Focus Groups', *Global Environmental Change* Vol. 11.

Sturgis, P. and N. Allum (2004) 'Science in Society: Re-Evaluating the Deficit Model of Public Attitudes', *Public Understanding of Science* Vol. 13.

Teske, N. (1997) *Political Activists in America: The Identity Construction Model of Political Participation*, Cambridge: Cambridge University Press.

Tompkins, E.L. (2006) 'Scenario-Based Stakeholder Engagement: A Framework for Incorporating Climate Change into Coastal Decision Making', presentation on 6 February 2006 at the National Center for Atmospheric Research, Boulder, CO.

Tribbia, J. (2007) 'Stuck in the Slow Lane of Behavior Change? A Not-So-Superhuman Perspective on Getting out of our Cars', in S.C. Moser and L. Dilling (eds), *Creating a Climate for Change: Communicating Climate Change and Facilitating Social Change*, Cambridge: Cambridge University Press.

Tudor, T.L., S.W. Barr and A.W. Gilg (2008) 'A Novel Conceptual Framework for Examining Environmental Behavior in Large Organizations: Case Study of the Cornwall National Health Service (NHS) in the United Kingdom', *Environment and Behavior* Vol. 40, No. 3.

Tversky, A. and D. Kahneman (1974) 'Judgments under Uncertainty: Heuristics and Biases', *Science* Vol. 185, No. 4157.

Verplanken, B. (2006) 'Beyond Frequency: Habit as Mental Construct', *British Journal of Social Psychology* Vol. 45, No. 3.

Verplanken, B. and H. Aarts (1999) 'Habit, Attitude, and Planned Behaviour: Is Habit an Empty Construct or an Interesting Case of Automaticity?', *European Review of Social Psychology* Vol. 10.

Verplanken, B. and S. Orbell (2003) 'Reflections on Past Behavior: A Self-Report Index of Habit Strength', *Journal of Applied Social Psychology* Vol. 33, No. 6.

Verplanken, B. and W. Wood (2006) 'Interventions to Break and Create Consumer Habits', *Journal of Public Policy and Marketing* Vol. 25, No. 1.

Weber, E.U. (2006) 'Experience-Based and Description-Based Perceptions of Long-Term Risk: Why Global Warming Does Not Scare Us (Yet)', *Climatic Change* Vol. 77, Nos 1–2.

Weinstein, N.D. (1980) 'Unrealistic Optimism about Future Life Events', *Journal of Personality and Social Psychology* Vol. 39.

Williams, A. (2008) 'That Buzz in Your Ear May Be Green Noise', *The New York Times*, 15 June.

A–Z Glossary

Maxwell T. Boykoff and
Chukwumerije Okereke

A

Adaptation

Adaptation generally refers to the process of modifications or adjustments in behaviour, aspects of operations or rules in order to respond to changes in the external environment. In the context of climate **politics** the term is used mostly in **climate change** discussions and refers to the changes that societies are supposed to make in order to respond to the negative impacts of unavoidable climate change. It is also used in discussions that focus on the tendency as well as the limit of the earth's natural system and the living organisms to adjust in ways that can accommodate the process of (natural and human-induced) climate change without resulting in catastrophic consequences. When the issue of global climate change became a major political topic in the late 1980s and early 1990s, the main focus was on **mitigation**— that is how to reduce **carbon dioxide** emissions in the **atmosphere** in order to prevent the incidence of human-induced climate change. The focus on mitigation is clearly reflected in the wordings of the **UN Framework Convention on Climate Change** (UNFCCC), which has as its objective the need to 'stabilize **greenhouse gas** concentration in the atmosphere at a level that would prevent dangerous interference with the climate system' although the word adaptation was subsequently mentioned in a number places in the Convention text. Adaptation received less attention in the early years mainly because Parties to the Convention requested more certainty on the effects of and **vulnerability** to climate change on different natural and social systems. In 2001 the **Intergovernmental Panel on Climate Change** (IPCC) reported that it was reasonably certain that climate change was already happening with considerable negative effects on several ecosystems and human settlements around the world. The major effects were said to be the general reduction in crop yield in most tropical regions, increased flooding of human settlements, water scarcity and the increase in water borne and vector-borne diseases such as malaria due to drastic changes in precipitation patterns. Those identified to be mostly vulnerable to the negative impact of unavoidable climate change were the Third Word countries especially the Least Developing Countries (LDC) and the Small Island Developing States (SIDS). The panel called for attention to be given to adaptation as well as mitigation in the global effort to tackle climate change. Since then a huge number of studies from both public and private organizations have been conducted to ascertain the scale of impact and the vulnerabilities of various ecosystems and human communities to climate change. Most of these results show that the developing countries which contribute little to climate change are the ones that are most vulnerable to the negative consequences. Subsequently the developing countries have been pushing for adaptation to be accorded a priority in the scheme of things in the United Framework Convention on Climate Change. In the 10th **Conference of the Parties** (COP) meeting in Buenos Aires Argentina 2004 a plan of action on adaptation and response measures was adopted as part of the responses to this campaign. There have been also other programmes including the establishment of a special needs fund for the Least Development Countries (LDC Fund) and a Five-year programme of work on impacts, vulnerability and adaptation all designed to help the developing countries to respond the impacts of climate change.

Adaptation Fund

The **UN Framework Convention on Climate Change** (UNFCCC) defines **adaptation** as an 'adjustment in natural or human systems in response to actual or expected climatic stimuli or their effects, which moderates harm or exploits beneficial opportunities'. Articles 4.3 and 4.4. of the UNFCCC mandate that new and 'additional' resources must be provided for vulnerable countries to 'adjust' to these climate stimuli. While it has been in the planning since the development of the **Kyoto Protocol** in 1997 in order to provide a mechanism through which adaptation activities are funded, the 'Adaptation Fund' came into being in 2007. Monies are generated through a levy of 2% from **Clean Development Mechanism** projects. Over half a million Certified Emissions Reductions (CER) credits from CDM projects have been set aside for this Fund. In setting it up in this way, though, the size of the Adaptation Fund is dependent upon the volume of CDM projects taking place. In 2009, the Adaptation Fund was reported to have raised approximately US $200–300m. per year. However, many academic scholars—including a number of authors in this volume, such as Lemos, Boyd, Parks and Roberts—claim that these funds are a mere fraction of what will be needed to meet adaptation demands in the years to come. As Lemos and Boyd have pointed out in Chapter 6, a 2007 UNFCCC assessment puts the need in the developing world between $28 billion and $67 billion a year by the year 2030. This is a relatively conservative estimate compared to many others, such as those made by the UN Development Programme ($86 billion/year) and Oxfam ($50 billion/year). As of the time of writing in 2009, the fund remains non-operational due to debates within the supervisory 16-country Adaptation Fund Board over dissemination of these monies. Moreover, at the time of writing, just under half of the amount of money promised to the Adaptation Fund has actually been delivered. Chapters 3 and 6 discuss the **politics** of these processes. Also, in June 2009 United Kingdom Prime Minister Gordon Brown was the first **Annex I/B** head of state to put forward a specific plan to allocate funding to developing countries for climate adaptation. He proposed to commit funding beginning in 2013, rising to $100 billion a year by 2020.

Additionality

Additionality is a term associated with the generation of funds for projects that help human societies adapt to **climate change**, particularly in the developing world. Articles 4.3 and 4.4. of the **UN Framework Convention on Climate Change** mandate that new and 'additional' resources must be provided for vulnerable countries to adapt to 'actual or expected climatic stimuli or their effects'. Generally, the requirement of 'additionality' refers to a criterion that monetary funds are allocated beyond 'business-as-usual' project activities. Projects that meet 'additionality' requirements are, then, those that make emissions reductions in additional to those that otherwise would have occurred anyway. Explicitly, the additionality requirement is part of the **Adaptation Fund**, where money is generated through a levy of 2% from **Clean Development Mechanism** (Article 12) projects. The generation of funding by way of additionality also marks the connection between **mitigation** activities and **adaptation** projects. Beyond the UN Adaptation Fund, funds are assembled through new multilateral or bilateral development projects, or Overseas Development Assistance (ODA). In practice, it is difficult to agree upon what endeavours meet the 'additionality' requirements. This is because it is difficult, if not impossible, to determine what projects are specifically climate adaptation projects and, therefore, what funding is specifically additional climate adaptation funding. Adaptation programmes can include initiatives such as dam projects and dykes, but scholars—such as Lemos and Boyd in Chapter 6 of this volume—caution that the additionality stipulation creates the conditions where climate and development projects become unnecessarily segregated. They comment that complex initiatives like income diversification schemes may become de-prioritized, as simple measures like the introduction of drought resistant crops can be more clearly linked to adaptation strategies. Moreover, they write, 'We suggest that because climate change is one among many stresses that define the **vulnerability** of people and ecosystems in less developed regions, it makes little sense to prioritize additionally over the need to integrate across policies to adapt to these multiple stresses […] Through additionality, adaptation policy at the global level divides and circumscribes processes that are indivisible at the local level and, in practice, disables the opportunities for complementarities and synergies in adapting to climate change'. Thus 'additionality' is one particularly contentious issue ongoing, in the **politics** of climate change.

Afforestation

Afforestation is the process of planting trees and forests in spaces that had previously not been forested within the last 50 years. This is contrasted with 'reforestation', which is planting trees on more recently deforested areas or degraded forest lands. These issues are moving to the fore of negotiations for the successor to the **Kyoto Protocol**, particularly as they become articulated in the **Reducing Emissions from Deforestation and Forest Degradation** (REDD) mechanism.

Agenda 21

Agenda 21 was one of four major products of the 1992 **Earth Summit** (the other three were the Rio Declaration, the Convention on Biological Diversity and the **UN Framework Convention on Climate Change**). At the time, Agenda 21 was touted as a 'blueprint' for sustainable development in the 21st century. It consisted of a Preamble and then major sections on social and economic dimensions, conservation and management of resources, strengthening the role of major groups, and means of implementation. Going into the Rio Summit (UNCED) in 1992, the Parties had already agreed on 98% of this document. The points that remained under discussion involved **consumption** and population issues. This document also promoted the **Global Environment Facility** (GEF) to fund sustainable development initiatives.

Alliance of Small Island States (AOSIS)

AOSIS is a coalition of 43 small island and low-lying coastal developing countries, founded in 1990. These countries represent 20% of the UN membership. These countries have come together through common interests of development challenges and environmental concerns. Within the UN **Conference of the Parties** (COP) negotiations, AOSIS acts as a lobbying group to raise the profile of issues such as **vulnerability** and **adaptation** funding. In addition, the AOSIS nations are logically concerned about the impact of **sea-level** rise. The **Intergovernmental Panel on Climate Change** has assessed that the global average sea level has risen 8 inches (20.5 cm) since 1900 and scientists predict a rise of another 4–37 inches (10–94 cm) by 2100. Many poorer island nations are not financially capable of building large dykes and levee systems to guard against gradual rises as well as increasingly threatening storm events. AOSIS members have called for more severe cuts in **greenhouse gas** (GHG) emissions, in order to limit this sea-level rise. In particular, citizens of member nations such as Kiribati and the Marshall Islands risk becoming the first wave of 'climate refugees'. Thus, AOSIS has been an active group to challenge the framing of issues from those focusing predominantly on economic costs to issues of environmental justice and distribution of impacts. The AOSIS member states are Antigua and Barbuda, Bahamas, Barbados, Belize, Cape Verde, Cook Islands, Cuba, Comoros, Cyprus, Dominica, Federated States of Micronesia, Fiji, Grenada, Guinea-Bissau, Guyana, Haiti, Kiribati, Jamaica, Maldives, Malta, Marshall Islands, Mauritius, Nauru, Niue, Palau, Papua New Guinea, Samoa, São Tomé and Príncipe, Saint Christopher and

Nevis, Saint Lucia, Saint Vincent and the Grenadines, Seychelles, Singapore, Solomon Islands, Suriname, Tonga, Trinidad and Tobago, Tuvalu, and Vanuatu. The four observers to AOSIS are American Samoa, Guam, Netherlands Antilles and the United States Virgin Islands.

Alternative fuels

This is a term that refers to several types of fuel advocated for use in transportation because they are less polluting than **fossil fuels**. The refining of petrol and diesel from crude petroleum is not a sustainable technology. The principal alternative fuels for road vehicles are: natural gas; liquefied petroleum gas (LPG); ethanol derived from wood, corn or sugar; rape methyl ester; hydrogen, preferably produced using electricity from solar energy; and methanol from natural gas or coal. Some produce lower **carbon dioxide** emissions than conventional fuels but are more expensive. These remain less desirable, in environmental terms, than renewables: the best choice depends on which of the environmental problems associated with burning fuel is most severe in each case. For example, methane in the form of compressed natural gas (CNG) has significant environmental advantages over diesel for large vehicles—such as buses, road sweepers and refuse collection trucks/lorries—that make frequent stops in urban areas. CNG-powered vehicles produce few **particulates** such as PM10s and the hydrocarbons they emit have less than half the ozone-forming potential of those from diesel fuel.

Annex I/B countries

The Kyoto treaty calls on a first phase of 40 industrialized countries (or Parties) to reduce emissions by on average 5.2% from 1990 levels by 2012. These are most of the countries that are in the **Organisation for Economic Co-operation and Development** (OECD), along with countries that have economies 'in transition'. The countries are: Australia, Austria, Belarus, Belgium, Bulgaria, Canada, Croatia, Czech Republic, Denmark, Estonia, Finland, France, Germany, Greece, Hungary, Iceland, Ireland, Italy, Japan, Latvia, Liechtenstein, Lithuania, Luxembourg, Monaco, Netherlands, New Zealand, Norway, Poland, Portugal, Romania, Russia, Slovakia, Slovenia, Spain, Sweden, Switzerland, Turkey, Ukraine, the United Kingdom and the USA. These are also called 'Annex B countries' because the list is located in 'Annex B' of the **Kyoto Protocol** document.

Antarctic ice sheet

The Antarctic ice sheet is the blanket of ice that covers the Antarctic continent. It forms the southern ice cap, which is maintained by snow accumulation and the release of icebergs into the Antarctic Ocean. The Western Antarctic ice sheet (containing about 10% of the world's ice), in particular, is highly vulnerable to global **climate change** and scientists are not sure how the ice sheet will respond (the Eastern Antarctic sheet, which is vastly larger, is more stable, as it rests within a bowl of mountains). A warmer world could produce more precipitation, including increased snowfall, causing the ice sheet to become thicker. However, increased air and ocean temperatures are also likely to have a melting effect, which could cause **sea levels** to rise dramatically, flooding many small island states and other low-lying areas. Sea levels from global climate change could rise by as much as 1 m by 2100. There is evidence that the Western Antarctic ice sheet has melted significantly in the geologically recent past, having a dramatic impact on sea levels and global climate. Alarming signs of instability are already evident in the west, particularly on the ice shelves of the Antarctic peninsula. Such ice shelves are important in maintaining the stability of the ice sheet itself, as they shield the land-based ice from direct contact with the melting influence of the ocean.

Antarctica

Antarctica has a strong relationship with the global ecosystem and an important role in the global climate system. Along with the **Arctic**, the Antarctic continent acts as a 'refrigerator', affecting the global **atmosphere** and ocean circulation. Its importance means that many countries carry out research in Antarctica, with 30 countries operating research stations (2006), although seven countries also maintain territorial claims on the continent (neither the USA nor Russia, like the USSR before it, recognize these claims). The 1961 Antarctic Treaty was designed to ensure that Antarctica would be used exclusively for peaceful purposes. Nuclear explosions and the disposal of radioactive wastes were forbidden. Some 12 nations with an interest in Antarctica (Argentina, Australia, Belgium, Chile, France, Japan, New Zealand, Norway, South Africa, the USSR, the United Kingdom and the USA) signed the Treaty, agreeing to the establishment of joint scientific research projects to encourage co-operative endeavours between the parties. Sovereignty claims were frozen by the Treaty and some developing countries contend that the membership conditions are exclusionary, although 35 other states have acceded (of which 16 have acquired consultative status by virtue of their scientific activities in Antarctica). The Treaty forbids the exploitation of living resources in Antarctica or any activity that would cause deterioration of those resources, which has resulted in a degree of protection for wild animals and the sparse plant life. However, there is concern about the environmental degradation of the continent. This has especially been brought about by depletion of the **ozone layer**, by the onset of global **climate change**, by industrial pollutants originating at lower altitudes, and by damage caused by humans, in the form of construction, waste, disturbance to plants and animals, and fuel spillages. In October 1991 a draft agreement was signed by 24 countries in Madrid, Spain, to ban mineral and petroleum exploration in Antarctica for at least 50 years. The agreement, the Protocol on

Environmental Protection, calls for the Antarctic to be declared a natural reserve devoted to peace and science. It includes new regulations for wildlife protection, waste disposal, marine pollution and continued monitoring. It entered into force on 14 January 1998. However, no controls have been imposed on tourism, which has grown dramatically since the Protocol was signed, from 4,800 people in 1991, to 45,000 by 2008. There were growing concerns about the impact of relatively large numbers of visitors on such a delicate ecosystem and, at their consultative meeting in April 2009, treaty members agreed to ban cruise ships carrying more than 500 passengers and to limit parties going ashore at any one time to 100 people.

Anthropogenic climate change

Anthropogenic **climate change** is changes in the climate that are attributed to various human activities. This term comes from the Greek root word 'anthropos', which means 'man'. Anthropogenic climate change is also often referred to as the 'enhanced **greenhouse effect**'. Anthropogenic sources include fossil fuel burning (primarily coal, gas and oil) and land use change. Current heavy reliance on carbon-based sources for energy in industry and society has led to significant human contributions to climate change, noted in particular through increases in temperature as well as **sea-level** rise. This particular period of time has been referred to by Paul Crutzen as the 'Anthropocene Era'. In the climate science community, there has emerged a consensus that human activity has significantly driven climate change in the past two centuries, and that climate change since the Industrial Revolution has not been merely the result of natural fluctuations. Detection (of climate change) and attribution (to human activities) research has improved significantly, particularly over the last decade of work. For many decades, climate scientists have stated with increasing confidence that humans play a distinct role in changes in the climate. Prominently, the **Intergovernmental Panel on Climate Change** (IPCC)—a group of climate scientists and academic researchers from around the world—has noted this consensus. This has also been supported by numerous science organizations.

The Arctic

The Arctic generally refers to the north polar regions, but it has also become used to denote the territory lying within the Arctic Circle and to the landscape, climate and plant and animal life found in those regions. Both the Arctic and **Antarctica** play a very large part in maintaining the earth's heat balance. Since a large part of the earth's water is frozen in the ice fields, snow and glaciers of the polar regions, the possible melting caused by **global warming** could have world-wide repercussions. Melting could cause catastrophic **sea-level** rises and add to **climate change**. Both polar areas only absorb energy during their respective summer period and radiate heat throughout the year. Each year the outflow of energy must be balanced, more or less, by the inflow, otherwise the polar regions would become progressively colder. The vastly different geography of the two polar regions means that there are equally large differences in the way they influence the global climate. Unlike Antarctica, which is a huge land mass with bordering oceans and covers about three times the area of the Arctic, the northern region is an ocean, largely or almost entirely covered with sea ice, depending on the season (save the less fluctuating ice sheet of Greenland). The Arctic Ocean has the land of three continents at its perimeter: North America, Asia and Europe. However, the continental shelves that extend into the Arctic Ocean make it one of the world's most nutrient-rich seas and most fertile fishing grounds. Another difference between the polar regions is that the earth is also nearest the Sun during the Antarctic summer, so its **atmosphere** receives 7% more solar radiation than reaches the northern atmosphere during the Arctic summer. The southern limits of the Arctic are more difficult to define and include areas of Scandinavia warm enough to support reptiles. Some ecologists set the limit as the boundary where the sparse scrub of the polar tundra and the conifer-dominated taiga forest meet. Only the top 50 cms of the tundra thaw each summer, but many species of migratory birds use it as their breeding ground. The protection of flora and fauna and the exploitation of the mineral resources of the region are the subject of the Arctic Treaty and other international agreements. Many scientists believe global warming could melt the tundra's permafrost. Aside from destroying the tundra's ecosystem, they fear melting would release vast amounts of methane, which would accelerate the **greenhouse effect**.

Asia-Pacific Partnership on Clean Development and Climate

The Asia-Pacific Partnership on Clean Development and Climate (AP6) is a partnership by six countries—Australia, People's Republic of China, India, Japan, Republic of Korea (South Korea) and the USA—to achieve a reduction in **greenhouse gas** (GHG) emissions. This group was assembled in July 2005 at an Association of Southeast Asian Nations (ASEAN) Regional Forum meeting, and accounts for around 50% of the world's GHG emissions. These six countries agreed to co-operate on the development and transfer of technology, energy security, national air pollution and clean economies. They set up eight task forces, focused on aluminium (aluminum), buildings and appliances, cement, cleaner use of fossil energy, coal mining, power generations and transmission, **renewable energy** and distributed generation, and steel. These partnerships have emerged as a parallel (and some say competing) process to those in the UN, and these agreements remain voluntary declarations of intent, with no mandatory enforcement mechanisms or commonly agreed emissions reduction goals in place. Critics posit that this is largely rhetoric with little substantive action; since this agreement went into effect, none of the six countries have reduced GHG emissions.

Atmosphere

The atmosphere is an envelope of gases surrounding the earth and bounded by gravitational attraction. The global atmosphere extends 500 km above the surface of the earth. It is a mixture of gases constituting air, which is generally composed of 78.1% nitrogen (as N_2), 20.9% oxygen (as O_2), 0.9% argon, 0.03% **carbon dioxide** (CO_2), and a number of trace gases (such as CH_4 at 700 parts per billion and nitrous oxide at 275 parts per billion) (see **parts per million/parts per billion**). The atmosphere is a very dynamic and rapidly changing physical system. Along with the ocean, it drives the climate system and distributes energy throughout the planet. The troposphere is the lowermost atmospheric region, from the earth's surface to 12 km. It is a well-mixed region of the atmosphere and also a turbulent one. Here is where weather systems of clouds, surface winds and water vapour circulate around the planet. Next is the tropopause, at about 12 km, the area between the troposphere and stratosphere. Jet streams drive weather in this region and airplanes often take advantage of this area of general stability. The next layer is the stratosphere, which is between 12 km and 50 km above earth. This is followed by the mesosphere, the thermosphere and the exosphere.

B

Bali Roadmap

This refers to the beginning of a two-year process leading to a potential agreement in Copenhagen, Denmark in December 2009 for a successor to the **Kyoto Protocol** (see **Copenhagen Conference**). It is also known as the 'Bali Action Plan'. This plan was assembled at the 13th **Conference of the Parties** to the **UN Framework Convention on Climate Change** in Bali, Indonesia in December 2007. Essentially, this document pledged for co-ordination and co-operation in working towards an agreement for 'deep' reductions in **greenhouse gas** emissions. The term 'deep' did not get translated into an actual percentage of reductions, however. Also contained in this action plan was mention of the need to address **adaptation** measures in order to protect citizens, particularly in developing countries, against present and future climate impacts, forest protection by 'policy approaches and positive incentives', as well as the transfer of clean technologies from industrialized countries to developing nations.

Berlin Mandate

This is the name of a prominent decision that was reached at the **UN Framework Convention on Climate Change** (UNFCCC) first **Conference of the Parties** (COP) meeting, held in Berlin, Germany in 1995. It arose from country delegates' concerns about their ability to meet the terms in the UNFCCC. The Berlin Mandate declared that there should be a two-year Analytical and Assessment Phase (AAP). This mandate also established that there were 'common but differentiated responsibilities' that different countries have in fulfilling UNFCCC obligations. In practice, this exempted non-Annex I countries (non-industrialized countries) from participating in the first phase of explicit commitments of **targets and timetables** for reductions in **greenhouse gas** emissions. This Berlin Mandate was seen to be codified recognition of the difference between 'luxury' and 'survival' emissions between countries, as well as a declaration that made explicit some nascent concerns over justice, **vulnerability** and differentiated impacts from **anthropogenic climate change**. The US Senate reacted to this proposal by passing the July 1997 Byrd-Hagel Resolution, stating that they would not ratify a treaty without the full participation of developing nations in this first phase of commitments. Upon its passage 95–0, Resolution co-author Chuck Hagel (Republican, Nebraska) proudly declared, 'The Byrd-Hagel Resolution is a complete rejection of the Berlin Mandate'. This is seen as one of the early battles waged in an ongoing war (and impasse) over rights and responsibilities of greenhouse gas emissions and reductions between the Global North and Global South.

Brazilian Proposal

The 'Brazilian Proposal' refers to a proposal made by the Brazilian delegation in May 1997 during the lead up to the **Kyoto Protocol** treaty agreement. This Proposal aimed to develop a formula for differentiated emissions reductions targets based on *cumulative* **greenhouse gas** (GHG) emissions over time. This approach accounts for historical contributions to **climate change**, rather than taking a snapshot of GHG emissions levels in 1990, and is, then, more sensitive to legacies of colonialism and uneven development. This was not adopted formally in the Kyoto Protocol, but remains a proposal that continues to receive some traction (along with the Chinese '**offshoring emissions**' proposal). This also seeks to build from the 'common but differentiated responsibilities' statement made in the 1995 **Berlin Mandate**.

Brundtland Report

This is the report of the World Commission on Environment and Development, set up by the General Assembly of the UN in 1983. It was named after Gro Harlem Brundtland, the former Norwegian Prime Minister who chaired the body. The brief of the Commission was to draw up a global agenda for change and, in particular, to devise a strategy for achieving sustainable development for the year 2000 and beyond. This commission put forward a broad definition for 'sustainable development' which has been widely adopted. The report stated that sustainable development is 'development that meets the needs of the present generation without compromising the ability of future generations to meet their needs'. This definition has been subject to a wide range of interpretations. The report also urged the replacement of chemically dependent agriculture by sustainable agriculture and that there be a shift from export crops to food crops for local **consumption**. It recommended that 'soft' energy systems (**renewable energy** plus energy conservation measures) should be adopted, describing them as the best way towards a sustainable future. The report also urged industry to assess the potential impact of new technologies before their employment, so that their production, use and disposal do not put too much stress on environmental resources. The report set out seven goals for the future: to revive economic growth; to change the quality of growth; to meet essential needs for jobs, food, energy, water and sanitation; to ensure a sustainable level of population; to conserve and enhance the resource base; to re-orientate technology and management risk; and to merge environment and economics in decision-making.

C

Carbon Capture and Storage

Carbon capture and storage (CCS) most commonly refers to the capture of **carbon dioxide** from the **atmosphere** from large industrial sources, then compressing, transporting and injecting it into underground geological formations or the deep ocean for long-term storage. At present, it remains mostly a theoretical proposal for mitigating carbon dioxide emissions from **fossil fuels**—coal, oil, natural gas—which in turn contribute to **climate change**. CCS has also been referred to when discussing some other emergent sequestration techniques (see **carbon sequestration**). Among them is 'air capture', where carbon dioxide is removed or 'scrubbed' from the lower troposphere and stored indefinitely in geological formations; also there is 'biochar', where biological material—such as plankton from the ocean—is buried underground permanently. Proponents of CCS techniques tout them as feasible first steps towards decarbonization of industry. However, critics consider them to be far-fetched distractions from more significant and fundamental commitments to carbon dioxide emissions reductions from industry. At present, governments such as that of the United Kingdom are discussing the mandated installment of CCS technology with all-new coal-fired power plants. Meanwhile, the governments of Germany and the USA have been funding pilot projects to develop this **geoengineering** strategy. These are reported to potentially reduce carbon dioxide emissions by up to 90% from power plants fitted with CCS. Furthermore the **Intergovernmental Panel on Climate Change** has mentioned the **mitigation** gains that can be achieved through the integration of CCS methods among a suite of initiatives in the coming decades. However, due to a number of ongoing and unresolved challenges with CCS implementation on a large and co-ordinated scale—for example, there are concerns of leakage from long-term storage into the atmosphere thereby reducing the intended mitigation gains—CCS remains a contentious initiative.

Carbon Dioxide

Carbon Dioxide (CO_2) is a chemical compound made up of one carbon atom and two oxygen atoms. While it is a trace gas in the **atmosphere** in terms of volume, it is of central interest in atmospheric chemistry due to its capacity to trap incoming solar radiation in the atmosphere. For this reason, over time it has become known as a **greenhouse gas** (GHG), where increases of CO_2 into the atmosphere cause **climate changes**, which include increases in temperature or **global warming**. Other greenhouse gases include Methane (CH_4), Nitrous Oxide (N_2O), tropospheric ozone (O_3), halocarbons (CFCs, HFCs, HCFCs) and water vapour (H_2O_v). CO_2 is the principle GHG that contributes to climate change and global warming, as increases in CO_2 have contributed most to climate change compared to other greenhouse gases over time. CO_2 is part of larger carbon cycles on earth. All living things are composed primarily of carbon, so the cycling of carbon through the various spheres can provide indications of the health of the planet. Unlike other GHGs, CO_2 is not broken down or destroyed through chemical reactions. Aside from time spent in the atmosphere mainly as CO_2, carbon also moves through the biosphere, hydrosphere and lithosphere. For example, atmospheric CO_2 is taken out of the atmosphere and up into the biosphere through photosynthesis. The carbon can then stay in this 'reservoir' until the forest dies and decomposes, is cut down, or is burned. At this time, carbon is then released again to the atmosphere mainly as CO_2. There are many reasons why CO_2 is so influential in climate change; among them, CO_2 has a long 'residence time', where emissions can stay in the atmosphere for up to 200 years. For instance, emissions from a 1911 Model T Ford are potentially in the atmosphere today. This also means that even if all CO_2 emissions were halted today, declines in atmospheric CO_2 would only begin after the CO_2 cycled out of the atmosphere into another reservoir. Furthermore, CO_2 is the greenhouse gas changing most directly because of human activities. It is important to understand that there are also natural sources of CO_2 emissions. These include plant decomposition and volcanic activity, which contribute to a baseline 'natural **greenhouse effect**' that makes the world habitable. Without them, the earth would on average be about 60°F (15.6°C) cooler and the planet would be covered with ice. With this natural greenhouse effect, humans have been able to live and enjoy benefits such as forest and food growth. After time in the atmosphere, CO_2 cycles into a '**sink**'. For example, carbon is taken up in the biosphere through photosynthesis in forests. The carbon can stay in this 'reservoir' until the forest dies and decomposes, is cut down, or is burned. Measurements of atmospheric CO_2 concentration over time show that atmospheric CO_2 concentrations have now risen to approximately 385 parts per million (ppm) (see **parts per million/parts per billion**).

Carbon Dioxide equivalent

Carbon dioxide equivalent (CDE or CO_{2e}) is a metric designed to enable more clear comparison between **greenhouse gases** based on their **global warming** potential and radiative forcing, as compared to **carbon dioxide**. These then incorporate the comparative heat capacities and residence time in the **atmosphere** for various greenhouse gases such as methane and nitrous oxide. This comparison then provides a combined expression of the amount of greenhouse gases in the atmosphere (in parts per million) (see **parts per million/parts per billion**).

Carbon Markets

There have emerged many capitalist economic ideas that have gained salience in climate policy circles regarding **anthropogenic climate change** solutions. For example, market-based **greenhouse gas** (GHG) permits to be bought and sold have been introduced in places such as the **European Union** in order to create an explicit cost to pollute. Furthermore, investments by companies in **renewable energy** technologies in countries of the Global South can earn 'credits' for GHG emissions reductions, and thereby spur technological shifts in energy production in developing countries. These economic initiatives have been incorporated in the **Kyoto Protocol** as 'flexible mechanisms' in order to create more opportunities to achieve emissions reductions. However, a number of participants have cautioned that this could lead to the overwhelming privatization and commodification of the 'global public good' of our shared **atmosphere**. Carbon markets are essentially trading systems through which countries, businesses and other entities can buy or sell units of GHG emissions, most commonly **carbon dioxide** and methane.

Carbon offsets (compliance, voluntary)

Carbon offsets are market tools designed to facilitate the **mitigation** of **greenhouse gas** (GHG) emissions into the **atmosphere**. Many consider these instruments appealing because they enable a more 'flexible' and cost-effective approach to achieving emissions reductions as an individual, firm or country can pay for emissions reductions in places potentially very distant to the source of emissions. Due to uniform mixing of GHGs in the atmosphere, the global effects of GHG emissions provide an opportunity for global systems of carbon offsetting on more localized activities, such as transportation and electricity use. There are two principle markets of carbon offsets: compliance and voluntary. Compliance carbon offset markets are large-scale industrial and government-dominated systems. For example, the **Clean Development Mechanism**—established in Article 12 of the **Kyoto Protocol**—represents a market in compliance carbon offsets. Voluntary carbon offset markets are smaller-scale endeavours, where individuals and firms voluntarily participate. For instance, an individual or company may pay for a group to plant trees in India to offset emissions from air travel. Offset projects can manifest in a range of initiatives, such as wind farm development, reforestation projects, methane capture or biomass energy development. These carbon offsets provide opportunities to counteract possibly carbon-intensive lifestyle choices. Proponents posit that this illuminates some strengths of the financial instrument: carbon offsets raise awareness about **anthropogenic climate change** and provide an opportunity for many to offset their GHG emissions in an accessible way. However, in so doing, critics argue that they lessen the pressure to make more substantive lifestyle changes, and provide emotional salve to otherwise unsustainable behaviours. None the less, carbon offsets represent an increasingly utilized market instrument to mitigate GHG emissions contributing to anthropogenic **climate change**.

Carbon Sequestration

Carbon sequestration is a **geoengineering** technique that removes carbon from the **atmosphere** and stores it for the long term in forests, soils, oceans, or underground in depleted oil and gas reservoirs, coal seams and saline aquifers. These aim to mitigate the effects of **greenhouse gas** emissions on the atmosphere. Carbon can be sequestered in a variety of ways, such as capturing **carbon dioxide** during the processes of petroleum refining and power generation. Carbon can also be sequestered through projects such as 'air capture' and 'biochar' (see **Carbon Capture and Storage**).

Carbon Tax

As discussions on how to tackle the challenge of **global warming** become more intense and widespread, an increasing number of people are beginning to advocate the imposition of direct taxes on businesses and private individuals to reflect their emissions of **greenhouse gases**. Across the world, there are already several types of energy taxes that are mostly weighted against producers. There are equally a growing number of green taxes that are designed to encourage people to behave in an environmentally benign manner. The idea of asking companies and individuals to pay directly for the emissions of climate-warming gases in the form of taxes is a relatively new one, but none the less gathering momentum. Already the government of the city of Québec in Canada has announced plans to introduce a carbon tax under which companies will pay an extra 0.8 cents on every litre of gas sold. The money raised from this tax will be used to fund green projects such as the installation of **renewable energy** facilities. Similarly, in New Zealand, the government has announced plans to introduce an extra cost for using electricity, petrol and gas as part of the efforts to limit the use of greenhouse gas emissions and generate funds for climate-friendly projects. In Europe, the **European Union** (EU) has considered the option of imposing a carbon tax among its 27 member states to complement the **European Union Emissions Trading Scheme** and other national greenhouse emissions reduction policies. There is every indication that carbon tax would be one of the more popular instruments on the list of policies that could be used by governments in combating the challenge of **climate change**.

Certified Emission Reductions (CERs)

CERs are credits that have been generated through the **Clean Development Mechanism** (CDM) Executive Board, through Article 12 of the **Kyoto Protocol**. CERs can be banked, bought and sold through the **European Union**

Emissions Trading Scheme in order for **Annex I/B** Parties to comply with their emissions reduction targets. CERs can be issued for projects that meet two basic criteria: first, they must address sustainable development needs of the host developing country; and second the projects must contribute to the reduction of **greenhouse gas** emissions, as defined by Kyoto Protocol stipulations. A CER represents one tonne of CO_2-equivalent greenhouse gas emissions achieved through an approved CDM project.

Chlorofluorocarbons

Chlorofluorocarbons are a set of **greenhouse gases** that are compounds consisting of carbon, hydrogen, chlorine and fluorine, also commonly referred to as CFCs. These are human creations, first invented by Thomas Midgley in 1928 and marketed in the following years by Dupont Chemical under the trade name 'freon'. They were introduced as chemicals to enable refrigeration and air conditioning, and were also used for packaging, insulation, solvents and aerosol propellants. It was not until 1972 that scientists revealed that CFCs deplete the **ozone layer** and also contribute to **climate change**. Therefore, in the 1980s the **Montréal Protocol** sought to discontinue their use. The Protocol stated that CFCs must be phased out in industrialized countries in the 1990s and in industrializing countries in the following decade. However, a number of countries have filed for exemptions, while enforcement in other countries remains limited. For example, the USA sought an exemption so that farmers could continue using methyl bromide to grow things such as strawberries in California's Central Valley. Overall, these CFCs have since largely been replaced by hydrochlorofluorocarbons (HCFCs) and hydrofluorocarbons (HFCs). However, these gases still have a smaller heat trapping capacity, thereby still contributing to **anthropogenic climate change**. CFCs emitted today can remain in the **atmosphere** around 100–200 years, while HFCs remain in the atmosphere for about 12 years. Furthermore, these gases have heat-trapping capacities about 5,000–010,000 times the capacity of **carbon dioxide**.

Clean Development Mechanism (CDM)

The CDM is defined in Article 12 of the **Kyoto Protocol**, as a 'flexible mechanism' to assist with the implementation of **greenhouse gas** emissions **mitigation** objectives. The CDM essentially is a tool designed for developed countries designated in **Annex I/B** in the Kyoto Protocol to earn certified emissions reduction credits (CERs) when they invest in projects in developing countries that meet two basic criteria: they must address sustainable development needs of the host developing country, and the projects must contribute to the reduction of greenhouse gas emissions, as defined by Kyoto Protocol stipulations. Furthermore, for CDM projects to be approved for the purposes of Kyoto Protocol credited emissions reductions, the projects must be determined to meet **additionality** objectives. Additionality, as stated above, is the concept where emissions reductions from CDM projects are deemed to be 'additional' to emissions reductions that otherwise would have occurred anyway. Whether a project has or has not fulfilled these criteria is decided upon by a CDM Executive Board, which inevitably wields a significant amount of power through interpretation. Their decisions are guided by terms established in the **UN Framework Convention on Climate Change**. Overall, this more 'flexible' approach to achieving emissions reductions is argued to be more cost effective, and thus more appealing, than straightforward and mandated emissions reductions in the Annex I/B countries themselves.

Climate change

The climate on earth is moderated by input from energy from the Sun and the loss of this back into space. Incoming solar radiation enters the earth's **atmosphere** and is partly absorbed or trapped, while being partly reflected back into space. The composition of the atmosphere dictates the balance between these forces and this is called the 'planetary energy budget'. Certain atmospheric gases are critical to this balance and are known as **greenhouse gases** (GHGs). These GHGs include **carbon dioxide** (CO_2), methane (CH_4), nitrous oxide (N_2O), tropospheric ozone (O_3), halocarbons (CFCs, HFCs, HCFCs) and water vapour (H_2O_v). Emissions of GHGs into the atmosphere cause climate changes, which include increases in temperature. The terms 'climate change' and '**global warming**' signify slightly different things. 'Climate change' is a term that accounts for changes in many climate characteristics, such as rainfall, ice extent and **sea levels**. Global warming refers to a more specific facet of climate change: the increase in temperature over time. Clearly, temperature increases do not occur in isolation from other climate characteristics. Rather, many other sources and feedback processes contribute to changes across time and space. Temperature (particularly increases in temperature) is seen as the most clear and distinguishable climate characteristic that indicates more general climate change.

Common but Differentiated Responsibility (CDR)

A concept in international environmental law which basically provides that developing countries might need to take lighter responsibilities than the developed countries in the collective effort to deal with global environmental problems. The CDR is generally regarded as an equity principle through which it is acknowledged that although all the countries of the world share a common need to respond to the threats of global environmental degradation and drastic changes in the global environment, the developed countries need to bear greater responsibility as they are on balance more responsible for causing the problem. The concept also serves as a means of recognizing that certain environmental standards agreed for the developed countries might not be suitable for the developing countries given these latter countries' special economic and developmental needs. At the same time, CDR embodies recognition of the wide disparities in the economic, scientific and technological capabilities of states and the logic that governments should make contributions that are commensurate to their capabilities in the collective search for solutions to global environmental challenges.

Conference of the Parties (COP) meetings

The entry into force of the UNFCCC set forth future Conference of the Parties meetings (COPs) to delineate more specifics of the treaty. Most prominent is the third Conference of the Parties (COP3) that took place in Kyoto, Japan and produced the **Kyoto Protocol**. This Protocol outlines more specific **targets and timetables** for Annex I/II Parties to reduce anthropogenic **greenhouse gas** emissions. To date, the Kyoto Protocol has been signed by 140 countries and, despite US non-ratification, entered into force in February 2005.

Consumption

Within carbon-based industry and society there are uneven patterns of consumption and consequent CO_2 emissions. One way to consider anthropogenic CO_2 emissions is on a country level. At this scale, the USA and People's Republic of China are ahead, accounting for approximately 25% of global CO_2 emissions each. Russia (7%), Japan (5%) and India (5%) are the third-, fourth- and fifth-largest CO_2 emitters, respectively. These five countries are then followed in order by Germany, the United Kingdom, Canada, Italy and Republic of Korea (South Korea). Emissions are increasing at a faster rate in what is often called the 'Global South'. Another way this is considered is through per-capita—or individual—CO_2 emissions. The USA leads in per capita emissions, with 19.1 metric tons per year. Meanwhile, the individual emissions of a typical citizen in China are less than one-eighth that of a US citizen. The individual emissions of a Russian or Japanese citizen are both about one-half that of a US citizen, while a citizen of India emits less than 1/20th that of a US citizen. This per capita approach provides a very different picture of CO_2 emissions. Different perspectives like these can serve to reshape and broaden views on current and future plans for CO_2 emissions reductions policies and programmes. Thus, consumptive habits are differentiated on many scales. Emissions from the Global North account for about two-thirds of total global emissions each year. However, emissions in the Global South are increasing at a faster rate than those in the Global North. It is important to distinguish between what has been called 'luxury' emissions (such as driving an SUV to the corner store for a pint of ice-cream) and 'survival' emissions (such as burning wood for cooking). This was a concept first introduced in 1991 by Anil Agarwal and Sunita Narain. Moreover, many of the carbon-based energy-intensive—and hence emissions-intensive—activities that take place in the Global South are done to service demands in the Global North. According to J. Martinez-Alier and R. Muradian, approximately 80% of raw materials that are produced in the Global South are consumed in the Global North.

Contraction and Convergence

Contraction and convergence is a concept that refers to a long-term strategy for reducing global **greenhouse gas** (GHG) emissions. This is a process where overall GHG emissions are reduced (contraction),while emissions reductions from the Global South would be less aggressive than those of the Global North through per capita allocation, so as to enable development in the Global South as well as flexibility for a transition from carbon-based energy sources to **renewable energy** sources. This proposal has gained support from a number of policy participants with a particular sensitivity to issues of climate justice and equality. Eventually, all emissions **entitlements** would converge at an equal per capita emissions level, dependent upon particular geography and political economy.

Copenhagen Conference

The Copenhagen Conference or UN Conference on Climate Change was scheduled to take place in the Danish capital in December 2009. It was to include the 15th **Conference of the Parties** to the **UN Framework Convention on Climate Change** and the fifth meeting of the parties to the **Kyoto Protocol**. According to the **Bali roadmap** agreed in Indonesia in 2007, the Conference was to agree the framework for **climate change mitigation** efforts beyond 2012.

D

Dangerous Anthropogenic Interference

This term 'dangerous anthropogenic interference' appears prominently in the objective of the **UN Framework Convention on Climate Change** (UNFCCC). Article 2 states that co-ordinated international efforts must be made to 'achieve **stabilization** of the **greenhouse gas** concentrations in the **atmosphere** at a level that would prevent dangerous anthropogenic interference with the climate system'. There remain many contentious discussions regarding what threshold will constitute this; while some argue that it has already been crossed, others place this threshold at 450 parts per million (ppm) or 560 ppm (a doubling of pre-industrial levels) of CO_2 in the atmosphere (see **parts per million/parts per billion**). It may actually prove to be a distraction to determine exactly what level of anthropogenic interference constitutes 'dangerous'. However, the concept has mobilized public and policy attention for efforts to decarbonize the 21st century economy and society and is, therefore, a helpful heuristic.

Declaration of The Hague

The Declaration of The Hague was the first document drawn up by an inter-governmental meeting in which national leaders expressed a willingness to diminish their sovereignty in specific areas for the sake of the planet. The meeting was arranged in March 1989 by the Prime Ministers of the Netherlands (the host), Norway and France. As the implications of the twin problems of **global warming** and ozone depletion emerged from the latest research, the Governments of these countries were concerned about the difficulties of obtaining the unprecedented degree of international co-operation needed to avert ecological disaster. The declaration was a statement of principles, not an action plan. However, it proposed new institutions that would be needed to finance and facilitate activities such as the transfer of energy-efficient technologies between countries and provide **chlorofluorocarbon** (CFC) substitutes to developing countries in exchange for their agreement to limit **carbon dioxide** and CFC emissions.

Dobson units

Dobson units (DU) are used for measuring the total amount of ozone in a vertical column of air above the earth's surface; the method was perfected in

1956 by George Dobson, a British pioneer of stratospheric ozone and first president of the International Ozone Commission. He had long suspected seasonal changes occurred in the **ozone layer**, but he made his first measurements at Halley Bay, in **Antarctica**, almost 25 years before the ozone hole was observed by his colleagues. When Dobson made his first measurements the ozone level was 150 DU less than calculations suggested it should have been. He initially suspected faulty equipment. However, readings made the following year confirmed the pattern. Measurements made elsewhere in the world did not repeat the pattern. However, throughout the 1960s the seasonal decrease in ozone levels at Halley Bay were monitored. Then the depletion, now known as the ozone hole, was confirmed by Joe Farman and Jonathan Shanklin of the British Antarctic Survey, between 1982 and 1985. A reassessment of satellite photographs revealed the development of a hole every spring since 1970. Serious depletion was then confirmed over the **Arctic**, showing that ozone depletion was not restricted to the southern hemisphere.

E

Earth Summit (Rio 1992) – *see* UN Conference on Environment and Development (UNCED).

Earthwatch

Earthwatch is a global environmental assessment programme, which was included in the Action Plan for the Human Environment adopted by the UN Conference on the Human Environment in 1972. It has four main aims: to provide a basis on which to identify specific knowledge and to take the steps to find it; to generate the new knowledge needed to guide decision-making; to gather and evaluate specific data in order to discern and predict important environmental conditions and trends; and to distribute knowledge to scientists and technologists, and provide useful and up-to-date information to decision-makers at all levels. The Earthwatch programme of the **UN Environment Programme** has four main arms: the Global Environment Monitoring System (GEMS); the Global Resource Information Database (GRID); the International Register of Potentially Toxic Chemicals (IRPTC); and INFOTERRA, the global information system.

Emissions Trading

Emissions trading is a market-based approach used by governments to control or achieve reductions in the emissions of **greenhouse gases** (GHGs). In an emissions trading scheme, the government, in close consultation with companies, scientists and other stakeholders such as environmental **non-governmental organizations** (NGOs) sets a limit on the amount of a pollutant that should be emitted within a given time period. After setting the limit (or cap), governments distribute the total amount of emissions permissible among companies and other emitting entities in the form of allowances or credits. Entities that emit more than their allocated allowance (credits) are expected to buy emission credits from those that pollute less. Conversely, entities that use less than their allocated quota are allowed to sell their credits to those that pollute more. This way the government is able to control the total amount of emissions of a given pollutant within the system, while allowing companies and other polluting entities the flexibility to cut emissions in the ways that best suit them. There are many emissions trading systems around the world. Some of the best known include the US Sulfur Dioxide (SO_2) trading system established under the Clean Air Act of 1990. The system, which is managed by the US Environmental Protection Agency, sets an overall national limit on SO_2 emissions and requires hundreds of participating facilities to reduce their SO_2 emissions or buy tradable permits from those that emit less. The first trades were executed in 1992 at around US \$300 per tonne of SO_2. The system is widely acclaimed to have succeeded in cutting emissions by over 50% between 1992 and 1998. Other examples include the emissions trading systems in volatile organic compounds adopted by the state of Illinois in 1997 and the 1998 Chile Offset scheme for the control of air pollution in Santiago. More recently, emissions trading in **carbon dioxide** and other GHGs have fast gained huge popularity. Trading in these gases followed the adoption of the **Kyoto Protocol** on the **UN Framework Convention on Climate Change** (UNFCCC) in 1997. Under the Protocol emissions reduction quotas are allocated to the developing countries and nations that emit less than their quota of GHGs are allowed to sell emission credits to polluting countries. In 2002, the United Kingdom opened the first national scheme in the world for trading GHGs. The scheme, which ran from April 2002 to December 2006, had about 33 companies as direct participants and was reported to have achieved emissions reductions of over 7.2m. tonnes of SO_{2e} over its lifetime. However, by far the biggest known emissions trading scheme today is the **European Union Emissions Trading Scheme**. Emissions trading has been lauded in some quarters as one of the best ways to reduce the emissions of pollutants in the most cost effective way. Proponents argue that the schemes work better than control and command mechanisms in which emission limit values are imposed on particular facilities, in that the scheme allows companies the flexibility to determine where and how best to reduce emissions. However, some critics, mainly environmental justice NGOs, argue that emissions trading, as other market mechanisms, allows big and rich polluters to buy their way out of their pollution without doing much to reduce emissions. They also argue that emissions trading diverts attention from the wider systemic and collective socio-political changes needed to tackle global environmental problems.

Entitlements

Amartya Sen first framed the concept of entitlements in the seminal work *Poverty and Famines: An Essay on Entitlement and Deprivation* (1981). This was written as an effort to expand upon and improve the narrow economic conceptions of hunger, famine and deprivation that dominated Western development model perspectives. Sen took on the 'conventional' conceptions of poverty (food per capita) as he stated, 'starvation is the characteristic of some people not *having* enough food to eat. It is not the characteristic of there *being* not enough food to eat. While the latter can be cause of the former, it is but one of many *possible* causes. Whether and how starvation relates to food supply is a matter for factual investigation'. Taken in its time, these comments represented a significant break from orthodox and hegemonic thinking regarding poverty at the time. Sen thus offered an approach to poverty and deprivation analyses, putting activities such as food production within a network of relationships. It was an entitlement and endowment approach. In this book, entitlement relations, accepted in a private ownership market economy, were primarily defined in four ways: 1) trade-based entitlement; 2) production-based entitlement; 3) own-labour entitlement; and 4) inheritance and transfer entitlement. Among the strengths of this entitlement approach is the ability to consider the larger architectures of well-being, and to consider humans as more than rational economic actors to those seeking to meet wider **livelihood** needs.

European Environment Agency (EEA)

The EEA is a **European Union** (EU) institution established in Copenhagen, Denmark, in November 1994. Non-EU members were permitted to join and it was the first EU institution to admit the accession states of 2004, including some with a legacy of severe environmental damage. It was set up to produce reliable, objective and comparable information for those involved in developing European environmental policy and to give early warning of impending environmental problems. The EEA is supported by the national information systems incorporated into the European Environment Information and Observations Network (EIONET). Specific tasks are carried out under contract by European Topic Centres in priority fields, which include inland waters, marine and coastal environments, air quality, air emissions, nature conservation, soil, forests, land cover, and catalogue and data sources. One of the Agency's aims is to reform the existing environmental information system, in such a way that Europe can benefit from the results of years of measurements and monitoring. The Agency also aims to incorporate European information into international environmental monitoring programmes, for example those of the UN agencies, and to co-operate with other EU and international bodies and programmes. In February 2004 the EEA and the European Commission launched the European Pollutant Emission Register, the first Europe-wide record of industrial discharges into air and water. The EEA publishes a report on the state of the European environment every three years.

European Union (EU)

The EU consists of these member states: Austria, Belgium, Cyprus, Czech Republic, Denmark, Estonia, Finland, France, Germany, Greece, Hungary, Ireland, Italy, Latvia, Lithuania, Luxembourg, Malta, the Netherlands, Poland, Portugal, Slovakia, Slovenia, Spain, Sweden and the United Kingdom. They have formed an organization through common commitments to economic and **politics** integration. These include international governance agreements such as a collective commitment in **Annex I/B** to **targets and timetables** in the **Kyoto Protocol**, for 8% **greenhouse gas** emissions reductions below 1990 levels by 2012. These also involve a common market for goods and services, and common currency (the Euro). There are some exceptions to participation in various facets of these agreements, but on the whole these then provide more influence on the international stage than member states would otherwise achieve individually. The EU was established on 1 November 1993 and is headquartered in Brussels, Belgium where the European Commission, European Parliament and Council of the European Union carry out executive and legislative tasks.

European Union Emissions Trading Scheme (EU ETS)

The EU ETS is an agreement between the **European Union** (EU) member nations to monitor and report on national **carbon dioxide** emissions levels each year, and reduce emissions at an agreed rate in large emitting installations. At present, it represents the largest international trading scheme that incorporates activities from large industrial polluters. Under the auspices of the EU, National Allocation plans have been developed and tradeable allowances have been allocated. The first EU ETS trading period was from January 2005 to December 2007. The second period began in January 2008 and will run to December 2012, to coincide with the first Kyoto commitment period. Initial allocations have been determined on a case-by-case basis, taking into account a range of factors such as costs of plant retrofits and prevalence of extreme weather events (heatwaves, cold snaps). Beyond this initial allocation, plant operators then buy or sell allowances from other actors (be they other plants, traders or governments) in order to stay below their allocation limit. The early trading came under criticism for a number of reasons. Among them, some considered the permits undervalued because they were given away free. Also, some considered the number of industries involved in EU ETS to be too low to be effective. In response, following allocation periods may auction nearly two-thirds of the permits, and other industrial sectors such as commercial aviation may be included.

F

Flexibility Mechanisms

Flexibility mechanisms (also called 'flex mex' or 'Kyoto Mechanisms') are tools that enable **Annex I/B** Parties to meet their **Kyoto Protocol** commitments through actions outside their own borders. These are market-based measures that are argued to be more cost-effective **greenhouse gas** emissions reductions strategies. They are outlined in the Kyoto Protocol as **Joint Implementation** (Article 6), the **Clean Development Mechanism** (Article 12), and **Emissions Trading** (Article 17). It is stated that Annex I/B countries can meet requirements of flexibility mechanisms after they have ratified the Kyoto Protocol, they have established an emissions accounting scheme at the national level, and they have agreed to report emissions reductions information on an annual basis. These mechanisms were first introduced in the UN **Conference of the Parties** negotiations by the USA in 1995 in Berlin, Germany. Their inclusion in the climate agreement was seen to be a concession by the **European Union** (EU) to encourage the USA to ratify and abide by the terms of the emergent Kyoto Protocol. However, as time went on, the EU embraced and developed the principles of these procedures—for example, through the **European Union Emissions Trading Scheme**—while US President George W. Bush withdrew from the Kyoto Protocol in 2001.

Fossil Fuels

Fossil fuels are formed through heat and pressure over geologic time through the decomposition of organic matter. The term 'fossil' refers to the remains of this organic matter and is sometimes colloquially discussed as the energy derived from dinosaurs. This process has taken hundreds of millions of years to provide the fossil fuels we use today. Fossil fuels vary in energy content and volatility. Common fossil fuels are petroleum, coal and natural gas. Fossil fuel burning produces **carbon dioxide**, which is a principle **greenhouse gas** contributing to **climate change**. At present, the US Department of Energy estimates that approximately 85% of energy is derived from coal, oil and natural gas. Meanwhile, the remaining 15% comes from hydropower, solar, wind, tidal, nuclear and geothermal energy generation.

Fourth Assessment Report

The Fourth Assessment Report (AR4) was produced in 2007 and is an aggregate of scientific understanding of **climate change** from peer-reviewed research up to the end of 2005, as compiled by the UN **Intergovernmental Panel on Climate Change**. As its name indicates, this is the fourth major assessment, after the First Assessment Report (FAR) in 1990, the Second Assessment Report (SAR) in 1995 and the Third Assessment Report (TAR) in 2001. AR4 is composed of three major sub-reports assembled from three associated working groups, and a final synthesis report. Each report also contains a '**Summary for Policymakers** (SPM)' and a 'Technical Summary (TS)'. The SPM from Working Group 1 was released in January 2007 and covered the 'Physical Science Basis'. Working Group 2 produced a report in April 2007 on 'Impacts, **Adaptation** and **Vulnerability**', and Working Group 3 produced a report in May 2007 on '**Mitigation**'. The full reports were released in September 2007 and the synthesis report was circulated in November 2007. Among the top statements made in AR4 was the statement on **anthropogenic climate change** that '[m]ost of the observed increase in global average temperatures since the mid-20th century is very likely due to the observed increase in anthropogenic **greenhouse gas** concentrations'. The Synthesis Report covered six main topics: 1) observed changes in the climate; 2) causes of climate change; 3) climate change impacts over time; 4) adaptation and mitigation options, and their relation to sustainable development; 5) long-term scientific and socio-economic perspectives on climate change; and 6) key uncertainties.

Friends of the Earth (FoE)

FoE is an international pressure group that operates in dozens of countries. It started in the USA as an off-shoot of the conservation group the Sierra Club. It is a non-party group that lobbies governments and politicians on all environmental issues and works to increase public awareness. FoE is very active in campaigning against the construction of new nuclear power stations and in establishing safety levels for existing nuclear facilities. The organization campaigns against: air, sea and land pollution, ozone depletion, acid rain and **carbon dioxide** build-up; and the use of whale products, damaging aerosol propellants, leaded petrol, food additives and non-returnable bottles. FoE's activities include campaigns for recycling, increased use of bicycles and public transport, alternatives to tropical hardwoods, better energy conservation and home insulation, and the adoption of catalytic converters in cars to reduce emissions that cause photochemical smog.

G

G77

The Group of 77 (G77) is an umbrella group of developing countries that serves as a platform for the articulation of views on issues of common concern, especially with respect to deliberations within the UN or UN-sponsored treaties. In addition to articulating views, the G77, being an officially recognized intergovernmental organization, frequently sponsors motions during UN deliberations. It also produces joint declarations, action programmes and agreements on issues pertaining to global development, political economy and environmental sustainability. G77 is generally regarded as the official of the developing countries in global environmental negotiations. The forum was very active during the Third UN Conference on the Law of the Sea (1968–82) regularly providing a basis for internal consultation and the strengthening of developing countries' positions on a number of thorny issues. The forum has also been very active in the UN Conferences on Climate Change, including the **UN Framework Convention on Climate Change**. It has provided the platform on which the less industrialized countries have been able to highlight issues of justice and equity implicated in **climate change**. The G77 was formed in June 1964 by 77 developing countries that were signatories to a joint declaration of issues at the end of the first session of the UN Conference on Trade and Development (UNCTAD) held in Geneva, Switzerland. Today about 130 developing countries are members of the group.

Geoengineering

Geoengineering as an idea is the deliberate modification of the earth's environmental processes in order to make them more amenable to human societal needs and desires, writ larger. In practice, geoengineering is a tremendously controversial set of proposals due in part to the contested nature of goals and objectives—such as what is 'optimal' and 'desired'—of such projects. Often, geoengineering initiatives are associated with countering the effects of **greenhouse gas** emissions and **anthropogenic climate change**. Prominent among these activities are **carbon sequestration** projects. Examples include **carbon capture and storage** (CCS), enhancing cloud reflectivity (or 'albedo'), and ocean fertilization. These projects aim to mitigate the effects of heat-trapping emissions through technology-led ingenuity.

Global climate justice movements

Climate change and the pursuit of global justice are vitally linked: those most responsible for human-induced climate change are typically not the most vulnerable or experience the detrimental impacts of those changes in the climate. Historically, environmental movements for global justice have sought to contest environmental degradation as well as collective human disenfranchisement from the factors and institutions that give rise to and perpetuate unjust conditions. These movements have contested political, economic, social, cultural and environmental factors that shape this uneven terrain: from colonial and imperialist legacies to unequal power and protection, as well as access to resources and decision-making. Specific to climate change, climate justice movements have challenged inequities regarding differential **consumption** of carbon-based energy and adverse impacts from that consumption. Moreover, these movements have raised questions regarding responsibility; in other words, who can and should take action to alleviate the detrimental impacts from human-induced climate change. Moreover, human rights-based approaches seek a more just approach to accessible, flexible and equitable opportunities for alternatives to carbon-based industry and society, and to decarbonize energy demands. There is also sensitivity to 'inter-generational equity', or how future generations will be impacted by current carbon-based consumption. This leads to two broad forms of action: **adaptation** and **mitigation**. Adaptation is the alteration of an organism or the capacity to make changes to suit conditions different from those normally encountered. Differential **vulnerability** engenders challenges for some human populations to adapt to climate change. Mitigation is an intervention that reduces the sources of **greenhouse gases**. This can take shape through efficiency improvements (such as greater automobile fuel efficiency), fuel switching to less carbon-intensive fuels (such as switching from oil to natural gas for power generation), or mode switching to renewable technologies (such as solar or wind power). Mitigation can also include enhancements of **sinks**, and is often a more technologically-centred and controversial approach.

Global Environment Facility (GEF)

GEF is the largest multinational fund devoted to assisting developing countries fund projects and programmes that help protect the environment. The Fund is designated to six focal issues, including **climate change**, biodiversity, international waters, land degradation, the **ozone layer** and persistent organic pollutants. Accordingly, GEF functions as the Financial Mechanism for the **UN Framework Convention on Climate Change**, the UN Convention on Biological Diversity, the Stockholm Conference on Persistent Organic Pollutants and the Convention on Desertification. GEF is also in charge of disbursing grants to the developing countries under the **Montréal Protocol**. GEF was established in 1991 by the UN Environmental Programme (UNEP), the UN

Development Programme (UNDP) and the **World Bank**, all of which serve as implementing agencies for the Fund. GEF's activities are overseen by an independent board of directors, comprising representatives from 32 constituencies (16 from developing countries, 14 from developed countries and two from countries with transitional economies). The Council meets twice each year for three days, in which time they develop, evaluate and adopt GEF programmes.

Global Ocean Observing System (GOOS)

GOOS is a scheme that was established by the Intergovernmental Oceanographic Commission and the **World Meteorological Organization**. It is a permanent monitoring network, which feeds data about the oceans into research programmes on **climate change**.

Global Warming

Global warming refers to increases in the average atmospheric surface temperature on earth. These increases are attributed to adjustments made in the energy distribution between the spheres, where the rising temperature in the **atmosphere** compensates for energy imbalances elsewhere (this is called the 'planetary energy budget'). Broadly, emissions of **greenhouse gases** (GHGs) into the atmosphere cause changes in the climate. 'Global warming' refers to a specific facet of **climate change**: the increase in temperature over time. Many consider temperature to be climate change's 'fingerprint'. The GHGs that influence this energy budget and the warming of the globe include **carbon dioxide** (CO_2), methane (CH_4), nitrous oxide (N_2O), tropospheric ozone (O_3), halocarbons (CFCs, HFCs, HCFCs) and water vapour (H_2O_v).

Greenhouse Effect

The greenhouse effect is the process by which the earth is warmed through the retention of some of the Sun's energy by the **atmosphere**. Scientists discovered long ago that the functions of some trace gases in the atmosphere mimic those of the glass in a greenhouse, hence the name. Just as the glass of the greenhouse is transparent to sunlight but opaque to the infrared radiation emitted by the warm surfaces within, so certain atmospheric gases including water vapour, **carbon dioxide**, methane and **chlorofluorocarbons** (known collectively as **greenhouse gases**—GHGs) allow sunlight to pass unimpeded but absorb the radiation from the earth's surface. It is the absorbed radiation that is responsible for the warming of the land, atmosphere and the oceans. The earth receives energy from the Sun mostly in the form of ultraviolet radiation. About 30% of this ultraviolet radiation is reflected directly back to the Sun as ultraviolet rays, while about 70% is absorbed by the earth's surface. The absorbed energy is subsequently released gradually by the earth's surface in the form of infrared radiation with the intensity of the radiation increasing in proportion to the atmospheric temperature. Hence, the greater the amount of GHGs in the atmosphere, the more infrared radiation is absorbed and, subsequently, the higher the atmospheric temperature. On average, the atmospheric concentration of GHGs has increased by more than 15% in the last 100 years or so. Scientists attribute this increase mainly to the burning of **fossil fuels** such as gas, coal and oil, all of which result in the release of large amounts of GHGs to the atmosphere. Scientists believe that the rapid increase in GHGs in the atmosphere is responsible for the increase in mean temperature of the atmosphere over the last few decades. This condition is widely referred to as **global warming**. There are many uncertainties over the rate at which GHGs accumulate and the resulting consequences, but scientists on the **Intergovernmental Panel on Climate Change** have estimated that a doubling of the present level of carbon dioxide concentration (or its equivalent to other gases) could cause a rise in the average temperature of 1–3.5°C and that such an increase may occur by mid-to-late 21st century unless steps are taken to reduce the emissions of GHGs. Scientists say that in order to avert dangerous changes in the climate, it is necessary to cut global emissions of GHGs by up to 50% of the 1990 level. However, under the **Kyoto Protocol** agreed at a **Conference of the Parties** to the **UN Framework Convention on Climate Change** in December 1997, nations agreed to reduce emissions of GHGs at the global level by about 6.2% by 2012. Most approaches to emissions reduction involve increasing the efficiency with which energy is used, as well as the use of **renewable energy** sources as alternatives to fossil fuels.

Greenhouse Gases (GHGs) – *see* **Carbon Dioxide.**

Greenpeace

One of the first of the environmental pressure groups, Greenpeace was founded in 1971, dedicated to campaigning against abuse of the natural world, through non-violent direct-action protests. All of its protests are backed by scientific research. Greenpeace began when a group of US citizens and Canadians chartered a ship and went to Amchitka Island, Alaska, where a series of nuclear tests was planned. As a result of their presence only one test was carried out. The island subsequently became a bird sanctuary. Greenpeace continued in this active style, protesting about the slaughter of seals, against whaling and the dumping of waste at sea. Their methods, which often put campaigners in great personal danger, have made headlines around the world, bringing remote issues directly to the public's attention. In 1987 it raised its World Park **Antarctica** flag in an attempt to prevent exploitation of the continent. In the first decade of the 21st century its campaigns were aimed at: catalysing an energy revolution to address **climate change**; defending the oceans against wasteful and destructive fishing; protecting the world's forests and all the plants, animals and people that depend on them; working for disarmament and peace; creating a toxin-free future; and promoting sustainable agriculture.

Group of Eight (G8)

The G8 has roots in the response to the 1973 oil shock and subsequent recession. The group's formation was initiated by France, which sought more co-ordinated governance structures in an increasingly economically intertwined world. The G8 consists of heads of state from France, Russia, the United Kingdom, Italy, Germany, Canada, the USA and Japan. These countries form a coalition with meetings each year on a rotating basis and with a rotating 'presidency', which sets the agenda. For instance, in 2005 the then UK Prime Minister Tony Blair hosted the G8 Summit in Gleneagles, and put **climate change** and poverty on the agenda as the two main points for discussion. From this 2005 meeting came a 'Gleneagles Plan of Action on Climate Change, Clean Energy and Sustainable Development'. This plan supported energy efficiency improvement, **renewable energy**, and ongoing clean energy research and development. Associated with these meetings are quarterly G8 meetings of finance ministers, and annual gatherings of G8 foreign ministers and G8 environment ministers. For example, in April 2009 environment ministers gathered in Siracusa, Italy where climate change was at the top of the agenda in the lead up to the December 2009 UN **Conference of the Parties** meeting in Copenhagen, Denmark (see **Copenhagen Conference**). In recent years, France and the United Kingdom have sought to include a 'plus five' (or 'outreach five') set of key developing countries, to include their voices and interests in ongoing discussions. These countries are Mexico, People's Republic of China, India, South Africa and Brazil. Also, there is support to include Egypt and expand the entire group from a 'G8+5' to a 'G14'. These meetings are intended to increase dialogue among member nations in ongoing 21st century global challenges, such as climate change.

H

'Hot Air'

This phrase refers to concern that some **Annex I/B** Parties could meet their emissions reductions target stated in the first phase of the **Kyoto Protocol** with minimal effort. As a result, these countries could flood the market with tradable emissions credits, thereby reducing the incentive for other countries to contribute to greater overall emissions reductions, instead just buying up these credits that are not going to be needed. This gap between allocations and actual emissions is what is considered to be 'hot air'. Due primarily to the collapse of the Soviet Union—and associated economic downturn—during the benchmark period of emissions reductions and allocations from 1990 onwards, particular countries like Russia and the Ukraine reduced their **greenhouse gas** emissions far below their allocations. The credits achieved through this difference between allocation and actual emissions were then commodities that have effectively been created and traded 'out of thin air', instead of forcing other governments to reduce greenhouse gas emissions within their own borders or by other means.

I

Integrated Assessment

Integrated assessment is an analytical method designed to combine models and observations from physical, social, political, economic and biological sciences. This method also accounts for interactions therein. In so doing, integrated assessment seeks to put forward a coherent framework for evaluating causes, consequences and actions related to global environmental change issues such as **climate change**.

Intensity Targets

Intensity targets represent an alternative way to calculate and achieve reductions in **greenhouse gas** (GHG) emissions. Rather than a consideration of emissions reduction in and of themselves, intensity targets are based upon a ratio of carbon emissions reductions and gross domestic product (GDP). For example, on 14 February 2002, US President George W. Bush announced a new strategy to set a voluntary greenhouse gas intensity target for the USA. He declared a target of 18% 'intensity' reductions between 2002 and 2012. With continuing GDP growth, economists determined that this translated into actually allowing for total GHG emissions to increase by 12% over that time period. This plan was met with some suspicion, as Bush had withdrawn from the emissions reductions targets of the **Kyoto Protocol** in the previous year. Proponents call this way of accounting and planning for emissions reductions to be more sensitive to economic costs than straightforward emissions reductions targets as delineated in the Kyoto Protocol. Critics charge that this is a more nefarious form of '**hot air**', cooking the books or 'blowing smoke'. As such, focusing on intensity targets can present the appearance of GHG emissions reductions. However, as long as GDP growth outpaces emissions growth, it produces a negative value. Adding to the complexity of appearance and possible actual emissions growth or reduction, GDP calculations are laden with controversial elements and ways of making calculations.

Intergovernmental Panel on Climate Change (IPCC)

The IPCC is a body established by two UN agencies, the **World Meteorological Organization** (WMO) and the **UN Environment Programme** (UNEP) in 1988 to assess scientific, technical and socio-economic information relevant for the understanding of **climate change**, its potential impacts and options for **adaptation** and **mitigation**. The IPCC does not itself carry out scientific research on climate change, nor does it engage in the monitoring or gathering of raw climate data. Rather, the panel bases its assessments on peer-reviewed and published scientific literature and technical reports. The bulk of the members of the IPCC comprise government scientists but a significant number of independent academic scientists, researchers and scholars from various countries of the world also participate regularly in the activities of the IPCC. Over 2,500 scientific experts and 850 authors contribute to the works of the IPCC. The panel is open to all members of the UN and the WMO. The first meeting of the IPCC took place in November 1988 in Geneva, Switzerland where three expert or working groups were set up. Working Group I has the function of assessing the scientific aspects of the climate system and climate change. Working Group II assesses the impact of climate change on socio-economic and natural systems, while Working Group III assesses policy options for limiting **greenhouse gas** emissions as well as options for adaptation. Each Working Group has two Co-Chairs, one from the developed and other from the developing world, as well as a technical support unit. The first reports (called Assessment Reports) of the three Working Groups were presented in an IPCC meeting in Sweden in August 1990. These reports played a significant role in galvanizing activities and government support for the negotiation of the **UN Framework Convention on Climate Change** (UNFCCC) between 1990 and 1992. The IPCC reports are updated every five years. The Second Assessment reports were published in 1995, the third in 2001 and the fourth in 2007. The Fifth Assessment Report work has begun, for release in 2013. To date, the IPCC reports, despite some controversies relating to objectivity and bias, continue to provide the basis for much of governments' position and negotiation on climate change. For example, the Second Assessment Report provided key input to the negotiations that led to the adoption of the **Kyoto Protocol** to the UNFCCC in 1997. Apart from these comprehensive reviews the IPCC also produces hundreds of special reports, technical papers, summary reports and CD ROMs on various aspects of climate change. The governing body of the IPCC is a Panel that meets in plenary sessions about once every year. The Panel adopts IPCC reports, decides on work plans for the Working Groups, on the structure of reports, and on budget and procedures. A secretariat, which is hosted by the WMO in Geneva, oversees the day-to-day operations of the group.

International Council for Science (ICSU)

The ICSU, formerly known as the International Council of Scientific Unions, is a non-governmental group of scientific organizations representing 80 national academies of science, 20 international unions and 26 other bodies called scientific associates. The object of ICSU is to achieve the free exchange of scientific information and co-operation between the world's scientific communities. To accommodate the spread of activities in which many of the member unions are involved, ICSU has established 13 scientific committees with experts from a multiplicity of scientific disciplines. One of them is the Scientific Committee on Problems of the Environment (SCOPE), which directs attention to developing countries. SCOPE was formed in 1969 in response to environmental concerns emerging at the time. Its first task was to prepare a report on global environment monitoring for the UN Conference on the Human Environment in Stockholm, Sweden. The mandate of SCOPE is: to assemble, review and assess the information available on human-induced environmental changes and the effects of these changes on humans; to assess and evaluate the methods of measuring environmental parameters; and to provide an intelligence service on current research and a body of informed advice.

International Environmental Agreements (IEAs)

IEAs are treaties, conventions, or protocols that are set up to address environmental problems that have international implications. They are initiated by national governments agreeing to take action to limit environmental damage and can involve a dynamic range/complex web of actors. The fundamental objectives of IEAs include the desire to move from non-co-operative behaviour to co-operative behaviour in regard to the use of common resources, and the development of mechanisms for joint decision-making in regard to these common resources. An example of an IEA is the **UN Framework Convention on Climate Change**, and the subsequent **Kyoto Protocol**. There are five basic steps in the development of an international environmental treaty. First is the identification of needs and goals. Second, are the negotiations, which can include a pre-negotiation negotiation to frame the parameters of the debate and set timetables for deliberations. At this stage, consensus processes are most common. Third is adoption and signature. In IEAs only countries vote: the UN Charter prohibits a decision-making role for **non-governmental organizations**. The fourth step is **ratification**, unless Parties agree to be bound simply by signature. This typically involves national-level legislative processes. Fifth, the IEA enters into force after sufficient ratification. This threshold is set in earlier negotiations. IEAs must be assembled in accordance with the rules of the Vienna Convention of 1969. The Vienna Convention defines an IEA as an agreement 'concluded between States in written form and governed by international law, whether embodied in a single instrument or in two or more related instruments and whatever its particular designation'. The Vienna Convention governs the major aspects of treaties (including negotiations, conclusion, interpretation, amendment and termination).

International Monetary Fund (IMF)

The IMF is a specialized agency of the UN. It was established in 1947 to promote international monetary stability, the growth of world trade and the stability of foreign exchange. It also gives financial assistance to the 184 member countries when they have balance of payments problems, and smoothes multilateral payments and financial arrangements among member states. The IMF works in close collaboration with the **World Bank** and **World Trade Organization** (WTO).

International Renewable Energy Agency (IRENA)

IRENA was established at a conference in Bonn, Germany, in January 2009, to provide practical advice and support for developing and industrialized states and to promote a rapid transition to the sustainable use of **renewable energy** throughout the world. IRENA is an intergovernmental organization, which had 136 signed-up member states when it decided to locate its interim headquarters in Abu Dhabi, in the United Arab Emirates in June 2009.

International Union for Conservation of Nature and Natural Resources (IUCN)

The IUCN has been, since 1956, the official name of what was founded as the International Union for the Protection of Nature (IUPN). Between 1990 and March 2008 the 'World Conservation Union' was used as a simpler name, in conjunction with the IUCN acronym; since 2008 the IUCN has instead pre-ferred to use the short name of 'International Union for Conservation of Nature'. It is an independent, global organization that promotes the world-wide conservation of wildlife, habitats and natural resources. It was founded in 1948 to alleviate the worst effects of human influence on the environment from industrial and urban development. It is also concerned about excessive exploitation of the earth's natural resources. The IUCN's members include governments and conservation organizations representing more than 100 countries. It has close links with several UN agencies.

J

Joint Implementation

This is one of the so-called flexible mechanisms put in place by the **Kyoto Protocol** to make it easier for industrialized countries to meet their emissions reduction commitments under the Protocol. Specifically, Joint Implementation allows industrialized countries to sponsor or collaborate with Eastern European countries (countries in transition) in the establishment of low-carbon development projects. The idea is that by sponsoring such low carbon development projects, it would be possible to reduce the amount of emissions that would have otherwise occurred if the country in transition were to follow the cheaper but high-carbon development pathways. At the same time, it is considered that investing in such projects would provide the opportunity for the transfer of technology while allowing the industrialized countries to make emissions reductions in locations where they would get the highest result per investment. Accordingly, the policy provides that both the investment and the host country share the emission reduction credits that accrue from following the more carbon efficient developmental pathway. The policy is, though, not restricted to deals between developed countries and those in transition, but also allows for collaboration between two or more industrialized countries.

Jusscannz

In negotiations of environmental treaties, particularly climate treaties, a number of regional coalitions have emerged that share commons interests. Among them is JUSSCANNZ, which is a group of developed countries. JUSSCANNZ is a clunky acronym that signifies the founding members Japan, United States, Switzerland, Canada, Australia, Norway and New Zealand. This block now also includes Russia and Iceland. JUSSCANNZ was formed with an interest in focusing on the economic impacts of the **Kyoto Protocol**, and calling for developing country participation in the first phase of the Treaty.

K

Kyoto Protocol

International negotiations over anthropogenic global climate policy have most prominently taken shape as the Kyoto Protocol. This Protocol was the product of the **UN Framework Convention on Climate Change** (UNFCCC), drafted at the 1992 **UN Conference on Environment and Development** (UNCED) or '**Earth Summit**'. The Protocol was adopted in Kyoto, Japan on 11 December 1997. The Protocol came into force in 2005 following its **ratification** by Russia. The Kyoto Protocol provides detailed guidelines and policy mechanisms that allow governments to take more specific and measurable action to combat **climate change** in line with the objective of the UNFCCC. The most outstanding aspect of the Protocol is that it commits industrialized countries to legally, individually binding targets to reduce their **greenhouse gas** (GHG) emissions. Under the Protocol, the Annex 1 (industrialized countries) agree to cut their (cumulative) GHG emissions by at least 5% from the 1990 base line between 2008 and 2012, which is known as the first commitment period. Remarkably, the Protocol allocates all the industrialized countries with specific emission reduction quotas based on a number of criteria including historical emissions, level of technological advancement, extent of dependence on fossil fuel and peculiar development challenges. For example, the **European Union** has a quota of -8%, which it was expected to distribute among its then 15 member states, the USA has a quota of -7%, Canada, Japan and Hungary have each a quota of -6%, Norway has +1%, while Australia has +8%. The Kyoto Protocol also details a series of rules and project-based mechanisms such as the **Clean Development Mechanism** (CDM) and **Joint Implementation** (JI), through which country Parties might collaborate to meet their emission reduction targets (Kyoto targets). The Protocol also provides for the trading of emissions among Annex I Parties as a means of achieving emissions reductions. Despite these provisions for collaboration among Parties and for **emissions trading**, the Protocol requires that contracting Parties must put in place strong domestic measures to reduce GHG emissions. The Protocol provides for the review of its commitments, so that these can be strengthened over time. Negotiations on targets for the second commitment period started in 2005, by which time Annex I Parties must have made 'demonstrable progress' in meeting their commitments under the Protocol. Only Parties to the Convention can become Parties to the Protocol, but this involves a separate ratification process. At present, about 175 Parties have ratified the Protocol. The USA was opposed to the Protocol and indicated its intention not to ratify.

L

Least Developed Countries (LDCs)

This is the term used to refer to the poorest countries on earth. Countries meet LDC criteria through factors such as low income, low public health, low levels of education and literacy, and overall economic **vulnerability**. At present these are the 49 countries considered to be LDCs by the UN General Assembly: Afghanistan, Angola, Bangladesh, Benin, Bhutan, Burkina Faso, Burundi, Cambodia, Central African Republic, Chad, Comoros, Democratic Republic of Congo, Djibouti, Equatorial Guinea, Eritrea, Ethiopia, Gambia, Guinea, Guinea-Bissau, Haiti, Kiribati, Laos, Lesotho, Liberia, Madagascar, Malawi, Maldives, Mali, Mauritania, Mozambique, Myanmar (Burma), Nepal, Niger, Rwanda, Samoa, São Tomé and Príncipe, Senegal, Sierra Leone, Solomon Islands, Somalia, Sudan, Tanzania, Timor-Leste, Togo, Tuvalu, Uganda, Vanuatu, Yemen and Zambia. Only Cape Verde and Botswana have moved out of—or 'graduated' from—LDC status.

Livelihoods

Utilization of the concept 'livelihoods' has been a successful way through which to investigate human well-being, security, **vulnerability**, **entitlements**, capabilities and perspectives on development as they relate to **anthropogenic climate change**. Livelihood investigations work to link these issues to appropriate livelihood-enhancement policy measures. In 1992 R. Chambers and G. Conway defined livelihoods as, 'the means of gaining a living, including livelihood capabilities, tangible assets, and intangible assets [...] employment can provide a livelihood, but most livelihoods of the poor are based on multiple activities and sources of food, income and security'. Tangible assets refer to material goods such as cattle, land and equipment, while non-tangible assets mean claims and access.

Lulucf

This is an acronym that refers to Land Use, Land-Use Change, and Forestry. This also encompasses activities that involve biodiversity conservation and management. At present, approximately one-fifth of anthropogenic **greenhouse gas** (GHG) emissions are attributed to land use and land cover change activities. The **Intergovernmental Panel on Climate Change** has assembled two reports on LULUCF. Land-use change—such as agriculture, fires, land clearing for development—is one of the primary contributors to GHG emissions and, therefore, contributes to **climate change**. These activities, and associated goals and objectives for **mitigation**, are outlined in Article 3.3 of the **Kyoto Protocol**.

M

Marrakech Accords

These are a set of agreements that were outlined and agreed at the seventh **Conference of the Parties** (COP-7) meeting to the **UN Framework Convention on Climate Change**, in 2001. These accords made explicit the guidelines for how the **Kyoto Protocol** provisions were to be made operational. These guidelines included the development and implementation of an **Adaptation Fund**, as well as the details of the **Flexibility Mechanisms**: **Joint Implementation** (Article 6), the **Clean Development Mechanism** (Article 12), and **Emissions Trading** (Article 17).

Millennium Development Goals

Over 190 countries and approximately 24 international organizations have agreed to the principles and targets outlined by the Millennium Development Goals. These are a set of eight goals that were agreed at the UN Millennium Summit in 2000, and derived from the UN Millennium Declaration. The goals also involve 21 associated targets to reach by particular periods of 2010, 2015 and 2020. These goals are 1) end poverty and hunger; 2) achieve universal primary education; 3) promote gender equality and empower women; 4) reduce child mortality; 5) improve maternal health; 6) combat HIV/AIDS, malaria and other diseases; 7) ensure environmental sustainability; and 8) develop a global partnership for development. An example of an associated target is to halve the proportion of people without consistent access to basic sanitation and safe drinking water by 2015. Some of these aspirational as well as concrete goals and targets are on track, while progress towards reaching others is falling far short. Progress also varies by region, where sub-Saharan Africa continues to make little progress towards these development goals, while the People's Republic of China does so quite rapidly overall. Funding for programmes remains a key challenge. However, **Group of Eight** (G8) countries co-operated with the **World Bank** and **International Monetary Fund** to establish a 'Multilateral Debt Relief Initiative' to promote debt forgiveness.

Mitigation

Mitigation is an intervention that reduces the sources of **greenhouse gases** (GHGs) or enhances **sinks** for GHGs. This can take shape through efficiency improvements (such as greater automobile fuel efficiency), fuel switching to less carbon-intensive fuels (such as switching from oil to natural gas for power generation), or mode switching to renewable technologies (such as solar or wind power). Mitigation can also include enhancements of sinks, and is often a more technologically-centred and controversial approach.

Montréal Protocol

The Montréal Protocol was signed in 1987 by 24 countries, which agreed to reduce **chlorofluorocarbon** (CFC) production by 50% by 1999. By the end of the 20th century most countries in the world were parties to the Protocol, which was a product of the **Vienna Convention for the Protection of the Ozone Layer**. In a series of amendments to the Convention in the early 1980s, known as the London Amendments and Copenhagen Amendments, countries agreed to phase out CFC production completely by 1996 in the industrialized world. Developing countries were allowed over 10 years longer to phase out their production of ozone-depleting substances. In part because developing countries were still producing CFCs in the late 1990s, a 'black' market (illegal trade) in CFCs appeared in the industrialized countries. Many developing countries started to phase out their production with the assistance of a Multilateral Fund contributed to mainly by industrialized countries. At the end of the 1990s the People's Republic of China was the largest producer and consumer of CFCs. One of the main alternatives to CFCs, the hydrofluorocarbons (HFCs), are major **greenhouse gases** and are now meant to be regulated under the **Kyoto Protocol**. The other main alternative is hydrochlorofluorocarbons (HCFCs), which are also ozone-depleting substances, albeit much less damaging than CFCs. Even so, HCFCs were also to be phased out completely in all countries by 2030. The other main ozone-depleting substance regulated under the Montréal Protocol is methyl bromide, a potent greenhouse gas and dangerous pesticide used mainly on grapes, strawberries, cut flowers and tomatoes. The USA is the largest producer and consumer of methyl bromide, closely followed by Israel, in terms of production. As a result of the Montréal Protocol, by 2000 some forms of CFC appeared to have reached their maximum concentration in the **atmosphere**, but the **ozone layer** had not yet started to recover. Ozone depletion was expected to continue long into the 21st century because CFCs persist for many decades in the atmosphere.

N

National Adaptation Plan of Action (NAPA)

In 2001 at the seventh **Conference of the Parties** (COP-7) meeting in Marrakech, Morocco, delegates agreed to establish a programme where **Least Developed Countries** (LDCs) could identify and prioritize their **adaptation** needs (see **Marrakech Accords**). These were then articulated in National Adaptation Plans of Action for each country. In the years since COP-7, countries have worked to develop these plans, and present them to the international donor community in order to co-ordinate possible funding through the UN and other multilateral or bilateral agreements.

No regrets options

This phrase 'no regrets options' refers to the introduction of policies, measures and technologies that mitigate **greenhouse gas** (GHG) emissions and also have 'co-benefits'. These co-benefits could include reduced energy costs, increased energy security and the like. Considering these gains, investments in these actions are considered to be worthwhile even if GHG emissions reductions are not a consideration. For example, in the USA, Senators from coal-producing regions may be less hesitant to support federal-level actions to mitigate GHG emissions if combine-cycle gas turbine technologies—capturing heat from coal-burning and then generating more energy with it—are funded in their districts. Irrespective of the gain in GHG emissions reductions, these turbines can boost energy efficiency and lower electricity costs in their areas. Therefore, this term refers to possible activities in climate **politics** that may gain the support of certain sectors of the policy community that may otherwise not be willing to support actions to reduce GHG emissions.

Non-Governmental Organizations (NGOs)

These are private, voluntary, non-profit organizations that act in the public interest on wide-ranging issues such as human rights, child welfare, poverty alleviation, humanitarian aids, women's rights, etc. NGOs educate the public on their issues of focus. They also sometimes lobby governments to act or make favourable policies with regard to the issues of concern. NGOs also mobilize the public to action and often function as advocates on behalf of people on given issues. Environmental NGOs have played a crucial part in the development of environmental awareness and of key environmental policies, as well as multilateral environmental agreements across the globe. **Greenpeace** played an essential role in the development of the Basel Convention on the Transboundary Movement of Hazardous Wastes and their Disposal, while **Friends of the Earth** played an important role in getting bottling companies in Europe to introduce recyclable bottles, and conservation organizations such as the **International Union for Conservation of Nature and Natural Resources** have been active in promoting various multilateral environmental agreements since the 1960s. Throughout the world, there are more than 7,000 international NGOs that are concerned with environment and development, with millions of supporters. In all, it is estimated that globally there are well over 20,000 such NGOs ranging from small grassroots agencies to influential international groups like Greenpeace and Friends of the Earth. The growth of environmental NGOs has been dramatic ever since the UN Conference on the Human Environment in Stockholm in 1972. This growth is often said to be a result of the increased rate of environmental degradation world-wide, the increase in socio-economic globalization, which has increased interaction among different groups across the world, as well as changes in the functions of government, which allow private organizations to play more active roles in governance.

Non Nation-State Actors

Non nation-state actors (NNSAs) (also called non-state actors) are those who operate in climate **politics** from outside national-level government agencies. NNSAs include **non-governmental organizations** (NGOs), cities, mass media, multinational corporations and various social movement organizations. In investigations of climate politics and policy, there is often a focus on government officials explicitly shaping policy action. However, research centres such as the UK-based Tyndall Centre for Climate Change Research have expanded considerations to encompass the influences of these NNSAs on ongoing climate politics and codified climate policies.

North–South tensions (legacies of colonialism)

In 1991 Anil Agarwal and Sunita Narain wrote a seminal piece that traced differential impacts in the Global North and Global South, entitled 'Global Warming in an Unequal World: A Case of Environmental Colonialism'. They discussed concerns of 'intra-generational equity', or inequality across segments of the contemporary global community. They considered vastly different levels of **consumption**—and hence GHG emissions—across populations, and called for a rights-based approach to determinations regarding what constitutes a fair share of atmospheric space. Many others have examined the economic structures that support carbon-based industry, which, in turn, have grown to fuel, support and encourage particular forms of consumption with related GHG emissions. Others have looked at political-economic impacts critically exploring for whom the economy potentially 'booms'. This leads to further analysis regarding emissions reductions based on historical rates of emissions at a per capita and country level. Since the end of the Cold War, this North–South axis has been considered the dominant consideration for ongoing international politics. Furthermore, research by Piers Blaikie, Terry Cannon, Ian Davis and Ben Wisner has asserted that impacts are not merely a result of detrimental events associated with **climate change**, but rather are the product of the combination of a trigger event and social, political and economic factors that differentially structure people's lives and **livelihoods**. Many of the poor in the Global South are highly dependent on natural resources, while also having a limited capacity—and less infrastructural support—to adapt to changes in the climate. Moreover, these challenges manifest through varied concerns over future impacts of climate change.

O

Offshoring emissions

The concept of offshoring emissions refers to **greenhouse gas** (GHG) emissions that are generated by a country through the production of material goods for **consumption** elsewhere. GHG emissions accounting schemes—such as those developed through the **UN Framework Convention on Climate Change**—at present account for the emissions from production of goods rather than emissions from goods imported and consumed in a particular country. A 2009 paper by Peters et al. in *Geophysical Research Letters* found that 6% of emissions in the People's Republic of China are attributed to the production of export goods for consumption in Europe. They determined that if these country-level emissions profiles were recalculated to account for this production-consumption issue, the progress towards **targets and timetables** established in the **Kyoto Protocol** would look very different. For instance, the United Kingdom, which has achieved 18% reductions below 1990 GHG emissions levels, would instead amount to a 20% increase in GHGs since 1990. Thus, Chinese climate negotiators have introduced this recalculation as a possible point for discussion in ongoing **Conference of the Parties** talks. The calculation of emissions from production rather than consumption is one complex factor among many that reveal systemic challenges for ongoing climate **politics** and policy.

Organisation for Economic Co-operation and Development (OECD)

With headquarters in Paris, the OECD was established in 1948 as part of the Marshall Plan for rebuilding Europe after the Second World War. It gained a great deal of momentum and influence over the decades that followed. At present, the OECD is an international organization of 30 countries that share characteristics of relatively highly developed nations (with Turkey, Poland and Mexico perhaps as exceptions), with free market economies and representative democracies. The members are: Australia, Austria, Belgium, Canada, Czech Republic, Denmark, Finland, France, Germany, Greece, Hungary, Iceland, Republic of Ireland, Italy, Japan, Luxembourg, Mexico, Netherlands, New Zealand, Norway, Poland, Portugal, Republic of Korea (South Korea), Slovakia, Spain, Sweden, Switzerland, Turkey, the United Kingdom and the USA. Most of the OECD countries make up the bulk of **Annex I/B** Parties to the **Kyoto Protocol**, with commitments to reduce **greenhouse gas** emissions on average by 5.2% from 1990 levels by 2012.

Organization of Petroleum Exporting Countries (OPEC)

This group of petroleum exporting countries is often referred to in shorthand parlance as 'OPEC' and includes these 12 nation-states: Algeria, Angola, Ecuador, Iran, Iraq, Kuwait, Libya, Nigeria, Qatar, Saudi Arabia, the United Arab Emirates (UAE) and Venezuela. Indonesia has been a member of OPEC in the past. OPEC member nations possess about two-thirds of the world's oil reserves. However, with the development of energy production from tar sands, and **renewable energy** sources, this power and influence can be considered under threat. In principle, this group works to control the flow of oil onto the world market, thus influencing the price through the duel factors of supply and demand. However, many other factors, such as political stability and weather, play roles in shaping OPEC decisions and actions on this 'flow of oil'. The stated goals of OPEC include efforts to stabilize international oil markets (avoiding large fluctuations in price) in order to continue the steady income to OPEC member nations. These efforts often fall short of their goals, though, as evidenced by the 1973 oil crisis and the 2008 oil shock.

Ozone layer

The ozone layer, or ozonosphere, is the protective layer of ozone in the stratosphere, found at a level between 15 km and 30 km above the earth, and which prevents harmful ultraviolet (UV-B) radiation, a potential cause of skin cancer and a threat to plant life, from reaching the ground. The fragile shield is being damaged by chemicals released on earth. The main chemicals depleting stratospheric ozone were **chlorofluorocarbons** (CFCs), used in refrigerators, aerosols, and as cleaners in many industries, and halons, used in fire extinguishers. The damage is caused when these chemicals release highly reactive forms of chlorine and bromine. It is hoped that the international phasing out of such chemicals will allow the ozone layer to regenerate by the middle of the 21st century.

P

Particulates

These are tiny flecks of soot and similar substances in the **atmosphere**. A principal source of particulates is black exhaust smoke from road vehicles. Among road vehicles, 77% of particulates are produced by heavy goods vehicles, 10% by buses, 7% by light delivery vehicles and 6% by cars. A diesel engine produces far more particulates than a petrol engine. Particulates in vehicle exhausts mainly consist of carbon and unburnt compounds from the fuel or lubricating oil. Particulates are also produced by tyre wear, the chimneys of power stations, industrial process plants and even such activities as barbecues and fireworks. Secondary particulates may form in the atmosphere and include nitrates and sulphates created from nitrogen oxides and sulphur dioxide. Small particles of solid or liquid may form aerosols. Particulate traps are devices attached to diesel vehicles to prevent particulates from the engine being discharged into the atmosphere. Such traps were initially too bulky to be fitted to smaller vehicles. Engineers have experimented with designs for burning off the trapped particulates, but this solution was complicated by the difficulty of destroying the particulates without increasing the amounts of nitrogen oxides produced.

Parts per million/parts per billion

Parts per million (ppm) or parts per billion (ppb) are ways of describing the amounts of trace gases in the earth's **atmosphere**. Although these gases may be small in concentration, they are of great importance in terms of contributing to what comprises the **greenhouse effect**. At the time of writing, with slight seasonal variation, there were about 385 ppm of the principle **greenhouse gas carbon dioxide** in the atmosphere. Ppm or ppb are defined as the number of parts by weight of a suspended or dissolved constituent per million/billion parts by weight. In other words, it can be described as parts of the gas per million/billion parts of the air. As a molecule, a ppm is about 1 milligram per litre of water (1 mg/L = ppm).

Policies and Measures (PAMs)

This phrase refers to actions, technologies, practices and processes that can be promoted in UNFCCC member nations in order to catalyse efforts to **mitigation** of **greenhouse gas** emissions, and meet established reduction commitments. PAMs are also discussed often as public–private partnerships, in order to encourage the participation of business and industry in meeting national targets. PAMs might also incorporate concessions and exchanges for participation. For example, the 2009 proposal by the US Environmental Protection Agency for fuel efficiency increases in new personal automobiles can potentially help the USA more capably achieve the commitments to reductions in greenhouse gas emissions made in the successor treaty to the **Kyoto Protocol**. This US fuel-efficiency measure can significantly contribute to emissions reductions as well as energy security. Essentially, PAMs seek to co-ordinate and harmonize common goals and objectives to keep more carbon out of the **atmosphere**.

Political ecology

While there are some disagreements over its exact genesis, Alexander Cockburn, Eric Wolf and Grahame Beakhurst are often given credit as foundational contributors in the 1970s to what has emerged as a political ecology perspective. Michael Watts asserts that political ecological perspectives were triggered particularly by 1) peasant studies of exploitation, social differentiation and the role of the market among the Third World rural poor; and 2) the growth of Marxist development studies (world systems theory, dependency, structural Marxism, etc.). In 1987, Piers Blaikie and Hal Brookfield defined political ecology as an approach that 'can encompass interactive effects, the contribution of different geographical scales and hierarchies of socioeconomic organizations (e.g. person, household, village, region, state, and world) and the contradictions between social and environmental changes through time'. It is an effort to understand multi-scale and complex nature-society relations through an analysis of access, control over resources, and implications for environmental health and sustainable **livelihoods**. Similarly, in 2000 P. Stott and S. Sullivan defined political ecology as 'a concern with tracing the genealogy of narratives concerning "the environment", with identifying power relationships supported by such narratives, and with asserting the consequences of hegemony over, and within, these narratives for economic and social development, and particularly for constraining possibilities for self-determination'. Among valuable writing projects to understand the roots and tenets of political ecology as well as mobilize its analytical tools for case-study explorations are two books: Tim Forsyth's *Critical Political Ecology* (2003) and Paul Robbins's *Political Ecology* (2004). Overall, political ecology approaches emphasize environmental and social variability, and also pay attention to contestations across scales in regards to resource access and use.

In short, political ecology is a critical recognition and exploration of the dynamics, properties, and meanings of 'politicized environments'.

Politics

In this volume, 'politics' are considered as the management and contestations of policies, through social relations infused with power, authority and varying perspectives. Roger Pielke, Jr has defined politics as 'bargaining, negotiation and compromise in the pursuit of desired ends'. Politics involve proposals, ideas, intentions, decisions and behaviours, with a focus on processes that prop up, challenge, lurk behind, support and resist explicit actions.

Post-modern thought

Post-modern writings emerged to significantly question and radically transform dominant Western industrialized nation-led conceptions of social, economic and political modernity. It grew in a rhizomatic form, emphasizing fragmentation and elusiveness of terms and definition. This perspective deconstructed modernization project myths and 'grand narratives' to reveal more accurate narratives of local people/struggles, and marginalized/disempowered groups. Post-modern thought is distinguished from modernization by a break from faith in objective truths and scientific certainty, greater attention paid to contributions of power and access to knowledge formation and articulation, and investigations and discussions of who benefits from what constructions of truth.

Precautionary Principle

The precautionary principle is Principle 15 of the Rio Declaration (1992). It states, 'Where there are threats of serious or irreversible damage, lack of full scientific certainty shall not be used as a reason for postponing cost-effective measures to prevent environmental degradation'. This principle aims to provide an informed and cautious basis for action in the face of uncertainty. It is most often applied in the context of the impact of human actions on the environment and human health, given the complicity of the system and the fact that most of the relationship and cause effect are extremely difficult to predict in details. The logic of the precautionary principle is that it is better to err on the side of caution, especially when some of the possible consequences of policies or actions on human health or the natural environment might be irreversible. The precautionary principle is widely accepted in international circles and is frequently mentioned in regional, multilateral and global environmental treaties.

Proxy Data

Proxy data are data from which past climates and past **climate changes** can be derived indirectly. These are vitally important to tracing the past in order to help inform contemporary and future climate changes. Climate proxy data can come from a wide range of human sources such as vintner and gardening diaries, ship captains' logs and records from trading posts. Climate proxies are obtained also from what are considered natural sources, such as ice cores, tree rings, corals and sediment cores. Together, these proxy data have provided evidence that recent increases in atmospheric CO_2 exceed the bounds of natural variability experienced during the preceding 900,000 years. While there has been discussion of the passing of the 'peak' in economically recoverable global oil that is commercially available for **consumption**, many in the climate science community consider the atmospheric concentration of **greenhouse gases** to be of more pressing concern, and proxy data provide substantive assistance in helping to understand these changes.

Q

Quantified Emissions Limitation and Reduction Commitments (QELROs)

Used to describe the legally binding targets and timetables set out in the Kyoto Protocol for Annex I/B Parties. These QELROs make explicit the limits and reductions for greenhouse gas emissions in the first phase, 2008–12.

R

Ratification

Ratification is the formal approval of an agreement, convention, treaty or protocol. This happens after a head of state signs the agreement. This is often carried out by a legislative body. Ratification is typically the fourth of five major steps through which an international agreement, convention, treaty or protocol passes (see **International Environmental Agreements—IEAs**). In IEAs only countries vote: the UN Charter prohibits a decision-making role for **non-governmental organizations**. The fifth step is when the IEA enters into force after sufficient ratification. This threshold is set in earlier negotiations.

Reducing Emissions from Deforestation and Forest Degradation (REDD)

At present, approximately one-fifth of anthropogenic **greenhouse gas** emissions are attributed to land use and land-cover change activities. Therefore, ongoing international climate **politics** consider what happens to forests to be critical to goals and objectives of substantive emissions reductions in the 21st century. REDD is a set of mechanisms and financial incentives proposed as part of the successor to the **Kyoto Protocol**. This set of mechanisms was first proposed at the 13th **Conference of the Parties** (COP-13) in Bali, Indonesia in 2007. Many competing interests have mobilized to influence the content of REDD mechanisms, as the carbon credits associated with deforestation and forest degradation projects can be both ecologically critical and financially lucrative endeavours. For example, indigenous movements and forest-dependent communities have been organizing in recent years to potentially receive credits for forest conservation that they can then trade for monetary value. These credits are thus seen as opportunities to address persistent legacies of colonialism and uneven development. Concurrently, a number of multi-national corporations have taken interest in possible profits that can be derived from the commodification of forested lands in this way. Ongoing climate politics regarding REDD include discussions about how to determine what constitutes forested land (for example what percentage of tree cover must exist in different biomes), how to distribute benefits from forest conservation, how to incorporate historical deforestation rates into targets, and how to monitor, report and verify forest conservation activities. These are merely some of the vital issues that makes the politics of REDD a high-stakes and highly contentious ongoing issue.

Renewable Energy

This is energy derived from ongoing natural processes or resources that are naturally regenerative. Unlike, for example, **fossil fuels**, of which there is a finite supply, renewable energy is obtained from sources that are essentially inexhaustible, as these resources are not depleted in the process of energy generation. Renewable sources of energy include hydroelectricity, wood, waste, wind, tidal and wave power, biomass, geothermal and solar thermal energy (such as photovoltaics). Historically, mankind has been harnessing energy from a number of these sources in a bid to maintain life on earth, but it was not until recently that they began to attract wide interest the world over. The main reason for renewed interest in renewable energy relates first to increased concern over the limit of the non-renewable sources and second to concern about **climate change**. Renewables are considered as desirable alternatives because, unlike fossil fuels (coal and petroleum), the generation of power from renewable sources does not lead to the emission of undesirable gases such as sulphur oxides (which causes acid rain) and **greenhouse gases** (responsible for climate change). Accordingly, renewable energy is widely seen as a major link in the global transition from a high-to a low-carbon economy. It is for this reason that both industries and governments alike have been committing large sums of money into the research and development of renewable energy over the last two decades or so. These investments have been yielding some positive results. For example, there has been about a 30% increase in the amount of energy generated through wind sources globally over the last two decades. Indeed, it is now thought that energy from renewable sources accounts for about 10% of global energy and this is set to increase over the next few years. In 2005, 4% of the UK's electricity supply came from renewable sources and the government has set a target of 10% of electricity supply from renewable energy by 2010. Many other governments across the world, including those of the **European Union**, have also set similar targets to increase their supply of energy from renewable sources. The main challenges involved in generating energy from renewable sources relate to cost, quantity and stability. At present, it costs far more to generate energy from non-renewables compared with fossil fuels. Besides this, it is extremely difficult to derive a steady and high amount of energy from renewable sources, as production is affected by natural variations in metrological conditions.

Rio Convention – *see* UN Conference on Environment and Development (UNCED).

S

Sea level

Rises in sea level are a possible consequence of **climate change**. During the 20th century the mean sea level rose by 15 cm and during the 21st century it could rise by a further 15 cm to more than 1 m as a result of **global warming**. Revised estimates by the **Intergovernmental Panel on Climate Change**, published in 2007, expected the rise in sea level by 2100 to be between 18 cm and 59 cm, even without the contribution of melting polar ice. Predicting how quickly the polar ice sheets—particularly the immense **Antarctic ice sheet** and Greenland ice sheet—might melt is extremely difficult, but the Greenland ice sheet alone is estimated to contain enough water to raise sea level by 6 m. In 2009, based on analysis of growth rings of trees, ice-core samples and estimates of the variation in sea level caused by temperature over the previous 2,000 years, some scientists were putting the **sea-level** rise by 2100 at 1.2 m. Contrary to common belief, projected sea-level rises would be primarily a result of the thermal expansion of oceans owing to higher oceanic temperatures. It was not known for sure whether the polar ice caps and ice sheets would melt, releasing their enormous store of fresh water. As one of the projected impacts of climate change is increased precipitation, it is possible that the polar ice caps could increase somewhat, owing to more snowfall. If one of the land-based ice sheets were to break off as a result of climate change, it could cause a catastrophic rise in sea level. Even the more conservative projected rise could endanger many low-lying regions and small island states. This is because there are many regions that would actually be inundated by such a rise and also because storm surges would reach further inland as a result of the higher sea level. This concern prompted the formation of the **Alliance of Small Island States** (AOSIS) as a negotiating bloc in the **Kyoto Protocol** negotiations.

Sinks

As related to **climate change**, sinks (also called 'carbon sinks') are reservoirs that store carbon through processes and mechanisms by which **greenhouse gases** (GHGs) are removed (or 'sequestered') from the **atmosphere** (see **carbon sequestration**). Natural sinks are forests and vegetation, where **carbon dioxide** is removed from the atmosphere through photosynthesis. Artificial sinks can involve the removal of carbon dioxide through **carbon capture and storage** techniques. The earth's carbon dioxide exists in a number of sinks. The largest is the deep ocean water, which contains approximately 38,000 Gigatons of Carbon (GtC). The cycle is regulated by solubility pump and biological pump processes. The ocean sink is so large relative to the atmosphere, that the release of just 2% of the carbon stored in the ocean would double the amount of atmospheric carbon dioxide. The second-largest sink is terrestrial vegetation, containing about 1,500 GtC, with around 500 GtC also in the soil. A third sink is actually the atmosphere itself, holding roughly 750 GtC. Each year, about 20% of CO_2 cycles through the atmosphere (in and out). Some uncertainties regarding specific amounts stored in each reservoir remain, as more carbon is taken up from the atmosphere than can be accounted for in ocean and terrestrial sinks. This discrepancy has been referred to as the 'missing sink'.

Special Report on Emissions Scenarios (SRES)

The SRES was developed in 2000 through the **Intergovernmental Panel on Climate Change** (IPCC) to describe future **greenhouse gas** (GHG) emissions pathways, contingent on a range of possible human activities and decisions made to 2100. The SRES was used as a basis for driving global circulation models (GCMs) and thus arriving at possible future climate scenarios. The SRES improved upon earlier IS92 models, which informed the IPCC Second Assessment report in 1995. Within SRES, there have been 40 individual scenarios developed, varying chiefly by future GHG emissions, fossil fuel **consumption**, technological development, land use practices, economic development and policy actions. The fundamentals of a number of these assumptions have been called into question, thereby questioning the validity of the SRES as a helpful tool to understand possible futures. For instance, the growth rate of global emissions used in these scenarios varies between 1.4% and 3.4%. The actual growth rate since 2000 has been 3%, causing critics to argue that these assumptions are too conservative. The 40 scenarios are grouped into themes, which are more similar to one-another in their assumptions. These are called A1F1, A1B, A1T, A2, B1 and B2. To take an example of A1 families, these are characterized by 1) a global peak in population at 9 billion in 2050, declining thereafter; 2) convergent world income and well-being/decreasing inequality; 3) rapid economic growth; and 4) development and deployment of efficient technologies. Sub-themes vary by rapidity of adoption of **renewable energy** sources, economic growth rates, etc. In contrast, the B1 theme is marked by 1) similar population growth; but 2) reductions in carbon intensity of material production; 3) rapid introduction and deployment of renewable technologies; 4) an emphasis on global governance; and 5) rapid economic growth, but shifts towards service and information economies. The B1 scenario thus represents a world with lower GHG emissions from A1 as projected out to 2100.

Square brackets

This phrase alludes to the [symbols] that are placed around treaty text under negotiation, in order to note that the language inside these square brackets is still under discussion. Thus, square brackets can be considered an instructive manifestation of climate politics meeting climate policy. The contestations and negotiations that are undertaken to resolve the language yet to be agreed can involve horse trading and other concessions. Of note, when working into the late hours of agreeing to Kyoto Protocol treaty text, then Chair. Raul Estrada Oyuela took a strong and firm leadership role to get country delegations to agree to the final text, thereby avoiding the failure of the negotiations. 'The Estrada Factor' now refers to the strong negotiations and concessions that are needed in resolving these square brackets disputes. Negotiations for the successor treaty to the Kyoto Protocol have been explicitly under discussion since the release of the 53-page outline of the potential agreement—square brackets and all—in Bonn, Germany in June 2009. From volumes of comments, suggestions and recommendations, this outline seeks to find consensus among 192 Parties on GHG emissions reductions, beginning with the next commitment period in 2013.

Stabilization

The objective of the **UN Framework Convention on Climate Change** (UNFCCC) is found in Article 2. This article requires Parties to 'achieve stabilization of the **greenhouse gas** concentrations in the **atmosphere** at a level that would prevent **dangerous anthropogenic interference** with the climate system'. This Article is intended to be the standard by which the Parties' commitments under the climate regime are measured. It also states that 'stabilization' should be pursued in an appropriate time frame for 'ecosystems to adapt naturally to **climate change**, to ensure that food production is not threatened and to enable economic development to proceed in a sustainable manner'. Since the entry into force of the UNFCCC, there has been increasingly politicized discussion and debate over the precise meaning behind the statement in Article 2 regarding the 'stabilization of the greenhouse gas concentrations [...] at a level that would prevent dangerous anthropogenic interference'. Contestation has centred on what level of greenhouse gas concentrations constitutes 'dangerous anthropogenic interference'. Many climate scientists, such as Stephen H. Schneider of Stanford University, assert that this threshold has already been surpassed. For instance, as of 2009 atmospheric CO_2 concentrations have risen to approximately 385 parts per million (ppm) (see **parts per million/parts per billion**), marking a 38% increase in emissions from pre-industrial levels of approximately 280 ppm, and a level not reached in the last 650,000 years.

Stern Review

The 'Stern Review' is a United Kingdom economic assessment of the effect of **climate change** on the global economy. It gains its name from the lead author, Lord Nicholas Stern, and calls climate change a 'market failure'. The report was released in October 2006 and surveys the evidence on the economic impact of **anthropogenic climate change**, the cost involved in taking action to 'stabilize' the climate (as stated in Article 2 of the **UN Framework Convention on Climate Change**), and the policy alternatives that can feasibly decarbonize United Kingdom industry and society. Key to the assessment is the use of a low-discount rate, where they determine that present and early actions will have great benefits for humans and the environment over the long term. The Stern Review determines that the allocation of 1% of global annual gross domestic product (GDP) to mitigate and adapt to climate change will avoid losses of up to 20% of GDP in the future. Two years later (in 2008), Lord Stern increased the recommendation to 2% of GDP, as anthropogenic climate change was unfolding more rapidly than previously thought. In comments on the Stern Review from HM Treasury, Oxford economist Cameron Hepburn claimed that 'when the history of the world's response to climate change is written, the Stern Review will be recognized as a turning point'.

Subsidiary Body for Implementation (SBI)

The SBI is one of two permanent standing committees of the **UN Framework Convention on Climate Change** (UNFCCC) (along with the **Subsidiary Body for Scientific and Technological Advice**). The SBI acts as a bridge for implementation between the UNFCCC and the **Conference of the Parties** (COP). The SBI focuses on assisting governments to fulfil the terms of the UNFCCC and the **Kyoto Protocol**.

Subsidiary Body for Scientific and Technological Advice (SBSTA)

The SBSTA is one of two permanent standing committees of the **UN Framework Convention on Climate Change** (UNFCCC) (along with the **Subsidiary Body for Implementation**). The SBSTA acts as a bridge between Parties to the UNFCCC and **Kyoto Protocol**, and scientific or technical bodies, such as the **Intergovernmental Panel on Climate Change**. The SBSTA is thus a group designed to increase co-ordination at the climate science-policy interface.

Summary for Policymakers

The comprehensive, thorough and intensively reviewed chapters of the **Intergovernmental Panel on Climate Change** assessment reports are also condensed as a Summary for Policymakers (SPM). These summaries are designed to provide clear reference points for more extensive treatment in other parts of the report. The wording of each of these is approved in detail at plenary meetings, and this is done to reach consensus agreement on the science and on the best way of presenting the science to policy-makers with accuracy and clarity. The production of these SPMs can be a highly contentious and arduous affair.

Sunspots

These are the dark areas that appear periodically on the surface of the Sun. A sunspot is a vortex of gas associated with magnetic activity. Each one is 2,000–3,000 km in diameter, and they appear darkest at the centre. Sunspots appear in the mid-latitudes of the disc and migrate towards the equator. They seldom occur individually but appear in groups of two or three, and tend to be short-lived, forming and disappearing again over two or three weeks. However, the frequency and size of sunspots fluctuates, reaching a peak roughly every 11 years. There are also minor peaks within the 11-year cycle, and a 22-year cycle (consisting of two of the 11-year cycles). Certain scientists claim that sunspot activity has a greater influence on **climate change** than variations attributed to the **greenhouse effect**. The earth depends on the Sun for its existence as a planet hospitable to life, and solar energy is the major factor determining the climate. Hence, conditions on the sun and conditions on earth are inextricably linked. Although the Sun's rays may appear unchanging, its radiation does vary. Sunspots have been observed for centuries and vary dramatically over decades. At the beginning of the 19th century only 45 sunspots per year were recorded, whereas in the middle of the 1950s over 190 sunspots per year were observed. Temperatures on earth in the mid-1950s were notably higher than at the start of the 19th century. Between 1645 and 1715 very few sunspots were seen by astronomers. This period of diminished solar activity became known as the Maunder minimum, after Walter Maunder, a British astronomer, who was the first to notice their reduction and a reduction in solar radiation. Until recently, the Maunder minimum was not taken too seriously until it was realized that it coincided with a particularly cold period, known as the Little Ice Age, which lasted until the early 19th century. It has been estimated that the Little Ice Age experienced a reduction in temperature large enough to correlate with a 0.5% decrease in solar radiation, an enormous reduction in terms of the consequences for the earth's climate.

T

Targets and Timetables

This phrase refers to the commitments to **greenhouse gas** emissions reductions for **Annex I/B** Parties in the first phase of the **Kyoto Protocol**. Targets and timetables first took shape through a recognition of 'common but differentiated responsibilities' that different countries have in fulfilling **UN Framework Convention on Climate Change** (UNFCCC) obligations in the **Berlin Mandate** in 1995. However, the explicit commitments were made in the 1997 treaty, where the following countries delineated reduction commitments from 1990 levels by 2012: Australia, Austria, Belarus, Belgium, Bulgaria, Canada, Croatia, Czech Republic, Denmark, Estonia, Finland, France, Germany, Greece, Hungary, Iceland, Ireland, Italy, Japan, Latvia, Liechtenstein, Lithuania, Luxembourg, Monaco, Netherlands, New Zealand, Norway, Poland, Portugal, Romania, Russia, Slovakia, Slovenia, Spain, Sweden, Switzerland, Turkey, Ukraine, the United Kingdom and the USA. For example, the USA agreed to 7% GHG emissions reductions, signed by then President Bill Clinton in 1998 (this commitment was never ratified in the US Senate, however). Article 4 of the Kyoto Protocol stated that **European Union** (EU) commitments could be met through an aggregate effort, taking into account individual country circumstances, such as relative levels of economic development and associated abilities to decarbonize industry. This is also colloquially referred to as the 'EU bubble'. The 15 countries of the EU in 1997 then sorted out responsibility for meeting the overall treaty obligation of 8% GHG emissions reductions. For example, the United Kingdom agreed to 12.5% GHG emissions reductions from 1990 levels and Germany agreed to 20% reductions. Meanwhile, Portugal was allowed a 27% GHG emissions increase during the first commitment period.

Technology Transfer

Technology transfer refers to a broad set of processes that share experience, knowledge, tools and information in order to assist in more effective climate **mitigation** and **adaptation** activities. For example, renewable technologies can be shared between research and development in the USA and India, so that rural electrification programmes can avoid the pitfalls of fossil fuel energy sources and subsequent centralized energy generation and distribution.

Terrestrial Initiative in Global Environmental Research (TIGER)

TIGER is a £20m. international research project, organized by the British Natural Environment Research Council. It was designed to discover the interaction between peat bogs, grassland, agricultural crops, forests and tundra, and **climate change**. The conclusions reached after the first five years of research, published in 1996, contradicted accepted ideas about the probable impact of climate change on soil, plant and animal life over the following 50 years. The purpose of the project was to monitor the effects of **global warming** on the terrestrial environment as thoroughly as other research had studied the **atmosphere** and oceans. Its discoveries provided answers to global and more-local problems that had bewildered scientists. On a global scale, the researchers answered the question of the fate of 1,500,000m. metric tons of **carbon dioxide** discharged into the atmosphere each year: it is absorbed by forests, shrubs and other vegetation. Another project discovered a previously unknown but common process by which methane, a significant **greenhouse gas**, is released into the atmosphere by plants growing in profusion on millions of hectares of peat bog, while another such gas, nitrous oxide, was found to be produced by intensively managed pasture more than was predicted. The research also proved how it is possible for a species of wildlife to become threatened by a seemingly small change in the climate of its normal ecosystem. Plants play a greater role than had been thought in recycling water vapour back into the atmosphere, thus influencing cloud cover and the amount of heat the earth absorbs. The process is known as vegetation feedback. Drought was discovered to be a bigger driver of ecosystems' reaction to change than expected. The TIGER project also identified many similar processes, all of which are critical factors previously missing from the equations that meteorologists and climatologists used to predict climate change. Subsequent revised forecasts of climate change showed that the United Kingdom, North America and Africa would be cooler than previously predicted, while India, South-east Asia, and parts of the People's Republic of China and the Russian Federation would be much hotter.

Toronto Conference on the Changing Atmosphere

This was held in 1988, in Canada, under the auspices of the **UN Environment Programme** (UNEP), and urged a global reduction in carbon emissions by 2005. The meeting concentrated on energy efficiency. Moreover, policies discussed at Toronto that were designed to reduce carbon emissions included a gradual increase in tax on motor vehicle fuel and the introduction of a **carbon tax** weighted to the carbon content of all **fossil fuels**. Coal, for example, would be taxed more heavily than natural gas because of its greater carbon content. The Toronto Conference led to the **UN Framework Convention on Climate Change** and the **Kyoto Protocol**.

U

UN Conference on Environment and Development (UNCED)

UNCED was held in June 1992 in Rio de Janeiro, Brazil. It took place over 12 days and brought together a number of heads of government, while there were senior officials of over 179 countries present. Otherwise known as the 'Earth Summit', it was also attended by a record number of non-governmental organizations and over 8,000 journalists. The purpose of the meeting was to adopt a new global strategy for economic development that did not compromise the quality of the global environment. The Earth Summit was, in effect, an attempt by the world community to design a framework and adopt practical steps that were needed to achieve global sustainable development. The path to Rio started with the release of the Report of the World Commission on Environment and Development (WCED) (the Brundtland Report) in 1987. The Report contained serious warnings of the growing threat to earth's system from environmental degradation, pollution, industrial economic development and world poverty, and called on the UN to convene a global conference where these threats and possible solutions might be addressed. Five years later, at the insistence of the UN, the world gathered in Rio with fanfare and expression of optimism designed to encourage the world leaders to embrace the path of change required to save the earth. In the end, five main documents were agreed. The first was a 27-point Rio Declaration, which endorsed the commitment to pursue sustainable development and to eradicate global poverty. The second was Agenda 21, which is a 40-chapter plan of action on how governments at all levels, businesses and individuals might go about pursuing the objectives of sustainable development. The heads of government also adopted two important conventions: the UN Framework Convention on Climate Change and the Convention on Biological Diversity. The latter document was a statement on sustainable forest management. Although more than 20 years on it is doubtful the extent to which the objectives of Rio have been achieved, the Earth Summit has remained one of the most significant in the history of environmentalism, not the least for its role in raising the profile of environmental concern to a global level.

UN Conference on the Human Environment (UNCHE, Stockholm 1972)

The UN General Assembly organized the Conference on the Human Environment in 1972 (or the 'Stockholm Conference') in Stockholm, Sweden 'to serve as a practical means to encourage, and to provide guidelines for, action by Governments and international organizations designed to protect and improve the human environment, and to remedy and prevent its impairment, by means of international co-operation, bearing in mind the particular importance of enabling developing countries to forestall occurrence of such problems'. At the time, the Stockholm Conference was one of the largest and most successful UN conferences undertaken, as 113 countries had representation (although only India and the host country Sweden were represented by their heads of state). Three major products emerged from the Stockholm Conference. First, there was the 'Stockholm Action Plan', which identified the environmental issues requiring international action. It contained over 100 priority recommendations for planning and managing human settlements for environmental quality, addressing the environmental aspects of natural resources management, identifying and controlling pollutants of broad international significance, exploring and strengthening the educational, informational, social and cultural aspects of environmental issues, and addressing the integration of development and environment. Second, the Stockholm Conference launched the **UN Environment Programme** (UNEP), to then act as a general authority over environmental issues. Its mission was 'to facilitate international co-operation in the environmental field, to keep the world environmental situation under review so that problems of international significance receive appropriate consideration by Governments, and to promote the acquisition, assessment and exchange of environmental knowledge'. Third, from the conference came the 'Stockholm Declaration on the Human Environment'. This provided groundwork for subsequent acceptance of the concept of 'sustainable development' as promoted by the Brundtland Commission (in 1987; see **Brundtland Report**). The Declaration emphasized the importance of integrating environment and development, reducing or eliminating pollution and limiting the use of ecosystem services and resources. It also delineated the role that international co-operation and, thus, international law must play in facilitating action to address global environmental challenges.

UN Environment Programme (UNEP)

The UNEP is an agency that evolved from the UN Conference on the Human Environment, held in Stockholm in 1972. The UNEP is now accepted as the agency responsible for co-ordinating environmental activities within the UN system. The UNEP's global base is in Nairobi, Kenya. It is one of only two UN programmes headquartered in the developing world (the other is UNEP's sister agency, UN HABITAT, which is also located in Nairobi). The UN neither awards contracts, nor executes environmental programmes.

Its main responsibility is to stimulate awareness on environmental matters as well as to provide leadership and encourage partnership in caring for the environment. The UNEP executes these functions mainly by inspiring, informing and providing the platform for international co-operation on the environment. Since its inception, the UNEP has played a crucial role in the area of issue definition and agenda setting. It has functioned as a catalyst for the elaboration of many important environmental regimes, including the Basel Convention on the Control of Transboundary Movements of Hazardous Wastes and their Disposal and the **UN Framework Convention on Climate Change**. In performing its functions, the UNEP works closely with other UN agencies, environmental **non-governmental organizations** like the **International Union for Conservation of Nature and Natural Resources**, as well as with environmental scientists, industrialists and decision-makers. The UNEP also functions to provide important help to developing countries in their bid to care for the environment. To this end, it works with scientists, policy-makers and environmental activists in these countries to promote or strengthen relevant institutions for the wise management of the environment. It also facilitates the transfer of knowledge and technology for sustainable development from the more industrialized to the less industrialized countries. The UNEP has six regional offices around the world and serves as host for several environmental convention secretariats, including the Ozone Secretariat, the **Montréal Protocol**'s Multilateral Fund, the Convention on International Trade in Endangered Species of Wild Fauna and Flora (CITES), the Convention on Biological Diversity, the Convention on Migratory Species and the Basel Convention.

UN Framework Convention on Climate Change (UNFCCC)

The UNFCCC is a voluntary and non-binding declaration of standards, goals and objectives that represents international co-operation to reduce human-made **greenhouse gas** emissions that contribute to **climate change** (known also as 'anthropogenic emissions'). This Convention—modelled after the **Vienna Convention on Protection of the Ozone Layer**—established a general framework for emissions reductions. The text begins with a series of declarations. The first states that 'Parties' (participating countries) in the UNFCCC, '[a]cknowledg(e) that change in the earth's climate and its adverse effects are a common concern of humankind'. The UNFCCC document comprises 26 Articles, ranging in issues from defining terms (Article 1), to the financial mechanism (Articles 11 and 21), to requirements for the entry of the UNFCCC into force (Article 23). The objective of the Framework is found in Article 2, to 'achieve **stabilization** of the greenhouse gas concentrations in the **atmosphere** at a level that would prevent **dangerous anthropogenic interference** with the climate system'. Articles 4, 10 and 12 contain statements regarding more specific commitments of the Parties, based on 'common but differentiated responsibilities'. Article 4(2) of the UNFCCC text distinguishes between three groupings of Parties to the convention, based on present levels of industrialization: Annex I Parties (all industrialized countries), Annex II Parties (all industrialized countries except those of the former Soviet bloc in the process of economic transition to market economies, in light of the fall of the Soviet Union in 1991), and all Parties (including developing countries). Furthermore, Article 4(2)b notes that 'the aim' for these Annex I countries is to return to 1990 levels of anthropogenic emissions. Articles 10 and 12 outline the rules by which Annex I Parties must 'adopt national policies and take corresponding measures on the **mitigation** of climate change, by limiting anthropogenic emissions of greenhouse gases and protecting and enhancing greenhouse gas **sinks** and reservoirs'. As stated, these emissions reductions are to be based on factors such as a Parties' level of dependence 'on income generation form the production, processing and export, and/or **consumption** of **fossil fuels** and associated energy-intensive products and/or the use of fossil fuels for which such Parties have serious difficulties in switching to alternatives'. Moreover, Article 4 (3–5) notes that developed countries shall assist developing countries reach anthropogenic emissions reductions goals through **technology transfer** as well as various forms of financial assistance. The text of the Convention was adopted at the UN Headquarters in New York on 9 May 1992. It was then opened for signature to leaders at the June 1992 **UN Conference on Environment and Development** (UNCED) in Rio de Janeiro, Brazil, a conference also commonly referred to as the 'Rio Conference' or the '**Earth Summit**'. Overall, 154 countries signed the UNFCCC. Notably, US President George Bush, Sr was one of the signatories, and the US Senate ratified it on 15 October 1992. Through associated and sufficient **ratification** through other signatories' legislative bodies, the UNFCCC entered into force on 21 March 1994. The UNFCCC has endured much scrutiny. First, critics charge that the few specific obligations to curb **anthropogenic climate change** contained in the document have allowed for considerable discretion in application. Second, the proposed emissions reductions are deemed to be merely symbolic as they do not significantly mitigate greenhouse gas emissions. Third, legacies of colonialism shaping contemporary inequality and associated levels of greenhouse gas emissions are underemphasized in this UNFCCC country-level emissions reductions approach, and rhetorical acknowledgements (such as the **Berlin Mandate** in 1995) have proven insufficient. However, proponents counter that this approach is a productive first step that encourages Parties to be involved in the process, before then potentially signing on to binding agreements that follow.

V

Vienna Convention for the Protection of the Ozone Layer

This Convention was the first drawn up to deal with the destruction of the **ozone layer**. The international agreement came after a conference in 1985, and was adopted by 21 states and the European Communities (which became known as the **European Union** in 1993). It called for a halt in the production of **chlorofluorocarbon** (CFC) gases and for procedures to reduce all emissions of CFC gases. The producers of CFCs, mainly found in the developing world, would not sign the Convention until they received guarantees of compensation. The Convention led to the **Montréal Protocol**, signed in Canada in 1987, which mandated the phase-out of the production and **consumption** of ozone-depleting substances such as CFCs and hydrochlorofluorocarbons (HCFCs)—CFCs in all countries by 2010 and HCFCs, by 2030. A multilateral fund has been established by the **UN Environment Programme**, the UN Development Programme and the **World Bank** to help developing countries with the costs of complying with the Protocol and provide for the necessary **technology transfer**.

Vulnerability

Vulnerability has been defined as the degree to which a person, community or system is susceptible to, or unable to cope with, adverse effects of **climate change**. These include climate variability and extremes, such as floods and drought. Vulnerability has been defined more specifically in many ways, as it relates to hazards and disasters, public health, psychology, engineering and security. In relation to climate change, definitions focus on the human-environment relationship, which encompasses cultural values, political economy, social systems and environmental perceptions. Robert Chambers defines vulnerability as the exposure to contingencies and stress, and difficulty coping with them. He discussed it as having an external side of risks, shocks and stress to which an individual or household is subject, and an internal side of defencelessness, meaning a lack of means to cope without damage or loss. Definitions share common characteristics that vulnerability is expressed as a function of the character, magnitude and rate of climate variation to which a system is exposed, its sensitivity, and its adaptive capacity.

W

World Bank

The World Bank comprises the International Bank for Reconstruction and Development (IBRD), which raises money on international financial markets and lends at commercial rates of interest, and the International Development Agency (IDA), which provides loans at concessional rates of interest to the poorest countries from member subscriptions, donations and grants from the IBRD. The World Bank Group also includes a further three institutions: the International Finance Corporation (IFC), which lends money to the private sector with government guarantees, the Multilateral Investment Guarantee Agency (MIGA) and the International Centre for Settlement of Investment Disputes (ICSID). The World Bank operates as a multinational development agency with 184 member nations, and was formed to give loans and technical assistance to the poorer countries of the world. It was established in 1945 after the Bretton Woods conference of 1944, at which Canada, the United Kingdom and the host nation of the USA established a system of international financial rules. The World Bank, with its headquarters in Washington, DC, is the largest of the multilateral development banks, investing many billions of dollars per year in developing countries. It is controlled by member countries which vote according to the size of their donations. The USA is the largest shareholder at 16.9%. As it is a commercial operation, any loans the Bank makes must be repaid, so that funding is mostly given to those projects that are likely to be profitable. The World Bank works in collaboration with its sister organization, the **International Monetary Fund** (IMF). The World Bank has been criticized by environmental organizations, because many of the projects it has funded have had adverse effects on the environment and on local people, including many large dams and irrigation schemes, road construction through forested areas, and livestock-rearing programmes. In 1983 the pressure on the World Bank began to mount, and was spearheaded by **non-governmental organizations**. In 1986 there was a co-ordinated campaign against the Polonoreste road-building and colonization project in Brazil. This resulted in a vote against a loan to Brazil, the first time that environmental reasons were cited for such a delay. In 1987 the World Bank published a report, Environment: Growth and Development, setting out new environmental guidelines for future activities. Future projects, it said, would be obliged to have three objectives: economic growth, poverty alleviation and environmental protection. A new enlarged Environment Department was formed in 1990. The Bank reviewed its energy lending for a number of years prior to the endorsement of a new strategy, Fuel for Thought: Environmental Strategy for the Energy Sector, by the Executive Board in July 1999. This began a radical change in the environmental consequences of the Bank's lending practices, because the main goal outlined in the paper was to promote the environmentally sustainable development of energy resources. This process resulted in a single policy document that was endorsed in July 2001, Making Sustainable Commitments: An Environment Strategy for the World Bank, which aimed to improve the quality of life of a population, to improve the quality of economic growth, and to protect the quality of the regional and global commons. Sustainable development was recognized as fundamental to the Bank's aim to achieve lasting poverty alleviation.

World Health Organization (WHO)

The WHO is a specialized agency of the UN, formed in 1948 to foster international co-operation for improved health conditions. It took over epidemic control, quarantine measures and drug standardization from the Health Organization of the League of Nations and the International Office of Public Health. The WHO aims to promote the highest possible level of health for all people, defined as a state of complete physical, mental and social well-being, not just the absence of disease or infirmity. It is funded by member governments and an allocation from the technical assistance programme of the UN. Its administrative headquarters are in Geneva, Switzerland. A WHO Commission on Health and Environment reported to the June 1992 **Earth Summit**, its conclusions forming the basis of the WHO Global Strategy for Health and Environment. In 1996 a report prepared in conjunction with UNEP and the **World Meteorological Organization** considered the impact of **climate change** on human health.

World Meteorological Organization (WMO)

The WMO was created in 1950 in order to provide an international body to co-ordinate activities in climatology, meteorology, operational hydrology, geophysical sciences and their outputs. It took shape from its predecessor, the International Meteorological Organization (IMO), which was established in 1873. The WMO became recognized as an agency of the UN in 1951, and now has 188 member states and territories. From its headquarters in Geneva, Switzerland the WMO has convened three climate councils: the first took place in 1979, the second in 1990 and the third in 2009. The third meeting (WCC-3) sought to appraise progress in seasonal to multi-decadal climate predictions and to further integrate their uses in decision-making processes across a range of sectors (e.g. food, water, energy, health and tourism). The WMO has contributed to the founding of a number of important organizations, initiatives and programmes. Examples include the creation of the **Intergovernmental Panel on Climate Change** in 1988 in conjunction with the **UN Environment Programme**, a World Weather Watch Programme (WWW) and the International Polar Year (IPY). The WWW objectives are to provide meteorological and related geophysical and environmental information to decision-makers. These activities aim particularly to improve instrumentation and observational methods, and help strengthen operational capacities (particularly in developing countries). The IPY was an initiative rolled out in March 2007 running until March 2008 to raise the profile of polar issues. Jointly sponsored by the WMO and the **International Council for Science**, the IPY focused on the **Arctic** and **Antarctica** polar regions, and encompassed approximately 200 projects that engaged with physical, biological and social areas of research.

World Ocean Circulation Experiment (WOCE)

WOCE was a critical component of the **World Meteorological Organization**'s World Climate Research Programme during 1990–2002. With the participation of some 30 countries, WOCE was the largest ever international study of the physics of the oceans and their role in regulating the climate of the planet. The ocean has an enormous capacity to store heat. The top 3 m of the ocean have a greater heat capacity than the entire **atmosphere**. The oceans determine the timescale and regional patterns of **climate change**. Ocean currents transport huge amounts of energy, absorbed from the Sun, from the tropical latitudes towards the poles. The surface layer of the ocean acts as an energy buffer. Some of its heat is transferred back into the atmosphere and some of it is transferred into the ocean interior. Huge swathes of water at great depths then move like a gigantic conveyor belt, forming vast currents of thermal energy that move towards the poles, while immense 'rivers' of cold water flow towards the equator from the **Arctic** and **Antarctica**. Precise measurements of these great ocean currents are difficult to make; hence, one aspect of WOCE was a Hydrographic and Chemicals Tracer Study, which analysed samples of seawater from thousands of different areas and depths. However, vast amounts of energy are also released into the atmosphere, and this heat influences the winds, rainfall patterns and regional temperatures. Consequently, a critical part of WOCE was a Satellites and Surface Meteorology Project, measuring interactions between the sea and atmosphere. Through WOCE, scientists collected vital data in order to develop realistic computerized ocean circulation modelling experiments, demonstrating how the ocean links with the atmosphere to influence climate. Scientists aimed to produce reliable forecasts on the changes in energy levels in the oceans and what they would mean for the climate pattern of the world. WOCE led to a longer-term plan for systematic monitoring of the ocean on a global basis, the **Global Ocean Observing System** (GOOS). The substantial legacy of data and literature generated by WOCE was an invaluable resource on which the international scientific community could build.

World Trade Organization (WTO)

The WTO is an international institution established in 1995 with powers to administer, implement and enforce the agreements that collectively constitute the General Agreement on Tariffs and Trade (GATT). GATT came into being in 1948 with the aim of creating a free global trading system which, with the **International Monetary Fund** (IMF) and the **World Bank**, would establish the 'economic foundations for world-wide peace and prosperity'. By mid-2009 there were 153 members of the WTO, accounting for 95% of world trade and including the massive economy of the People's Republic of China, as well as Taiwan (entering as Chinese Taipei), Ukraine and Viet Nam. When the GATT was originally drawn up, there was little or no awareness that the liberalization of trade might have environmental implications, but by the 1990s there was increasing concern about the relationship between trade and environmental protection. A number of controversial cases ensured that the WTO was at least more cognizant of environmental sensitivities by the early 2000s. There was also increased awareness that the liberalized global trading system had not, hitherto, been of effective benefit in reducing poverty, and there was discussion of reforming the institution. The WTO is essentially an intergovernmental organization making contractual agreements between governments. The major decision-making body is the Ministerial Conference, which generally meets once every two years. Day-to-day decisions are made by the General Council in Geneva, Switzerland. The WTO is a trade organization and is not responsible for setting, evaluating or enforcing environmental policies, but disputes about environmental regulations are frequently brought before the WTO. It is increasingly feared that WTO rules may conflict with multilateral environmental agreements. There is concern regarding the trade impacts of the **Kyoto Protocol** to the **UN Framework Convention on Climate Change**, and the potential environmental impacts of the Trade-Related Investment Measures agreement. In an attempt to allay such fears, the WTO established the Committee on Trade and Environment as the first step in incorporating environmental considerations into international trade policy. There has been criticism that the Committee is biased strongly in favour of trade, but it is, nevertheless, an international forum where governments from the developed and developing countries can discuss conflicts between trade and environmental issues.

World Wide Fund for Nature (WWF)

The WWF is one of the largest international nature conservation organizations. It was formed in 1961 and until 1988 was known as the World Wildlife Fund. The WWF raises funds, mostly from the general public, for conservation projects. Its aim is to conserve nature by preserving genetic species and ecosystem diversity. The WWF's international campaigns have brought about a growing awareness of environmental issues and of the threats to the natural environment. The WWF works closely with the **International Union for Conservation of Nature and Natural Resources** (IUCN) and has played a part in implementing international laws and agreements on conservation, including the Convention on International Trade in Endangered Species of Wild Fauna and Flora. In collaboration with IUCN and the **UN Environment Programme**, the WWF launched the World Conservation Strategy in 1980.

X

Xeric

Xeric most frequently refers to a kind of moisture regime that is adapted to dry climate. It is also associated with taxonomic classifications for soils. Soils are a vital component of carbon cycling on earth, between and among the **atmosphere**, oceans and terrestrial systems. Along with terrestrial vegetation, soils are the second-largest carbon reservoir (or **sink**) on earth. Terrestrial vegetation contains approximately 1,500 Gigatons of Carbon (GtC), and soils contain about 500 GtC. Xeric moisture regimes are distinct from Aquic, Aridic or Torric, Perudic, Udic and Ustic moisture regimes. Xeric moisture regimes are typically temperate desert or Mediterranean climate regions with dry summer months and moist winter months, receiving an average rainfall of less than 10 inches (25.5 cm). These regimes only require a small amount of moisture and rain falls in the winter when evapotranspiration is minimal.

Y

Yemen

This is a representative country designated as a Least Developed Country (LDC) by the United Nations General Assembly. These are considered LDCs through factors such as low income, low public health, low levels of education and literacy, and overall economic vulnerability. At present there are 49 countries considered LDCs by the United Nations General Assembly: Afghanistan, Angola, Bangladesh, Benin, Bhutan, Burkina Faso, Burundi, Cambodia, Central African Republic, Chad, Comoros, Democratic Republic of Congo, Djibouti, Equatorial Guinea, Eritrea, Ethiopia, Gambia, Guinea, Guinea-Bissau, Haiti, Kiribati, Laos, Lesotho, Liberia, Madagascar, Malawi, Maldives, Mali, Mauritania, Mozambique, Myanmar, Nepal, Niger, Rwanda, Samoa, São Tomé and Príncipe, Senegal, Sierra Leone, Solomon Islands, Somalia, Sudan, Tanzania, Timor-Leste, Togo, Tuvalu, Uganda, Vanuatu, Yemen and Zambia. Only Cape Verde and Botswana have moved out of—or 'graduated' from—LDC status.

Z

Zero emissions

Zero emissions represent a goal and objective of decarbonizing energy production and **consumption**. The term is often associated with the 'carbon economy' and is called the zero-carbon economy. Such a discursive move marks a shift in focus from 20th-century carbon-based industry and society to aspirational movements in the new millennium. Tools used to help achieve this goal of zero emissions include policy actions, **carbon markets** and **flexibility mechanisms** in the **Kyoto Protocol**. Through this kind of variety of economic, political, ecological and cultural initiatives, new actors and more citizens are stepping in to work towards carbon reductions and, eventually, zero emissions.

Maps

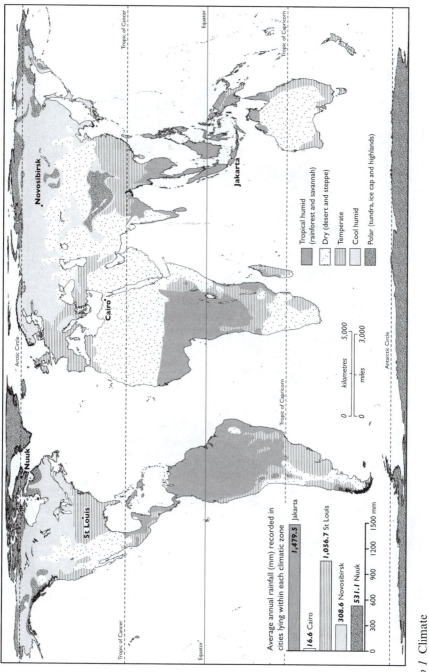

Map 1 Climate
Source: Food and Agriculture Organization of the United Nations (FAO), Sustainable Development Department (2006).

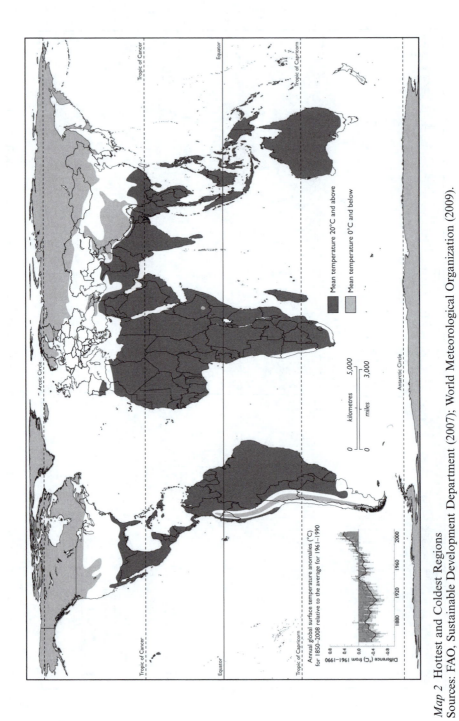

Map 2 Hottest and Coldest Regions
Sources: FAO, Sustainable Development Department (2007); World Meteorological Organization (2009).

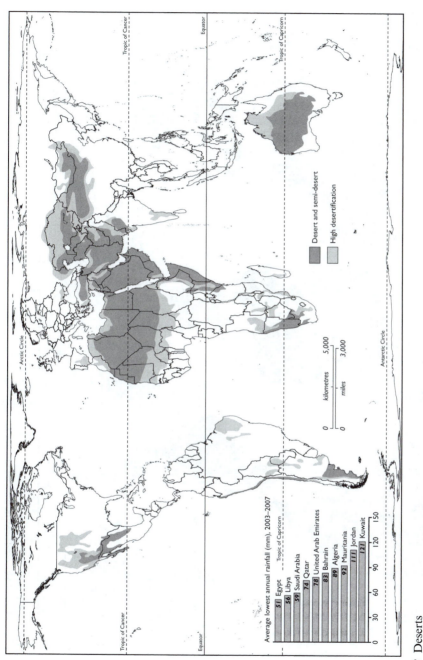

Average lowest annual rainfall (mm), 2003–2007

Egypt	51
Libya	56
Saudi Arabia	59
Qatar	74
United Arab Emirates	78
Bahrain	83
Algeria	89
Mauritania	92
Jordan	111
Kuwait	121

Map 3 Deserts
Source: FAO, Land and Water Development Division (2003 and 2009).

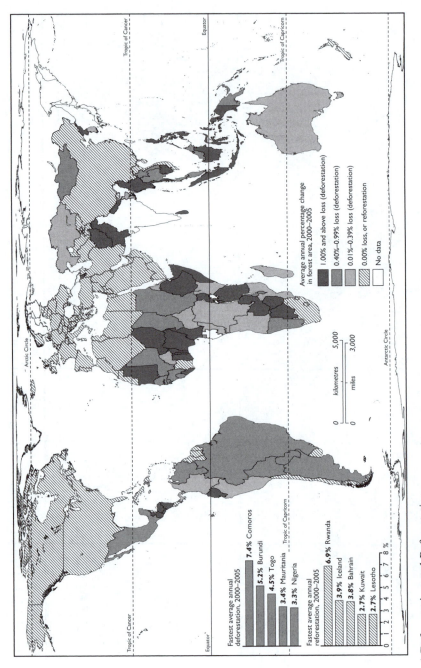

Map 4 Deforestation and Reforestation
Source: FAO, Global Forest Resources Assessment (2005).

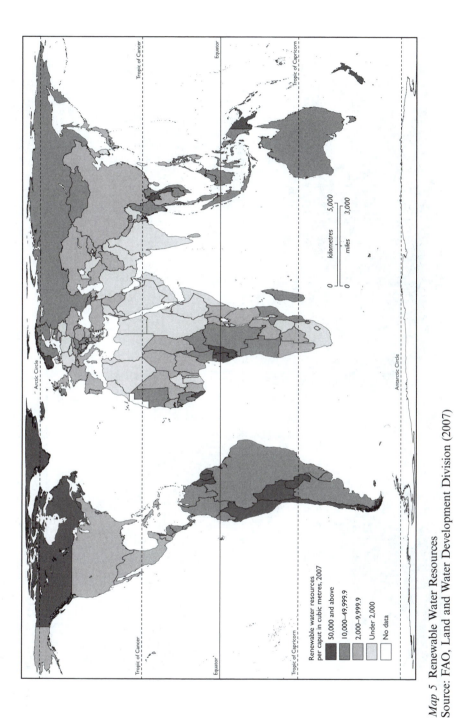

Map 5 Renewable Water Resources
Source: FAO, Land and Water Development Division (2007)

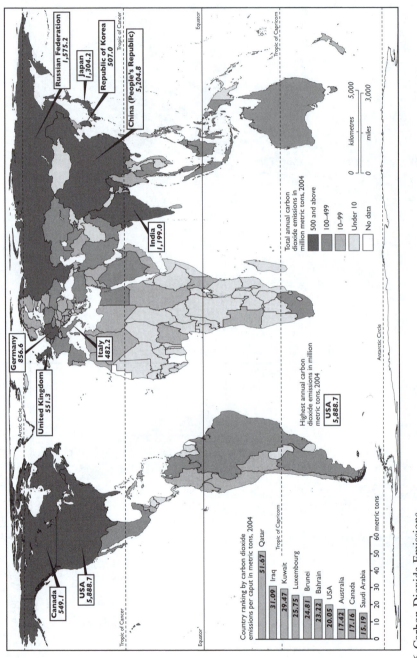

Map 6 Carbon Dioxide Emissions
Sources: World Resources Institute, Climate Analysis Indicators Tool (2005); United Nations Department of Economic and Social Affairs, Population Division (2004).

Statistics

Table 1 Population Change

Annual rate of population change, %	2005	2006	2007
Albania	0.6	0.6	0.3
Algeria	1.5	1.5	1.5
American Samoa	2.3	2.2	1.0
Andorra	0.3	1.1	0.4
Angola	2.9	2.8	2.8
Antigua and Barbuda	1.3	1.3	0.8
Argentina	1.0	1.0	0.9
Armenia	-0.3	-0.3	-0.3
Aruba	1.3	0.9	-0.3
Australia	1.3	1.5	1.5
Austria	0.7	0.6	0.4
Azerbaijan	1.0	1.1	1.0
Bahamas	1.2	1.2	1.2
Bahrain	2.0	1.9	1.9
Bangladesh	1.8	1.8	1.6
Barbados	0.4	0.3	0.3
Belarus	-0.5	-0.4	-0.3
Belgium	0.6	0.7	0.7
Belize	3.2	2.0	2.1
Benin	3.2	3.1	3.0
Bermuda	0.4	0.4	0.3
Bhutan	2.2	1.8	1.3
Bolivia	1.9	1.9	1.7
Bosnia and Herzegovina	0.5	-0.1	-0.1
Botswana	1.1	1.2	1.2
Brazil	1.4	1.3	1.2
Brunei	2.2	2.1	1.9
Bulgaria	-0.5	-0.6	-0.7
Burkina Faso	3.1	3.0	2.9
Burundi	3.8	3.9	3.9
Cambodia	1.7	1.7	1.7
Cameroon	2.2	2.1	2.0
Canada	1.0	1.0	1.0
Cape Verde	2.3	2.3	2.2
Cayman Islands	2.2	2.2	1.7
Central African Republic	1.6	1.7	1.8
Chad	3.4	3.1	2.8
Chile	1.1	0.8	1.0
China, People's Republic[1]	0.6	0.6	0.6
Colombia	1.4	1.4	1.2
Comoros	2.1	2.2	2.0
Congo, Democratic Republic	3.2	3.2	2.9
Congo, Republic	2.2	2.2	2.1
Costa Rica	1.7	1.6	1.4
Côte d'Ivoire	1.7	1.8	1.9
Croatia	0.0	0.0	-0.1
Cuba	0.1	0.1	-0.1
Cyprus[2]	2.4	1.9	1.8
Czech Republic	0.3	0.3	0.6
Denmark	0.3	0.4	0.4

(continues on the next page)

Table 1 (continued)

Annual rate of population change, %	2005	2006	2007
Djibouti	1.7	1.8	1.8
Dominica	0.7	0.5	0.5
Dominican Republic	1.5	1.5	1.4
Ecuador	1.1	1.1	1.0
Egypt	1.8	1.8	1.7
El Salvador	1.4	1.4	1.3
Equatorial Guinea	2.3	2.4	2.4
Eritrea	3.9	3.6	3.1
Estonia	-0.2	-0.2	-0.1
Ethiopia	2.6	2.6	2.5
Faroe Islands	0.0	0.0	0.2
Fiji	0.6	0.6	0.6
Finland[3]	0.3	0.4	0.4
France	0.6	0.8	0.6
French Polynesia	1.5	1.4	1.3
Gabon	1.6	1.5	1.5
Gambia	2.9	2.8	2.6
Georgia	-1.0	-0.9	-0.8
Germany	-0.1	-0.1	-0.1
Ghana	2.1	2.1	2.0
Greece	0.4	0.4	0.4
Greenland	0.0	-0.3	0.0
Grenada	0.7	1.5	0.0
Guam	1.6	1.5	1.3
Guatemala	2.5	2.5	2.4
Guinea	1.9	2.0	2.1
Guinea-Bissau	3.0	3.0	2.9
Guyana	0.1	-0.1	-0.1
Haiti	1.6	1.6	1.7
Honduras	1.9	2.0	1.7
Hong Kong	0.4	0.6	1.0
Hungary	-0.2	-0.2	-0.2
Iceland	1.6	2.3	2.3
India[4]	1.4	1.4	1.2
Indonesia	1.4	1.1	1.2
Iran	1.5	1.5	1.3
Ireland	2.2	2.4	2.4
Isle of Man	0.9	0.9	0.9
Israel[5]	1.7	1.8	1.7
Italy	0.7	0.6	0.7
Jamaica	0.5	0.5	0.4
Japan	0.0	0.0	0.0
Jordan	2.3	2.3	3.2
Kazakhstan	0.9	1.1	1.1
Kenya	2.6	2.6	2.6
Kiribati	1.2	1.2	1.6
Korea, Democratic People's Republic	0.4	0.4	0.3
Korea, Republic	0.4	0.3	0.2
Kuwait	3.0	2.5	2.4
Kyrgyzstan	1.0	0.9	1.0

(continues on the next page)

Table 1 (continued)

Annual rate of population change, %	2005	2006	2007
Laos	1.6	1.7	1.7
Latvia	-0.5	-0.5	-0.5
Lebanon	1.1	1.1	1.0
Lesotho	0.8	0.7	0.5
Liberia	2.7	3.9	4.8
Libya	2.0	2.0	1.9
Liechtenstein	0.9	0.4	0.9
Lithuania	-0.6	-0.6	-0.5
Luxembourg	0.8	2.4	2.6
Macao	1.2	0.9	0.5
Macedonia, former Yugoslav Republic	0.2	0.1	0.0
Madagascar	2.8	2.7	2.6
Malawi	2.5	2.6	2.5
Malaysia	1.8	1.8	1.7
Maldives	1.6	1.7	1.7
Mali	3.0	3.0	3.0
Malta	0.5	0.6	0.8
Marshall Islands	3.3	3.3	1.7
Mauritania	2.8	2.7	2.5
Mauritius	0.8	0.8	0.7
Mayotte	4.5	3.6	3.6
Mexico	1.0	1.1	1.0
Micronesia, Federated States	0.6	0.5	0.3
Moldova	-1.2	-1.1	-1.1
Monaco	0.3	0.3	0.3
Mongolia	1.6	1.2	1.1
Montenegro	-1.9	-1.1	-0.1
Morocco[6]	1.0	1.2	1.2
Mozambique	2.2	2.1	1.9
Myanmar	0.8	0.9	0.8
Namibia	1.3	1.3	1.3
Nepal	2.0	2.0	1.7
Netherlands	0.2	0.2	0.2
Netherlands Antilles	1.2	1.3	1.3
New Caledonia	1.9	1.5	1.6
New Zealand	1.1	1.2	1.0
Nicaragua	1.3	1.3	1.3
Niger	3.5	3.5	3.3
Nigeria	2.4	2.4	2.2
Northern Mariana Islands	2.6	2.2	2.0
Norway	0.7	0.8	1.0
Oman	1.1	1.6	2.1
Pakistan[7]	2.4	2.1	2.1
Palau	0.5	0.5	0.5
Palestinian Autonomous Areas[8]	3.3	4.0	2.5
Panama	1.8	1.7	1.6
Papua New Guinea	2.2	2.2	2.0
Paraguay	1.9	2.0	1.7
Peru	1.2	1.1	1.1
Philippines	2.0	2.0	1.9

(continues on the next page)

Table 1 (continued)

Annual rate of population change, %	2005	2006	2007
Poland	0.0	-0.1	-0.2
Portugal	0.5	0.3	0.2
Puerto Rico	0.4	0.4	0.4
Qatar	4.1	3.1	1.8
Romania	-0.2	-0.2	-0.2
Russian Federation	-0.5	-0.5	-0.6
Rwanda	2.0	2.5	2.8
Saint Christopher and Nevis	2.1	0.8	0.8
Saint Lucia	1.4	0.7	1.2
Saint Vincent and the Grenadines	0.5	0.5	0.5
Samoa	0.7	0.8	0.7
San Marino	0.7	1.4	1.0
São Tomé and Príncipe	1.7	1.6	1.8
Saudi Arabia	2.6	2.4	2.2
Senegal	2.6	2.5	2.8
Serbia[9]	-0.3	-0.4	-0.3
Seychelles	0.5	2.0	0.5
Sierra Leone	3.6	2.8	1.8
Singapore	2.4	3.1	4.2
Slovakia	0.1	0.1	0.1
Slovenia	0.2	0.3	0.6
Solomon Islands	2.5	2.4	2.3
Somalia	3.0	3.0	2.9
South Africa	1.2	1.1	0.4
Spain[10]	1.6	1.6	1.7
Sri Lanka	1.1	1.1	0.3
Sudan	2.1	2.2	2.2
Suriname	0.6	0.6	0.5
Swaziland	1.0	0.6	0.6
Sweden	0.4	0.6	0.7
Switzerland	0.6	0.6	0.9
Syria[11]	2.7	2.7	2.5
Tajikistan	1.3	1.4	1.5
Tanzania	2.6	2.5	2.4
Thailand	0.7	0.7	0.6
Timor-Leste	5.4	5.4	3.5
Togo	2.7	2.7	2.6
Tonga	0.4	0.5	0.8
Trinidad and Tobago	0.3	0.4	0.3
Tunisia	1.0	1.0	1.2
Turkey	1.3	1.3	1.2
Turkmenistan	1.4	1.4	1.3
Uganda	3.2	3.2	3.4
Ukraine	-0.7	-0.7	-0.9
United Arab Emirates	3.9	3.5	2.7
United Kingdom[12]	0.6	0.6	0.7
United States Virgin Islands	-0.1	-0.1	-0.1
United States of America	1.0	1.0	0.7
Uruguay	0.1	0.3	0.1
Uzbekistan	1.2	1.2	1.4

(continues on the next page)

Table 1 (continued)

Annual rate of population change, %	2005	2006	2007
Vanuatu	2.6	2.5	2.3
Venezuela	1.7	1.7	1.6
Viet Nam	1.3	1.2	1.2
Yemen	3.0	3.0	3.0
Zambia	1.8	1.9	1.9
Zimbabwe	0.7	0.8	1.3
World	*1.2*	*1.2*	*1.1*

Notes:
[1] Excluding Hong Kong and Macao, listed separately.
[2] Excluding settlers from Turkey in the 'Turkish Republic of Northern Cyprus'.
[3] Including the Åland Islands.
[4] Including the Indian-controlled part of Jammu and Kashmir.
[5] Including the Golan region, annexed from Syria, and East Jerusalem.
[6] Including the disputed territory of Western Sahara.
[7] Excluding Azad Kashmir and the Northern Areas.
[8] Comprising the West Bank, including Israeli-occupied East Jerusalem, and the Gaza Strip.
[9] Including Kosovo until February 2008.
[10] Including Ceuta and Melilla.
[11] Including the Israeli-occupied Golan region.
[12] Including Northern Ireland.
Source: Europa World Online, www.europaworld.com.

Table 2 Population Density

Population density per sq. km (at mid-year)	2005	2006	2007
Albania	109.7	110.3	110.7
Algeria	13.8	14.0	14.2
American Samoa	288.6	298.5	298.5
Andorra	141.0	143.2	143.2
Angola	12.9	13.3	13.7
Antigua and Barbuda	187.8	190.0	192.3
Argentina	13.9	14.1	14.2
Armenia	101.5	101.2	100.9
Aruba	518.1	523.3	523.3
Australia	2.7	2.7	2.7
Austria	98.2	98.7	99.1
Azerbaijan	96.9	98.0	99.0
Bahamas	23.2	23.5	23.7
Bahrain	978.4	997.3	1,016.2
Bangladesh	1,064.5	1,083.3	1,101.2
Barbados	679.1	681.4	683.7
Belarus	47.1	46.9	46.7
Belgium	343.3	345.5	348.1
Belize	12.7	13.0	13.2
Benin	75.4	77.8	80.1
Bermuda	1,207.5	1,207.5	1,207.5
Bhutan	16.6	16.9	17.1
Bolivia	8.4	8.5	8.7
Bosnia and Herzegovina	73.8	73.8	73.7
Botswana	3.2	3.2	3.2
Brazil	21.9	22.2	22.5
Brunei	64.9	66.3	67.5
Bulgaria	69.7	69.3	68.9
Burkina Faso	50.8	52.4	53.9
Burundi	282.4	293.6	305.2
Cambodia	77.1	78.4	79.8
Cameroon	37.4	38.2	39.0
Canada	3.2	3.3	3.3
Cape Verde	125.6	128.6	131.3
Cayman Islands	171.8	175.6	179.4
Central African Republic	6.7	6.8	7.0
Chad	7.9	8.2	8.4
Chile	21.6	21.7	21.9
China, People's Republic[1]	136.3	137.0	137.9
Colombia	39.4	39.9	40.4
Comoros	322.2	329.8	336.2
Congo, Democratic Republic	25.1	25.9	26.6
Congo, Republic	10.6	10.8	11.0
Costa Rica	84.7	86.1	87.3
Côte d'Ivoire	57.6	58.7	59.8
Croatia	78.5	78.5	78.4
Cuba	102.5	102.5	102.4
Cyprus[2]	81.9	83.6	85.1
Czech Republic	129.8	130.2	131.0
Denmark	125.7	126.1	126.7

(continues on the next page)

Table 2 (continued)

Population density per sq. km (at mid-year)	2005	2006	2007
Djibouti	34.7	35.3	35.9
Dominica	95.9	95.9	97.2
Dominican Republic	194.3	197.3	200.1
Ecuador	48.0	48.5	49.0
Egypt	72.7	74.0	75.3
El Salvador	316.9	321.4	325.7
Equatorial Guinea	17.3	17.7	18.1
Eritrea	37.4	38.7	40.0
Estonia	29.8	29.7	29.7
Ethiopia	66.3	68.1	69.8
Faroe Islands	34.3	34.3	34.3
Fiji	45.1	45.3	45.6
Finland[3]	15.5	15.6	15.6
France	111.9	112.8	113.4
French Polynesia	61.4	62.2	63.1
Gabon	4.8	4.9	5.0
Gambia	143.2	147.2	151.1
Georgia	64.2	63.6	63.1
Germany	230.9	230.7	230.4
Ghana	94.5	96.5	98.4
Greece	84.1	84.5	84.8
Grenada	307.2	313.0	313.0
Guam	307.8	311.5	315.1
Guatemala	116.7	119.7	122.6
Guinea	36.6	37.3	38.2
Guinea-Bissau	44.2	45.6	46.9
Guyana	3.4	3.4	3.4
Haiti	335.0	340.4	346.4
Honduras	60.8	62.0	63.0
Hong Kong	6,171.2	6,211.1	6,273.6
Hungary	108.4	108.3	108.1
Iceland	2.9	3.0	3.0
India[4]	345.7	350.5	354.8
Indonesia	114.7	116.0	117.4
Iran	41.9	42.5	43.1
Ireland	59.3	60.7	62.2
Isle of Man	132.9	134.6	134.6
Israel[5]	313.7	319.4	324.9
Italy	194.5	195.6	197.0
Jamaica	241.5	242.7	243.6
Japan	338.1	338.0	338.1
Jordan	61.0	62.4	64.4
Kazakhstan	5.6	5.6	5.7
Kenya	61.1	62.7	64.4
Kiribati	122.1	123.3	125.8
Korea, Democratic People's Republic	192.4	193.1	193.7
Korea, Republic	484.7	485.9	487.0
Kuwait	142.3	145.9	149.5
Kyrgyzstan	25.7	26.0	26.2
Laos	23.9	24.3	24.7

(continues on the next page)

Table 2 (continued)

Population density per sq. km (at mid-year)	2005	2006	2007
Latvia	35.6	35.4	35.2
Lebanon	383.8	388.0	392.0
Lesotho	65.3	65.7	66.1
Liberia	35.2	36.6	38.4
Libya	3.3	3.4	3.5
Liechtenstein	218.8	218.8	218.8
Lithuania	52.3	52.0	51.7
Luxembourg	176.7	181.0	185.6
Macao	16,310.3	16,482.8	16,551.7
Macedonia, former Yugoslav Republic	79.1	79.2	79.2
Madagascar	31.8	32.6	33.5
Malawi	111.6	114.5	117.5
Malaysia	77.8	79.2	80.5
Maldives	989.9	1,006.7	1,023.5
Mali	9.4	9.7	9.9
Malta	1,278.5	1,284.8	1,294.3
Marshall Islands	348.1	359.1	370.2
Mauritania	2.9	3.0	3.0
Mauritius	609.3	614.2	619.1
Mayotte	481.3	500.0	518.7
Mexico	52.5	53.1	53.6
Micronesia, Federated States	156.9	158.3	158.3
Moldova	114.7	113.4	112.2
Monaco	16,000.0	16,500.0	16,500.0
Mongolia	1.6	1.7	1.7
Morocco[6]	42.4	42.9	43.4
Mozambique	25.7	26.2	26.7
Myanmar	70.9	71.5	72.1
Namibia	2.5	2.5	2.5
Nepal	184.1	187.8	191.0
Netherlands	393.0	393.6	394.5
Netherlands Antilles	232.5	236.3	238.8
New Caledonia	12.6	12.8	13.0
New Zealand	15.3	15.5	15.6
Nicaragua	41.9	42.4	43.0
Niger	10.5	10.8	11.2
Nigeria	155.4	159.1	162.6
Northern Mariana Islands	175.1	179.4	183.8
Norway	14.3	14.4	14.5
Oman	8.1	8.2	8.4
Pakistan[7]	195.7	199.7	204.0
Palau	39.4	39.4	39.4
Palestinian Autonomous Areas[8]	602.3	627.1	642.7
Panama	42.8	43.5	44.2
Papua New Guinea	13.1	13.4	13.7
Paraguay	14.5	14.8	15.0
Peru	21.2	21.5	21.7
Philippines	281.9	287.5	293.0
Poland	122.1	121.9	121.7
Portugal	114.2	114.6	114.9

(continues on the next page)

Table 2 (continued)

Population density per sq. km (at mid-year)	2005	2006	2007
Puerto Rico	436.7	438.4	440.1
Qatar	69.3	71.4	72.7
Romania	90.8	90.6	90.4
Russian Federation	8.4	8.3	8.3
Rwanda	350.6	359.3	369.7
Saint Christopher and Nevis	178.4	178.4	182.2
Saint Lucia	267.9	269.5	272.7
Saint Vincent and the Grenadines	305.9	308.5	308.5
Samoa	65.0	65.3	66.1
San Marino	459.0	475.4	475.4
São Tomé and Príncipe	152.8	154.8	157.8
Saudi Arabia	10.3	10.6	10.8
Senegal	59.7	61.3	63.0
Serbia[9]	96.0	95.6	95.3
Seychelles	182.4	186.8	186.8
Sierra Leone	77.9	80.1	81.5
Singapore	6,033.9	6,224.9	6,490.8
Slovakia	109.9	109.9	110.0
Slovenia	98.7	99.0	99.5
Solomon Islands	17.1	17.6	18.0
Somalia	12.9	13.2	13.6
South Africa	38.5	38.9	39.0
Spain[10]	85.8	87.2	88.7
Sri Lanka	300.2	303.5	304.4
Sudan	14.7	15.0	15.4
Suriname	2.8	2.8	2.8
Swaziland	65.1	65.5	65.9
Sweden	20.0	20.2	20.3
Switzerland	180.1	181.3	182.9
Syria[11]	102.0	104.8	107.4
Tajikistan	45.8	46.4	47.1
Tanzania	40.7	41.8	42.8
Thailand	122.8	123.6	124.4
Timor-Leste	66.8	70.4	73.0
Togo	110.2	113.3	116.3
Tonga	132.4	133.7	135.0
Trinidad and Tobago	258.2	259.0	259.9
Tunisia	61.3	61.9	62.6
Turkey	92.0	93.1	94.3
Turkmenistan	9.9	10.0	10.2
Uganda	119.8	123.8	128.0
Ukraine	78.0	77.5	76.8
United Arab Emirates	52.8	54.7	56.2
United Kingdom[12]	248.4	249.9	251.7
United States Virgin Islands	314.1	314.1	311.2
United States of America	30.2	30.5	30.7
Uruguay	18.8	18.8	18.8
Uzbekistan	58.5	59.2	60.1
Vanuatu	17.6	18.1	18.5
Venezuela	29.0	29.5	30.0

(continues on the next page)

Table 2 (continued)

Population density per sq. km (at mid-year)	2005	2006	2007
Viet Nam	250.9	253.9	257.1
Yemen	39.3	40.5	41.7
Zambia	15.3	15.5	15.8
Zimbabwe	33.6	33.9	34.3

Notes:
[1] Excluding Hong Kong and Macao, listed separately.
[2] Excluding settlers from Turkey in the 'Turkish Republic of Northern Cyprus'.
[3] Including the Åland Islands.
[4] Including the Indian-controlled part of Jammu and Kashmir.
[5] Including the Golan region, annexed from Syria, and East Jerusalem.
[6] Including the disputed territory of Western Sahara.
[7] Excluding Azad Kashmir and the Northern Areas.
[8] Comprising the West Bank, including Israeli-occupied East Jerusalem, and the Gaza Strip.
[9] Including Kosovo until February 2008.
[10] Including Ceuta and Melilla.
[11] Including the Israeli-occupied Golan region.
[12] Including Northern Ireland.
Source: Europa World Online, www.europaworld.com.

Table 3 Life Expectancy

Expectation of life, 2006	Females	Males	Both
Albania	80	73	76
Algeria	73	71	72
Angola	44	41	42
Argentina	79	71	75
Armenia	75	68	72
Australia	83	79	81
Austria	83	77	80
Azerbaijan	75	70	72
Bahamas	76	70	73
Bahrain	77	74	76
Bangladesh	65	63	64
Barbados	80	74	77
Belarus	74	63	69
Belgium	82	77	79
Belize	74	70	72
Benin	57	55	56
Bermuda	81	76	79
Bhutan	67	64	65
Bolivia	67	63	65
Bosnia and Herzegovina	77	72	75
Botswana	50	50	50
Brazil	76	69	72
Brunei	80	75	77
Bulgaria	76	69	73
Burkina Faso	53	50	52
Burundi	50	48	49
Cambodia	61	57	59
Cameroon	51	50	50
Canada	83	78	80
Cape Verde	74	68	71
Central African Republic	46	43	44
Chad	52	49	51
Chile	81	75	78
China, People's Republic[1]	74	70	72
Christmas Island	76	69	73
Comoros	64	62	63
Congo, Democratic Republic	47	45	46
Congo, Republic	56	54	55
Costa Rica	81	76	79
Côte d'Ivoire	49	47	48
Croatia	79	72	76
Cuba	80	76	78
Cyprus	82	77	79
Czech Republic	80	73	76
Denmark	80	76	78
Djibouti	56	53	54
Dominican Republic	75	69	72
Ecuador	78	72	75
Egypt	73	69	71
El Salvador	75	69	72

(continues on the next page)

Table 3 (continued)

Expectation of life, 2006	Females	Males	Both
Equatorial Guinea	52	50	51
Eritrea	60	55	57
Estonia	78	67	73
Ethiopia	54	51	52
Faroe Islands	81	76	79
Fiji	71	66	69
Finland[2]	83	76	79
France	84	77	81
French Polynesia	77	71	74
Gabon	57	56	57
Gambia	60	58	59
Georgia	75	67	71
Germany	82	76	79
Ghana	60	59	60
Greece	82	77	79
Guam	78	73	75
Guatemala	74	66	70
Guinea	57	54	56
Guinea-Bissau	48	45	46
Guyana	69	63	66
Haiti	62	59	60
Honduras	73	66	70
Hong Kong	85	79	82
Hungary	77	69	73
Iceland	83	79	81
India	66	63	64
Indonesia	70	66	68
Iran	72	69	71
Ireland	82	77	79
Israel	82	78	80
Italy	84	78	81
Jamaica	73	70	71
Japan	86	79	82
Jordan	74	71	72
Kazakhstan	72	61	66
Kenya	55	52	53
Korea, Democratic People's Republic	69	65	67
Korea, Republic	82	75	78
Kuwait	80	76	78
Kyrgyzstan	72	64	68
Laos	65	63	64
Latvia	76	65	71
Lebanon	74	70	72
Lesotho	43	43	43
Liberia	46	44	45
Libya	77	71	74
Lithuania	77	65	71
Luxembourg	82	76	79
Macao	83	78	80
Macedonia, former Yugoslav Republic	76	72	74

(continues on the next page)

Table 3 (continued)

Expectation of life, 2006	Females	Males	Both
Madagascar	61	57	59
Malawi	48	47	48
Malaysia	76	72	74
Maldives	69	67	68
Mali	56	52	54
Malta	81	76	79
Mauritania	66	62	64
Mauritius	77	70	73
Mexico	77	72	74
Micronesia, Federated States	69	68	68
Moldova	72	65	69
Mongolia	69	66	67
Montenegro	77	72	74
Morocco	73	69	71
Mozambique	43	42	42
Myanmar	65	59	62
Namibia	53	52	52
Nepal	64	63	63
Netherlands	82	78	80
Netherlands Antilles	79	71	75
New Caledonia	78	73	75
New Zealand	82	78	80
Nicaragua	76	70	72
Niger	56	57	56
Nigeria	47	46	47
Norway	83	78	80
Oman	77	74	76
Pakistan	66	65	65
Palestinian Autonomous Areas	74	71	73
Panama	78	73	75
Papua New Guinea	60	55	57
Paraguay	74	69	72
Peru	74	69	71
Philippines	74	69	71
Poland	80	71	75
Portugal	82	75	78
Puerto Rico	83	74	78
Qatar	76	75	75
Romania	76	69	72
Russian Federation	73	59	66
Rwanda	47	44	46
Saint Lucia	76	73	74
Saint Vincent and the Grenadines	74	69	71
Samoa	75	68	71
San Marino	85	79	82
São Tomé and Príncipe	67	63	65
Saudi Arabia	75	71	73
Senegal	65	61	63
Serbia[3]	76	70	73
Seychelles	76	69	72

(continues on the next page)

Table 3 (continued)

Expectation of life, 2006	Females	Males	Both
Sierra Leone	44	41	42
Singapore	82	78	80
Slovakia	78	70	74
Slovenia	81	74	78
Solomon Islands	64	63	63
Somalia	49	47	48
South Africa	52	49	51
Spain[4]	84	78	81
Sri Lanka	78	72	75
Sudan	60	57	58
Suriname	73	67	70
Swaziland	40	42	41
Sweden	83	79	81
Switzerland	84	79	82
Syria	76	72	74
Tajikistan	69	64	67
Tanzania	53	51	52
Thailand	75	66	70
Timor-Leste	58	56	57
Togo	60	56	58
Tonga	74	72	73
Trinidad and Tobago	72	68	70
Tunisia	76	72	74
Turkey	74	69	71
Turkmenistan	67	59	63
Uganda	51	50	51
Ukraine	74	62	68
United Arab Emirates	82	77	79
United Kingdom[5]	81	77	79
United States Virgin Islands	80	77	79
United States of America	81	75	78
Uruguay	80	72	76
Uzbekistan	71	64	67
Vanuatu	72	68	70
Venezuela	77	72	74
Viet Nam	73	68	71
Yemen	64	61	62
Zambia	42	41	42
Zimbabwe	42	43	43

Notes:
[1] Including Hong Kong and Macao, listed separately.
[2] Including the Åland Islands.
[3] Including Kosovo until February 2008.
[4] Including Ceuta and Melilla.
[5] Including Northern Ireland.
Source: Europa World Online, www.europaworld.com.

Table 4 Energy Consumption

Consumption of commercial energy per head, kg of oil equivalent	2003	2004	2005
Albania	687.0	667.8	761.6
Algeria	1,044.7	1,034.5	1,058.3
Angola	600.8	604.1	615.0
Argentina	1,571.4	1,648.6	1,644.5
Armenia	659.7	703.4	847.7
Australia	5,681.3	5,639.5	5,978.3
Austria	4,063.7	4,067.9	4,173.7
Azerbaijan	1,492.6	1,558.8	1,648.6
Bahrain	10,410.1	10,584.4	11,214.3
Bangladesh	148.8	151.4	157.8
Belarus	2,632.3	2,730.2	2,720.0
Belgium	5,728.5	5,575.1	5,406.5
Benin	304.2	306.1	304.3
Bolivia	503.8	552.6	578.0
Bosnia and Herzegovina	1,181.5	1,231.5	1,312.5
Botswana	1,035.5	1,002.2	1,032.2
Brazil	1,065.3	1,111.4	1,121.5
Brunei	7,495.2	7,369.5	7,064.7
Bulgaria	2,511.6	2,434.3	2,591.7
Cameroon	399.9	400.1	392.1
Canada	8,294.8	8,399.8	8,416.5
Chile	1,652.2	1,743.4	1,814.5
China, People's Republic[1]	1,055.9	1,221.0	1,316.3
Colombia	624.1	621.7	636.0
Congo, Democratic Republic	289.8	289.5	288.8
Congo, Republic	298.1	301.2	332.1
Costa Rica	879.7	869.3	882.8
Côte d'Ivoire	370.8	379.0	422.0
Croatia	1,976.4	1,985.2	1,999.8
Cuba	936.2	951.5	905.5
Cyprus	3,716.4	3,398.2	3,367.6
Czech Republic	4,369.3	4,484.2	4,417.1
Denmark	3,858.1	3,739.7	3,620.8
Dominican Republic	868.3	821.1	776.8
Ecuador	740.8	769.3	799.4
Egypt	786.7	791.0	841.5
El Salvador	700.0	681.6	694.2
Estonia	3,642.4	3,835.4	3,785.8
Ethiopia	287.1	287.7	287.8
Finland[2]	7,203.3	7,240.4	6,664.2
France	4,510.6	4,542.7	4,533.5
Gabon	1,340.1	1,332.9	1,333.4
Georgia	600.8	626.3	717.6
Germany	4,206.2	4,220.0	4,180.3
Ghana	393.5	378.7	396.6
Greece	2,710.3	2,754.6	2,789.7
Guatemala	603.2	610.6	628.4
Haiti	248.4	241.0	269.1
Honduras	547.2	575.8	566.3

(continues on the next page)

285

Table 4 (continued)

Consumption of commercial energy per head, kg of oil equivalent	2003	2004	2005
Hong Kong	2,482.2	2,580.5	2,653.2
Hungary	2,600.4	2,607.9	2,752.2
Iceland	11,694.1	11,975.5	12,219.0
India	461.1	482.1	490.9
Indonesia	777.6	799.9	813.9
Iran	2,077.3	2,216.0	2,352.2
Ireland	3,753.3	3,724.0	3,676.0
Israel	3,085.0	3,048.9	2,815.7
Italy	3,136.6	3,142.2	3,159.8
Jamaica	1,543.1	1,540.9	1,444.7
Japan	4,034.9	4,166.1	4,151.6
Jordan	1,070.7	1,229.9	1,310.7
Kazakhstan	3,038.5	3,225.8	3,461.9
Kenya	460.4	481.2	484.5
Korea, Democratic People's Republic	850.9	866.4	898.3
Korea, Republic	4,335.3	4,435.8	4,426.4
Kuwait	9,563.0	10,322.7	11,099.8
Kyrgyzstan	541.4	548.6	544.0
Latvia	1,899.1	1,985.0	2,050.0
Lebanon	1,520.6	1,361.2	1,390.5
Libya	3,173.0	3,272.2	3,218.4
Lithuania	2,620.8	2,662.1	2,515.0
Luxembourg	9,472.2	10,324.4	10,457.4
Macedonia, former Yugoslav Republic	1,313.7	1,327.9	1,346.3
Malaysia	2,351.2	2,208.6	2,388.8
Malta	2,237.8	2,339.9	2,351.9
Mexico	1,581.5	1,619.0	1,712.4
Moldova	837.7	861.9	917.3
Morocco	371.2	393.0	458.3
Mozambique	497.3	502.8	497.1
Myanmar	290.4	296.8	307.0
Namibia	645.7	670.6	682.8
Nepal	336.3	337.5	338.5
Netherlands	4,990.2	5,046.9	5,015.3
Netherlands Antilles	9,008.4	9,292.2	8,889.9
New Zealand	4,253.8	4,263.7	4,090.3
Nicaragua	587.6	611.5	610.5
Nigeria	724.3	719.1	734.2
Norway	5,946.2	6,156.0	6,948.5
Oman	5,079.7	4,771.2	5,569.9
Pakistan	466.9	489.1	490.0
Panama	835.8	801.2	804.0
Paraguay	702.6	694.4	673.5
Peru	439.9	489.6	506.3
Philippines	518.4	531.4	528.5
Poland	2,394.3	2,403.9	2,435.9
Portugal	2,468.9	2,528.0	2,575.1
Qatar	19,177.5	20,140.4	19,877.3
Romania	1,794.2	1,778.4	1,772.3

(continues on the next page)

Table 4 (continued)

Consumption of commercial energy per head, kg of oil equivalent	2003	2004	2005
Russian Federation	4,423.7	4,459.6	4,517.5
Saudi Arabia	5,587.8	5,873.4	6,067.6
Senegal	248.6	260.1	258.4
Singapore	5,355.3	6,113.7	7,056.1
Slovakia	3,462.9	3,406.1	3,495.6
Slovenia	3,511.0	3,589.4	3,656.6
South Africa	2,578.7	2,789.6	2,721.9
Spain[3]	3,240.0	3,334.1	3,345.7
Sri Lanka	448.9	479.8	476.7
Sudan	468.1	488.0	498.6
Sweden	5,706.2	5,914.1	5,781.7
Switzerland	3,661.3	3,671.9	3,651.0
Syria	994.8	977.8	947.7
Tajikistan	492.0	509.3	527.9
Tanzania	469.5	499.9	530.3
Thailand	1,428.7	1,551.5	1,587.8
Togo	343.8	323.0	319.8
Trinidad and Tobago	8,459.4	9,408.4	9,598.7
Tunisia	837.4	876.2	842.7
Turkey	1,114.3	1,151.2	1,182.3
Turkmenistan	3,646.6	3,256.6	3,380.7
Ukraine	3,031.5	3,039.2	3,040.8
United Arab Emirates	11,242.1	11,528.1	11,435.8
United Kingdom[4]	3,900.2	3,898.8	3,884.2
United States of America	7,850.1	7,930.0	7,892.9
Uruguay	761.9	867.1	875.1
Uzbekistan	1,988.6	1,911.0	1,797.7
Venezuela	2,070.4	2,184.5	2,292.8
Viet Nam	546.8	612.2	617.2
Yemen	292.2	311.1	318.9
Zambia	612.6	616.1	620.6
Zimbabwe	739.3	714.1	741.1
World	*1,711.5*	*1,769.9*	*1,796.4*

Notes:
[1] Including Hong Kong and Macao (Hong Kong listed separately).
[2] Including the Åland Islands.
[3] Including Ceuta and Melilla.
[4] Including Northern Ireland.
Source: Europa World Online, www.europaworld.com.

Table 5 Global Concentrations of Carbon Dioxide (CO_2)

Year	Carbon dioxide concentrations, parts per million
1744	276.8
1764	276.7
1791	279.7
1816	283.8
1839	283.1
1843	287.4
1847	286.8
1854	288.2
1869	289.3
1874	289.5
1878	290.3
1887	292.3
1899	295.8
1903	294.8
1905	296.9
1909	299.2
1915	300.5
1921	301.6
1927	305.5
1935	306.6
1943	307.9
1953	312.7
1959	315.98
1960	316.91
1961	317.64
1962	318.45
1963	318.99
1965	320.04
1966	321.38
1967	322.16
1968	323.05
1969	324.63
1970	325.68
1971	326.32
1972	327.45
1973	329.68
1974	330.25
1975	331.15
1976	332.15
1977	333.9
1978	335.51
1979	336.85
1980	338.69
1981	339.93
1982	341.13
1983	342.78
1984	344.42
1985	345.9
1986	347.15

(continues on the next page)

Table 5 (continued)

Year	Carbon dioxide concentrations, parts per million
1987	348.93
1988	351.48
1989	352.91
1990	354.19
1991	355.59
1992	356.37
1993	357.04
1994	358.89
1995	360.88
1996	362.64
1997	363.76
1998	366.63
1999	368.31
2000	369.48
2001	371.02
2002	373.1
2003	375.64
2004	377.38
2005	379.67
2006	381.84
2007	383.55
2008	385.34

Notes: Data before 1958: Neftel, Friedli, Moore et al. (1994) *Historical Carbon Dioxide Record from the Siple Station Ice Core* (reported online by the Carbon Dioxide Information Analysis Center at cdiac.esd.ornl.gov/ftp/trends/co2/siple2.013). Bern, Switzerland: University of Bern. Data after 1958: C. D. Keeling, T. P. Whorf and the Scripps Institute of Oceanography (2005) *Atmospheric CO2 Concentrations (ppmv) derived from in-situ air samples collected at Mauna Loa Observatory, Hawaii* (reported online by the Carbon Dioxide Information Analysis Center at cdiac.ornl.gov/ftp/trends/co2/maunaloa.co2). Mauna Loa: Scripps Institute of Oceanography.

Source: EarthTrends, earthtrends.wri.org; provided by the World Resources Institute, www.wri.org.

Table 6 Carbon Dioxide (CO_2) Emissions, metric tons per capita

Country	2004	2005	2006
Afghanistan	0.029	0.028	0.027
Albania	1.619	1.438	1.356
Algeria	3.734	4.206	3.979
Angola	0.582	0.612	0.639
Anguilla	3.649	4.188	4.125
Antigua and Barbuda	4.967	4.946	5.058
Argentina	4.066	4.102	4.434
Armenia	1.204	1.441	1.452
Aruba	22.668	22.450	22.260
Australia	16.963	18.010	18.120
Austria	8.417	8.782	8.626
Azerbaijan	4.019	4.225	4.170
Bahamas	6.292	6.521	6.532
Bahrain	25.422	27.156	28.816
Bangladesh	0.246	0.262	0.267
Barbados	4.374	4.509	4.569
Belarus	6.615	6.568	7.067
Belgium	10.938	10.520	10.278
Belize	2.940	2.967	2.903
Benin	0.290	0.302	0.355
Bermuda	8.601	8.799	8.771
Bhutan	0.600	0.616	0.588
Bolivia	1.007	1.042	1.219
Bosnia and Herzegovina	6.192	6.542	6.988
Botswana	2.416	2.465	2.567
Brazil	1.851	1.873	1.862
British Virgin Islands	3.878	3.997	4.443
Brunei	16.614	15.801	15.475
Bulgaria	5.810	6.068	6.251
Burkina Faso	0.057	0.057	0.055
Burundi	0.021	0.022	0.024
Cambodia	0.255	0.267	0.287
Cameroon	0.221	0.209	0.201
Canada	17.334	17.347	16.720
Cape Verde	0.541	0.586	0.594
Cayman Islands	11.078	11.018	11.134
Central African Republic	0.057	0.056	0.059
Chad	0.038	0.039	0.038
Chile	3.622	3.648	3.650
China, People's Republic	3.907	4.285	4.621
Colombia	1.216	1.317	1.392
Comoros	0.113	0.110	0.108
Congo, Democratic Republic	0.037	0.037	0.036
Congo, Republic	0.539	0.445	0.397
Cook Islands	3.834	4.458	4.838
Costa Rica	1.671	1.682	1.786
Côte d'Ivoire	0.419	0.439	0.364
Croatia	5.195	5.189	5.198
Cuba	2.155	2.209	2.630
Cyprus	8.856	8.970	9.210

(continues on the next page)

Table 6 (continued)

Country	2004	2005	2006
Czech Republic	11.363	11.256	11.273
Denmark	9.386	8.645	9.934
Djibouti	0.580	0.588	0.596
Dominica	1.564	1.676	1.735
Dominican Republic	2.142	2.101	2.117
Ecuador	2.302	2.348	2.373
Egypt	2.144	2.381	2.249
El Salvador	0.940	0.944	0.955
Equatorial Guinea	9.181	8.968	8.789
Eritrea	0.175	0.166	0.118
Estonia	13.902	13.550	13.077
Ethiopia	0.073	0.070	0.074
Faeroe Islands	14.090	14.072	13.973
Falkland Islands	16.060	17.255	17.180
Fiji	2.335	2.010	1.932
Finland	12.936	10.445	12.676
France[1]	6.469	6.467	6.244
French Guiana	4.552	4.428	4.444
French Polynesia	3.130	3.342	3.168
Gabon	1.253	1.449	1.569
Gambia	0.203	0.197	0.201
Georgia	0.869	1.073	1.245
Germany	9.946	9.723	9.742
Ghana	0.304	0.332	0.402
Gibraltar	12.976	13.230	13.161
Greece	8.778	8.912	8.666
Greenland	9.555	9.697	9.770
Grenada	2.070	2.230	2.292
Guadeloupe	4.737	4.834	4.848
Guatemala	0.932	0.934	0.903
Guinea	0.152	0.151	0.148
Guinea-Bissau	0.175	0.170	0.169
Guyana	1.955	2.018	2.039
Haiti	0.192	0.190	0.192
Honduras	1.106	1.139	1.032
Hong Kong	5.570	5.823	5.474
Hungary	5.724	5.832	5.731
Iceland	7.599	7.390	7.421
India	1.220	1.255	1.311
Indonesia	1.437	1.463	1.457
Iran	6.118	6.281	6.645
Iraq	3.030	3.166	3.248
Ireland	10.802	10.628	10.378
Israel	10.257	9.513	10.344
Italy[2]	8.028	8.012	8.062
Jamaica	3.952	3.789	4.503
Japan	10.266	10.166	10.109
Jordan	3.582	3.848	3.617
Kazakhstan	11.397	11.652	12.636

(continues on the next page)

Table 6 (continued)

Country	2004	2005	2006
Kenya	0.305	0.308	0.332
Kiribati	0.284	0.279	0.314
Korea, Democratic People's Republic	3.399	3.535	3.577
Korea, Republic	10.362	9.906	9.891
Kuwait	31.078	33.285	31.166
Kyrgyzstan	1.118	1.070	1.059
Laos	0.248	0.249	0.248
Latvia	3.052	3.068	3.260
Lebanon	4.260	4.362	3.780
Liberia	0.187	0.214	0.219
Libya	9.153	9.275	9.190
Lithuania	3.873	4.087	4.164
Luxembourg	24.460	24.805	24.518
Macao	4.760	4.883	4.684
Macedonia, former Yugoslav Republic	5.530	5.526	5.341
Madagascar	0.152	0.150	0.148
Malawi	0.083	0.079	0.077
Malaysia	6.924	7.146	7.194
Maldives	2.587	2.297	2.894
Mali	0.050	0.049	0.048
Malta	6.488	6.430	6.296
Marshall Islands	1.584	1.487	1.582
Martinique	4.381	4.529	4.706
Mauritania	0.560	0.557	0.547
Mauritius	2.598	2.747	3.076
Mexico	3.949	4.118	4.140
Mongolia	3.346	3.414	3.625
Montserrat	13.019	12.379	12.034
Morocco	1.339	1.559	1.469
Mozambique	0.096	0.090	0.097
Myanmar	0.206	0.218	0.207
Namibia	1.304	1.349	1.383
Nauru	14.170	14.143	14.117
Nepal	0.102	0.117	0.117
Netherlands	11.027	10.719	10.288
Netherlands Antilles	20.359	20.144	22.834
New Caledonia	11.074	11.962	12.358
New Zealand	7.585	7.348	7.365
Nicaragua	0.795	0.761	0.783
Niger	0.078	0.070	0.068
Nigeria	0.707	0.806	0.672
Niue	2.194	2.247	2.296
Norway	10.782	13.119	8.615
Oman	12.533	12.552	16.250
Pakistan	0.836	0.848	0.886
Palau	5.860	5.830	5.801
Palestinian Autonomous Areas	0.608	0.732	0.767
Panama	1.813	1.851	1.955

(continues on the next page)

Table 6 (continued)

Country	2004	2005	2006
Papua New Guinea	0.755	0.760	0.745
Paraguay	0.706	0.649	0.663
Peru	1.228	1.363	1.401
Philippines	0.928	0.904	0.792
Poland	8.068	7.948	8.343
Portugal	6.041	6.218	5.672
Qatar	48.397	58.667	56.243
Moldova	1.958	2.101	2.041
Réunion	3.252	3.204	3.168
Romania	4.265	4.247	4.574
Russian Federation	10.367	10.528	10.925
Rwanda	0.082	0.083	0.084
Saint Helena	1.740	1.719	1.697
Saint Christopher and Nevis	2.570	2.761	2.726
Saint Lucia	2.277	2.320	2.338
Saint Pierre and Miquelon	9.830	10.400	10.394
Saint Vincent and the Grenadines	1.640	1.631	1.653
Samoa	0.844	0.858	0.851
São Tomé and Príncipe	0.611	0.673	0.662
Saudi Arabia	15.014	15.544	15.784
Senegal	0.463	0.474	0.353
Serbia and Montenegro	5.248	4.769	5.096
Seychelles	9.120	8.145	8.643
Sierra Leone	0.186	0.180	0.173
Singapore	11.913	13.763	12.829
Slovakia	6.908	6.997	6.952
Slovenia	7.470	7.466	7.583
Solomon Islands	0.390	0.380	0.371
Somalia	0.030	0.031	0.020
South Africa	8.736	8.534	8.588
Spain	8.027	8.214	8.026
Sri Lanka	0.626	0.606	0.618
Sudan	0.287	0.298	0.287
Suriname	5.081	5.259	5.356
Swaziland	0.925	0.907	0.896
Sweden	6.039	5.697	5.604
Switzerland	5.470	5.570	5.611
Syria	3.600	3.525	3.528
Tajikistan	0.839	0.886	0.963
Tanzania	0.116	0.132	0.136
Thailand	4.286	4.303	4.296
Timor-Leste	0.174	0.165	0.158
Togo	0.230	0.215	0.191
Tonga	1.371	1.329	1.323
Trinidad and Tobago	21.103	23.384	25.294
Tunisia	2.245	2.256	2.264
Turkey	3.150	3.405	3.645
Turkmenistan	8.317	8.639	9.002
Uganda	0.065	0.081	0.091
Ukraine	6.954	6.975	6.855

(continues on the next page)

Table 6 (continued)

Country	2004	2005	2006
United Arab Emirates	33.460	33.061	32.848
United Kingdom	9.254	9.190	9.395
United States of America	19.532	19.481	18.994
Uruguay	1.753	1.802	2.061
Uzbekistan	4.517	4.233	4.287
Vanuatu	0.419	0.409	0.415
Venezuela	5.177	5.707	6.311
Viet Nam	1.169	1.198	1.231
Wallis and Futuna Islands	1.708	1.945	1.936
Yemen	0.935	0.956	0.976
Zambia	0.203	0.206	0.211
Zimbabwe	0.818	0.880	0.838

Notes:
[1] Including Monaco.
[2] Including San Marino.
Source: UN Millennium Development Goals Indicators, millenniumindicators.un.org /unsd/mdg/SeriesDetail.aspx?srid=751&crid (accessed 2 September 2009).

Table 7 Global Mean Surface Temperature

Year	Mean surface temperature, degrees centigrade
1880	13.75
1881	13.8
1882	13.77
1883	13.76
1884	13.7
1885	13.7
1886	13.75
1887	13.65
1888	13.74
1889	13.85
1890	13.63
1891	13.72
1892	13.68
1893	13.68
1894	13.67
1895	13.73
1896	13.83
1897	13.88
1898	13.75
1899	13.83
1900	13.9
1901	13.84
1902	13.73
1903	13.69
1904	13.66
1905	13.75
1906	13.8
1907	13.61
1908	13.66
1909	13.65
1910	13.67
1911	13.66
1912	13.66
1913	13.68
1914	13.85
1915	13.91
1916	13.7
1917	13.6
1918	13.68
1919	13.8
1920	13.81
1921	13.87
1922	13.76
1923	13.8
1924	13.79
1925	13.84
1926	13.99
1927	13.87
1928	13.89

(continues on nextpage)

Table 7 (continued)

Year	Mean surface temperature, degrees centigrade
1929	13.75
1930	13.93
1931	13.99
1932	13.94
1933	13.83
1934	13.95
1935	13.89
1936	13.96
1937	14.08
1938	14.11
1939	14.03
1940	14.05
1941	14.11
1942	14.03
1943	14.1
1944	14.2
1945	14.07
1946	13.96
1947	14.01
1948	13.96
1949	13.94
1950	13.85
1951	13.96
1952	14.03
1953	14.11
1954	13.9
1955	13.9
1956	13.83
1957	14.08
1958	14.08
1959	14.06
1960	13.99
1961	14.08
1962	14.04
1963	14.08
1964	13.79
1965	13.89
1966	13.97
1967	14
1968	13.96
1969	14.08
1970	14.03
1971	13.9
1972	14
1973	14.14
1974	13.92
1975	13.95
1976	13.84
1977	14.13

(continues on the next page)

Table 7 (continued)

Year	Mean surface temperature, degrees centigrade
1978	14.01
1979	14.09
1980	14.18
1981	14.27
1982	14.05
1983	14.26
1984	14.09
1985	14.06
1986	14.13
1987	14.27
1988	14.31
1989	14.19
1990	14.38
1991	14.35
1992	14.13
1993	14.14
1994	14.24
1995	14.38
1996	14.3
1997	14.4
1998	14.57
1999	14.33
2000	14.33
2001	14.48
2002	14.56
2003	14.55
2004	14.49
2005	14.63

Notes: Data from Goddard Institute for Space Studies (GISS) (2006) NASA GISS Surface Temperature Analysis (GISTEMP), New York: GISS, data.giss.nasa.gov/gistemp. Source: EarthTrends, earthtrends.wri.org; provided by the World Resources Institute, www.wri.org.

Table 8 Ratification of environmental treaties

Country	Cartagena Protocol on Biosafety	Framework Convention on Climate Change	Kyoto Protocol to the Framework Convention on Climate Change	Convention on Biological Diversity
Afghanistan		●		●
Albania	●	●	●	●
Algeria	●	●	●	●
Angola		●	●	●
Antigua and Barbuda	●	●	●	●
Argentina	○	●	●	●
Armenia	●	●	●	●
Australia		●	●	●
Austria	●	●	●	●
Azerbaijan	●	●	●	●
Bahamas	●	●	●	●
Bahrain		●	●	●
Bangladesh	●	●	●	●
Barbados	●	●	●	●
Belarus	●	●	●	●
Belgium	●	●	●	●
Belize	●	●	●	●
Benin	●	●	●	●
Bhutan	●	●	●	●
Bolivia	●	●	●	●
Bosnia and Herzegovina		●	●	●
Botswana	●	●	●	●
Brazil	●	●	●	●
Brunei Darussalam		●		●
Bulgaria	●	●	●	●
Burkina Faso	●	●	●	●
Burundi	●	●	●	●
Cambodia	●	●	●	●
Cameroon	●	●	●	●
Canada	○	●	●	●
Cape Verde	●	●	●	●
Central African Republic	●	●	●	●
Chad	●	●		●
Chile	○	●	●	●
China	●	●	●	●
Colombia	●	●	●	●
Comoros	●	●	●	●
Congo	●	●	●	●
Congo, Dem. Rep. of the	●	●	●	●
Costa Rica	●	●	●	●
Côte d'Ivoire		●	●	●
Croatia	●	●	●	●
Cuba	●	●	●	●
Cyprus	●	●	●	●
Czech Republic	●	●	●	●
Denmark	●	●	●	●

(continues on the next page)

Table 8 (continued)

Country	Cartagena Protocol on Biosafety	Framework Convention on Climate Change	Kyoto Protocol to the Framework Convention on Climate Change	Convention on Biological Diversity
Djibouti	•	•	•	•
Dominica	•	•	•	•
Dominican Republic	•	•	•	•
Ecuador	•	•	•	•
Egypt	•	•	•	•
El Salvador	•	•	•	•
Equatorial Guinea		•	•	•
Eritrea	•	•	•	•
Estonia	•	•	•	•
Ethiopia	•	•	•	•
European Community	•	•	•	•
Fiji	•	•	•	•
Finland	•	•	•	•
France	•	•	•	•
Gabon	•	•	•	•
Gambia	•	•	•	•
Georgia	•	•	•	•
Germany	•	•	•	•
Ghana	•	•	•	•
Greece	•	•	•	•
Grenada	•	•	•	•
Guatemala	•	•	•	•
Guinea	•	•	•	•
Guinea-Bissau		•	•	•
Guyana	•	•	•	•
Haiti	○	•	•	•
Honduras	•	•	•	•
Hungary	•	•	•	•
Iceland	○	•	•	•
India	•	•	•	•
Indonesia	•	•	•	•
Iran, Islamic Rep. of	•	•	•	•
Ireland	•	•	•	•
Israel		•	•	•
Italy	•	•	•	•
Jamaica	○	•	•	•
Japan	•	•	•	•
Jordan	•	•	•	•
Kazakhstan	•	•	○	•
Kenya	•	•	•	•
Korea, Rep. of	•	•	•	•
Kuwait		•	•	•
Kyrgyzstan	•	•	•	•
Laos	•	•	•	•
Latvia	•	•	•	•
Lebanon		•	•	•

(continues on the next page)

Table 8 (continued)

Country	Cartagena Protocol on Biosafety	Framework Convention on Climate Change	Kyoto Protocol to the Framework Convention on Climate Change	Convention on Biological Diversity
Lesotho	•	•	•	•
Liberia	•	•	•	•
Libyan Arab Jamahiriya	•	•	•	•
Lithuania	•	•	•	•
Luxembourg	•	•	•	•
Macedonia, former Yugoslav Republic	•	•	•	•
Madagascar	•	•	•	•
Malawi	•	•	•	•
Malaysia	•	•	•	•
Maldives	•	•	•	•
Mali	•	•	•	•
Malta	•	•	•	•
Mauritania	•	•	•	•
Mauritius	•	•	•	•
Mexico	•	•	•	•
Moldova, Rep. of	•	•	•	•
Monaco	○	•	•	•
Mongolia	•	•	•	•
Montenegro	•	•	•	•
Morocco	○	•	•	•
Mozambique	•	•	•	•
Myanmar	•	•	•	•
Namibia	•	•	•	•
Nauru	•	•	•	•
Nepal	○	•	•	•
Netherlands	•	•	•	•
New Zealand	•	•	•	•
Nicaragua	•	•	•	•
Niger	•	•	•	•
Nigeria	•	•	•	•
Norway	•	•	•	•
Palestinian Autonomous Areas				
Oman	•	•	•	•
Pakistan	•	•	•	•
Panama	•	•	•	•
Papua New Guinea	•	•	•	•
Paraguay	•	•	•	•
Peru	•	•	•	•
Philippines	•	•	•	•
Poland	•	•	•	•
Portugal	•	•	•	•
Qatar	•	•	•	•
Romania	•	•	•	•
Russian Federation		•	•	•

(continues on the next page)

Table 8 (continued)

Country	Cartagena Protocol on Biosafety	Framework Convention on Climate Change	Kyoto Protocol to the Framework Convention on Climate Change	Convention on Biological Diversity
Rwanda	●	●	●	●
Saint Kitts and Nevis	●	●	●	●
Saint Lucia	●	●	●	●
Saint Vincent and the Grenadines	●	●	●	●
Samoa (Western)	●	●	●	●
São Tomé and Principe		●	●	●
Saudi Arabia	●	●	●	●
Senegal	●	●	●	●
Serbia	●	●	●	●
Seychelles	●	●	●	●
Sierra Leone		●	●	●
Singapore		●	●	●
Slovakia	●	●	●	●
Slovenia	●	●	●	●
Solomon Islands	●	●	●	●
South Africa	●	●	●	●
Spain	●	●	●	●
Sri Lanka	●	●	●	●
Sudan	●	●	●	●
Suriname	●	●	●	●
Swaziland	●	●	●	●
Sweden	●	●	●	●
Switzerland	●	●	●	●
Syria	●	●	●	●
Tajikistan	●	●	●	●
Tanzania	●	●	●	●
Thailand	●	●	●	●
Timor-Leste		●	●	●
Togo	●	●	●	●
Tonga	●	●	●	●
Trinidad and Tobago	●	●	●	●
Tunisia	●	●	●	●
Turkey	●	●		●
Turkmenistan	●	●	●	●
Uganda	●	●	●	●
Ukraine	●	●	●	●
United Arab Emirates		●	●	●
United Kingdom	●	●	●	●
United States of America		●	○	○
Uruguay	○	●	●	●
Uzbekistan		●	●	●
Vanuatu		●	●	●
Venezuela	●	●	●	●
Viet Nam	●	●	●	●
Yemen	●	●	●	●

(continues on the next page)

Table 8 (continued)

Country	Cartagena Protocol on Biosafety	Framework Convention on Climate Change	Kyoto Protocol to the Framework Convention on Climate Change	Convention on Biological Diversity
Zambia	•	•	•	•
Zimbabwe	•	•		•

• Ratification, acceptance, approval, accession or succession.
○ Signature
Note: Information is as of September 2009. The Cartagena Protocol on Biosafety was signed in Cartagena in 2000, the United Nations Framework Convention on Climate Change in New York in 1992, the Kyoto Protocol to the United Nations Framework Convention on Climate Change in Kyoto in 1997 and the Convention on Biological Diversity in Rio de Janeiro in 1992.
Source: United Nations Treaties Collection (http://treaties.un.org).

Monthly Carbon Dioxide Concentration
parts per million

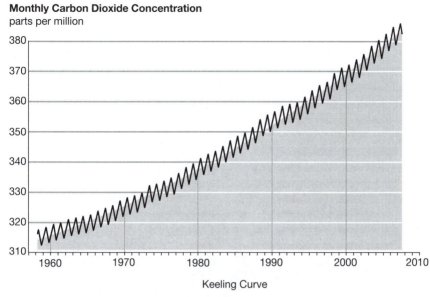

Keeling Curve

Figure 1 Monthly Carbon Dioxide Concentration
The 'Keeling Curve', a measure of atmospheric carbon dioxide concentrations, plotted up to 2007.
Source: CO_2 program, Scripps Institution of Oceanography, University of California San Diego.